Globalization, Consumption and Popular Culture in East Asia

Globalization, Consumption and Popular Culture in East Asia

Tai Wei Lim
Wen Xin Lim
Xiaojuan Ping
Hui-Yi Tseng

NUS, Singapore

NEW JERSEY · LONDON · SINGAPORE · BEIJING · SHANGHAI · HONG KONG · TAIPEI · CHENNAI · TOKYO

Published by

World Scientific Publishing Co. Pte. Ltd.
5 Toh Tuck Link, Singapore 596224
USA office: 27 Warren Street, Suite 401-402, Hackensack, NJ 07601
UK office: 57 Shelton Street, Covent Garden, London WC2H 9HE

British Library Cataloguing-in-Publication Data
A catalogue record for this book is available from the British Library.

GLOBALIZATION, CONSUMPTION AND POPULAR CULTURE IN EAST ASIA

ISBN 978-981-4678-19-3

Desk Editor: Jiang Yulin

Typeset by Stallion Press
Email: enquiries@stallionpress.com

Printed in Singapore

Contents

Section 1

Introduction

Chapter 1

Introduction

Tai Wei LIM

In the era of globalization, popular cultures originating from different localities worldwide are able to reference the universalistic influences from the US, aspects of which are hybridized with local cultures. In this process of interpenetration and adaptation of exogenous Western culture, the polycentric dispersions of the Japanese, Korean and Chinese popular cultures provide fertile materials for studying production and fandom consumption in the region. The different production centers in these three countries transcend national and traditional cultural boundaries, facilitating cultural hybridity. Through the mechanics of globalization, popular cultures originating from different countries are reinforced by the universalistic global trends from the US, and then intermediated, reinterpreted or hybridized with local cultures to attain cultural resonance with regional audiences.

This edited volume studies the platforms for interpenetration, adaptation, innovation and hybridization of exogenous Western culture and popular culture in (North) East Asia, which, together collectively shaped the way popular cultures are produced, consumed and innovated today. This multidisciplinary volume, through the use of concepts and theories related to the anthropogenic origins, political economy, and historical research, attempts to examine the workings of state policies, mass media, celebrity impact and fandom consumption of popular cultural products in (North) East Asia, especially in Japanese, Korean, Taiwan/HK and mainland Chinese markets. A number of specific case studies are examined in the publication.

We set out in this publication to examine various kinds of popular culture in East Asia and its reception by global consumers. In doing so, we were also interested to examine regional indigenization of global popular cultural trends in trying to be independent, unique and original. In writing and editing this publication, we acknowledge the crucial importance of the heterogeneity of different varieties of popular culture in East Asia but at the same time, understand that the creative industries in these three East Asian settings exhibit high permeability when it comes to exchanges of ideas between themselves. In studying popular culture within the setting and contextualization of a regional backdrop, we acknowledge the important presence of the framework of a universal and global popular cultural industry in which East Asian originated popular culture was conceptualized, shaped, innovated, improved upon and distributed.

Shaped by ideas from global trends in popular culture, the production houses and studios based in East Asia hybridize local cultures with fashionable global trends into easily consumable commodified units tailored made for its domestic markets. Upon reaching a critical level of popularity within the home audience, successful products are then tested in familiar neighboring regional markets. And, if the receptivity towards that products proves positive, the popular cultural products are then regionalized and distributed region-wide, sometimes simultaneous with a global launch, sometimes preceding or subsequent to a global launch. Popular cultural soft power is mutually-reinforcing in the sense that East Asian economies work with each other and influence each other to become cool and creative (a process of creative cross-pollination), but yet at the same time trend-spots global popular cultural elements for selective incorporation into their textual and visual imaginations and body of works.

This publication has a multidisciplinary area studies and interdisciplinary Asian studies (Japanese studies, Chinese studies, economics, area studies) approach in a field dominated by sociologists and anthropologists. Having an eclectic approach can open the field of inquiry wider to implications of globalization, innovation, development of creative clusters and consumption with specific empirical examples. It is probably one of the few if not the first monograph (not a review volume) to cover J-pop, K-pop and Chinese popular culture. It provides comparative insights of different popular cultures in the region.

Definition of Popular Culture

There are no universal definitions of popular culture. How one under-
stands popular culture is dependent on the context in which the term is
used and whether a particular definition stands the scrutiny of cultural
relativism. For the readers, it would be helpful to have a working definition of what popular culture is, and also perhaps some examples of popular culture. With references to J-pop, K-pop, Cantopop and *Tai Liu*, it may
be possible to give some examples of what pop culture means in the
context of these particular strains of popular culture, e.g. referring to
music, dressing, Korean drama serials, Japanese anime and so forth.

Based on the narratives covered in this writing, several definitions are
offered here. They range from the amorphous, broad and encompassing
definitions to more precise and carefully crafted detailed definitions. For
example, in defining the term "popular culture," Jonathan Pickering is less
concerned about the boundaries of dichotomous global-local definitions
of popular culture and conceptualizes it as a feature that encompasses
"entertainment, sport and other practices of everyday life."[1] In other
words, popular culture is fully integrated into lifestyles and everyday
experiences. The American and Japanese middle classes as well as their
lifestyles and consumption patterns inspired emulation and inspiration for
the rest of the world.[2] This may be visible in the emerging economies like
India, China and the Gulf region where evidence may be detected through
popular culture, entertainment, material acquisitions, branding, new and
traditional media, and consumption patterns.[3]

Offering another perspective, John Hannigan sees popular culture as
part of a homogenizing process that is reinforced by large quantities of
images interacting and interfacing with market-driven forces to influence

---

[1] Jonathan Pickering, "Globalisation: A Threat to Australian Culture?" *Journal of Australian Political Economy* 48 (December 2001): 47.

[2] Justin Dargin and Tai Wei Lim, *Energy, Trade and Finance in Asia: A Political and Economic Analysis* (London: Pickering and Chatto, 2011).

[3] Justin Dargin and Tai Wei Lim, *Energy, Trade and Finance in Asia: A Political and Economic Analysis* (London: Pickering and Chatto, 2011).

the lives and worldviews of the receivers of such culture.[4] Popular culture may be more easily identifiable by younger generations and students located in a particular region. Japanese popular culture (J-pop) and more recently Korean popular culture (*hanliu* in Chinese, *hallyu* from Korean pronunciation, *hanryū/kanryū* in Japanese or K-pop)[5] may fit this role in integrating the East Asian market culturally and contribute to common appreciation and consumption of such culture within the global rubric and context of American-driven popular cultural trends.

Popular culture generated in East Asia is utilized as a case study to find out if regional strains of popular culture contain elements of soft power (i.e. if the concept of soft power indeed exists) and can be applied to popular culture. The creative industries in these three East Asian settings are likely to find more exchanges and permeability, developing hybridized and unique forms of popular culture in the process within the setting and contextualization of a regional backdrop. It is within the framework of a universal and global popular cultural industry that East Asian-originated popular culture was conceptualized, shaped, innovated, improved upon and distributed.

Some academic works focus exclusively on defining specific East Asian popular cultures in country-specific area studies settings. For example, in my study, I discovered that traces of Japanese popular culture can be found integrated into the daily lives of Japanese people and they can be classified into tangible and intangible categories. In the tangible category, Japanese popular cultural representations can be found in the form of physical promotional items displayed at outlets that are patronized by the general public. Other than Japanese popular culture, some scholars studying K-pop defined Korean popular culture as a fusion between East and West. For example, Woongjae Ryoo "explores a regionally specific phenomenon and logic of transnational popular cultural flow as an example

---

[4]John Hannigan, "Culture, Globalization, and Social Cohesion: Towards a De-territorialized, Global Fluids Model," *Canadian Journal of Communication* 27, no. 2/3 (2002), http://search. proquest.com/docview/219574482?accountid=10371 (accessed June 16, 2011).

[5]J-pop or K-pop usually refers to popular music only while *kanryu/hallyu* refers to the "Korean wave/popular culture". The definition of K-pop may be a bit narrower and different from *kanryu*.

to illustrate the complexity involved in the cultural hybridization and the implications that it has on the globalization of culture" (Ryoo, 2009).[6] He also argues that the impact of the Korean wave has not only permeated popular culture but is also a measure of positive lifestyle for many Asians (Ryoo, 2009, p. 144).[7]

Importance of the Subject Area

Regardless of how one defines the term popular culture, we believe that popular culture is no longer a fringe subject matter but has mainstreamed academically due to its far-reaching implications for other subject matters like the study of soft power (political science), creative industries and clusters (business and urban planning), resonance with audiences (cultural anthropology), public policy-making (public administration), consumption (economics), subtext readings of virtual idols (psychoanalysis), impact of an aging population (demographics), cultural aspects of otakus (area studies), etc. Therefore the subject matter of popular culture has become an eclectic interdisciplinary subject that encompasses a wide spectrum of expertise. The importance of popular culture as an academic subject is also reflected by the academic publishing industry's increasing interest in the subject area. Some trends and news update are discussed selectively in the section below.

Sensing a strong market in this area, in October 2013, a much larger publisher Routledge made the fateful decision of taking over 15 "cutting-edge" journals from Intellect and focusing in the fields of visual and performing arts, film, media and cultural studies. Routledge itself has a number of books on Chinese popular culture, including recent ones on the dynamically changing Hong Kong popular cultural scene with the introduction of multimedia technologies as well as production and consumption of local media. Much of Intellect and Routledge's offerings in popular cultural studies tends to be general coverages of popular culture as a theoretical subject,

---

[6]Woongjae Ryoo, "Globalization, or the logic of cultural hybridization: The case of the Korean Wave," *Asian Journal of Communication* 19, no. 2 (2009).
[7]Woongjae Ryoo, "Globalization, or the logic of cultural hybridization: The case of the Korean Wave," *Asian Journal of Communication* 19, no. 2 (2009).

focusing on universalistic Western popular culture or country-based studies. These are all very important. This edited volume contributes to this important body of literature by adopting an area studies-based approach but one with comparative perspectives of Japan, China and Korea.

Japanese popular cultural soft power has spilled over to neighboring countries and consumer markets, changing and modifying the lifestyles of fandom communities in those regions. They draw reactions from the critical mass media in the receiving audiences. In Lin's chapter, she discusses how the media stereotypes otakus and their subculture in China, creating negative connotations about this community. The Chinese media is not the only participant in image construction of dedicated groups of popular culture as otakus were first marginalized in Japan where the term came from. Lim's chapter on Akihabara however points out that perceptions of sub-cultural groups do change and the otaku community has somehow transformed their marginalized image to that of cool consumers based on the consumption power they possess and their ability to influence design trends and creative processes.

Research Objectives

This book aims to discuss the burgeoning fan communities and sustained proliferation of popular culture with East Asian origins, particularly the Japanese, Korean and Chinese genres. The polycentric dispersions of the East Asian cultures are influential forces with the support of extensive distribution and reception networks within and beyond the region. In its form and makeup, popular culture from different production and originating centers transcend national and traditional cultural boundaries, facilitating cultural hybridity and ideational cross-pollination aided by globalization. Underlying the production of the East Asian popular culture is the closely-intertwined relationships among the iron triangle of production companies (producers), fans (consumers) and the states (regulators), which evolve into the contemporary system of sales, distribution and production in the popular culture industries.

The publication also discusses how consumption emanates soft power — through the encouragement of consumption in regionally rising middle classes and/or marketing efforts of production networks in the region. The writings will also examine soft power reinforced by the concept of cultural resonance with regional audiences. Structurally, Japanese and Korean popular cultures not only serve as forerunners for regional developing economies with emerging consumers like China, but also provide a platform for interpenetration, adaptation, innovation and hybridization of exogenous Western culture and traditional popular culture in historical China, which then leads to the establishment of the current local-regional-global cultural network. While Japan has prided itself on producing and exporting its own fantastical pop culture, Korean entertainment has gained popularity and global recognition in melodrama and musical market share.

Several questions are raised in this writing. First, historically, how did relationships within the iron triangle of production companies (producers), fans (consumers) and the state (regulators) evolve to the current contemporary system of sales, distribution and production in the popular culture industries? How does the proliferation of culture change in the digital era? Second, what sort of influence does popular culture have on regional audiences? Do the cultural products resonate with a regional audience through collective consumption, contents-based depictions of normative values and network-based peer pressure? Third, how does consumption emanate soft power — through the encouragement of consumption in regionally rising middle classes and/or production networks in the region? How can a government leverages on its cultural advantages to stretch its national influence? These questions will be discussed and analyzed in this volume and they will be discussed and contextualized in the case studies of J-pop, K-pop and Chinese popular culture. Before proceeding to an explanation of the layout and organizational structure of chapters in the publication, it may be useful to discuss some of the existing literatures written on the topic of Northeast Asian popular culture.

Literature Review

The unifying element in all the case studies covered in the volume is the unmistakable influence of American popular culture in all of its Northeast Asian carnations. Regardless of whether it is J-pop, K-pop, C-pop, Mandopop, Cantopop or *Tai Liu*, the roots of postwar East Asian popular

culture cannot escape the American influence. Existing literatures studying the universalistic characteristics of American popular culture urge
caution in conceptualizing it as a hegemonic entity. Ian Condry argues
against defining American popular culture as a ubiquitous and broad
entity, and to avoid defining it as a uniform entity "wherever it appears"
and instead differentiate definitions according to their local features and
characteristics.[8]

Condry and other scholars propose defining popular culture as a form
of constant negotiation between globalized culture and localization.
Jonathan Pickering is less concerned about the boundaries of dichotomous
global-local definitions of popular culture and conceptualizes it as a feature that encompasses "entertainment, sport and other practices of everyday life."[9] In other words, popular culture is fully integrated into lifestyles
and everyday experiences. The American and Japanese middle classes as
well as their lifestyles and consumption patterns inspired emulation and
inspiration for the rest of the world.[10] This may be visible in the emerging
economies like India, China and the Gulf region where evidence may be
detected through popular culture, entertainment, material acquisitions,
branding, new and traditional media, and consumption patterns.[11]

John Hannigan sees popular culture as part of a homogenizing process
that is reinforced by large quantities of images interacting and interfacing
with market-driven forces to influence the lives and worldviews of the
receivers of such culture.[12] The idea of a "homogenizing" universal
American popular culture makes the formation of regional identifications

---

[8] Ian Condry, "Japanese Hip-Hop and the Globalization of Popular Culture," in *Urban Life:
Readings in the Anthropology of the City*, eds. G. Gmelch and W. Zenner (Prospect Heights,
IL: Waveland Press, 2002), 372.

[9] Jonathan Pickering, "Globalisation: A Threat to Australian Culture?" *Journal of Australian
Political Economy* 48 (December 2001): 47.

[10] Justin Dargin and Tai Wei Lim, *Energy, Trade and Finance in Asia: A Political and
Economic Analysis* (London: Pickering and Chatto, 2011).

[11] Justin Dargin and Tai Wei Lim, *Energy, Trade and Finance in Asia: A Political and
Economic Analysis* (London: Pickering and Chatto, 2011).

[12] John Hannigan, "Culture, Globalization, and Social Cohesion: Towards a De-territorialized,
Global Fluids Model," *Canadian Journal of Communication* 27, no. 2/3 (2002), http://
search.proquest.com/docview/219574482?accountid=10371 (accessed June 16, 2011).

of popular culture less crucial. American popular culture is also easily consumable, understood and integrated into desirable urbanized middle class lifestyles. Therefore, the argument may not be so much whether American popular culture is consumed in different regions of the world but how it is indigenized, emulated and customized in various forms in various regions of the world. American popular culture is not challenged by alternatives but is studied closely, indigenized, innovated and systematically recreated by other strains of popular culture. Having examined existing literatures that debate the universality or particularistic features of US popular culture, it would be useful to compare them with the localized features of individual Northeast Asian popular cultures and also examine what existing literatures have to say about them.

Likewise, just as Northeast Asian popular culture draws upon elements of universalistic American popular culture, successful strains of Northeast Asian popular culture also need to adapt to a global audience and diminish its local features when marketing those products overseas. Regional strains of popular culture have to universalize their popular cultural features in order to adapt to a global audience that may not be as sensitive to regional cultural instincts and idiosyncrasies. For an important work in this aspect, one may refer to the book *Pikachu's Global Adventure: The Rise and Fall of Pokemon* edited by Joseph Tobin (Durham and London: Duke University Press, 2004). Articles in this edited volume indicate that Japanese popular culture has to be modified and translated in terms of marketing, advertising, distribution, dialogue and characters foregrounding in order to appeal to the American kids consumer market (largest in the world) and also English-speaking audiences around the world. Therefore, American popular culture consumed in regional variations undergoes the opposite process. Universal American popular culture is particularized to fit regional contexts, environments and idiosyncrasies.

If American popular culture is universal and far-reaching, most existing literatures tend to study Northeast Asian popular culture as a regional phenomenon. Within the region itself, Chinese-language popular culture takes on a center-periphery format as continental mainland Chinese culture continually interacts with its periphery in Taiwan and Hong Kong to create new forms of popular culture. One spin-off from this interaction is the historical emergence of Cantopop.

Existing literatures examine how Chinese popular culture is the outcome of an interplay and interactions between mainland China and its periphery (e.g. Taiwan and Hong Kong). For example, through the study of Cantopop fandom in Hong Kong, one may comprehend how Hong Kong society has undergone socio-cultural transformations in the regional and global contexts. In discussing the general history of Cantopop, lyricists and prominent singers, Zhi-hua Huang wrote probably the first comprehensive and systematic book in 1990 to outline the historical development of Cantopop and analyze why it became popular in the 1970s and 1980s.[13]

Later in 2003, Wong Jum Sum, also known as Jim Wong 黃霑, a famous lyrics writer and music composer in Hong Kong entertainment industry, has periodized Hong Kong popular music history into four historical periods up till 1997 based on his rich experience in the industry.[14] Wong interprets the musical styles in each period and gives the reasons behind the popularity of Cantopop in each historical period, but he also foresees the decline of Cantopop and thinks that it would be an unavoidable trend.[15] It is because Cantonese, as one of the dialects of Chinese language, is difficult to market to other non-Cantonese areas, especially in mainland China, where Mandarin is the main language of communication, and Mandopop itself has been rising internationally and exerting its strong cultural power in the past two decades.

More recently, Liu Jing-zhi, as a musician, studies the melody, lyrics, genre of Hong Kong Cantopop, together with its history.[16] Also, Liu devotes a chapter to studying 15 major composers of Hong Kong popular music. Generally, the developmental history of Cantopop and its several important leading figures are usually included into the existing literatures,

---

[13] Zhi-hua Huang, *Yueyu Liuxingqu Sishi Nian* 粤語流行曲四十年 [40 Years of Cantonese Popular Music] (Hong Kong: Joint Publishing, 1990).

[14] Jum Sum Wong, "The Rise and Decline of Cantopop: A Study of Hong Kong Popular Music (1949–1997)" (PhD diss., University of Hong Kong, 2003).

[15] *Ibid.*, 183.

[16] Jing-zhi Liu, *Xianggang Yinyueshi Lun: Yueyu Liuxingqu, Yansu Yinyue, Yueju* 香港音樂史論：粤語流行曲，嚴肅音樂，粤劇 [Historical Discussion on Hong Kong Music: Cantonese Popular Music, Serious Music, Cantonese Opera] (Hong Kong: Commercial Press, 2013).

but publications that study its fandom, a much larger community compared to the music producers, are relatively few. Wong and Lee's chapter in this edited volume is an updated contribution to the existing literature, surveying historical narratives of Cantopop's emergence and evolution. It comes at an appropriate time as Hong Kong is searching for its cultural identity after a period of turmoil in the Occupy Central movement in end-2014.

Identity issue, it seems, is also present in the case study of Taiwan. Tseng's chapter studies and reviews the issue of identity in existing academic literature in great details. Tseng examines this issue not from the perspective of historical studies but from the viewpoint of reception of culture. She cites three kinds of receptions by audiences towards popular culture.[17] The first form is hegemonic reception, where the ideology reflects and reinforces the domination of the ruling class. The masses are generally deemed to consent to this predisposed form of culture production. However, in an age when communication and global information dissemination are made possible because of technological advancement of the internet, this authoritarian style of culture production now has little market. Effectively, there is no longer a clearly hegemonic popular culture as the regime's control over society and the social superstructure continues to erode.

The second type Tseng proposes is a negotiated form of reception, where some ground is left for expressing emotions such as anger "without

---

[17] Paul Graves-Brown, Siân Jones and Clive Gamble (authors and eds.), *Cultural Identity and Archaeology: The Construction of European Communities* (Psychology Press, 1996); Michael Thompson, "The problem of the center: An autonomous cosmology," in *Essays in the Sociology of Perception*, ed. M. Douglas (London: Routledge & Kegan Paul, 1982), 302–328. For more discussion of culture and cultural rights, see Michael Thompson, Richard Ellis and Aaron Wildavsky, *Cultural Theory* (Boulder, CO: Westview, 1990); Gunnar Grendstad, Per Selle, Michael Thompson (eds.), *Cultural Theory as Political Science* (Routledge, 2003); John Storey, *Cultural Theory and Popular Culture: An Introduction* (Routledge, 2015); Peter Jones, "Bearing the Consequences of Belief," Journal of Political Philosophy 2, no. 1 (1994): 24–43; Jacob T. Levy, "Classifying Cultural Rights," in *Ethnicity and Group Rights: Nomos XXXIX*, eds. Will Kymlicka and Ian Shapiro (New York: New York University Press, 1997); Chandran Kukathas, "Are There Any Cultural Rights?" Political Theory 20 (1995): 105–139; James Johnson, "Why Respect Culture?" American Journal of Political Science 44, no. 3 (2000): 405–418.

confronting the social mechanics of domination *per se*."[18] Expression of individuality and feelings does not directly challenge the regime's status quo political hegemony, but neither does it reflect consent. Instead, it carves out a private sphere for the individual apart from the collective one in her/his life, by institutionalizing a zone of indifference when negotiating between the two. The existence of this private sphere offers an outlet for simply ignoring the imperatives of state authorities and opting out of the cultural world that the state tries to dominate.

The third form of reception is emancipatory, including what Miklós Haraszti calls "Maverick Artists," referring to those artists "willing to sacrifice the privileges of the assimilated in order to retain their independence" although "by so doing they are doomed to eke [sic] out a meager existence as fringe-dwellers in a state-owned cultural desert crowded with mirages."[19] Explicit producers and consumers of this type of culture are still few, with their main forms of expression like satirical literatures or rock-and-roll music. In her chapter, Tseng will apply these three forms of cultural reception to her case study of Taiwan.

Wong and Lee's as well as Tseng's chapters show intense self-reflection on the part of fans in enjoying and consuming popular cultural products. Cantopop facilitates Hong Kongers' search for identity given its contributive role in Hong Kong's cultural history and Taiwanese consumers are showing complex and nuanced reactions and reception of popular culture. But not all responses to popular culture are inward-looking or self-reflective. Emanating outwards instead of self-reflecting internally, other forms of Northeast Asian popular culture are reaching out globally for more consumer markets and soft cultural influence. In this aspect, a major force in the Northeast Asian popular cultural scene is K-pop. Scholars in existing literatures have tried to define this phenomenon. The Korean wave — "*Hallyu*" in Korean — refers to a surge in the international visibility of Korean culture, beginning in East Asia in the 1990s and continuing more recently in the North America, Latin America, the Middle East, and parts of Europe.[20] Scholarly works have

---

[18] *Ibid.*

[19] See, note 17.

[20] Mark Ravina, "Introduction: conceptualizing the Korean Wave," Southeast Review of Asian Studies 31 (2009): 3–9.

tried to understand the underlying factors for K-pop's success in the world. A survey conducted by the National Institute of Education (NIE) in Singapore with local female fandom has identified the elements in Korean dramas that the fans found "most attractive" include "touching storylines," "beautiful scenery" in the dramas coupled with "excellent cinematography," "good looking actors and actresses," "trendy fashion," "nice music," and etc.[21]

Aesthetics, it seems, is a major attraction in popular culture for fans. W.X. Lim, Ping and T.W. Lim's co-authored chapter details how such attractive aesthetics in the case of K-pop is packaged and marketed to a global audience. But promoting local popular culture globally is not without problems or challenges. We have reviewed existing literatures that examine US popular culture as a source of universal influence on Northeast Asian popular culture as well as those that focus on the developmental histories of individual Northeast Asian popular culture and how local factors shape their development. Inevitably, some existing works have pointed out the link between globalization and localization. Some scholars even appropriate the political scientific term of soft power to describe this nexus. William Tsutsui and Saya Shiraishi are two scholars who discuss about this point. Tsutsui believes that Japanese soft power has set the pace and example for future popular cultural trends in East Asia, including the current Korean popular cultural craze in Asia, and perhaps China Central Television (CCTV) drama series in the future based on the precedent that Japan has set.[22] The creative industries in these three East Asian settings are likely to find more exchanges and permeability, developing a pan-East Asian popular culture in the process within the setting and contextualization of an East Asian backdrop. Connected with this process is the construction of self-identity and regional features of such exchanges.

The idea of soft power has evolved along with narratives focusing on popular cultural soft power. From Joseph S. Nye's idea of getting someone

---

[21] Brenda Chan and Xueli Wang, "Of prince charming and male chauvinist pigs: Singaporean female viewers and the dream-world of Korean television dramas," *International Journal of Cultural Studies* 14, no. 3 (2011): 294.

[22] William Tsutsui, *Japanese Popular Culture and Globalization* (Ann Arbor, MI: Association for Asian Studies Inc., 2010), 71.

to do what you want without the use of force,[23] Tsutsui has argued that it has been transformed from an academic to a general purpose term. Shiraishi goes further to adapt the term for use in popular culture by privileging the element of resonance or the ability to tug at the emotive element of major sections of the populace in Asia. In the case of East Asia, Japanese, Korean, Taiwanese, Hong Kong and Chinese popular culture have aggregated the collective aspirations, imaginations and fascinations of regional audiences.

If popular culture carries the promise of soft power and cultural influences, then who are the major targets and consumers of popular culture in Northeast Asia? Ultimately, most existing academic literatures state that the target audiences and consumers for Northeast Asian popular cultural products within and outside the region are still the burgeoning middle class that is growing alongside the East Asian economies. Geoffrey McNicoll classifies the phenomenon of popular culture growth as a form of urban middle class culture that is soaked in J-manga and anime, Hong Kong movies and Western IT technologies.[24] Consumption patterns therefore appear to offer a form of homogenizing effect on regional populations, socializing them in similar aesthetic appreciation, entertainment options, fashion trends and creative development. For example, John Lie noted that, *collectively*, Japanese and Koreans in Japan used to consuming popular sweets and confectionary for example manage to name Lotte as a major processed food firm in Japan.[25] Joseph Tobin suggests that intra-regional consumption still has a long way to go, given China's market potentialities and growing Japanese marketing networks in popular cultural products.[26]

---

[23] For further reading, see Joseph S. Nye, *Soft Power: The Means to Success in World Politics* (New York: Public Affairs, 2004).

[24] Geoffrey McNicoll, "Demographic Future of East Asian Regional Integration," in *Remapping East Asia: The Construction of a Region*, ed. T. J. Pempel (Ithaca and London: Cornell University Press, 2005), 71.

[25] John Lie, *Zainichi (Koreans in Japan): Diasporic Nationalism and Postcolonial Identity* (Oakland, CA: University of California Press, 2008), 191.

[26] Joseph Tobin, "Conclusion: The Rise and Fall of the Pokemon Empire," in *Pikachu's Global Adventure: The Rise and Fall of Pokémon*, ed. J. Tobin (Durham and London: Duke University Press, 2004), 268.

At the individual level, when middle class consumer markets are atomized into its fundamental units, the fans or collectively the fandom make up the core group of the consumers. Fandom in pop music takes on different meanings. A "fan" may be defined as one who consumes actively popular cultural products related to a particular idol or idols (i.e. their music and/or related by-products). Roy Shuker for example defines fans as participants who often attend concerts, collect their idols' records and goods, and discuss news related to their idols with other fans.[27] Nissim Otmazgin and Irina Lyan define the multiple roles of fans as consumers as well as "marketers, mediators, translators, and localizers of globalized culture."[28] In this sense, fans play an important role in testing whether a particular popular cultural product is well-received by local consumers and localizing those cultural products in order to suit the tastes of local consumers. Paul Booth further expands the scope of fandom from individual fans of specific idols to everyone else. In his work *Digital Fandom*, he suggests that "everyone is fan of something" and we all "based part of our identity on our appreciation of that fandom."[29]

With the implications of identity-building and collective behavior, some existing literatures and works discuss how popular cultural consumption is a process of constant negotiation between individual choices and normative collective identity/behavior. Despite the fact that becoming part of a fandom is a subjective and personal choice, participation in the activities is never a solitary activity. Lewis points out that once fans group together to share their common interests, they will soon construct their own identity, which he defines as "coherent identities for themselves" and these "individuals" share common practices as well.[30] As a result, fandom usually appears as a community. From the viewpoint of social history, every community has a close and inevitable relationship

---

[27] Roy Shuker, "Record Collecting and Fandom," in *Popular Music Fandom: Identities, Roles and Practices*, ed. M. Duffett (New York and London: Routledge, 2013), 166.

[28] Nissim Otmazgin and Irina Lyan, "Hallyu across the Desert: K-pop Fandom in Israel and Palestine," *Cross-Currents: East Asian History and Culture Review* 9 (December 2013): 70.

[29] Paul Booth, *Digital Fandom: New Media Studies* (New York, Bern, Berlin, Bruxelles, Frankfurt am Main, Oxford, Wien: Peter Lang, 2009), 20.

[30] Lisa A. Lewis, *The Adoring Audience: Fan Culture and Popular Media* (New York: Routledge, 1992).

with group identity formation. For example, social historians believe that identity is "public and relational."[31] In other words, it is contextual: dependent on the external environment and specific situations; and based on interactions with others and how others perceive an individual. An individual's self-identity requires recognition by others to construct that identity. There is a need to distinguish an individual's unique identity from others. The shape and characteristics of the chosen identity are shaped by the social environment which it is located in. Therefore, an identity formation process is never private and individual. Social historians view the society as a collective construct rather than the personal experience of numerous individuals.[32] It is the sum of individuals which makes up a group. With social historians focusing on the construction of social structure, which refers to the interaction among individuals and groups, and studying social structure within a community, they are able to find out how individuals operate within a particular society.[33]

When individual fans and their atomized narratives are aggregated into a collective, then a subculture is born. When individual fandom is studied collectively, scholars then look closely at the concept of a "subculture". According to notable scholars in the field, the term "subculture" became a key concept in analyzing young members of deviant groups with unified dressing and acting style in early 20th century, a definition that was predominantly accepted by scholars from the Chicago School of academics (Bennett and Kahn-Harris, 2004, p. 7)[34] in this subject area. Becker (1964, p. 9) came up with the concept of "labeling" to explain the formation of identity for those subculture members.[35] According to him, a society constructs its own norms by making rules and labeling those who failed to

---

[31] Charles Tilly, "Citizenship, Identity and Social History," in *Citizenship, Identity and Social History*, ed. C. Tilly (New York and Melbourne: Cambridge University Press, 1996), 6–7.

[32] Donald M. MacRaild and Avram Taylor, *Social Theory and Social History* (New York: Palgrave Macmillan, 2004), 83.

[33] *Ibid.*, 7.

[34] Andy Bennett and Keith Kahn-Harris, "Introduction," in *After Subculture: Critical Studies in Contemporary Youth Culture*, eds. A. Bennett and K. Kahn-Harris. (New York: Palgrave Macmillan, 2004), 7.

[35] Howard S. Becker, *Outsiders: Studies in the Sociology of Deviance* (New York: Free Press, 1963), 9.

obey those rules as outsiders, while the existence of the subculture community provided a way of normalization for outsiders (1964, pp. 1–8).[36] Those who have been stigmatized are reinforced by their subculture labels, which means they would behave according to the rules of the subculture of their belonging in order to fit in.

Based on this conflict model, the Birmingham Centre for Contemporary Cultural Studies (CCCS) further developed a theoretical framework using field researches of juvenile delinquency in local communities of England during 1950s and 1970s.[37] Young people in this study were adopting subculture as a collective reaction towards social structural changes. On the one hand, the affluence of the society encouraged consumerism amongst the upper income socio-economic classes of the society and then extended it into the working class. On the other hand, the hierarchy of a society, as well as its limited career opportunities for upward mobility, remained unchanged for the lower socio-economic classes. As a result, youths from the working class are facing a consumption culture in which they do not fit in socio-economically. Subculture has been employed as a form of reactionary resistance towards the cultural changes, as well as a re-creation of their identities (Bennett & Kahn-Harris, 2004, pp. 4–6).[38]

The theoretical framework raised by CCCS, as well as the concept of "subculture," has been criticized by later scholars. Several criticisms which could help in the understanding of an otaku identity will be reviewed in this writing. One criticism is that the enjoyment youths gained while consuming subculture has been overlooked by CCCS. According to Simon Frith (1983, pp. 219–220), those young "stylists" of subculture would switch groups and alter their identities just for fun in their leisure time.[39] George H. Lewis (1992, p. 141) believes those musical communities formed around common interests can be better classified as "taste cultures."[40] It is

---

[36] *Ibid.,* 1–8.

[37] John B. Mays, *Growing Up in the City: A Study of Juvenile Delinquency in an Urban Neighbourhood* (Liverpool; Liverpool University Press, 1954).

[38] Bennett and Kahn-Harris, "Introduction," 4–6.

[39] Simon Frith, *Sound Effects: Youth, Leisure and the Politics of Rock* (London: Constable, 1983), 219–220.

[40] George H. Lewis, "Who Do You Love? The Dimensions of Musical Taste," in *Music and Communication, 2nd edition,* ed. James Lull (London: Sage, 1987), 141.

similar tastes and mutual understanding and appreciation of the contents that created the community. Similar to the observation made by Frith (1983, pp. 219–220),[41] Andy Bennett argues that the identity of members in a subculture community is temporal and floating, in that both their boundaries and memberships changed over time (Bennett, 1999, p. 600).[42] In fact, he prefers to avoid the term "subculture" and use the concept "tribes" raised by Michel Maffesoli, which focuses on the fluid nature of the culture groups (Bennett, 1999, pp. 599–600).[43] However, those criticisms might not be applicable with all social contexts. For example, Hilary Pilkington investigated the fandom community of rock music, which is a well-developed subculture, in post-Soviet modernizing Russia (2004, pp. 119–133).[44] She found that the identities of those Russian youths were predicated upon the symbolic meaning of the behavior and performance in appreciating the music rather than enjoyment brought about by music gatherings and parties (2004, pp. 121–128).[45]

Besides the criticisms mentioned above, many other scholars, including Bennett, question the presumption of the relationship between subculture and working class identity (1999, p. 602).[46] Based on empirical observation of an urban dance club in England, he believes that instead of re-creating tradition, consumerism provides new self-constructed identities for youths to choose from (1999, p. 602).[47] Though researches done by CCCS and following discussions are focusing on young people, some scholars notice that the members of a subculture are not restricted only to young people. When these young members grow up, some of them remain ardent consumers of the subculture and the products it offers. Instead of being only a passing stage in their lives, their subcultural identity becomes

---

[41] Frith, *Sound Effects*, 219–220.

[42] Andy Bennett, "Subcultures or Neo-tribes? Rethinking the Relationship between Youth, Style and Musical Taste," *Sociology* 33, no. 3 (1999): 600.

[43] *Ibid.*, 599–600.

[44] Hilary Pilkington, "Youth Strategies for Glocal Living: Space, Power and Communication in Everyday Cultural Practice," in *After Subculture: Critical Studies in Contemporary Youth Culture*, eds. A. Bennett and K. Kahn-Harris. (New York: Palgrave Macmillan, 2004), 119–133.

[45] *Ibid.*, 121–128.

[46] Bennett, "Subcultures or Neo-tribes," 602.

[47] *Ibid.*, 602.

a part of their lifelong identities. Those researchers suggest that the cultural products the interest groups consumed formed their "taste of mind," and continuing this consumption behavior gives them a sense of "youthfulness" (Bennett and Kahn-Harris, 2004, pp. 10–11).[48]

In summary, the Chicago School and CCCS emphasized the symbolic value and social/class identity behind the subculture group, while later scholars pay more attention to the actual meaning of the content for the youths and also notice the fluctuation and diversity of the identity amongst fan groups and same-interest groups.

Chapterization and Organization of this Publication

Chapters in this publication are organized into four sections focusing on the area studies of Japan, Korea, China and Taiwan. We included a chapter on the debate on particularism and universalism which can pave the way for important discussions on the global American culture as a comparative element before looking at each of the four East Asian locations in detail. These four locations are often known to be the major consumers and/or producers of popular culture in East Asia and their strains of popular culture are known as J-pop (abbreviation for Japanese popular culture), K-pop (abbreviation for Korean popular culture) and, for Taiwan and China, the advent of *Tailiu* for Taiwanese popular culture, Mandopop (Mandarin-language popular culture), Cantopop (popular culture in the Cantonese-language medium), and C-pop or Chinese popular culture.

J-pop Section

In order to study the ecology of a creative cluster, we have chosen to focus on the case study of a physical location that is regarded as the thriving center of Japanese popular culture. In the center of Japan's multi-stakeholder Cool Japan campaign as well as globalized fan-driven consumption of Japanese popular culture, lies the cultural center of Akihabara in Tokyo. In this section of the publication, Tai Wei Lim examines the organic historical growth of the creative cultural retail cluster, Akihabara,

---

[48] Bennett and Kahn-Harris, "Introduction," 10–11.

and contributions made by its multi-stakeholders, the role of fandom and policy inputs in the development.

Akihabara is simultaneously a creative industry production and retail center, a social networking/tourism platform and a symbol of fan-driven consumption. The fluid ecology of Akihabara itself is made up of multi-stakeholders, dynamically interacting with each other with no clear center or hegemonic principal players. The seminar examines the organic historical growth of this creative cultural retail cluster, contributions made by its multi-stakeholders, the role of fandom and policy inputs in its development, and concludes with a short discussion on future trends for Akihabara. This is one of the few publications to look at creative industrial clusters like Akihabara. The last major trade professional publication to do so was in 2004.

K-pop Section

In the K-pop section of this publication, Wen Xin Lim discusses how the Korean state policies and media agencies promote and export Korean cultural products that transcend the national boundary. This section traces the success of the (South) Korean transnational cultural trends, known as the "Korean Wave," which have been sweeping across East Asia since the 1990s and continuing on more recently to the United States, Latin America, the Middle East, and various parts of Europe. The success of Korean Wave encompasses not only its cultural products, including TV drama, K-pop, movies and online games, but also represents a sizable business potential for a full range of (South) Korean corporations ranging from cosmetics, food, fashion to tourism.

The factor of technology

By examining the Korean Wave which started in the 1990s, one can identify and analyze the shift of "Korean Wave" from its origins in the cultural industry to becoming a content provider in the creative industry in the digital era. With the emergence of social media, the Korean entertainment industry is now rapidly changing its conventional business model to target consumers in the vibrant sunrise markets made possible by the digital and online revolutions. W.X. Lim will discuss how the radical transformation of (information and) communication technologies helps the "Korean Wave" to gain hitherto popularity, with the media agencies and government's cultural policies playing a central role to promote and facilitate the circulation and distribution of Korean cultural products.

In the section on the Korean case study, we examine the following research questions. Besides cultural hybridization taking place between Western universalism (popular culture disseminated and consumed globally) and East Asian exoticism (particularistic products that are specific in language medium use and cultural nuances) that is pivotal in attracting transnational audiences, what are the other factors that led to the overseas expansion of the "Korean Wave"? What are the roots of the "Korean Wave" — the remarkable global rise in popularity of South Korean popular culture over the past decade? What role does globalization play in this?

Historically, it all began in 1994 when the Presidential Advisory Board on Science and Technology submitted a report to then president, Kim Young-sam, advocating the Korean government to promote media production as a national strategic industry using the reference point of overall revenues earned by the Hollywood blockbuster, *Jurassic Park*, to compare with the equivalent total foreign sales of 1.5 million Hyundai cars.[49] Against this backdrop was the unexpected success of the Korean movie *Sopyonje* in 1993 which attracted more than a million viewers for the first time in the history of Korean cinema.[50] In the wake of this phenomenal success, the Korean government started realizing the potential of the cultural industry which could possibly benefit the Korean economy.

Through a closer look at the recent phenomenon of the unprecedented overseas proliferation of the Korean popular culture, as well as studying the cultural policies and a paradigm shift of Republic of Korea (ROK) economic policies under different leaderships, W.X. Lim constructs a

---

[49] Beng Huat Chua and Koichi Iwabuchi, *East Asian Pop Culture: Analysing the Korean Wave* (Hong Kong: Hong Kong University Press, 2008), 17.
[50] Doobo Shim, "Waxing the Korean Wave," Asia Research Institute Working Paper Series No. 158, June 2011.

set of explanations, respectively pointing to cultural factors, government support, media agencies and technological development as core factors and explanations that led to the global success of the "Korean Wave."

Since the "Korean Wave" has swept across the globe, elevating South Korea's international image and generating positive economic implications for South Korea's economy, this section on K-pop will also look into a case study of how K-pop has interacted with one particular Southeast Asian country. Singapore is one of the early recipient countries of K-drama (Korean TV drama) and K-pop due to its cultural, political and economic proximity with South Korea. Despite being a small consumer market in terms of population size, Singapore is the gateway for K-pop's cultural entry to Southeast Asia. It is an important commercial, technological and trading hub for South Korean products in the region. Besides serving as a model for Singapore, the success of K-pop also offers Track II cultural diplomacy potential for the two countries to cooperate in this field. There are however limitations to soft power, commercial successes and reach of any popular culture. In order to be sustainable, what started out as particularistically Korean may eventually evolve to be universally attractive instead of culturally specific.

Section on China

Xiaojuan Ping looks at the recent phenomenon of reality TV shows in China. Ping's chapter reveals how reality show grasps the characteristics of an era, reflecting contemporary social values in a certain society. Information and entertainment are intertwined in the Chinese reality shows, which reflect the consumerism trends in Chinese society.[51] Cultural products have been important components of consumerism in China as its mass entertainment function for satisfying and soothing inner desires is increasingly demanded by Chinese consumers. China's socio-economic transition is accompanied by environmental pollution, sky-rocketing real estate price, and other social injustices, which have left some Chinese people increasingly anxious and frustrated with life. Reality show, to some extent,

---

[51]Li Li, 奇观社会的文化密码: 电视真人秀的游戏规则研究 (Chengdu: Sichuan University Press, 2015).

provides an imaginary solution or at the very least escapism from these conundrums. With issues empathized by ordinary Chinese people at all socio-economic levels, it sends incessantly positive messages and energies to the Chinese society.

Anying Lin differs from Ping's study by examining the reception of foreign cultures by Chinese audiences, particularly focusing on the phenomenon of the Japanese otaku culture in her chapter *Yuzhaizu: A study of otaku identity in mainland China*. Through empirical studies, textual analysis, semi-structured interviews, surveys and literature reviews under Chinese context, three major aspects will be concentrated: (1) attributes of otaku population and their multiple identities in mainland China; (2) the national policy changes and its influences to otaku's identity building process; (3) their perception of otakuism and the fandom, as well as their perceived relationship with mainstream culture and Japanese culture.

Lin points out that watching Japanese animation and reading manga are important shared childhood memories for many children born after the mid-1970s in mainland China. According to media agencies like the Xinhua News Agency (2006), since 1981, the national television channels of mainland China started to import Japanese animation. And from 1986, many local televisions also imported a large number of Japanese animations based on their own programming initiatives. Until early this century, the cartoon and youth programs of both national and local televisions were monopolized by Japanese.[52] Among those imported works with mixed qualities, some influencing and classical pieces among Japan and other foreign otaku world were included,[53] which became well-known among younger generations.

Since 2000, the State Administration of Press, Publication, Radio, Film and Television has issued several regulations to reduce the frequency of Japanese animation broadcast. In 2000, direct censorship of animations

---

[52] The Beijing News, "Guang Dian Zong Ju Fa Bu Xin Gui: Huang Jin Shi Duan Jin Bo Jing Wai Dong Hua," *Xin Hua Agency*, August 13, 2006, accessed May 14, 2013, http://news.xinhuanet.com/politics/2006-08/13/content_4954807.htm.

[53] For example, *The Super Dimension Fortress Macross*, where the world "otaku" might have first originated, and *Neon Genesis Evangelion*, which appealed to a whole new generation of otaku fans, were imported and broadcasted on public TV channels during the 1980s and 1990s.

run by the Chinese government was established.[54] From 2006, no foreign-produced animations were allowed during children program's primetime, which is 17:00–20:00 in mainland China.[55] And since 2008, foreign-produced animations were forbidden in all national and local TV channels.[56] Though some of those regulations claimed to protect and promote local animation productions, Japanese animations were still popular among children. According to a survey mainly targeting people under 13 years old conducted by official media, just before the 2006's new restriction was issued, 59% of the responders enjoyed cartoon/animation programs most among all TV programs, 68% of them loved Japanese animations, and 81% of them believed they would only watch local products which attracted them even without any foreign works competing on TV.[57] Further, even with these regulatory restrictions in place, people can still easily watch and download Japanese animations on the internet or buy discs at a very low price legally or illegally (Yang, 2006).[58] According to Genqiang Zhang (2009, p. 94), Japanese animation still took up 60% of the market in mainland China.[59]

Lin noted that the story of print manga is less complicated. Passion towards Japanese manga broke out spontaneously since 1990s, and the government and legitimate channels played little role in it. According to

---

[54] The State Administration of Press, Publication, Radio, Film and Television, *Guo Jia Guang Bo Dian Ying Dian Shi Zong Ju Guan Yu Jia Qiang Dong Hua Pian Yin Jin He Bo Fang Guan Li De Tong Zhi*, March 20, 2000. http://big5.mofcom.gov.cn/gate/big5/tfs.mofcom.gov.cn/article/date/i/n/cp/200212/20021200058991.shtml.

[55] Beijing Evening News, "Jiu Xiang Xin Gui Jin Qiu 9 Yue Qi Shi Xing, Huang Jin Shi Duan Jin Bo Jing Wai Dong Hua," *Xin Hua Agency*, August 30, 2006, accessed January 23, 2015, http://news.xinhuanet.com/politics/2006-08/30/content_5026353.htm.

[56] The State Administration of Press, Publication, Radio, Film and Television, *Guang Dian Zong Ju Guan Yu Jia QiangDian Shi Dong Hua Pian Bo Chu Guan Li De Tong Zhi*, Feburary 9, 2008. http://www.sarft.gov.cn/articles/2008/02/19/20080221111624750711.html.

[57] The Beijing News, "Guang Dian Zong Ju Fa Bu Xin Gui."

[58] Yang Meng, "Zhuang Jia Cheng Ping Bi Jin Kou Dong Hua Bu Li Yu Guo Chan Dong Hua Zhi Zuo Fa Zhan," *The Mirror*, June 9, 2006, accessed May 14, 2013, http://news.163.com/06/0812/13/2OB258OE0001124J.html.

[59] Genqiang Zhang, "'Yu Zhai Zu' De San Chong Shen Fen," *China Youth Study*, no. 3, (2009): 94.

practitioners from press industry, most classical Japanese manga works had their pirated versions/copies in early 1990s and readers also had access to the latest and most popular current manga in Japan. Those products were distributed by small book stores around schools or via internet. But, even under this circumstance, Japanese manga are still best-selling among imported foreign manga/comics (Ifeng Reading, 2011).[60]

The introductions of animation and manga through both authorized and illegal channels in last decades created a dedicated fandom of Japanese animation and manga with sizable numbers in mainland China, within which further developed the hardcore otaku community. However, for a long period of time, it is widely believed that animation and manga are only targeting small children under 12, and they are bad influences to adolescents and young adults, which distract students' attention away from school duties (Wang, 2011, p. 60).[61] Therefore, these tried to conceal their communities' existence from the general public to escape the media spotlight. It was not until the late 2000s that mainstream media started to pay attention to the existence of those obsessive adolescent and young adult fans. This media recognition coincided with the importation of the word "*Yuzhaizu* (御宅族)," a Chinese translation from Japanese word "otaku" borrowed from Taiwan. Under the label of "*Yuzhaizu*," or "*Zhai* (宅)" for short, the group began to acquire the status of a deviant community in the society. Media scrutiny and debates related to the definition of "*Zhai*" are important components of Chinese otakus' identity building, which would be discussed in Lin's chapter in detail.

The story also would not be complete without inputs and a section on Taiwan and Hong Kong. In some ways, rather than the periphery, these locations are important laboratories for understanding Chinese popular culture. They have also interacted with Japanese and other foreign popular cultures much earlier than mainland China, and at a time when the four dragons or tiger economies developed earlier than China

---

[60] Ifeng Reading, "Ri Ben Man Hua Sui Hong Yin Jin Huo Li Tai Nan," *ifeng.com*, April 21, 2011, accessed May 14, 2013, http://book.ifeng.com/yeneizixun/special/tongnianduwu/wenzhang/detail_2011_04/21/5891010_0.shtml.

[61] Wei-jia Wang, "On the Cultural Differences Between China and Japan Through the Word 'Otaku'," *Journal of Hefei University (Social Science)* 28, no. 6 (2011): 60.

which was just starting its economic reforms from 1979 onwards. Consequently, their brushes with commodified and commercialized popular cultural products came much earlier.

Katherine Tseng's chapter is a complex self-reflective piece on popular culture and the Taiwanese identity. She argues that, while it is difficult to summarize this ongoing process, it is discernible that a synthesis of a rapidly evolving political-cum-cultural relation and an imbalanced development of "Taiwanization" and "de-Sinicization" has set the tone for identity construction in Taiwan. Democratization justifies liberalization not only in the political, but also cultural and societal arenas, strengthening the prospects for cultural diversity and vitality. Yet, Tseng argues that downsides remain. The dilemma of accommodating "Taiwanization" and "de-Sinicization" has continued. In her view, a consequence of dwindling economic performance is the hollowing-out of the cultural paradigm in Taiwan. As a result, the Taiwanese case of identity construction is reconsidering the relationship between what constitutes the cultural center and its periphery.

Cantopop is an early outcome of Chinese experiments with popular culture in the modern and contemporary (postwar) era. Cantopop, an acronym for Cantonese popular music, has its roots in Shanghai in the early 1920s. After over 60 years of localization in Hong Kong, the 1980s was Cantopop's golden age featuring many big names, for example, Anita Mui, Danny Chan, Alan Tam and Leslie Cheung, who are well-known domestically and internationally. This golden era also marked the start of Cantopop fandom in Hong Kong. Joining the fan clubs of these artistes was once a prevalent social phenomenon among the youths. As the lyrics of the hit song *A Fans Murder Case at Broadcast Drive* (1993) described, banners with artistes' names written in bright colors were seen at every music show in Hong Kong, fans waiting for their favorite stars were blocking all exits of the concert or the sites of performance venues for 24 hours. Writing the artistes' names on walls at public areas was a common but illegal practice of fandom in Hong Kong.

Examining fandom development in Hong Kong from a historical approach through the use of archival materials, such as newspapers and magazines, Elim Wong and Wilson Lee's chapter does not only survey the history of Cantopop fandom in Hong Kong, it also highlights the unique characteristics of Hong Kong pop fandom. While the rise of J-pop (Japanese pop music) in the 1990s and the importation of K-pop (Korean pop) music in the early 2000s may have influenced Hong Kong popular music industry, one should not overlook the characteristic feature of cultural diversity in Hong Kong society and the music that it generates, as well as how these musical works are received and appreciated in Hong Kong. The influence exerted by fandom activities on the works is also discussed in this chapter.

The last chapter is a conclusion of the major points mentioned by the various writers and it will spot the commonalities amongst the major arguments and raised by the writings in this edited volume. In highlighting the commonalities, the volume demonstrates that issues of cultural self-identity, receptivity of audiences to popular culture, sense of aesthetics, social acceptability of new ideas and worldviews, patterns of consumption and lifestyle habits are constantly shaped and influenced by technological advancements, shifting social values and norms, international trends and marketing campaigns by the state, private sector and fandom communities.

Chapter 2

Particularism within the Context of Universalistic Popular Culture: A Historiographical Survey Approach in the Literature Review of Soft Power in East Asia[1]

Tai Wei LIM

Introduction — Universalism and Particularism

The strength of American popular culture is hardly neglected by scholarly circles and instead is often assumed and taken for granted. The consumption of American popular culture takes place almost subconsciously and without deliberate awareness, given its ubiquitous presence and its appeal. Conceptually, American popular culture is global and universal in nature, driving and encompassing much of the popular trends that one can observe on multimedia, social media, new and old media.[2] Hollywood, fast food cuisine, virtual technologies and more amorphous ideas of fashion and lifestyle choices are all examples of American popular culture.

---

[1]This is a revised paper presented in the 4th Annual Conference of the Association of International Relations Theme: International Relations: Theory and Global Developments and incorporating comments from the 9 June 2011 conference and/or its participants. (This paper is submitted for CD-Rom conference proceedings: 4th Annual Conference of the Association of International Relations.)

[2]My informant in the landscaping and design industry pointed out that in tangible material culture like food and fashion, the US is also in a leading position. (I would like to acknowledge George Ho's contributions here.)

Definitional debates over what makes up popular culture are important but they fall outside the scope of this paper and should be the subject
of important dedicated studies to it. Based on the narratives covered in this
writing, several definitions are offered here. They range from the amorphous, broad and encompassing definitions to more precise and carefully
crafted detailed definitions. Ian Condry argues against defining American
popular culture as a ubiquitous and broad entity and to avoid defining it
as a uniform entity "wherever it appears" and instead differentiate definitions according to their local features and characteristics.[3]

Jonathan Pickering is less concerned about the boundaries of dichotomous global-local definitions of popular culture and conceptualizes it as a
feature that encompasses "entertainment, sport and other practices of everyday life."[4] In other words, popular culture is fully integrated into lifestyles and
everyday experiences. The American and Japanese middle classes as well as
their lifestyles and consumption patterns inspired emulation and inspiration
for the rest of the world.[5] This may be visible in the emerging economies
like India, China and the Gulf region where evidence may be detected
through popular culture, entertainment, material acquisitions, branding,
new and traditional media, and consumption patterns.[6]

John Hannigan sees popular culture as part of a homogenizing process
that is reinforced by large quantities of images interacting and interfacing
with market-driven forces to influence the lives and worldviews of the
receivers of such culture.[7] The idea of a "homogenizing" universal American
popular culture makes the formation of regional identifications of popular

---

[3] Ian Condry, "Japanese Hip-Hop and the Globalization of Popular Culture," in *Urban Life:
Readings in the Anthropology of the City*, eds. G. Gmelch and W. Zenner (Prospect Heights,
IL: Waveland Press, 2002), 372.

[4] Jonathan Pickering, "Globalisation: A Threat to Australian Culture?" *Journal of Australian
Political Economy* 48 (December 2001): 47.

[5] Justin Dargin and Tai Wei Lim, *Energy, Trade and Finance in Asia: A Political and
Economic Analysis* (London: Pickering and Chatto, 2011).

[6] Justin Dargin and Tai Wei Lim, *Energy, Trade and Finance in Asia: A Political and
Economic Analysis* (London: Pickering and Chatto, 2011).

[7] John Hannigan, "Culture, Globalization, and Social Cohesion: Towards a De-territorialized,
Global Fluids Model," *Canadian Journal of Communication* 27, no. 2/3 (2002), http://search.
proquest.com/docview/219574482?accountid=10371 (accessed 16 June 2011).

culture less crucial. American popular culture is also easily consumable, understood and integrated into desirable urbanized middle class lifestyles. Therefore, the argument may not be so much whether American popular culture is consumed in different regions of the world but how it is indigenized, emulated and customized in various forms in various regions of the world. American popular culture is not challenged by alternatives but is studied closely, indigenized, innovated and systematically recreated by other strains of popular culture.

Five narratives or interpretations are examined here to interpret the association of American popular culture with globalization and its ubiquity with global consumers. The first perspective by Jack Banks argues that the development of American popular culture (using the case study of Music Television or MTV) is motivated by commercial market-driven factors and, in doing so, it has a homogenizing effect on global popular culture due to the ability of the US popular cultural production system in providing sizable airtime to its pre-selected stars which, in return, generates local resistance and counteracting movements to resist being overwhelmed by this global homogenizing effect.[8] Market-driven commercialism and its strong links with globalization's facilitation of trade and commerce form a powerful universal framework to examine popular culture by imagining it as a dominant entity within a transnational space that is resisted only at its fringes. Are there alternatives to this core-periphery analysis?

Condry provides a valuable second perspective through comparative analysis by comparing American popular culture with Japanese hip-hop through his informative article *Japanese Hip-Hop and the Globalization of Popular Culture*.[9] Adopting an approach that highlights localization of American popular culture through local intermediation, Condry examines

---

[8] Jack Banks, "MTV and the Globalization of Popular Culture," *International Communication Gazette* 59, no. 1 (February 1997): 43–45, 57.

[9] My informant, George Ho, who is an avid listener of music in all forms including jazz and selected Japanese tracks opined: "Although the music[al] arrangement of Japanese and American hip hop music is close to each other, the lyrics are much different, e.g. US hip hop [may include themes like] (sex, drugs and violence), Japanese hip hop [may include themes like] (social status, love, meaning of life). Indigenization depends on how and to what extent the local people [in different parts of the world, including Japan] decode the global popular culture."

the issue from the margins — unraveling the deceptive cloaking of localized strains of popular culture by globalized culture.[10] According to Condry, the central element in differentiating between local interpretations as opposed to American or globalized perspectives of popular culture lies in indigenous values and local socialization processes as local-area educational system, family values/environment, and the daily encounters and experiences.[11] Resistance, in other words, is not predicated upon local assertions of identity to avoid being overwhelmed by commercialization. Instead, Condry's interpretation of the limits of globalized popular culture is derived from everyday experiences and socialization processes. Life experiences are cumulative, resulting in local interpretations of global popular culture; it is not driven by anxiety about excessive commercialization and homogenous consumption.

Differing from the imagery of a globalized homogenous popular cultural world or the model of marginal indigenization and interpretation of a dominant core, Pickering argues that globalized culture is polycentric in makeup and not homogenous.[12] He makes an important argument with regards to *reception* of popular culture — that the process is not passive but rather an interactive one in which the receiver of popular culture actively integrate, indigenize, and navigate their interpretations of popular culture.[13] In other words, not only are there local readings of global culture but the process is active, interactive and value-add as localization enhances innovation of received global culture and offers greater diversity to the original offerings.

The fourth narrative by Hannigan offers a sophisticated look at the relationship between culture and globalization. His interpretation conceptualizes culture as something transnational with no bases, highly mobile with little physical resistance, connected with metropolitan pulses and lifestyles, and able to travel multi-directionally and autonomously with little restraint.[14] Instead of anxieties over commercialization, homogenization or the need to erect defensive mechanisms to limit the reach of

---

[10] Condry, "Japanese Hip-Hop," 373.

[11] *Ibid.*, 374.

[12] Pickering, "Globalisation," 47.

[13] *Ibid.*, 51.

[14] Hannigan, "Culture, Globalization, and Social Cohesion."

globalization, Hannigan makes an interesting argument that the "chaotic" nature of globalization and popular cultural flows and its problematic random reach and directions lead to a lack of awareness over social traditions, cultures that may be geographically-bound and limited — he problematizes what he sees as the lack of discipline in globalization fluidity often transgressing and offending socially-established conventions.[15]

With these four narratives in mind, it may be possible to examine the legitimacy of local and regional indigenization of global popular cultural trends, whether indeed there are alternatives to American popular culture and, if so, to what extent can those strains of popular culture be considered independent, autonomous and original. This writing acknowledges the great importance of those analyses but is written for a conference on international relations and thus, privileges the international relations idea of soft power as a paradigm and angle in examining the conceptualization of popular culture as a form of soft power. The writing also acknowledges the crucial importance of different varieties of popular culture such as India's Bollywood and its strong appeal for consumers in East Asia, South Asia and the Middle East, and is fully aware of its great importance. With this in mind, this writing focuses on popular culture generated in East Asia as a case study to find out if such regional strains of popular culture contain elements of soft power and, in addition, if the concept of soft power indeed exists and can be applied to popular culture.

This writing acknowledges the important interpretation of East Asian strains of popular culture are global in nature rather than regional. It does not argue that East Asian generated popular is parochial, regional and has no global influence, in fact, reality is quite the opposite. Many aspects of Japanese, Korean and Taiwanese popular culture are global in nature reaching many audiences in the Pacific and translated into many languages. But the paper asserts that East Asian-based popular culture is a subset of global trends in the universe of popular culture driven at its core by American popular culture. East Asian and other regional strains of popular culture are the intangible projections emanating from the hub of American popular cultural core.

---

[15] *Ibid.*

Why is this so? Efforts, financial resources and time are generally required for any formation of regional identity, much less a universal one. Given that US is a generator of new ideas, knowledge and creative know-how for much of the then developing world's postwar developmental phase, its popular cultural industries have been an offshoot of this systemic role in postwar architectural construction.

Secondly, American ideas are generally germinated in English and then either transmitted overseas in English or translated into various regional languages for mass consumption elsewhere. While interpreted differently by different scholars, English has become the *de facto* working language for the world, almost universally. Therefore, back to the hub and spokes model, linguistically, the melting pot of the English language is universal in nature since it is based on global trade and commercial foundations. Other regional strains and varieties of popular culture are mainly germinated in other languages, this feature alone does not preclude the possibility of globalizing it for regional audiences through indigenization, localization, translation and adaptation.

However, regional strains of popular culture have to universalize their popular cultural features in order to adapt to a global audiences that may not be as sensitive to regional cultural instincts and idiosyncrasies. For an important work in this aspect, one may refer to the book *Pikachu's Global Adventure: The Rise and Fall of Pokemon* edited by Joseph Tobin (Durham and London: Duke University Press, 2004). Articles in this edited volume indicate that Japanese popular culture has to be modified and translated in terms of marketing, advertising, distribution, dialogue and characters fore-grounding in order to appeal to the American kids consumer market (largest in the world) and also English-speaking audiences around the world. Therefore, American popular culture consumed in regional variations undergoes the opposite process. Universal American popular culture is particularized to fit regional contexts, environments and idiosyncrasies.

It is within this universal and global popular cultural industry that East Asian-originated popular culture was conceptualized, shaped, innovated, improved upon and distributed. The systemic origins of regional variations of popular culture typically (not always) arises from the production studios based in East Asia and shaped by popular trends, events and thinking in those societies and transformed into easily-consumable product units tailored made for its domestic markets. Upon reaching a critical level of popularity amongst the home audiences, it is then regionalized, first tested in familiar neighboring regional markets well-acquainted with products emanating from a particular source and, if the receptivity towards that products proves positive, the popular cultural products are then regionalized and distributed region-wide, sometimes simultaneous with a global launch, sometimes preceding or subsequent to a global launch.

This is the content component of the creative flying geese structure whereby ideas are exchanged and packaged in specialized units of production. From concept components akin to industrial design workshops of industrial products, these products are consumed by domestic markets that grow in sophistication and tastes. When costs of production become too high (various creative enhancements within the creative process) and/or are then sent to regional markets for testing the waters in the quest for market expansion, the production sites for such popular cultural products are then shifted overseas to nearby regional bases such as from Japan to Taiwan or Hong Kong (HK) either as franchises or joint ventures as indigenous production bases for Japanese popular cultural products.[16]

Popular Culture in East Asia — Examples

It may be possible that, sub-regionally, where there are similar groups of states, cultures and economies, for popular cultural strains to group and cluster ideas and popular cultural appreciation together and increase interactions before embarking on region-wide mass marketing process. In this process of marketing, self-identifications and common interpretations of the attractiveness of popular culture are sought. Popular culture may be more easily identifiable by younger generations and students located in a particular region. Japanese popular culture (J-pop) and more recently Korean popular culture (*hanliu* in Chinese, *hallyu* from Korean pronunciation, *hanryū/kanryū* in Japanese or K-pop)[17] may place this role in

---

[16] My informant, George Ho, a consumer of Japanese popular culture, pointed out that it includes Japanese comics franchised to Taiwanese and Hong Kong publishing companies.

[17] J-pop or K-pop usually refers to popular music only while *kanryu/hallyu* refers to the "Korean wave/ popular culture." The definition of K-pop may a bit narrower and different from *kanryu*.

integrating the East Asian market culturally and contribute to common appreciation and consumption of such culture within the global rubric and context of American-driven popular cultural trends.

Even between Korea and Japan which have a history of competitive instincts in popular culture,[18] Korean popular culture goods have been well-received in Japan. Kent E. Calder and Min Ye point out that the Korea movie (*Winter*), and TV series *Winter Sonata* with Korean superstar Bae Yong-jun and Rain (concert with 40,000 fans in Beijing and 20,000 in Tokyo) may be examples of *hanryū*.[19] John Lie's important publication on the mainstream acceptance of signifiers of Korean existence in Japan noted that it was the most well-watched TV drama in Japan and members of its Japanese following travelled to the actual place where the drama was shot in the hope of seeing Bae Yong-jun or *Yon-sama* (as he is known in Japan) in person.[20] According to Jung-sun Park, the reason for K-pop success lies in the ability to articulate the regional heartstrings, emotive feel and identity of past, present and future of nearby states.[21]

Sports stars and the 2002 Joint World Cup held by Japan and Korea were other visible manifestation of the effect of popular culture in pulling the two neighbors closer together in the realm of popular culture. Lie argues that celebrities in Japan who were public with their Korean heritage like venture capitalist Son Masayoshi and other Koreans or ethnic Koreans with Japanese nationality helped to bridge the relations between Japan and Korea.[22] Gilbert Rozman noted that Korean culinary cuisines were also another source of ideational awareness, for e.g. *kimchi* became a popular dish in Japan between 2001 and 2003, carrying on beyond

---

[18] My informant, George Ho, a fan in selected aspects of J-pop, stated that since 1945, Seoul imposed [a] ban on imports of Japanese pop[ular] cultural products such as music, movies, comics [etc]. The ban was gradually lifted from 1998. That signified the influence of political factors on the diffusion of Japanese pop[ular] culture in Korea.

[19] Kent E. Calder and Min Ye, *The Making of Northeast Asia* (Stanford, California: Stanford University Press, 2010), 12.

[20] John Lie, *Zainichi (Koreans in Japan): Diasporic Nationalism and Postcolonial Identity* (Berkeley, LA and London: University of California Press, 2008), 133.

[21] Jung-sun Park, "The Korean Wave: Transnational Cultural Flows in Northeast Asia," in *Korea at the Center: Dynamics of Regionalism in Northeast Asia,* eds. C. K. Armstrong *et al.* (Armonk and London: ME Sharpe, 2006), 252.

[22] Lie, *Zainichi (Koreans in Japan)*, 134.

2003.[23] According to Lie, *kimchi* was the most popular pickle in Japan, even more so than the customary pickle dish *takuan* (named after a Zen priest) that Japanese were used to.[24] Such exchanges may be classified under Track II diplomacy which T. J. Pempel included sports stars, dance groups, in addition to the J- and K-pop stars named above.[25]

As an East Asian pioneer in positioning its creative capacities for global consumption, Japanese electronic soft power has become regionalized and globalized. According to David Buckingham and Julian Sefton-Green, Nintendo's Pokemon franchise drew in US$5 billion in its first year in 1998.[26] *Anime* (animation) and *manga* (Japanese comics) are probably two of Japan's most well-known popular cultural exports. According to Taylor E. Atkins, one HK retailer makes sales of 50 Video Compact Discs (VCDs) on a daily basis while J-pop stars have a large following as well.[27] A more traditional popular cultural icon that is recognizable all over East Asia may be Doraemon which made its appearance in Vietnam (1993) and was utilized in Cambodia as a symbol of ethical behavior. Saya Shiraishi contends that such popular cultural icons break Japan out of its cultural isolationism and inward-looking tendencies.[28]

As examples of other forms of East Asian strains of popular culture building upon Japan's successes, HK has had a tradition of Cantopop songs, particularly appealing to Cantonese-speaking East Asians or, if translated into Mandarin, Chinese-speaking audience as well. Peter Katzenstein highlights Cantopop legend Jacky Cheung and HK comics

---

[23] Gilbert Rozman, *Northeast Asia's Stunted Regionalism: Bilateral Distrust in the Shadow of Globalization* (Cambridge: Cambridge University Press, 2004), 305.

[24] Lie, *Zainichi (Koreans in Japan)*, 149.

[25] T. J. Pempel, "Introduction: Emerging Webs of Regional Connectedness," in *Remapping East Asia: The Construction of a Region,* ed. T. J. Pempel (Ithaca and London: Cornell University Press, 2005), 12.

[26] David Buckingham and Julian Sefton-Green, "Structure, Agency and Pedagogy in Children's Media Culture," in *Pikachu's Global Adventure: The Rise and Fall of Pokémon,* ed. Joseph Tobin (Durham and London: Duke University Press, 2004), 13.

[27] Taylor E. Atkins, "Can Japanese Sing the Blues? 'Japanese Jazz' and the Problem of Authenticity," in *Japan Pop!: Inside the World of Japanese Popular Culture*, ed. T. J. Craig (New York: East Gate, 2000), 5.

[28] Saya S. Shiraishi, "Doraemon Goes Abroad," in *Japan Pop!: Inside the World of Japanese Popular Culture*, ed. T. J. Craig (New York: East Gate, 2000), 288–289.

artist Tony Wong's Jademan as examples.[29] Cantopop, however, appears to have contemporarily and recently been relatively and comparatively overshadowed by J-pop and the Korean wave although its cinematic gems continue to make regional impact. Given the high permeability of cultural flows and the fickle nature of its consumer base, popular cultural trends and fashion may be revived or ebb at different time periods.

Consumption and Production

Geoffrey McNicoll classified the phenomenon of popular culture growth as a form of urban middle class culture that is soaked in J-manga and anime, HK movies and Western IT technologies.[30] Consumption patterns therefore appear to offer a form of homogenizing effect on regional populations, socializing them in similar aesthetic appreciation, entertainment options, fashion trends and creative development. For example, Lie noted that, *collectively*, Japanese and Koreans in Japan used to consuming popular sweets and confectionary manage to name Lotte as a major processed food firm in Japan.[31] Tobin suggests that intra-regional consumption still has a long way to go, given China's market potentialities and growing Japanese marketing networks in popular cultural products.[32]

Japan, South Korea and China are teaching each other on how to be cool and creative through trilateral and bilateral soft power and popular culture projects. In fact, East Asian popular cultural industries have become so sophisticated that, like industrial production systems, they have graduated and specialized production systems and testing grounds. Park noted in his informative and important article that Taiwan and HK are prep platforms for Korean popular culture to see if they can succeed in Greater China and other

---

[29] Peter J. Katzenstein, "East Asia — Beyond Japan," in *Beyond Japan: The Dynamics of East Asian Regionalism,* eds. P. J. Katzenstein and T. Shiraishi (Ithaca and London: Cornell University Press, 2006), 13.

[30] Geoffrey McNicoll, "Demographic Future of East Asian Regional Integration," in *Remapping East Asia: The Construction of a Region*, ed. T. J. Pempel (Ithaca and London: Cornell University Press, 2005), 71.

[31] Lie, *Zainichi (Koreans in Japan)*, 191.

[32] Joseph Tobin, "Conclusion: The Rise and Fall of the Pokemon Empire," in *Pikachu's Global Adventure: The Rise and Fall of Pokémon*, ed. Joseph Tobin (Durham and London: Duke University Press, 2004), 268.

parts of East Asia.[33] Besides consumption, the production factor is just as important. Shiraishi's important study of Doraemon popular cultural icon indicates that, in an effort to pare down the budget used for manufacturing animation, economic factors determined the necessity and viability of relocating workspaces to other East Asian locations like Seoul and Taipei.[34]

This is reminiscent of the production structure found in Japan's industrialization in the postwar years when the flying geese model determined the viability of relocating Japan's production sites overseas when costs became too high in Japan. Japan is a large donor of aids and loans (including Japanese Official Development Assistance or ODA) to the East Asian region, helping to build infrastructure in East Asian economies. In the initial stage, Japan utilized Foreign Direct Investments (FDIs) to kick-start industrialization when local businesses lacked the skills to build up systems of production. Through joint ventures or training at these facilities, local companies acquired the skills and knowhow for industrialization which then fed an export system to accumulate profits that snowballed into further investments in industrialization, resulting in greater employment and economic development.

It also initiated a period of "Learning from Japan" in the 1990s when East Asian economies emulated and indigenized successful features (such as Japanese business management, productivity drive, social harmony, etc.) of Japanese economic growth and development. In his article *East Asia — Beyond Japan*, Peter Katzenstein argues that this was a process of "Japanization." The process appeared to slow down with Japanese long-drawn recession and the onset of the US-driven IT age. The globalized nature and soft power of the US appear to have allure for East Asian economies and thus, some of the leading economies in East Asia outside Japan began to hybridize Japanese learning with cutting-edge American ideas. According to Shiraishi, soft power may be based on "resonance," the ability of popular culture to strike a chord with sizable portions of the populations in Asia.[35]

Popular cultural development may be analogized as Japan's own popular cultural flying geese model that may become increasingly significant and important as Japan's creative industries boom and send production sites overseas based on labor costs, closeness to markets and

---

[33] Park, "Korean Wave," 248.

[34] Shiraishi, "Doraemon Goes Abroad," 300.

[35] *Ibid.*, 289

presence of expertise. Shiraishi's important work on Doraemon noted that Taiwan was one of the first recipients of Japan's iconic Doraemon franchise with its indigenous group of illustrators, periodicals and soft-cover series in place since the late 1970s in both comics and cartoon formats.[36]

Given contemporary levels of development and capabilities, the creative flying geese is likely to be much flatter than its industrial counterpart, given the greater proximity between Japan and its East Asian neighbors in terms of the levels of developmentalism. In their own ways, Korea, Taiwan and even China have caught up in technical capabilities, consumption capability and integration into the global hub of fashion trends and awareness. Rather than a flying geese model or a hub and spokes, the interactions now resemble complex interconnecting lines of influence, as they exchange creative ideas and trends with each other, mutually influencing each other in the end and reinforcing regional production capabilities in creative production. But other interpretations contest this closing of capabilities gap. David Leheny noted a trilateral project where HK filmmaker Kar-wai Wong featured Kaneshiro Takeshi (Jin Chengwu in Chinese) in his films *Chungking Express* and *Fallen Angels* and, in *Chungking Express*, Kaneshiro or Jin used a variety of Chinese dialects and Japanese language in his character's dialogue.[37] Leheny also provides other examples such as Wong's 2004 film *2046*; Kusanagi Tsuyoshi's starring in Korean-speaking Japanese movie *Hotel Venus* and Nakamura Tōru's main character in Korean film *Lost Memories*.[38] According to my informant, George Ho, "it appears that this trend still continue with the present film 'The Crossing 1'."

Conclusion

In conclusion, Table 2.1 relates East Asian popular cultural features with narratives discussing the relationship between popular culture and globalization discussed earlier in this chapter:

---

[36] *Ibid.*, 303.

[37] David Leheny, "A Narrow Place to Cross Swords: Soft Power and the Politics of Japanese Popular Culture in East Asia," in *Beyond Japan: The Dynamics of East Asian Regionalism*, eds. P. J. Katzenstein and T. Shiraishi (Ithaca and London: Cornell University Press, 2006), 215.

[38] *Ibid.*

TABLE 2.1. NARRATIVES AND FEATURES RELATED TO EAST ASIAN POPULAR CULTURE.

Author	Narrative Feature	Application to East Asian Popular Cultural Developments
Jack Banks	Commercialization	According to David Buckingham and Julian Sefton-Green, Nintendo's Pokemon franchise drew in US$5 billion in its first year in 1998.[39] *Anime* and *manga* are probably two of Japan's most well-known popular cultural exports. According to Taylor E. Atkins, one HK retailer makes sales of 50 Video Compact Discs (VCDs) on a daily basis while J-pop stars have a large following as well.[40]
Jack Banks	Homogenizing effect	John Lie noted that, *collectively*, Japanese and Koreans in Japan used to consuming popular sweets and confectionary for example manage to name Lotte as a major processed food firm in Japan.[41]
Ian Condry	Everyday experiences and socialization processes	According to Jung-sun Park, the reason for K-pop success lies in the ability to articulate the regional heartstrings, emotive feel and identity of past, present and future of nearby states.[42] Saya Shiraishi noted that soft power may be based on "resonance," the ability of popular culture to strike a chord with sizable portions of the populations in Asia.[43]

(Continued)

[39] Buckingham and Sefton-Green, "Structure, Agency and Pedagogy," 13.
[40] Atkins, "Can Japanese Sing the Blues?" 5.
[41] Lie, *Zainichi (Koreans in Japan)*, 191.
[42] Park, "Korean Wave," 252.
[43] Shiraishi, "Doraemon Goes Abroad," 289.

TABLE 2.1. *(Continued)*

Author	Narrative Feature	Application to East Asian Popular Cultural Developments
Ian Condry	Local interpretations of global popular culture	Saya Shiraishi's important work on Doraemon noted that Taiwan was one of the first recipients of Japan's iconic Doraemon franchise with its indigenous group of illustrators, periodicals and soft-cover series in place since the late 1970s in both comics and cartoon format.[44]
Jonathan Pickering	Reception of culture not passive but rather an interactive one	
	Receiver of popular culture actively integrate, indigenize and navigate their interpretations of popular culture	
Jonathan Pickering	Polycentric in makeup and not homogenous	Jung-sun Park notes in his informative and important article that Taiwan and HK are prep platforms for Korean popular culture to see if they can succeed in Greater China and other parts of East Asia.[45]
		David Leheny noted a trilateral project where HK filmmaker Kar-wai Wong featured Kaneshiro Takeshi (Jin Chengwu in Chinese) in his films *Chungking Express* and *Fallen Angels* and, in *Chungking Express*, Kaneshiro or Jin used a variety of Chinese dialects and Japanese language in his character's dialogue.[46]

[44] *Ibid.*, 303.
[45] Park, "Korean Wave," 248.
[46] Leheny, "Narrow Place to Cross Swords," 215.

John Hannigan	Transnational with no bases, highly mobile with little physical resistance	Saya Shiraishi contends that such popular cultural icons break Japan out of its cultural isolationism and inward-looking tendencies.[47]
John Hannigan	Connected with metropolitan pulses and lifestyles	Geoffrey McNicoll classified the phenomenon of popular culture growth as a form of urban middle class culture that is soaked in J-manga and anime, HK movies and Western IT technologies.[48]
John Hannigan	Able to travel multi-directionally and autonomously with little restraint	Cost factors: Saya Shiraishi's important study of Doraemon popular cultural icon indicates that, in an effort to pare down the budget used for manufacturing animation, economic factors determined the necessity and viability of relocating workspaces to other East Asian locations like Seoul and Taipei.[49]
John Hannigan	Lack of awareness over social traditions, cultures that may be geographically-bound and limited	

(Continued)

[47] Shiraishi, "Doraemon Goes Abroad," 288–289.
[48] McNicoll, "Demographic Future," 71.
[49] Shiraishi, "Doraemon Goes Abroad," 300.

TABLE 2.1. *(Continued)*

Author	Narrative Feature	Application to East Asian Popular Cultural Developments
	Lack of discipline in globalization fluidity often transgressing and offending socially-established conventions	
	"Chaotic" nature of globalization and popular cultural flows and its problematic random reach and directions	

Concluding Remarks and Trends: Soft Power?

William Tsutsui believes that Japanese soft power has set the pace and example for future popular cultural trends in East Asia, including the current Korean popular cultural craze in Asia, and perhaps China Central Television (CCTV) drama series in the future based on the precedent that Japan has set.[50] The creative industries in these three East Asian settings are likely to find more exchanges and permeability, developing a pan-East Asian popular culture in the process within the setting and contextualization of an East Asian backdrop. Connected with this process is the construction of self-identity and regional features of such exchanges.

The idea of soft power has evolved along with narratives focusing on popular cultural soft power. From Joseph S. Nye's idea of getting someone to do what you want without the use of force,[51] Tsutsui has argued that it has been transformed from an academic to a general purpose term. Shiraishi goes further to adapt the term for use in popular culture by privileging the element of resonance or the ability to tug at the emotive element of major sections of the populace in Asia. In the case of East Asia, Japanese, Korean, Taiwanese, HK and Chinese popular culture have aggregated the collective aspirations, imaginations and fascinations of regional audiences.

In terms of class analyses, soft power appears to be most applicable to the urban middle classes in East Asia. Within the urban middle classes, the narratives and discourses focus on consumption. This urban middle class often uses popular culture as a signifier for common identification, focusing on branding and engaging in popular cultural trend-spotting to build a common experience. In utilizing a consumption perspective on popular culture, narratives on soft power are built upon the idea of economic complementarity.

The basis of narratives of soft power in East Asia consumption is also predicated upon an electronic and technologically-driven process. One in

---

[50] William Tsutsui, *Japanese Popular Culture and Globalization* (Ann Arbor, MI: Association for Asian Studies Inc., 2010), 71.

[51] For further reading, see Joseph S. Nye, *Soft Power: The Means to Success in World Politics* (New York: Public Affairs, 2004).

which electronic pets, online discussions and robotic technologies attract common fascination from East Asian consumers amidst a global audience. The products of popular cultural soft power are also weightless and tend to be visually and experientially oriented. In the narratives that move fluidly between universalistic and particularistic elements, while there are some attempts to achieve Asian cultural identities and sensitivities on popular cultural trends, the same forces that created globalization and foster global popular cultural trends are also at play here. Globalized and universalistic appeal of American soft power for example permeates and interacts with East Asian popular cultural trends.

Popular cultural soft power is mutually-reinforcing in the sense that East Asian economies work with each other and influence each other to become cool and creative, but yet at the same time trend-spots global popular cultural elements for incorporation into their textual and visual imaginations and body of works. The East Asian popular cultural industries have developed production facilities and specialized teams region-wide. It has the commercial and industrial potential of a creative flying geese model since Japan had in the past set the pace for the development of the creative industries. There are also differential levels of consumption, for e.g. narratives noted the sequential dissemination of popular culture, for example HK and Taiwan as laboratories and platforms to test receptivity and reactions to popular cultural products before introduction to Chinese consumption.

Currently, more well-known exports from India related to its soft power are Bollywood movies and other forms of popular culture that may be well-received in the Middle East.[52] The cultural reach is not just one-way. For example, according to Arielle Kandel, India welcomed Israeli arts and cultural performances and the same applied the other way round to foster greater contacts between the two societies.[53]

---

[52] Justin Dargin and Tai Wei Lim, *Energy, Trade and Finance in Asia: A Political and Economic Analysis* (London: Pickering and Chatto, 2011).

[53] Arielle Kandel, "The Significant Warming of Indo-Israeli Relations in the Post-Cold War Period," *Middle East Review of International Affairs* 13, no. 4 (December 2009): 75, http://www.gloria-center.org/files/2010020372653.pdf (accessed 16 June 2011). This point was argued in the co-authored manuscript "Energy and Trade" to be published by Pickering and Chatto.

Simultaneously, there appears to be contacts that are increasingly people-to-people contact, e.g. in the field of education (tertiary education), cultural exchanges, art shows and exhibitions.[54] The inter-regional extension of popular cultural products and influence is another development reinforcing exchanges within the complex universal rubric of globalized popular cultural trends.

---

[54] Justin Dargin and Tai Wei Lim, *Energy, Trade and Finance in Asia: A Political and Economic Analysis* (London: Pickering and Chatto, 2011).

Section 2

Japan

Chapter 3

Introduction to the Section on Japan

Tai Wei LIM

In conceptualizing this section on Japan, I kept in mind the limitations of my writing. Throughout the narratives, I maintain the important caveat that Japanese popular culture is not necessarily universalistic and maintains its international, regional and local popularity through translation, dubbing and marketing intermediation that makes Japanese cultural products acceptable to children and consumers in its major destination markets. For the regional and local consumers, the element of resonance is equally important in enhancing the products emotive and cognitive connections with its audience. Japanese popular cultural products are attractive because they can strike a chord with the consumers in East Asia through cultural symbolisms and content-based aesthetics that appeal to viewers from a particular cultural region. The resonance factor is in addition to slick and effective marketing techniques.

Popular culture generated in East Asia is utilized as a case study to find out if regional strains of popular culture contain elements of soft power (if the concept of soft power indeed exists) and can be applied to popular culture. The creative industries in these three East Asian settings are likely to find more exchanges and permeability, developing a popular culture in the process within the setting and contextualization of a regional backdrop. It is within the framework of a universal and global popular cultural industry that East Asian-originated popular culture was conceptualized, shaped, innovated, improved upon and distributed. The systemic origins of regional variations of popular culture typically (but not always) arises from the production studios based in East Asia and shaped by popular trends, events and thinking in those societies and transformed into easily-consumable product units tailored made for its domestic markets.

Upon reaching a critical level of popularity amongst the home audiences, it is then regionalized, first tested in familiar neighboring regional markets well-acquainted with products emanating from a particular source and, if the receptivity towards that products proves positive, the popular cultural products are then regionalized and distributed region-wide, sometimes simultaneous with a global launch, sometimes preceding or subsequent to a global launch. Popular cultural soft power is mutually-reinforcing in the sense that East Asian economies work with each other and influence each other to become cool and creative but yet at the same time trend-spots global popular cultural elements for incorporation into their textual and visual imaginations and body of works.

US globalized popular culture plays several simultaneous functions. It serves as inspiration for other cultures to imitate, borrow and indigenize. It is also a universalistic force that appeals to a global audience as the world becomes gradually homogenized by globalization. Globalization promotes the standardization of tastes, sense of aesthetics, and common consumption experiences because of improved technologies in increasing the speed of information flow and digital technologies that disseminate intellectual products like online games, anime cartoons and digital manga available to large audiences who yearn for instant gratification.

Because of the fluid nature of cultural influences, flows and dissemination, different genres and varieties of products cross-influence each other substantially (the idea of cultural cross-pollination). Therefore, just as it is difficult and challenging to pinpoint original Korean, Japanese, Taiwanese or mainland Chinese sources of influence. Every individual popular cultural products receives multiple influences from various sources, culminating in unique designs and products. These designs are then sold and marketed by economies that developed earlier like Japan, Taiwan and South Korea to large consumer markets in China and East Asia. In exporting these products to China and East Asia as a whole, the idea of cultural soft power influence comes into play. But cultural influences are tempered with geopolitical realities, historical memories and other differences within the region. Therefore, sometimes, popular cultures experience separation of politics from cultural appreciation as regional audiences consume K-pop, J-pop, Cantopop and *Tailiu* products independent of political tensions.

More importantly, as Chinese, Japanese and Koreans consume each other's products, cultural cross-pollination takes place with popular cultures learning from each other. Such cross-influences are not exclusive as the rising urban middle-class consumers enjoy J-pop and K-pop simultaneously with consuming American popular cultural products. The consumption mode therefore is fluid and competitive, with different historical periods where certain popular cultural genres are more popular than others. The constantly-shifting creative equilibrium between East Asian popular culture and extensive cross-influences with other cultural influences form the crux of analysis for the chapter on universalism and particularism in this section. After a theoretical discussion on cultural influences, this section then zooms in Japanese popular culture and first introduces a quantitative chapter that outlines the market size, industries involved and product range of Japanese popular cultural creative industries. Here the stakeholders of creative producers, state agencies and fans form an important triangle of creative production ecology. Policy instruments, state-provided seed funding, tourism attraction and the deployment of popular culture franchises in mega-events are some of the major items discussed in this section on Japan.

With the overall size of the industry carefully outlined and discussed based on different benchmarks, the section then analyzes specific case studies and examples. The chapter on Akihabara is probably the most important case study on the nucleus of Japanese popular culture. It is also an important case study of a physical location where tangible entities like retailers, billboards, consumption centers and creative clusters can be found. In the center of Japan's multi-stakeholder Cool Japan campaign as well as globalized fan-driven consumption of Japanese popular culture, lies the cultural center of Akihabara in Tokyo. Akihabara is simultaneously a creative industry production and retail center, a social networking/ tourism platform and a symbol of fan-driven consumption. The fluid ecology of Akihabara itself is made up of multi-stakeholders, dynamically interacting with each other with no clear center or hegemonic principal players. The seminar examines the organic historical growth of this creative cultural retail cluster, contributions made by its multi-stakeholders, the role of fandom and policy inputs in its development, and concludes with a short discussion on future trends in Akihabara.

After the detailed examination of Akihabara as a creative production center, I turned my attention to the consumption side, at the national, local and individual levels. This chapter is based on my observation studies in Japan from 2012 to 2015 to provide a qualitative rather than a quantitative study of how Japanese popular culture is consumed in the cities of Tokyo and Fukuoka. The observations are random and unstructured to accentuate width and span of activities, physical locations, cultural rituals and lifestyles covered. The observations do not pretend to be comprehensive but rather provide a glimpse into how Japanese popular culture is consumed in every-day settings. Some of these observations are supported by visual materials. I selected three major angles for my observation fieldwork. I paid special attention to several activities and agencies in the ecology of creative production: marketing strategies and concepts utilized by creative producers as well as the role of the state and retailers in promoting popular cultural products; soft power harnessed by the state and local authorities in social campaigns/policies utilizing popular culture; and the presence of popular cultural products in daily life routines exposing, socializing and familiarizing young Japanese and other consumers of Japanese society with the stylized features and aesthetics of Japanese popular culture. These three areas make up the three major sections in this chapter. The chapter will then end off with a limitations section and some concluding remarks.

From the macro-level analysis of universalism and particularism, I narrowed down the perspective to an area studies level by focusing on Japan in this section. Then, case studies are utilized to look at popular cultural centers like Akihabara to examine the ideas, activities and ecology of fandoms and their influences on creative production. I then employed observation studies to look at the consumption side, on how different local districts market, disseminate and distribute popular cultural products.

Chapter 4

Size and Reach of the Japanese Popular Cultural Industry

Tai Wei LIM

One of the first things I set out to do when writing this publication's section on Japanese popular culture was to determine the size and reach of the industries and stakeholders involved. The challenge encountered was that there is no universal standard way to determine the size of the Japanese popular cultural industry. I then relied on secondary literature review to determine how other scholars or industry watchers measured the size of the Japanese popular cultural industry or its reach. I reviewed a combination of academic literature as well as media sources. The reasons for understanding how other scholars measure the size of the Japanese popular cultural industry is three-folds: (1) knowing its size would reveal the significance of studying this industry and its contribution to the Japanese economy; (2) accurate assessments of the importance of this industry could also facilitate comparative work, e.g. understanding the relative importance of J-pop vis-à-vis K-pop; (3) understanding how different stakeholders in the industry define the popular culture, creative industries, leisure and entertainment industries in Japan.

In English-language literature related to Japanese popular culture in the arts and social sciences, humanities fields, a number of scholarships tend to define Japanese popular culture according to its three components of Anime, Comic and Games (ACG) industries. According to Ichiya Nakamura who quoted the report by Megumu Onouchi, by 2003, the ACG industry made up 10% of the Japanese media entertainment market and

30% if character goods were added.[1] It was also about this time that the concept and idea of Cool Japan emerged, coined by observers who saw the potential for soft power in Japanese popular cultural exports. In terms of dollars and cents, in 2003, the ACG market was worth ¥34 trillion (approximately US$340 billion) and ¥10 trillion (approximately US$100 billion) each for comics and animations, respectively and ¥14 trillion (approximately US$140 billion) for games.[2]

Market size is only one of the many criteria used to measure and track the popularity of Japanese popular culture. Scholars have also used website hits to track popularity of Japanese popular culture. For example, Danielle Rich noted that in May 2010, *Google.com* ranked *Onemanga. com* website, a website that makes available fan-made products, as one of the world's 1000 most visited online sites (ranked 935th) with 4.2 million unique visitors per month.[3] These statistics show the reach and popularity of Japanese popular culture but there are limitations in interpreting the information. Website popularity does not necessarily indicate its profitability, industry size and revenues, all of which may be crucial for gathering state and private sector support for funding Cool Japan initiatives. At the same time, however, there is also a limitation to measuring only ACG industries quantitatively as there are trickle-down effects from ACG consumption to other industries. Prominent Japanese popular culture scholar Nissim Otmazgin quoted a *Manga Network* survey which studied 1200 manga fans in their early 20s in Western European countries like France, Italy, Germany and Switzerland and found out that majority of the manga consumers developed interest in "learning Japan (two-thirds), traveling to the country (three-quarters), meeting Japanese people and learning more about Japan (half), and some even expressed a wish to find

[1] Ichiya Nakamura, "Japanese Pop Industry DP-2003-002-E," dated 22 November 2003 in the Stanford Japan Center website [downloaded on 22 December 2014], available at http:// sjcr.stanford.edu/research/publication/DP/pdf/DP2003_002_E.pdf, 2.

[2] Ichiya Nakamura, "Japanese Pop Industry DP-2003-002-E," dated 22 November 2003 in the Stanford Japan Center website [downloaded on 22 December 2014], available at http:// sjcr.stanford.edu/research/publication/DP/pdf/DP2003_002_E.pdf, 5.

[3] Danielle Leigh Rich, "Global Fandom: The Circulation of Japanese Popular Culture in the US" (PhD diss., University of Iowa, 2011), 1.

a job related to Japan (15%)."[4] This potentially means that the language educational sector, travel agencies, headhunting companies and tourism industries may also benefit from greater consumption of ACG products but they may not be included comprehensively in studies on popular cultural or the ACG industries.

Future Challenges

The Ministry of Economy, Trade and Industry (METI) identified a number of challenges facing the Japanese popular cultural industry. The most well-known of all is probably the aging population which will lead to lower consumption of popular cultural and creative goods overall. This will mean that Japan needs to export more popular cultural products overseas to make up for a declining domestic market. The global size of the popular cultural market is US$624 billion (2011 figure) when "trade in creative goods and services" are taken into account.[5] Japan wants to occupy more of this global market share of popular cultural products and consumption. In 2012, the METI made its ambitions public. The "creativity-based" industries make up approximately ¥2 trillion share of the global market which is expected to have a value above ¥900 trillion in 2020 and Cool Japan has set the target to increase its share in 2020 to between ¥8 trillion and ¥11 trillion.[6]

There are certain quantitative indicators working in Japan's favor when it comes to greater consumption of Japanese popular cultural products. For example, Otmazgin noted that individuals learning Japanese language external to Japan went up from 127,161 in 1979 to 3.65 million in 2009, mainly due to "consumption of manga and anime by young

---

[4]Nissim Otmazgin, "Meta-Narratives of Japanese Popular Culture and of Japan in Different Regional Contexts: Perspectives from East Asia, Western Europe, and the Middle East," in *Representation of Japanese Contemporary Popular Culture in Europe, Regionines studijos (7)*, ed. K. Koma (Kaunas: Vytautas Magnus University, 2013), 89.

[5]Alan Wheatley, "Asian Style," dated June 2014 in Finance & Development (Washington DC: IMF), 2014, 15.

[6]Kazuaki Nagata, "Exporting culture via 'Cool Japan'," dated 15 May 2012 in Japan Times [downloaded 23 December 2014], available at http://www.japantimes.co.jp/news/2012/05/15/reference/exporting-culture-via-cool-japan/#.VJmN10oA.

audiences abroad."[7] Ability to read Japanese would facilitate non-Japanese consuming more Japanese popular cultural products. But this also means that, as Japan relies more on overseas markets for its popular cultural products, it will also become more vulnerable to economic conditions in those markets. Rich's thesis noted that *ICv2*'s report indicated that North American manga (comic) sales declined 20% in 2009 (having previously reached a peak of US$210 million in 2007) as *shojo* fans mature and stop purchasing manga as well as recessionary conditions in the US.[8] The same decline can also be spotted in the anime industry. In 2012, the *Japan Times* ran an article by Kazuaki Nagata indicating that the Japanese anime industry peaked at ¥16 billion in 2006 and declined to ¥9.2 billion in 2010.[9]

Regionally, Japan is trying to look into exporting more creative and popular cultural products to overseas markets like China. Up to 2008, J-pop music was doing relatively well in Chinese-speaking economies. It was more popular than American or Korean pop music in Hong Kong (45% of respondents surveyed by Otmazgin) and in the three major Chinese cities of Beijing, Shanghai and Guangzhou (23.7% of respondents surveyed).[10] But bilateral maritime disputes, historical memories and other political/geopolitical bilateral issues may have changed perceptions of J-pop in China. There are currently no major studies to look into the impact of political disagreements on Japanese popular cultural development. Regionally, there is also greater competition and high-quality products coming from South Korea. Some literatures that I came across defined cultural

---

[7]Nissim Otmazgin, "Meta-Narratives of Japanese Popular Culture and of Japan in Different Regional Contexts: Perspectives from East Asia, Western Europe, and the Middle East," in *Representation of Japanese Contemporary Popular Culture in Europe Regionines studijos (7)*, ed. K. Koma (Kaunas: Vytautas Magnus University, 2013), 84.

[8]Danielle Leigh Rich, "Global Fandom: The Circulation of Japanese Popular Culture in the US" (PhD diss., University of Iowa, 2011), 174–175.

[9]Kazuaki Nagata, "Exporting culture via 'Cool Japan'," dated 15 May 2012 in Japan Times [downloaded 23 December 2014], available at http://www.japantimes.co.jp/news/2012/05/15/reference/exporting-culture-via-cool-japan/#.VJmN10oA.

[10]Nissim Otmazgin, "Japanese Popular Culture in East and Southeast Asia: Time for a Regional Paradigm?" dated 8 February 2008 in Japan Focus [downloaded on 19 December 2014], available at http://www.japanfocus.org/-Nissim_Kadosh-Otmazgin/2660. [This essay originally appeared in *Kyoto Review of Southeast Asia*.]

exports in comparative terms. Japan's popular cultural industry exports US$23 billion worth of cultural products and, by contrast, according to the Korea Foundation for International Culture Exchange, the economic returns from South Korean popular cultural exports is approximately US$4.3 billion.[11] South Korean popular cultural products however will continue to increase in popularity and importance in Asia and beyond, and may one day catch up with Japan which relies mainly on domestic market shares.

State Help

In recognition of Japan's increasing reliance on popular cultural exports and the need to surmount the challenges highlighted above, the Japanese government is working with the private sector to provide more resources to the creative industry. The initial state-approved funds arrived in mid-2013. On 12 June 2013, *TIME* magazine reported that Japan's upper house of the Diet (Parliament) approved a US$500 million 20-year fund known as Cool Japan to integrate anime and manga to Japanese "movies, design, fashion, food and tourism."[12] In November 2013, the Japanese government increased the amount to a US$300 million (approximate conversion from ¥30 billion) 20-year Cool Japan fund to promote a wide variety of cultural goods and services.[13] When it was launched in mid-2013, the METI wanted it to attract private investors by late 2013 to reach an eventual investment target of US$600 million.[14] As of November 2013, contributions from private sector investment sources amounted to US$75 million.[15] According to Japan's METI's presentation document dated 18 November 2013, there are

[11] Alan Wheatley, "Asian Style," dated June 2014 in Finance & Development (Washington DC: IMF), 2014, 15–16.

[12] Roland Kelts, "Japan Spends Millions in Order to Be Cool," dated 1 July 2013 in Time.com website [downloaded on 23 December 2014], available at http://world.time.com/2013/07/01/japan-spends-millions-in-order-to-be-cool/.

[13] Alan Wheatley, "Asian Style," dated June 2014 in Finance & Development (Washington DC: IMF), 2014, 15.

[14] Roland Kelts, "Japan Spends Millions in Order to Be Cool," dated 1 July 2013 in Time.com website [downloaded on 23 December 2014], available at http://world.time.com/2013/07/01/japan-spends-millions-in-order-to-be-cool/.

[15] Ministry of Economy, Trade and Industry (METI), Cool Japan Initiative (Cool Japan Fund) [Powerpoint] dated 18 November 2013 (Japan: METI, 2013), Slide 6.

five clusters of products (content, fashion, clothing/food/housing, services, local products) that can lead to inbound tourists "seeking authenticity" in their visits to Japan.[16] Part of the rationale for building this fund is solving the problem faced by some companies (especially small- and medium-sized ones) that lacked funds for marketing, information dissemination, resources to build up confidence and experience to promote their products overseas.[17] According to the latest figures reported by Japan-based media, the Cool Japan Promotion Fund was initiated in mid-2014 and had a starting state investment of ¥37.5 billion (approximately US$370 million) led by former fashion elite businessman Nobuyuki Ota who will then invest this fund in cultural SMEs (Small and Medium-Sized Enterprises).[18] This figure matches the number reported by Alan Wheatley in the International Monetary Fund (IMF) publication *Finance and Development* but falls short of the end-2013 target mentioned in the *TIME* magazine's article.

The impetus for the fund also arose from what Japan has concluded as the tremendous boost that the Korean government has given to their own popular cultural industry and is following likewise. This is not the first time the Japanese state has come in to work with its popular cultural and creative industries. In the past, the Japanese government has designated Doraemon as an unofficial non-human Japanese ambassador to the world as well as the official mascot for the Tokyo Olympic Games in 2020, Prime Minister Taro Aso promoted manga culture, and government agencies also worked to promote products like Pokemon to American consumers. The fund works through government agencies and private sector entities contributing financial resources to a central fund which project groups, incubators and private companies can draw from.

---

[16] Ministry of Economy, Trade and Industry (METI), Cool Japan Initiative (Cool Japan Fund) [Powerpoint] dated 18 November 2013 (Japan: METI, 2013), Slide 2.

[17] Ministry of Economy, Trade and Industry (METI), Cool Japan Initiative (Cool Japan Fund) [Powerpoint] dated 18 November 2013 (Japan: METI), 2013, Slide 4.

[18] Matt Alt, "Will Cool Japan finally heat up in 2014?" Japan Times, January 9, 2014, accessed December 23, 2014, http://www.japantimes.co.jp/culture/2014/01/09/general/will-cool-japan-finally-heat-up-in-2014/.

Chapter 5

Centering Akihabara: The Positionality of Tokyo's Pop Cultural Nucleus in Cool Japan Industries and Globalized Fandom Consumption

Tai Wei LIM

Introduction

In the humanities and social sciences, the field of Japanese popular culture is dominated by anthropologists and media/cultural studies specialists with international relations (e.g. concept of soft power) and historians in the minority. This is understandable since familiar popular culture trends are to be associated with Japan's contemporary society and patterns of consumption. Historical research tends to focus on socio-cultural histories — of how individuals consume popular cultural items based on prevailing lifestyles, materialistic needs, socio-economic factors and normative values in a diachronic historical context. Other historical writings look at the subject area through multiple historical lens — e.g. the history of branding and marketing, social histories of consumers, socio-economic history of communities, etc. In this writing, I embedded contemporary consumption and creative production in a historical study and the historical context of globalization in order to analyze three important items. Historical developments are utilized as a context for analytical discussions in this writing.

I raise several questions in this writing. First, historically, how did relationships within the iron triangle of production companies (producers), fans (consumers) and the state (regulators) evolve to the current contemporary system of sales, distribution and production. Second, what sort of influence does the iron triangle have on regional audiences? Do the cultural products resonate with a regional audience through collective consumption, contents-based depictions of normative values and network-based peer pressure? Third, how does consumption emanate soft power — through the encouragement of consumption in regionally rising middle classes and/or production networks in the region? These three questions will be discussed and analyzed in this writing and they will be contextualized in the case study of Akihabara, Japan's premium Japanese popular cultural center.

I have benefitted from reading Jakob Nobuoka's persuasive article on Japanese Cultural Economy focusing on Akihabara as one of its case studies. His central arguments and thesis statement include how media mix (one image or narrative used in many categories of media including anime, manga, digital game, etc.), the capability to send contents-based narrative through various forms of media, and technologies is the basis for Japan creative industry competitiveness.[1] Agreeing with Nobuoka for most parts of this theoretical discussion of the cultural economy, I adopt his definition of the term as "the system of production, distribution, consumption and management of goods that primarily have a symbolic value which serves the preference to express culture."[2]

Historical Background

A signboard put up by the local authorities at the main retail street of Akihabara narrated the late pre-modern history of the district:

> This neighborhood was once called Kanda-Tashirocho. It is said that the name derives from the fact that in the late 18th century, land that had been used by a retainer of the Shogun was offered as alternative land for people who had been displaced from a nearby town to make way for a firebreak.

---

[1] Jakob Nobuoka, *Geographies of the Japanese Cultural Economy Innovation and Creative Consumption* (Sweden: Uppsala University Geografiska Regionstudier NR 83, 2010), 18–19.

[2] Jakob Nobuoka, *Geographies of the Japanese Cultural Economy Innovation and Creative Consumption* (Sweden: Uppsala University Geografiska Regionstudier NR 83, 2010), 29.

From a firebreak, the district has since evolved from a trading outpost to a train station trading stop in the modern period, and then a secondhand radio repair workshop district in the early postwar period operated by demobilized technicians and engineer military men. In the contemporary era, Akihabara the district is known to otakus affectionately as "Akiba" and the consumers that shopped there were the "Akiba kids." From the 1960s onwards, Akihabara's history reflected Japan's industrial development in manufacturing high-tech electronics, retailing the latest electronic gadget lines. This is how the signboard put up by the authorities near the Akihabara station on the side of the Denkimachi exit narrated the history of the district:

> The name of this neighborhood comes from a bridge Maebashi that crosses the Kanda River. Even before World War II, this area was home to many wholesalers and retailers in electric goods and today has become, under the name of Akihabara, one of the world's most famous shopping areas for electronic goods.

The signboard itself may be outdated, given that Akihabara is no longer a premium district for electronics goods shopping but a location increasingly infused with retailers in popular cultural products. The large electronics retail businesses have declined due to severe competition in the 1980s and 1990s, leaving only a select few large players behind (like Laox seen in the photograph below). The other factor that accounts for the electronics retail sector decline is the suburbanization of Japanese cities, resulting in the appearance of large chain branch stores that serve the needs of the middle classes residing in the suburban areas.

In the 1970s and 1980s, it was an electronic retailing district that was transformed into the center of otaku culture in the 1990s. In the 1980s, according to Patrick Marcias and Tomohiro Machiyama, Akihabara experienced a brisk sales period from retailing "illegal electronic devices like mini cameras, radio scanners, eavesdropping devices, and bootleg software," becoming a "hacker boom" and a "nerds" historical phase until digital encryption in the 1990s halted its advancement.[3] By the first decade

---

[3] Patrick Macias and Tomohiro Machiyama, *Cruising the Anime City* (Berkeley, CA: Stone Bridge Press, 2004), 81.

The photograph shows one of the last surviving corners of Akihabara that still retails electronic components and wires in the traditional open stall (*Yatai*) format. It is unclear if this corner can even survive the ongoing gentrification process in the lead-up to the Tokyo Olympics in 2020.

of the 21st century, Akihabara was firmly known as a place for otakus, a paradise whereby specialized comic books for self-identified communities (*doujinshi*) could acquire and consume their products throughout the year. Tora no Ana is an Akihabara-based chain store that sells products which are specialized for otakus and not easily understood or acceptable by the general public (e.g. sexual themes, homosexual fantasies, etc.).[4] The initial success of retailers like Tora no Ana inspired other niched popular cultural outfits to follow and this resulted in formation of clusters of competitive as well as complementary fellow retailers selling the same genre of products, making Akihabara a convenient one-stop location for popular cultural goods.

---

[4] Patrick Macias and Tomohiro Machiyama, *Cruising the Anime City* (Berkeley, CA: Stone Bridge Press, 2004), 22–23.

The clutter of wires at the last surviving corner of Akihabara that sells such products in open stalls. Wires used to dominate the retail industry here during Japan's fast-growth economic period.

In the first decade of the 21st century, Nomura Research Institute, Ltd. published an authoritative study which estimated the otaku population to be 1.72 million-strong with a market size of ¥411 billion.[5] This number does not include overseas markets, mainstream consumers who consume otaku products but do not identify themselves as otakus and closet otakus who hide their identities for various reasons. According to this study, the industries that the otakus engaged in are also multi-faceted, including comics, animation, idols, games, PC assembly, audio-visual equipment, mobile IT equipment, autos, travel, fashion, cameras and railways.[6] Nobuoka

---

[5]Nomura Research Institute, Ltd., "New Market Scale Estimation for Otaku: Population of 1.72 Million with Market Scale of ¥411 Billion," dated 6 October 2005 in the Nomura Research Institute (NRI) News Release [downloaded on 5 December 2014], available at https://www.nri.com/global/news/2005/051006.html.
[6]Nomura Research Institute, Ltd., "New Market Scale Estimation for Otaku: Population of 1.72 Million with Market Scale of ¥411 Billion," dated 6 October 2005 in the Nomura Research Institute (NRI) News Release [downloaded on 5 December 2014], available at https://www.nri.com/global/news/2005/051006.html.

A retro-looking gaudy in-your-face advertisement by electronics dealers/retailers recommending their latest products. These images are reminiscent of Akihabara in the 1980s and 1990s.

quoted the following figures from Ken Kitabayashi's study to indicate the respective population and market sizes of different kinds of otakus (2004 figures): manga otakus (1 million and ¥100 billion); anime otakus (200,000 and ¥20 billion yen); idols otakus (800,000 and ¥60 billion); games otakus (800,000 and ¥78 billion); PC assembly otakus (50,000 and ¥32 billion).[7] A decade later, Japanese Internet portal *My Navi* conducted an early 2014 survey of 5,663 individuals about to graduate from college or postgraduate school in March 2015 and 39.5% of the respondents self-identified themselves as otakus.[8]

---

[7] Jakob Nobuoka, *Geographies of the Japanese Cultural Economy Innovation and Creative Consumption* (Sweden: Uppsala University Geografiska Regionstudier NR 83, 2010), 76.
[8] Casey Baseel, "Are you otaku? Roughly 40% of Japanese college students say, 'Yes!'," dated 1 February 2014 in the Rocket News 24 website [downloaded on 5 December 2014],

Today, you can still find large electronics retailers in Akihabara like Laox interspersed with the Japanese popular culture retailers. These are the survivors of the electronics retailing shakeup in the 1990s.

Methodology

The methodology for this paper is three-folds. First, I employed textual analysis with interpretation of textual documents and secondary materials. Second, I utilized onsite observation studies of major Japanese popular cultural production and consumption centers in Tokyo, including locations like Akihabara and Ikebukuro during my summer 2014 fieldwork. Third, I performed the role of a collector of material artefacts, acquiring and amassing popular culture products in order to understand practitioners' motivation in consuming these items. The acquisition of material items facilitates my understanding of how fans acquire their social value and capital in their networked communities. The ability to

available at http://en.rocketnews24.com/2014/02/01/are-you-otaku-roughly-40-percent-of-japanese-college-students-say-yes/.

Electronics retailing continues to be a shared component of Akihabara's business activity, especially in the annual Akihabara Electric Town Summer Campaign in 2014. When the author did his fieldwork as part of a study tour in summertime 2014 in Akihabara, Doraemon was the official mascot for the summer campaign. This is a picture of a banner that hangs on public street lamps out in the main street of Akihabara.

display the latest figurine or to boast about the acquisition and experience of attending a balloted sold-out concert connotes social status and fan pride. It is a form of social ritual performed for acceptance by others within the community. Materialistic possession also drives individual incentives to consume the product through personal ownership and when this personal ownership becomes viral through social network promotion or internet publicity, a sense of collective identity and cultural resonance results. The question is whether such collective consumption repeated over many times and many products from either Japan or Korea can constitute a source of soft power?

Low-rise multi-storey buildings now house the leading Japanese popular culture retailers in Japan (and the world).

While I focus on the consumption aspects of popular culture in Japan, specifically the major center of Tokyo, I acknowledge the importance of the role played by the state in cultural policy formulation and the social context of consumption in anthropological studies. They are as important as the historical narrative. Because I was based in Hong Kong between 2010 to 2014, I was able to study overseas consumption of Japanese popular culture in one of the two major overseas markets for J-pop (Hong Kong and Taiwan). Here, it adds a comparative element to my study as I observed how overseas fans (fans in the first degree platform for Japanese popular cultural exports) consumed cutting-edge Japanese popular cultural products. This chapter cannot avoid having no discussions of Korean popular culture (K-pop or *Hallyu*), given that there are temptations and tendencies for scholars interested in East Asian popular culture to compare between the two. In the presentation of my previous papers on

The iconic Sofmap, a recognized giant in popular cultural retailing, offering both main-stream and niched product, is a must-stop for otaku pilgrimages.

Japanese popular culture, audience's questions in the Q&A section often inevitably raised enquiries and feedback for such comparisons.

Significance

Roblyn Simeon's journal article prefers to define this industry as a "contents industry" (including hardware to cultural exports) which makes up approximately ¥13 trillion (US$130 billion) in yearly retail sales and has become Japan's ranking business sector by 2006.[9] When sectorally segmented, the 2006 figures for the popular cultural industries' market

---

[9]Roblyn Simeon, "The Branding Potential And Japanese Popular Culture Overseas," *Journal of Diversity Management* 1, no. 2 (2006): 13.

size are in the following: the Visual Media (¥4,833.8 billion), Publishing and Newspapers/Image and Text (¥5,789 billion), Music and Audio (¥1,914.1 billion), and Video Games (¥1,144.2 billion) make up a total of ¥13.7 trillion.[10]

"A" for Anime of ACG Industries

The economic resilience of the creative industries was pointed out by Tsutomo Sugiura:

> According to Yoshimoto Mitsuhiro (2003), in the 1990s, when the Japanese economy had long been in depression, the number of employees in all creative industries increased by 16% from 1.2 million in 1996 to 1.4 million in 2001, while that of all industries decreased by 4.3% from 60.9 million to 58.3 million. In terms of revenues, creative industries as a whole earned ¥28 trillion (US$280 billion) in 1999, robust gain of 86% from ¥15 trillion (US$150 billion) in 1989, whereas all service industries earned ¥202 trillion (US$2,020 billion) in 1999, a gain of 69% from ¥119 trillion (US$1,190 billion) in 1989.[11]

According to Sugiura, the Japanese anime market rose from ¥4.6 billion (US$46 million) in 1975 to ¥200 billion (US$2 billion) in 2002, more than 60% of the global anime market (Marcadal, 2006).[12] At least from 2006, Japanese anime industry already makes up more than 60% of global output of cartoons.[13] In terms of practical contribution to the economy, Nissim Otmazgin and Eyal Ben-Ari provided some figures in their publication: anime industry has about 450 production companies and 5,000

---

[10] Jakob Nobuoka, *Geographies of the Japanese Cultural Economy Innovation and Creative Consumption* (Sweden: Uppsala University Geografiska Regionstudier NR 83, 2010), 71.

[11] Tsutomu Sugiura, "Japan's Creative Industries," in *Soft Power Superpowers*, eds. W. Yasushi and D. L. McConnell (Armonk, NY and London: ME Sharpe, 2008), 130.

[12] Marcadal, Raphaelle, "Le 'Japan cool' inode le planete (The 'Japan cool' is in flood on the planet)" [downloaded on 9 May 2016], available at http://japancool.typepad.com/japan_cool/2006/03/_soft_power_cul.html.

[13] Roblyn Simeon, "The Branding Potential And Japanese Popular Culture Overseas," *Journal of Diversity Management* 1, no. 2 (2006): 13.

animators.[14] Given the promising size and growth of the industry, the state is keen to be a stakeholder here. Other than the central government, local governments are keen to promote anime, for example the Tokyo Metropolitan Government sponsors the Tokyo International Anime Fair which in 2007 drew over 200 firms and 100,000 participants with an increasing number of foreign participants.[15] Ministry of Education, Culture, Sports, Science and Technology (MEXT) provides grants for outstanding Anime films limited to three awards annually.[16]

The large iconic Sofmap billboard featuring the anime flavor of the month in Akihabara.

[14] Nissim Otmazgin and Eyal Ben-Ari, "Cultural Industries and the State in East and Southeast Asia," in *Popular Culture and the State in East and Southeast Asia*, eds. N. Otmazgin and E. Ben-Ari (London and NY: Routledge Taylor and Francis Group, 2012), 19.

[15] KuKhee Choo, "Nationalizing 'cool': Japan's global promotion of the content industry," in *Popular Culture and the State in East and Southeast Asia*, eds. N. Otmazgin and E. Ben-Ari (London and NY: Routledge, 2012), 96.

[16] KuKhee Choo, "Nationalizing 'cool': Japan's global promotion of the content industry," in *Popular Culture and the State in East and Southeast Asia*, eds. N. Otmazgin and E. Ben-Ari (London and NY: Routledge, 2012), 93.

Another iconic anime in the 1980s with its own café franchise in Akihabara, one of the perennial stops in a typical otaku pilgrimage.

"C" for Comic of ACG Industries

The symbolic event for the manga industry is the Comiket convention in Tokyo where by 2003, it is estimated that more than ¥1 billion is transacted and exchanged in this event (an amount higher than the money spent at World Cup).[17] Comiket is described by Nobuoka as a "temporary innovative space, only present for a few days throughout the year" that is "also cyclical since the event reoccurs every year and also is becoming part of global cultural practices."[18] This transitional space provides *gentei* limited temporal space as a small window of opportunity for the fans to acquire their limited edition collections and fulfil other material yearnings. The

[17] Patrick Macias and Tomohiro Machiyama, *Cruising the Anime City* (Berkeley, CA: Stone Bridge Press, 2004), 119.

[18] Jakob Nobuoka, *Geographies of the Japanese Cultural Economy Innovation and Creative Consumption* (Sweden: Uppsala University Geografiska Regionstudier NR 83, 2010), 62.

A Gundam figurine can be found standing in front of the Gundam café entrance. A favorite corner for fans to pose with their favorite robotic character.

experience of queuing up and attending the event for fans from Japan and overseas living far away is an attractive one as these fans swagger and show off their insider information or the latest acquisitions. The consumption experience at this event also feeds the subjective of the two-dimensional world that otakus live in as they read and visually experience their favorite comic book contents.

In overseas markets, by 2004, English translations of manga become the fastest-growing sector of US-based publishing industry with yearly sales volume of approximately US$120 million.[19] Three years later, in the US alone, manga for all age groups expanded by 10% in 2007 in sales,

---

[19] Patrick Macias and Tomohiro Machiyama, *Cruising the Anime City* (Berkeley, CA: Stone Bridge Press, 2004), 19.

For mature adult fans, the Gundam café is also a bar for drinks.

attaining US$220 million, and almost an estimated 1,500 titles were released in 2007.[20] In North America, there are 1.5 to 2 million manga fans with sales of ¥300 billion (according to 2007 media statistics).[21] Domestically, in the decade of the 1990s, the manga industry produced 12 magazines with more than one million readers and approximately 50 magazines with 150,000 to a million copies circulated and by 2001, over 3.2 million different mangas come into circulation.[22] In practical

---

[20] Laura Tiffany, "Embracing Japanese pop culture," dated 11 May 2008 in NBCNews.com website [downloaded on 21 November 2014], available at http://www.nbcnews.com/id/24546355/ns/business-us_business/t/embracing-japanese-pop-culture/.

[21] Jakob Nobuoka, *Geographies of the Japanese Cultural Economy Innovation and Creative Consumption* (Sweden: Uppsala University Geografiska Regionstudier NR 83, 2010), 67–68.

[22] Jakob Nobuoka, *Geographies of the Japanese Cultural Economy Innovation and Creative Consumption* (Sweden: Uppsala University Geografiska Regionstudier NR 83, 2010), 67.

The Tokyo animation center is an important showcase for the leading and newest animation products for visitors to Akihabara.

contribution to the economy, in 2012, the manga sector hired about 4,000 cartoonists and 28,000 assistants.[23] Outside Japan, anime and manga-derived characters have become mainstream popular cultural icons and images. Sugiura noted that the French group Daft Punk uses anime by Keiji Matsumoto creator of *Uchuu Senkan Yamato* (*Space Battleship Yamato*), while Hollywood movies like *Kill Bill* (Quentin Tarantino) derive ideas from manga.[24] Sugiura made the following observation about the gaming industry:

---

[23] Nissim Otmazgin and Eyal Ben-Ari, "Cultural Industries and the State in East and Southeast Asia," in *Popular Culture and the State in East and Southeast Asia*, eds. N. Otmazgin and E. Ben-Ari (London and NY: Routledge Taylor and Francis Group, 2012), 19.

[24] Tsutomu Sugiura, "Japan's Creative Industries," in *Soft Power Superpowers*, eds. W. Yasushi and D. L. McConnell (Armonk, NY and London: ME Sharpe, 2008), 134.

Large billboards promoting game retailers at Akihabara. (Photo taken during fieldwork in summer 2014).

One English Web site devoted to the popular game Final Fantasy has received more than 59 million hits as of June 27, 2007, an indication of how many fans this game has attracted. In fact, according to BusinessWeek Rowley 2005, more than 35 million copies of the Final Fantasy series have been sold, and its online version has more than 300,000 subscribers worldwide.[25]

"G" for the Gaming Industry

In terms of revenue, Pokemon alone, is retailed in more than 140 countries with profits of over US$15 billion by August 2003.[26] Spin-offs for Pokemon which started off as a card game and then taken over by Nintendo as an

---

[25]Tsutomu Sugiura, "Japan's Creative Industries," in *Soft Power Superpowers*, eds. W. Yasushi and D. L. McConnell (Armonk, NY and London: ME Sharpe, 2008), 134.

[26]Anne Allison, *Millennial Monsters* (Berkeley, LA and London: University of California Press, 2006), 193.

electronic game include movie franchises. Within Japan, online game titles like World of Warcraft attracted 8.5 million participants online as of 27 March 2007, while portable games like Nintendo DS sold 35.61 million consoles by end 2006.[27] Overseas, by 2006, global sales of its movies amounted to a profit of US$91 million (the North American market generated US$85 million).[28] The gaming industry hires around 18,500 in 146 mainly small-scale firms.[29]

Spin-offs Related to the ACG

Figures for the ACG (Anime, Comic, Games industries) alone do not tell the whole story. The prevalence of a mixed media format in which products are simultaneously launched as animation, comics, games and other paraphernalia implies that there is an informal economy beyond the original ACG products. The informal economy can be based on franchises granted to independent producers carrying the local or/and overseas original brand name or design or fan-based products. Some of these products are lifestyle choices as popular cultural symbols are designed onto functional items which are then used by consumers in their daily lives. In such cases, lifestyle (the functionality of the products) is integrated with design aesthetics and cultural symbolisms (the ability to look cool when carrying such symbols around as a source of status). Sometimes, aesthetic symbolism even trumps functionality when an object used in daily life is not used for the primary purpose for which it was created but as a decorative item or accessory.

---

[27] Jakob Nobuoka, *Geographies of the Japanese Cultural Economy Innovation and Creative Consumption* (Sweden: Uppsala University Geografiska Regionstudier NR 83, 2010), 69.

[28] Anne Allison, *Millennial Monsters* (Berkeley, LA and London: University of California Press, 2006), 236.

[29] Nissim Otmazgin and Eyal Ben-Ari, "Cultural Industries and the State in East and Southeast Asia," in *Popular Culture and the State in East and Southeast Asia*, eds. N. Otmazgin and E. Ben-Ari (London and NY: Routledge Taylor and Francis Group, 2012), 19.

For the hardcore fans, visitors and overseas tourists alike, there are retailers at street corners in Akihabara trading in fandom products. This photo that I took in Akihabara during summer fieldwork 2014 shows a retailer specializing in dealing with secondhand products related to the popular singer-idol group AKB48.

There are spin-off products from ACG that have become industries by themselves, including the toy manufacturing and manga-recycling sectors. Akihabara also feeds other industries like the comics (manga)-recycling industries when unwanted and used manga books and volumes are recycled into toilet paper.[30] There are also independent firms ("indie" companies) that engage with small-scale musical or visual production assignment. There are also tourism-related venues for domestic and foreign tourists and visitors. In the 1990s, one of the more popular museums related to

---

[30] Patrick Macias and Tomohiro Machiyama, *Cruising the Anime City* (Berkeley, CA: Stone Bridge Press, 2004), 28.

Tourists and visitors also visit the Tokyo Anime Center to see the latest offerings, ideas and products from the creative cluster in Akihabara.

Akihabara was the Tetsuwan Atomu museum, featuring robotic displays and Atom Boy memorabilia.[31]

Toys Based on Manga and Anime

Toy products, not included in the traditional ACG industry, is another spin-off industry. In Mandarake which is the top-ranking retail chain store in used anime and manga headquartered in Nakano, more than a million items line the shelves, and some 45,000 manga titles, anime DVDs and toys are traded on a weekly basis.[32] The now ubiquitous and addictive capsule

---

[31] Anne Allison, *Millenial Monsters* (Berkeley, LA and London: University of California Press, 2006), 62.

[32] Patrick Macias, "10 of the best otaku shops in Tokyo," dated 1 February 2012 in The Guardian theguardian.com website [downloaded on 21 November 2014], available at http://www.theguardian.com/travel/2012/feb/01/top-10-otaku-shops-tokyo-anime-manga.

Photo of Gashapon machine outside a popular idol products retailer in Akihabara (taken during author's fieldwork in Akihabara in summer 2014).

toys "Gashapon" purchasable by turning a knob after inserting coins and then waiting for a toy to fall out. The innovative feature about this product is encouraging addictive desires to collect the entire range of figures in the capsules derived from popular anime and manga series, including the rare pieces.

The Gashapon toy retailing model is now well-known throughout East Asia. The intense demand for these small toys contained in plastic capsules spawned another industry far away in China. Japanese companies like Bandai (makers of Gashapon) hired Chinese artisans well-skilled in painting miniature objects (e.g. rice grain painting) and housed them in factories to manufacture Gashapon products on a large scale. Eventually, another idea emerged when SMEs (small and medium-sized enterprises) like Kaiyodo with their own independent product identities decided to team up with other industrial players like sweets confectioner Furuta Seika to produce Choco Eggs (Easter egg-shaped chocolates with hollow

A specialized Gashapon machine selling Gundam toys in front of the iconic Gundam café in Akihabara.

interiors encapsulating mini animal figurines) that sold six million units within months (by 2004, candy toys became an annual US$500 million industry and Gashapon itself became a US$310 million industry by 2004).[33]

Other Creative Ideas

Akihabara is also a generator of creative ideas in the Japanese popular cultural retailing industry. Nobuoka describes the "essence of Akihabara"

---

[33] Patrick Macias and Tomohiro Machiyama, *Cruising the Anime City* (Berkeley, CA: Stone Bridge Press), 2004, pp. 40–41, 43.

The success of all-girl bands in Akihabara has sparked off successive generations of imitators and innovators. The author saw a large billboard featuring idol wannabes in idol discovery searches.

as a "place for exchanging, promoting and testing ideas."[34] An early creative business model found in this district is hosting plastic boxes in Akiba shops and renting out to individual retailers to sell their products. Sometimes, these boxes capitalized on the *natsukashii* sentiments (nostalgia) for things used, rustic (*shibui*) and old. I have seen this retail business model replicated in Singapore and Hong Kong. The most well-known creative franchise in Akihabara is probably the AKB48 product line. Starting off as an idol group in Akihabara (AKB is short form for "Akihabara"), they now have an iconic café in the area and regional franchises in Jakarta (JKT48), Shanghai (SNH48) and other cities/regions.

---

[34] Jakob Nobuoka, *Geographies of the Japanese Cultural Economy Innovation and Creative Consumption* (Sweden: Uppsala University Geografiska Regionstudier NR 83, 2010), 38.

The Creative Ecology

Akihabara is a "space where different cultures, technologies and practices can meet, interact and develop."[35] It provides the platform for different sources of cultural and lifestyle influence to cross-pollinate and hybridize into unique products that are later introduced to the mass consumption market. As the origin of innovative retail business models and fashionable products, Akihabara also belongs to a space at the top of an architecture of ideas. The creative ecology of Akiba in this sense functions in the same manner as Silicon Valley where creative ideas are fermented in garage-size units resulting in products that first serve the consumption desires and needs of otakus. These products are sometimes the result of collaboration between different units specialized in their own fields but collectively working towards a final product. Sometimes, these collaborations become bigger units or get acquired by larger firms like Bandai. Some successful product ideas started small and fermented in humble units, but when picked up by a progressive otaku crowd and then mainstreamized for the general crowd of domestic consumers, they can eventually proliferate to become an internationally-known product line. Sometimes, Akihabara also gives space for subcultures to exist and interact with the main ecology of the district. Eventually, features of these subcultures would be subsumed into popular culture industry, hybridizing with more mainstream cultures to generate ideas and products that become acceptable to the mass consumers. An example is the gothic movement with its sado-masochistic tendencies and deliberate display of social rejection and ostracization coexisting with Lolita and Kawaii movements in Akihabara to evolve into new hybridized products, images and ideas like Gothic Lolita fashion or Kawaii figurines adapting gothic features that become palatable to more mainstream consumers.

This narrative of de-marginalizing different subcultures or innovative minority ideas related to Akihabara's production ecology contributes to the organic *laissez-faire* growth of creative ideas with little intervention and inputs from the state. At the same time, while the fermentation of ideas in

---

[35] Jakob Nobuoka, *Geographies of the Japanese Cultural Economy Innovation and Creative Consumption* (Sweden: Uppsala University Geografiska Regionstudier NR 83, 2010), 38.

Akihabara is organically conceived with little state intervention, when the select few ideas are actualized into popular products and gain traction with domestic and overseas consumers, the government becomes a stakeholder in its success and offers funding for the promotion of cultural items. Here Kukhee Choo's writing is instructive:

> The Agency for Cultural Affairs (Bunkacho), a subdivision in MET, oversee the cultural promotion of the content industry. The budget for Bunkacho in 2010, under the title "Cultural Transmission and Realization of Culture Arts Nation," was 102 billion Japanese yen. The areas of promotion included those to cultivate artistic creativity (14 billion Japanese yen), to preserve and utilize cultural artifacts (41.5 billion Japanese yen) and to transmit "excellent" Japanese culture abroad (41.4 billion Japanese yen).[36]

Some scholars notice the looming state presence. For example, Nobuoka detected the presence of state involvement in Akihabara:

> In the Akihabara article, I touch upon how policy-makers have begun to show interest in these topics and how subcultures have undergone a shift from being unnoticed or overlooked to becoming top issues for foreign trade and innovation policy. This shift can be notice in acts, such as Doraemon becoming a cultural ambassador, or when a former minister during his election campaign called himself a fan of manga in an opening ceremony in Akihabara.[37]

Indeed, in the case of Akihabara, the government is beginning to go beyond utilization of cultural symbolisms to reorganizing cultural spaces and economic geography of Akihabara itself although it is still early to tell how this process will evolve and the impact it will have on the popular cultural industries in Akihabara. The Ministry of Economy, Trade and

---

[36] KuKhee Choo, "Nationalizing 'cool': Japan's global promotion of the content industry," in *Popular Culture and the State in East and Southeast Asia*, eds. N. Otmazgin and E. Ben-Ari (London and NY: Routledge, 2012), 92.

[37] Jakob Nobuoka, *Geographies of the Japanese Cultural Economy Innovation and Creative Consumption* (Sweden: Uppsala University Geografiska Regionstudier NR 83, 2010), 71.

Industry (METI) also has another initiative that includes Akihabara (Town tourism, Electrical Town as well as Town management stakeholders). There are initiatives for Tokyo's creative clusters to be slowly cultivated by state agencies, e.g. the initiative of Creative Tokyo under the care of METI. In this initiative, the supporters of Creative Tokyo propose utilizing Japan's cultural capital to contribute to Japan's economy, attract foreign talents (including international creative personalities) and investments, accentuate businesses that reflect Japanese culture and lifestyle, boost domestic consumption, support overseas operations of Japanese firms, encourage information exchange, all with the aim of making Tokyo the most important creative hub in Asia.[38]

Literature Review

Fan-driven "Democratization"

Ian Condry detailed the concept of "collaborative creativity" in his important publication on the anime industry, noting that the creative process links studio productions with fan-created products.[39] In the field of anime, Condry quoted other scholars like William Kelly who argues that Japanese popular culture form is a distinctive entity that is forged through collaborative ventures between fans and producers.[40] Condry points out that a major point of debate faced by manga publishers and anime studios is that they tend to disagree with the concept that "free publicity" through non-official distribution is more important than illegal downloading and streaming.[41] Amongst the many English-language literatures that I came across in Japan, Condry's publication probably contains one of the most succinct explanations behind the origins and success of Japan's most successful idol

---

[38] Ministry of Economy, Trade and Industry (METI), "The Creative Tokyo Proposal," undated in METI website [downloaded on 9 December 2014], available at http://www.meti.go.jp/policy/mono_info_service/mono/creative/creative_tokyo/about/sengen_en.html.

[39] Ian Condry, *The Soul of Anime* (Durham and London: Duke University Press, 2013).

[40] William Kelly, *Fanning the Flames: Fans and Consumer Culture in Japan* (Albany: State University of New York Press, 2004); and Ian Condry, *The Soul of Anime* (Durham and London: Duke University Press, 2013), 21.

[41] Ian Condry, *The Soul of Anime* (Durham and London: Duke University Press, 2013), 24.

Miku Hatsune. Condry's narrative about Miku Hatsune's origins and her success is one good example of fan-driven creative production:

> Released in 2007 by Crypton Future Media, a small company in Sapporo, Miku Hatsune started out as a voice character in the music synthesizer software Vocaloid, which allows users to enter lyrics and melody that the soft can "sing." Cyrpton released an illustration and some body characteristics (height, weight, etc.) to go with the character, but interestingly, the company allowed the image to be used by anyone. Many Vocaloid users created songs and uploaded them to the Internet — for example, to the video-sharing website Nico Nico Douga (literally, "smile video"). Many of the uploaded songs were made into music videos with either moving or still images of the Miku character.[42]

Sharing is an effective marketing and distributional tool in this sense and the availability of digital technologies increases the speed and geographical reach by which such cyber products can reach their audiences. Sharing itself is also another ritual as fan clubs, official and unofficial, seize upon the latest gossips and news and proliferate them through smartphones, blogs and websites. When fans subtitle, create their own decorative items for concert, develop specific dance moves for use during concert, and translate foreign language products into their own language, they are developing a code through which fellow fans within the same community can speak to each other. Sharing bits of information such as concert dates, store discounts, and limited edition product sales when gathered together creates a collective narrative that contributes to identity building and coherence of the fan club, group or tribe dedicated to a particular idol, group or product. In some genres of Japanese popular culture, fans even integrate performance into the collective ritual of identity building. In the arena of cosplay for example, Kazumi Nagaike and Kaori Yoshida argue that fan gathering "not only functions as a science for fans' social activities, but also as a cultural arena for self-experience."[43] The proliferation of

---

[42] Ian Condry, *The Soul of Anime* (Durham and London: Duke University Press, 2013), 63.

[43] Kazumi Nagaike and Kaori Yoshida, "Becoming and Performing the Self and the Other: Festishism, Fantasy, and Sexuality of Cosplay in Japanese Girls'/Women's Manga," *Asia Pacific World* 2, no. 2 (Autumn 2011): 23.

popular cultural information through word of mouth is facilitated by the use of social media which enables the sharing of experience to be disseminated easily and cheaply.

Of course, not all information-sharing is cohesively harmonious, sometimes information is manipulated by networked individuals for showing off social status. Outside the communities themselves, fan groups and clubs work as active collaborators with the mass media and social media outfits to shape the form and contents of popular culture. Regardless of whether there are disagreements or common accolades amongst the fans, technology is an effective mediator to transmit fan information and news to a large audience within a short period of time. In the past, television played that role but with the advent of smartphones and social media software, the process has become interactive, allowing fans to have disproportionate access to large circles of dedicated fandom.

Vocaloid Fandom as Case Study

Other than the information exchange that acts as the software to lubricate the interactions and communications between fans in a club, hardware infrastructure is equally important. This includes physical assets such as publicity materials, events and conventions attendance, and fan-made merchandise, such as those depicted by Condry in the quotation below.

> "But the phenomenon around Miku shows that the character, more than the music software, is the platform on which people are building. I was one of the seven thousand people who attended the sold-out, one-day "Vocaloid-only" fan convention at the Sunshine City department store complex in the Ikebukuro section of Tokyo in November 2010. Almost five hundred fan groups had gathered to sell their wares — mostly CDs but also DVDs, books of drawing (irasuto), posters, videogames, jewelry, costumes, manga, and more. These activities cannot be explained only by capabilities of the voice synthesizer software, or in academic terms, the affordances of a computational platform. Rather, the creativity grows out of social energy arising from a collective interest in Miku."[44]

---

[44] Ian Condry, *The Soul of Anime* (Durham and London: Duke University Press, 2013), 63.

Three important general points follow from the quotation above. First, fans of Miku get to participate actively in the maturity of the product by adding more biographical, aesthetic and artistic details to her basic existence. Second, through collective social events, fans gather and develop common-interest groups and their own networked ecology, exchanging information and personal creative works with each other. Third, the allowance by the production company of wide personalized use of the images essentially democratizes and frees up the appropriation of Miku's original image in public space, an issue with implications on intellectual rights since it challenges the notion of artistic rights to a creative work. But the common thread that runs through all three points is that successful and cutting-edge Japanese popular cultural products rely on fan-based and fan-driven consumption. In essence, Condry is arguing about the importance of the social network between fans and how they are able to innovate products. One good example of the importance of this network to creative productive is fan-subbing which Condry defines as:

> ...the translation and dissemination of anime online by fans —
> a controversial practice that illuminates debates about culture, economy,
> and intellectual property in the digital era. Fansubbing refers to the practice
> whereby hundreds of fan groups digitize the latest anime broadcasts,
> translate them, add subtitles, and make the media available online.[45]

The Otakus

In some ways, fan-driven trends represent the "democratization"[46] of popular cultural consumption in Japan as fans actively participate in shaping the outcome of the products personally, contributing their value-addedness in creating new innovative items. Nobuoka argues that consumption satiates a particular desire for a product and satisfy the emotive needs of "novelty, adventure and defining self" as part of lifestyle

---

[45] Ian Condry, *The Soul of Anime* (Durham and London: Duke University Press, 2013), 161.

[46] Nobuoka describes this trend in cultural geographical terms, indicating "how users managed to contribute to innovation and dynamism by creating places and spaces that have become important institutions in the cultural economy." (Source: Jakob Nobuoka, *Geographies of the Japanese Cultural Economy Innovation and Creative Consumption* (Sweden: Uppsala University Geografiska Regionstudier NR 83, 2010), 31.

choices and the process of consumption.[47] It is a form of experience-based consumption and not just material accumulation and/or ownership. One group of consumers stands out amongst the fans in driving popular cultural trends — the otakus. Originally stereotyped as a group of nerdy individuals who rather spend their time in their idol-plastered bedroom playing electronic games, the otakus have become a major group of consumers in Japan due to their willingness to collect their idols' paraphernalia. Their consumption and fan inputs into content-based aspects of their favorite comic book, game or animation essentially shape and drive the popular cultural trends. Some management literatures classify them as a rising group of important consumers, alongside other products of Japan's demographic and social changes like the elderly, single women and freeter/"parasitic" singles living with their parents. Otakus have moved into the position of governing taste and, through this route, made their impact on shaping lifestyle choices, fashion sense and social status determinants. In playing these roles, otakus have accumulated cultural capital credentials. Producers have correspondingly made it their careers to track and predict otaku trends and fashion. Otakus may fulfill the role of being "creatives," defined by Nobuoka as "people who are creative," differentiating this group from the creators who produce, manufacture and make the products.[48] Producers therefore may selectively extract the creativity of otakus for their product designs.

Otakus have also spawned industries that are relatively recession-proof. Even the economic bubble burst in 1989 that started a long-lasting recession (which Abenomics is climbing out of) could not stop the growth of otaku consumption. Because of the resilience of this market, other stakeholders started to notice the otakus and connected with them through marketing research, intellectual studies, and tap into their knowledge and consumption patterns for exports.[49] The otaku culture spawned and mainstreamized in the

---

[47] Jakob Nobuoka, *Geographies of the Japanese Cultural Economy Innovation and Creative Consumption* (Sweden: Uppsala University Geografiska Regionstudier NR 83, 2010), 37.

[48] Jakob Nobuoka, *Geographies of the Japanese Cultural Economy Innovation and Creative Consumption* (Sweden: Uppsala University Geografiska Regionstudier NR 83, 2010), 27.

[49] Patrick Macias and Tomohiro Machiyama, *Cruising the Anime City* (Berkeley, CA: Stone Bridge Press, 2004), 15.

1990s was a different model from the Bubble Economy man in the eco-nomically booming 1980s. The idealized male individual worked in finance or for an advertising agency, wore Italian suit, drove a foreign luxury car, joined as a gym member and went clubbing.[50] The otakus spawned an alternative lifestyle that created their own universe of consumption. Besides games, anime and comics as well as the large array of paraphernalia that came with these three categories of products, otakus also indicated their own preferences for food, conversed in their own *lingo franca* and terminologies related to popular culture, and formed their own circles (*sakuru*), clubs and associations both in reality and online. Otaku consumption represents a deep integration between culture, lifestyle choices and the economic system.

Fans including the otaku fandom and their consumption habits created demand for retailers to satisfy. Akihabara reflected the contextual changes in the Japanese's economy. After serving consumers faithfully in retailing electronics throughout the 1970s and 1980s, the post-bubble economy period saw customers optimizing their budgets and shopping at malls in the suburbs instead of travelling to the Tokyo city to buy common electronics goods.[51] Tokyo as a stakeholder for adapting to changes in domestic con-sumption patterns and local economic development in Akihabara is visible. Choo covered this ambition in his writing:

> With locations such as Akihabara and concentrated Anime studios along the Central train line, Tokyo is indeed the global center of information on Anime. One of the most prominent examples of Tokyo establishing itself as a hub to promote Anime has been the construction of a life-size Gundam Robot status in Odaiba, Tokyo Bay, in the summer of 2009. Under the banner "Green Japan," Gundam was used as part of a bid for the 2016 Olympics Games that ended in failure.[52]

---

[50] Patrick Macias and Tomohiro Machiyama, *Cruising the Anime City* (Berkeley, CA: Stone Bridge Press, 2004), 15.

[51] Kaichiro Morikawa, "Otaku and the City: The Rebirth of Akihabara," in *Fandom Unbound Otaku Culture in a Connected World*, eds. M. Ito, D. Okabe and I. Tsuji (New Haven and London: Yale University Press, 2012), 134.

[52] KuKhee Choo, "Nationalizing 'cool': Japan's global promotion of the content industry," in *Popular Culture and the State in East and Southeast Asia*, eds. N. Otmazgin and E. Ben-Ari (London and NY: Routledge, 2012), 96–97.

Popular culture could be appropriated for economic growth as well as public campaigns to attract global events to come to Tokyo. While the bid for the Olympics failed the first time round, Tokyo succeeded in the second attempt when it successfully won the right to host the 2020 Olympics and Doraemon became the official mascot for the games. The state mechanism capitalized on anime characters that were already well known and established and utilized them for national initiatives. At the grassroots level, however, the directional trends and consumption habits/lifestyles remain the purview of a grand narrative that is made up of individual preferences and product evaluations by large numbers of dedicated fandom, including the otakus.

In the process of the urban construction of Akihabara as the retailing and intellectual center for Japanese popular culture, otakus were not stand-offish consumers but took part in shaping the production process, fashion trends and creative conceptualization of the products they consumed. The very idea of creative products connotes that value lies not in the material base used to make them but the value-addedness of innovation implemented in shaping these materials or decorating them to create symbolic designs that reflect certain cultural inclinations or lifestyle choices. Therefore consumer inputs like the ones offered by otakus are very important in such cases. Hiroki Azuma's volume *Otaku Japan's Database Animals* is arguably one of the most important works on contemporary otaku culture in the English language. In an interview with *Moe Manifesto* writer Patrick Galbraith, he made the following comment on the sophisticated nature of otaku fandom:

> As consumers, they want to know how the work is produced, so that they can break it down and reconstruct something else… What otaku are doing can also be seen in the remixing culture of hip-hop music, for example.[53]

Essentially, what Galbraith is arguing is that otaku fans add a value-addedness to the process of Japanese popular cultural production. They consume and simultaneously direct the consumption pattern, the

---

[53] Patrick Galbraith, *The Moe Manifesto* (Tokyo, Rutland, Vermont and Singapore: Tuttle Publishing, 2014), 172.

production process and the marketing directions. Because otaku consumption is a collective efforts of many different individual preferences, the process is not hegemonically-led but consists of contesting ideas that will eventually produce a general trend through aggregation of these preferences. Similarly, the opinions and views of otakus are not guided or led but each contribution of ideas when uttered becomes a component of the grand narrative that will then become the dominant ideas and concepts for each evolving stage of fandom and this will subsequently be displayed in Akihabara's gaudy district.

While male otakus have dominated academic and media discourses on the relationship between consumption and lifestyles, they are not the only group of players in the popular cultural universe. Celia Lury's persuasive publication *Consumer Culture* argues that individuals are not completely autonomous in their consumption decision-making process. They receive marketing influence from popular cultural producers (especially their marketing arm) and react in response — an impact-response relationship. But, in reacting, Lury noted that instead of a hegemonic response, consumers adopt multiple identities in consuming the product. In the case of Hello Kitty, she indicated that "Sanrio made a concentrated effort to tie together within a single individual different modes of self-presentation that chronologically correspond to girlhood, female adolescence, and womanhood: 'cut', 'cool', and 'camp'..."[54] Hello Kitty is morphed into different self-identities by discerning consumers who appropriate the image that best satisfies their public image-making priorities.

Polycentrism and Cross-pollination

Other than fan contributions, Condry also agrees with William Tsutsui that sources of influence on Japanese producers of creative works are now global in scope:

> In Japan, animators drew inspiration from Disney and from the animated Popeye and Betty Boop shorts by the Fleischer brothers, amongst others. The emphasis on characters with personalities is not uniquely

---

[54] Celia Lury, *Consumer Culture* (Cambridge and Massachusetts: Polity, 2011), 163.

Japanese, therefore, but the linking of characters to particular actors and performances — such as Mickey Mouse's borrowing from Buster Keaton in Steamboat Bill — tends to be more common in U.S. animation. This can be taken to extremes when animated characters are inextricably linked — for example, Robin Williams as Genie in *Aladdin* or Eddie Murphy as Donkey in *Shrek*.[55]

There are three implications arising from the long quotation above. First, it indicates the dynamic nature of cultural influences, often a process of receiving influence and trendspotting pulses, indigenizing these pulses and then re-influencing others. The section below elaborates on this point. The second implication is the presence of certain universal commonalities amongst different popular cultural products, in this case, the association of characters with personalities in US popular culture (in this case, the association of animation characters with the voices of Hollywood stars).

The debate whether Japanese popular culture is universalistic or particularistic can be resolved without taking sides. It is neither universal nor particularistic and this view may even be applicable to the general idea of cultural transmission itself since all forms of cultures cannot be clearly delineated from each other. Popular cultural trends often travel between different consuming markets. Japanese popular cultural products are translated and marketed to US consumer and audiences and vice versa and, in the midst of this exchange, these two groups of product co-influence each other. Such exchanges have been described variously in popular cultural literature, including the processes of cross-pollination of ideas, polycentrism, cross fertilization, etc. But they all essentially refer to the same phenomenon of learning from each other, influencing trends cross-culturally or indigenizing and imitating/emulating features to fit the local contexts.

Regional Reception

Japanese popular culture's past successes with regional audiences, particularly in East Asia is well-studied. Some scholarly works have used

---

[55] Ian Condry, *The Soul of Anime* (Durham and London: Duke University Press, 2013), 99.

the term "resonance" to describe the positive reception of regional audiences, arguing that content-based signifiers and symbols become associated with objects in the viewers' daily lives, thereby identifying their lifestyles and cultures with those found in Japanese popular culture. Other terminologies have been used in scholarly works to describe this scenario, including Yuk-ming Leung who argues that this is a form of hyper-reading, arguing the transnationality of the Japanese *Ganbaru* spirit in Japanese TV dramas as something reflecting the life experiences of the audiences in reality.[56]

The Cyberspace Future

What is the future shape of cyberidolism? On 22 October 2008, a Japanese male Taichi Takashita set up a webpage to appeal for support for the legal recognition of a marriage with an anime character Mikuru Asahina.[57] Takashita's rationale was that he lost interest in the three-dimensional world and wanted to live his own life in the two-dimensional counterpart, and his public petition was supported by 3000 people within two months, many of whom had their own preference of anime characters for marriage.[58] The otakus' obsessions, hobbies and interests have spawned new innovative lines of products one after another. Some of the otakus have given up being interested in the three-dimensional lives and realities that they live in and switched to a preference for the two-dimensional world. Nobuoka believes in the compatibility of the pragmatist school with the Akihabara experience received by otakus, fans and visitors, and emphasizes it is not the objective reality but the individuals' own subjective understanding or experience of reality that drives

---

[56]Chi Hang Wong, "From Passive Receivers to Distributing Consumers: The Changing Role of TV Drama Audiences in Hong Kong," *The Journal of Comparative Asian Development*, 9, no. 2 (December 2010): 225. This article quotes Leung's original source: Yuk-ming Leung, "Ganbaru and its transcultural audience: Imaginary and reality of Japanese TV dramas in Hong Kong," in *Feeling Asian Modernities: Transnational consumption of Japanese TV dramas*, ed. K. Iwabuchi (Hong Kong: Hong Kong University Press, 2004), 89–106.

[57]Ian Condry, *The Soul of Anime* (Durham and London: Duke University Press, 2013), 186.

[58]Ian Condry, *The Soul of Anime* (Durham and London: Duke University Press, 2013), 186.

creative ideas in Akihabara amongst all its stakeholders.[59] The cosplayers, the otakus, the manga readers, the gamers, the figurine collectors and the anime consumers are all engaged in their own subjective interpretation of reality when they consume fantasy and make-believe products found in Akihabara. The two-dimensional world is the subjective reality where otakus engaged in this experience live in.

The growing preference for a two-dimensional existence is also facilitated by the fact that otaku fans are now linked globally through cyberspace. Kaichiro Morikawa, a design theorist and professor at the School of Global Japanese Studies at Meiji University, describes this trend succinctly:

> Propelled by the spread of the Internet, communities of interest that do not depend on shared geographical locations or blood ties are growing in numbers and influence. These communities manifest themselves in various forms, including online portal sites and web forums devoted to particular interests and tastes.[60]

This means that fans do not need to physically travel to Akihabara to connect with other fans with similar interests. It also means that foreigners can now participate in the democratic shaping of Japanese popular culture from its center and core. Foreigners or individuals based outside Akihabara in other parts of Japan are able to get their voices heard through online portals and forums. Fandom has become truly global in participation and performance. It also means that any possibility of attempts at state regulation or dominance/monopolistic behavior by one single corporation is diminished. The whole process makes consumption and fandom trends more reactive to global pulses. It is important to note that the otaku and popular cultural communities, both online and in actual reality, are fluid and constantly evolving to adapt to external contexts and dynamically-changing fashion trends.

---

[59] Jakob Nobuoka, *Geographies of the Japanese Cultural Economy Innovation and Creative Consumption* (Sweden: Uppsala University Geografiska Regionstudier NR 83, 2010), 59.

[60] Kaichiro Morikawa, "Otaku and the City: The Rebirth of Akihabara," in *Fandom Unbound Otaku Culture in a Connected World*, eds. M. Ito, D. Okabe and I. Tsuji (New Haven and London: Yale University Press, 2012), 152.

Akihabara as a Constant Reference Point

But one location remains relatively constant in terms of popular cultural consumption and this is the J-pop mecca of Akihabara. Even with consumer tastes evolving constantly according to global, regional and local contexts and trends, Akihabara remains the constant center of Japanese popular culture as long as it continues to create value to the popular cultural industry. For the retailers, they need to carry innovative products that fit the trends and fashion senses of different groups of popular cultural consumers. For the producers, it remains a source of inspiration for consumer-driven ideas that they can translate into new products. For the consumers, it is a place where they can demonstrate and display their creative identity and exercise their power of showing preferences for different products offered in Akihabara.

As one of the few global nucleuses that reflect the trend physically, and universally recognized as the center of the Japanese popular cultural universe, according to Morikawa, Akihabara was shaped by otaku tastes in the 1990s when the retail outlets evolved from electronics retail to retailing personal computers as well as games.[61] The Comic Market also expanded in the 1990s with fanzines retailed throughout the year, along with the figurines that became popular when Evangelion became popular and spawned a following.[62] Messe Sanoh (games retailer), Kaiyodo (figurine manufacturer at Radio Kaikan) and Toranoana (fanzine and comic seller) were the pioneering J-pop cultural retailers that moved into Akihabara.[63] By 2009, at the peak of the *moe* (positive vibes towards made-belief cute-looking characters) movement, Akihabara became a *bishojo* retailing area. Akihabara

---

[61] Patrick Galbraith, *The Moe Manifesto* (Tokyo, Rutland, Vermont and Singapore: Tuttle Publishing, 2014), 159.

[62] Patrick Galbraith, *The Moe Manifesto* (Tokyo, Rutland, Vermont and Singapore: Tuttle Publishing, 2014), 159.

[63] Patrick Galbraith, *The Moe Manifesto* (Tokyo, Rutland, Vermont and Singapore: Tuttle Publishing, 2014), [downloaded on 9 May 2016], available at https://archive.org/stream/TheMoeManifestoAnInsidersLookAtTheWorldsOfMangaAnimeAndGaming/MoeManifesto_djvu.txt.

This is a photo of Radio Kaikan that hosted some of Japan's cutting edge popular culture-related figurine producers.

became the public space where private interests like *bishojo* were openly displayed, the analogy is equated with an otaku bedroom expanding into the streets of Tokyo.[64] An otaku fan naturally felt freer in this environment.

Akihabara did not only cater to otakus. Another range of products that arose was the emergence of cute or *kawaii* products popular with Japanese popular cultural consumers as well. The originators of the trend were attributed to girls in the 1980s who wanted adorable and cute idols that were not only sweet but had a strong fighting spirit and motivation.[65] This

---

[64] Patrick Galbraith, *The Moe Manifesto* (Tokyo, Rutland, Vermont and Singapore: Tuttle Publishing, 2014), 160.

[65] Manami Okazaki and Geoff Johnson, *Kawaii! Japan's culture of cute* (Munich, London and NY: Prestle, 2013), unpaginated introduction.

preference gave rise to a whole new empire of product merchandizing that started innocently from the emergence of letter-writing trends that undergirded product design booms characterized by the strong success of Hello Kitty for example.[66] Christine R. Yano calls the Hello Kitty popular cultural globalization "pink globalization" (feminine, cute, and sexual) equated with the global spread of *kawaii* products and franchises.[67] By 2002, in the US alone, Kitty products trawled US$100 million in earnings from its branded product lines and an additional US$400 million in licensing fees.[68]

Men were not left out of the pink or *kawaii* globalization. Out of this *kawaii* culture, Akihabara spawned its own variant, the maid cafes in which women dressed in maid costumes served tea and snacks to mainly male otaku customers. The maid café, appropriated from the *kawaii* movement, evolved with the tastes of otakus and then became mainstream when their popularity increased with tourists, non-otaku customers and regular consumers. Founded in 2008, MailDreamin with five branches in Akihabara, and the gender profile for its customers in terms of male to female ratio has grown to about six to four while tourists from Asia and particularly from France became the bulk of foreign consumers.[69] Maid cafes also innovated their own indigenous designs for customer satisfaction, including *kawaii* versions of household doorbells to give customers the impression that they are entering a residential area instead of a café joint.

---

[66] Manami Okazaki and Geoff Johnson, *Kawaii! Japan's culture of cute* (Munich, London and NY: Prestle, 2013), unpaginated introduction.

[67] Saya S. Shiraishi, "Doraemon Goes Abroad," in *Japan Pop!* ed. T. J. Craig (Armonk, NY and London: M.E. Sharpe, 2000), 154.

[68] Christine R. Yano, "Monstering the Japanese Cute," in *In Godzilla's Footsteps*, eds. W. M. Tsutsui and M. Ito (Hampshire: Palgrave MacMillan, 2006), 154 and Saya S. Shiraishi, "Doraemon Goes Abroad," in *Japan Pop!* ed. T. J. Craig (Armonk, NY and London: M.E. Sharpe, 2000), 154.

[69] Manami Okazaki and Geoff Johnson, *Kawaii! Japan's culture of cute* (Munich, London and NY: Prestle, 2013), 94.

Photo of a prominent and successful multi-storey maid café joint in Akihabara (second building from the right). This joint offers multi-lingual services with some floors of the maid café dedicated to customers speaking different languages.

Soft Power Element

Pink globalization shaped the lifestyle goods consumption patterns for legions of fans. The maid cafes become constructed environments that create the fantasy of being in a comic book environment or manga world. The Japanese Ministry of Foreign Affairs (MOFA) has even appointed Lolita models "*kawaii* ambassadors" due to their immense appeal.[70] In fact, Tokyo's *Diplomatic Bluebook 2006* mentioned:

> Japanese culture is currently attracting attention around the world as "Cool Japan". In order to increase interest in Japan and further heighten

---

[70]Manami Okazaki and Geoff Johnson, *Kawaii! Japan's culture of cute* (Munich, London and NY: Prestle, 2013), 113.

Ikebukuro's Hello Kitty Gift Gate. A *Kawaii* gateway in East Ikebukuro cementing mainstream appeal in Ikebukuro as the next center of popular culture in Japan.

the image of Japan, Ministry of Foreign Affairs (MOFA) is working with the private sector through overseas diplomatic establishments and the Japan Foundation to promote cultural exchanges while taking into consideration the characteristics of each foreign country.[71]

In 2009, Japan's Minister of Land, Infrastructure, Transport and Tourism, Tetsuzo Fuyushiba appointed Hello Kitty as the goodwill ambassador to advocate tourism to Japan from China and Hong Kong.[72] The focus on East Asian economies is strategic, as they represent

---

[71] Peng Er Lam, Japan Too Going After "Soft Power" in East Asian Institute National University of Singapore (EAI NUS) Background Brief No. 336 (Singapore: EAI NUS), 2007, p. 2 quoting Ministry of Foreign Affairs, Japan, Diplomatic Bluebook 2006, p. 208.
[72] William Tsutsui, *Japanese Popular Culture and Globalization* (Ann Arbor, MI: Association for Asian Studies, Inc., 2010), 66.

Ikebukuro also has a large-sized gaming center that is not found in Akihabara, drawing mainstream gamers to the district.

Skyscrapers hosting offices, hitech incubators, showrooms and mainstream executives (salarymen) have popped up in Akihabara that seems to be preparing for the post-pop culture era should Akihabara shifts from being a retail district to a financial/business center, just as the shift happened from electronics retailing to the pop-cultural scene in the 1990s.

Akiba Square is the entrance to a gleaming new skyscraper which houses offices, galleries and mainstream non-*otaku*ish tenants, as well as a highly-institutionalized Tokyo Anime Center for visitors (domestic and foreign). It remains to be seen whether this represents the new mainstream face of Akihabara or a new evolutionary phase replacing the organically-developed otaku district.

economic growth for Japan in the near future. In East Asian economies like Indonesia, economic growth is giving rise to a consuming class that is urbanized and modern, resonating with the lifestyles portrayed in Japanese manga and anime.[73]

Rising Rivals

Akihabara faces other rising popular cultural centers in Tokyo like East Ikebukuro. Currently, Ikebukuro specializes in products differing from

---

[73] Saya S. Shiraishi, "Doraemon Goes Abroad," in *Japan Pop!* ed. T. J. Craig (Armonk, NY and London: M.E. Sharpe, 2000), 302.

Akihabara such as Boy's Love products (in the Otome Road of East Ikebukuro or more mainstream products found in Sunshine City). Besides more mainstream emerging rivals, Akihabara also faces threat from gentrifications and mainstreamization of the district into a financial/business/retail sector. One can already find skyscrapers hosting hitech companies and showrooms slowly creeping upon the main street.

Chapter 6

Observation Studies Fieldwork in Japan from 2012–2015

Tai Wei LIM

This chapter is based on my observation studies in Japan from 2012 to 2015 to provide a qualitative rather than a quantitative study of how Japanese popular culture is consumed in the cities of Tokyo and Fukuoka. The observations are random and unstructured to accentuate width and span of activities, physical locations, cultural rituals and lifestyles covered. The observations do not pretend to be comprehensive but rather provide a glimpse into how Japanese popular culture is consumed in everyday settings. Some of these observations are supported by visual materials. I selected three major angles for my observation fieldwork. I paid special attention to several activities and agencies in the ecology of creative production: marketing strategies and concepts utilized by creative producers as well as the role of the state and retailers in promoting popular cultural products; soft power harnessed by the state and local authorities in social campaigns/policies utilizing popular culture; and the presence of popular cultural products in daily life routines exposing, socializing and familiarizing young Japanese and other consumers of Japanese society with the stylized features and aesthetics of Japanese popular culture. These three areas make up the three major sections in this chapter. The chapter will then end off with a limitations section and some concluding remarks.

Marketing Strategies and Gimmicks Accentuated by Creative Producers

In this section, I selected a handful of marketing concepts for discussion, including the idea of *gentei* (limited edition), *omotenashii* (welcome reception), *kawaii* (cute-ism) and *natsukashii* (nostalgia). By no means are these concepts comprehensive but they provide a sampling of some ubiquitous conceptual ideas found in Japanese popular cultural marketing. Conceptually, they are not unique as such marketing strategies can also be found in other countries and culture. The chapter examines them in the context of Japan, highlighting some of the local conditions, cultural nuances and lifestyles in this setting. The concept of *gentei* or limited edition is sometimes used in marketing local popular cultural products. The concept excites collectors of popular cultural products who are keen to purchase or acquire limited release products featuring their favorite popular cultural characters or icons so that they are able to swagger, boast or share news about their acquisitions with other members of the collecting community, either through personal networks or online platforms. For example, in my trips to Yamaguchi prefecture's aquarium, limited editions of Hello Kitty dolls specifically retailed in that aquarium were designed with the shape of Kitty wearing pink and blue dolphin suits, reflecting the famous dolphin shows found in that facility. Purchasing such products also serves as evidence that the consumers have visited some unique tourists, lifestyle, heritage or cultural sites. It is a form of recollection of the diachronic moments spent in that location. There is emotive attachment to the object collected, deriving satisfaction from visiting a place and these memories are now embodied in the collected object.

Memories can also take the form of yearning for the past. Besides *gentei*-ism, the element of nostalgia (*natsukashii*) is also sometimes highlighted for promoting popular culture products by invoking past (especially Showa-era) images like cartoon characters or advertisements (known as CMs or commercials in Japan) that promoted branded products. These images from the past are rehashed and updated for relevance and used in contemporary promotional campaigns that highlight certain nostalgic lifestyles or cultural norms less detectable in the current settings. The element of nostalgia is not only restricted to products originated in Japan but could also apply to foreign popular cultural characters and products from the past such as Betty Boop. These foreign characters and icons hark back to earlier historical periods of Japan's modernization drive or postwar recovery period. Due to yearnings by collectors for nostalgic popular cultural products, secondhand bookstores (*furuhonya*) collect and accumulate an inventory of rare and/ or classical publications related to Japanese popular culture. I visited the districts of Kanda and Waseda in Tokyo from 2013 to 2014 to collect some of these publications in order to view nostalgic popular cultural representations and images of postwar Japan. Some of these images are not only textual in nature but are role-played in contemporary life activities. More examples of such manifestations of nostalgia are discussed below using visuals.

Nostalgia and historical images of the past can also be housed in specific physical facilities for general enjoyment by the public. These images are carefully selected by the agencies that fund the facilities (e.g. the state, foundations, funding agencies, private sector entities or a combination of

Nostalgia for the past when taken to the extreme is manifested by this group of hard rock dancers. They are cosplaying in costumes datable to the 1950s and 1960s while dancing the twist and other dance styles of that era to the backdrop of rock and roll music in the public space of Ueno Park.

Nostalgia can also be discerned from the above photo of wall art near the Takadanobaba featuring a classic anime cartoon series, *Simba the Lion*. This cartoon was later translated into English and televised in the US, becoming a well-known character across the Pacific as well.

these stakeholders). An example of an institution important in the archiving of material artefacts and intangible assets as well as the propagation of the idea of nostalgia in Japanese popular culture is the museums. In the summer of 2014, I visited the Tokyo Toy Museum run by a non-profit organization (NPO). The museum featured environmentally-friendly, safe and healthy as well as traditional toys for visitors that included mainly kids and their parents. The museum also featured some pre-modern traditional toys as well as early postwar toys that Japanese children used to play with. The museum invoked nostalgia in the form of toys from the past to educate contemporary kids about toy-making/playing traditions in Japan. The museum also highlighted those ethically-conscious toy products (e.g. made in an environmentally-friendly way), relevant to lessons about contemporary consumption and lifestyles.

A photo depicting the entrance of the toy museum in Tokyo run by a non-profit organization (NPO).

During my fieldwork duration, another key word often heard or seen in the marketing campaigns was the concept of *omotenashii* which is heartfelt reception and welcome for visitors. The *omotenashii* campaign or visitor's welcome also deploys Japanese popular cultural icons that were visible as soon as visitors arrived at the Haneda airport in 2013. I witnessed popular boyband Arashi as well as trendy comic characters in *Dragonball* (a popular anime/manga series) posters immediately greeting visitors who exited from the immigration hall at Narita airport. The Arashi poster carried the message "Thank you for being one of Japan's 10 million visitors in 2013" while the Dragonball poster promised that "Tokyo will touch your heart." In the same period, a large-sized Arashi poster was hung up in the interior of the major interchange train station in Ueno, another major location that both Japanese and foreign visitors are likely to transit through. It is interesting that popular cultural images are the first images of Japan that greet arriving visitors after they step out from the immigration department. The same images are also found in a major transit station. In this sense, it is also a form of soft cultural influence through early exposure to Japanese popular culture for foreign visitors coming to Tokyo. For visitors arriving from East Asia in particular, these popular cultural icons are recognizable and enjoy a sizable following in the region.

Besides the abovementioned conceptual features of marketing campaigns, Japanese popular culture is also deployed in conventional marketing platforms like public posters. For example, during my research fellowship at the end of 2013, Au Smart Value hired the queen of Japan's *kawaii* movement, Kyary Pamyu Pamyu, to sing a catchy melody that featured the phrase "*mottainai*" that urged consumers to buy new smartphone products to avoid any regrets in missing out the deal. Pamyu Pamyu's ubiquitous images were also featured in the popular lifestyle magazine *Anan's* promotion campaign "Bite is An (translated from katakana Japanese characters)" and the popular commercial magazine *Chintai's* promotional posters. The ubiquitous deployment of images in marketing campaigns driven by the private sector resembled an information saturation strategy bombarding Japanese consumers and fans with multiple images of Pamyu Pamyu in many prominent commercial advertising outlets in Japan. These companies sold products used in the daily lives of the Japanese people like mobile phones, home rental informational magazines, etc. Like the Pamyu Pamyu phenomenon, in the same period, convenience store 7–11 in Japan was promoting house brand red wines by utilizing the images of aging but still popular boyband SMAP. While convenience stores and smartphone retailers are profitable businesses in Japan, images of Japanese popular cultural icons have also been utilized by less mainstream businesses keen to reverse perceptions of decline and reinforce positive messages of social acceptability. For example, controversial pachinko (pinball) businesses associated in the mass media with alleged gambling practices utilized anime and manga characters to promote their businesses, which were hit by mixed social reception, lower spending power due to recessionary conditions and an aging population.

Soft Power Implications

Images are not the only popular cultural instruments coveted by the private sector and other organizations for promotional activities. There is a prevailing mascot culture in Japan. The use of Doraemon as Japan's first non-human ambassador is ingenious as the character travels overseas and is given formalities and treated like an important cultural ambassadorial figure even though it is a human person dressed in a rubberized or foam suit. The popularity of Doraemon in East Asia ensures endearing reception in the travels of the non-human ambassador. This is conceivably a source of soft cultural power since audience reception is sometimes more positive and draws more media attention than political figures. The success of such non-human ambassadorship at the national and international levels is paralleled by similar efforts by the prefectural, town and city level local authorities to create indigenous mascots and cultural ambassadors to represent their locales. In Fukutsu City of Fukuoka, for example, I came across an owl mascot designed in stylized cute *kawaii* format representing the city. At the administrative unit level, mascots are also created for public facilities like coal museums and, sometimes, ambassadorial mascots make their rounds in local food produce markets, delighting shoppers who patronize local and organic food products. Similar to the coal museum, the fire-fighter museum in Tokyo also designed official mascots (along with the utilization of Hello Kitty images) to interact with children using materials related to fire-fighting. Therefore, mascots can assist in presenting extra-curricular activities and lessons in a more pleasant manner for children.

As part of a study tour from the Chinese University of Hong Kong to Saga University in the summer of 2013, I also interacted with the official mascot of Saga University, a stylized blue bird mascot. Many of these mascots, whether originating from national, prefectural or local initiatives, tend to have stylized *kawaii* (cute) features such as large eyes, short limbs, bright colors and rounded features to come across as harmless and innocent-looking. Very often, these characters are dressed in a flexible and maneuverable rubberized or foam suit. The latest sensation Funashi or the popular pear fairy character is a good example of strategic use of foam materials as the flexible rubber suit allows the character to bounce up and down as well as dance vigorously, creating a hyper-tensed character personality, much to the amusement of audiences. Humans dressed in character rubber and foam suits are also used in musicals featuring popular cultural characters. In June 2014 in Fukuoka, I attended an entertaining Precure musical performance for children and watched a number of rubberized or foamy suit characters entertain their young fans. The soft texture for the suits allows the performers to manipulate the arms and limbs easily during the performance, giving them room for dexterity during the musical.

Besides adopting rubber suit characters as the official mascots, some local districts in Tokyo have also embraced popular cultural symbols as

A generic Xmas tree character dressed in the typical rubberized or foamy suit, promoting commercial products and services in the festive season (photo taken by author in end 2013 in Tokyo). Foam or rubberized suits are a frequent sighting in Tokyo at commercial outlets and during festive seasons.

The classic and evergreen popular manga/anime character Astro Boy featured in banners along the streets of Takadanobaba which is a popular and hip retailing, restaurant and drinking hole for university students. There are several private universities located near this area which results in a constant stream of young consumers.

their official representatives. One district that I frequented during my observation study in Tokyo was Takadanobaba which featured a local district that has adopted Tetsuwan Atom or Astro Boy as its mascot or district icon. I was able to spot the Astro Boy icons at street level lamppost banners and wall art. This district's association with Astro Boy gives the local area its identity and incentivizes visitors to the district to remember the area vis-à-vis other districts in Tokyo. It can also attract fans of anime/manga, especially fans of Astro Boy to visit the district for photographic opportunities.

Popular culture can also provide Tokyo districts with their product specialization and retail identities. Many local districts in downtown Tokyo are specialized in retailing certain retail or service types of firms in commercial office spaces. For example Harajuku had a large selection of street fashion wear in different styles such as burlesque, gothic, hip hop,

The above photo was taking during my stay in Tokyo in end 2013. It depicts the popular manga anime character Astro Boy in a public wall art display in the Takadanobaba area. Tetsuwan Atom has been adapted as the mascot of the local district.

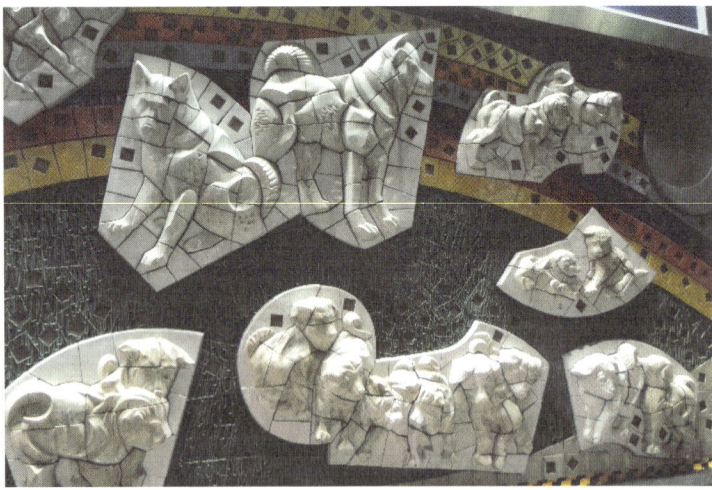

Public wall installation artwork installed at the Shibuya station that depicts Hachiko the dog who loyally waited for its owner to return despite the owner's absence.

Lolita, etc., all catering to niche groups of consumers. The district also has niche stores that retail foreign goods like American popular cultural products such as Star Wars and K-pop characters as well. Ura-Harajuku, the interior section of the Harajuku district, carries higher value-added products such as branded goods from Japan, the US and Europe. Sometimes, local urban legends and myths can become the subject of Japanese and foreign popular cultural themes. For example, the famous real-life story of a dog Hachiko who waited for its owner faithfully in Shibuya became the subject of a Hollywood film starring Richard Gere. Such international exposure lends color and popular cultural narrative to an otherwise local

Even in fashionable districts like Shibuya which have already become international icons for popular cultural fashion products, the use of popular cultural icons can sometimes value-add to its already-famous status. This large billboard facing the main road features popular anime character Sailor Moon advertising the final bargain sale at Shibuya 109, an iconic fashion house in Shibuya.

A man taking a photo of a gigantic billboard in Akihabara featuring the latest and most popular anime and manga characters.

area tale. When depicted in a Hollywood movie fronted by a well-known America actor, Hachiko the dog helps the Shibuya area develop its identity with its own local narratives and serves to distinguish and exceptionalize itself from other shopping and retail areas. Individuals sometimes visit the Shibuya station just to take photo of the spot where Hachiko the dog waited for its master.

In the more specialized districts that retail Japanese popular culture, cutting-edge products that are trendy or just released are featured with greater sophistication. Akihabara is the mecca of dedicated Japanese popular culture fans, including the uber collector crowd of the otaku male fans (some stereotype the otakus as stay-at-home "nerds," perhaps unfairly generalized). The district features and retails the most cutting-edge Japanese popular cultural products. When I was at the Tokyo Anime Center in the summer of 2014 in Akihabara, the long-haired vocaloid

Miku Hatsune was featured in this Center and other retail outlets, including the official Akihabara shop outlet of the Anime Center located just one floor below the Anime Center. I will discuss about Akihabara in greater details in Chapter 5.

Integral Part of Daily Lives

Traces of Japanese popular culture can be found integrated into the daily lives of Japanese people and they can be classified into tangible and intangible categories. In the tangible category, Japanese popular cultural representations can be found in the form of physical promotional items displayed at outlets that are patronized by the general public. At the local districts in Tokyo and Fukuoka that I visited, consciousness of the most popular anime and manga cartoons (for kids) remained strong. In one of the bookshops in suburban Fukuoka that I visited in 2013, an inflatable Anpanman (translated literally as the "Red Bean Paste Bread Man") stood at the entrance to welcome customers to a bookshop. Bookshops are not the only outlets in which mangas or comic books are consumed. During my summer 2014 stay in Tokyo, I also rented a manga-reading space that gave me access to a large manga library, food menu, free flow of drinks and game facilities. I also found restaurants that offered a limited selection of mangas that customers could borrow to read while having their meals. Besides bookshops, I visited a cinema in downtown Fukuoka in mid-2014 with the impending release of the Hollywood-produced Godzilla movie. The cinema became a roving display of historical images of Godzilla from the first film to the latest production. This display of the historical context of the films featuring the popular cultural icon was a delight for fans, especially youngsters, who had not been exposed to the early Godzilla films produced in Japan (also featuring men in rubberized Godzilla suits). But the event of that year in Tokyo which coincided with the Hollywood release of its version of the monster was a large installation of a half-body mockup of the creature in hip upper-class Roppongi neighborhood district.

A mockup of Godzilla whose body can emit light and whose mouth can spew out gas in the public park grounds of Roppongi in mid-2014. (Picture taken by the author during his stay in Tokyo at that time.)

Anpanman and other evergreen anime/manga favorites for kids have become synonymous with daily consumption activities even in suburban towns. In the intangible form, popular cultural icons and representations are deployed in community celebrations, *matsuri*s or festivals. For example, when I participated in a study tour's cultural night in 2013 in Saga city, our Japanese hosts dressed up like their favorite J-pop icon AKB48, mimed their songs and imitated their dance moves. They also made the efforts to sew together costumes that resembled those worn by their idols, a phenomenon that is part of the cosplaying culture where cosplayers dress up in clothes that resemble their idols' on-stage performance outfits. Like Kyary Pamyu Pamyu fans, AKB48 fans were also saturated with images of the top individual singers from the 100-member girl band. The ranking AKB48 members who won the annual elections where fans vote to pick the best singers eventually "graduated" to go solo or retire. Some of the select few who went solo eventually went on to achieve stardom and were featured in advertisements sponsored by firms with deep pockets like Mynavi.

A public display of the Anpanman character (from a popular televised anime cartoon series) dressed up in the local *matsuri* (festival) costume, in preparation for celebrating a local winter festival in the historic area of Kamakura, famous for its ancient giant sitting Buddha statue.

Rows of masks depicting popular cultural characters on display at a store in a local funfair event. Popular culture here is integrated with local events, reinforcing a sense of community. (Photo taken during winter 2015 in Fukuoka, Japan.)

A Power Rangers kite stuck on a tree during the extended New Year holiday season in 2015. (Photo taken in Fukuoka in winter 2015.)

The identity of Ishinomaki is clear from this picture as a manga/anime character is displayed in a "flying" position from the rooftop of the town's train station. (Photo taken by author during study trip in the summer of 2014.)

Popular culture also serves the important function of encouraging local tourism, something particularly important for towns recovering from natural disasters. Ishinomaki is an ideal town for studying the close integration of popular cultural images into an entire downtown area's physical architecture and landscape. During my summer 2014 visit to Ishinomaki, I was excited at the prospects of visiting a town well known for its manga and anime heritage and culture. It is also particularly significant because Ishinomaki is gradually recovering from the effects of the Great East Japan Earthquake and its popular culture heritage is an asset in this process.

Sometimes, marketing campaigns for popular cultural products are found on physical assets synonymous with the daily lives of the Japanese people. For example, visitors to Japan will immediately spot the ubiquitous vending machines in public spaces that retail everything from soft drinks to electrical appliances. In my observation studies in 2013, Japan's most popular girl band, AKB48, was also featured on the posters found on the vending machines, along with the classic Japanese anime *Space Battleship*

Windows at the building of the Ishinomaki train station creatively decorated with anime/manga characters. (Photo taken during study trip in the summer of 2014.)

Yamato. Socialization and exposure to stylized manga/anime characters start young in Japan as young children get exposed to anime and manga-like characters with rounded features, short limbs and big eyes in a variety of public spaces. This socialization process is not state-imposed but arose from a convergence of stakeholder interests and various agencies involved: including the producers who are keen to market their products and extract profits from it; the state that sometimes sees convenience in using popular cultural characters to promote economic and political policies; and the creative elites who derive satisfaction from originating and generating new, commercially viable and well-received products and designs. All of them derive social, financial and socioeconomic capital from successful anime, comic and gaming (ACG) products.

Popular cultural genres like anime and manga are sometimes utilized for public service campaigns. In such cases, anime and manga are helpful medium as they can convey socially sensitive messages in graphical form

Decorated glass windows with stain glass-like sticker designs featuring anime/manga characters. (Photo taken during a study trip to Sendai in the summer of 2014.)

or with humorous content. For example, the subway authorities used manga to advise passengers not to cause inconvenience to others by dozing off and falling asleep on other people's shoulders. In my stay in Tokyo in mid-2014, I also located posters featuring Kamen Riders providing updated information about Tokyo's metro railway. Other than socially-sensitive messages on public mannerisms (*manna* in Japanese language), popular culture is also utilized for potentially abrasive reminders found in our daily lives. For example, in December 2013, during my research fellowship in Tokyo, the canteen displayed bowing Hello Kitty images to apologize for closure during the New Year festive season. Rounded characters with no mouths, short limbs and large eyes present a harmless, cute and innocent image that reduces the abrasiveness of such social messages in daily routines. There are many other examples of Japanese popular cultures hybridizing with traditional cultures and customs whether in form, shape or contents. For example, *gentei*-ism can sometimes apply to seasonal products in

A running manga/anime character strategically decorating the space between two windows at an unidentified building located near the Ishinomaki train station. (Photo taken by the author during summer 2014 trip to Sendai.)

addition to limited edition series. During the Japanese New Year season leading up to 1 January 2014, I came across the traditional *otoshidama* prosperity packets (for New Year greetings) with Hello Kitty dressed in traditional kimono designs. Similarly, the universe of Hello Kitty franchise also churned out bento lunch boxes that had Kitty designs and came available in limited editions (*gentei*) when purchased with Kentucky Fried Chicken (KFC) products for ¥2,200 each. Besides New Year goods, another example of hybridized traditional-contemporary cultural products is found in designs on traditional textiles. In June 2014, during my visit to a recycling shop in Fukuoka, I spotted a traditional *yukata* (traditional summer dressing that resembles a dressed-down kimono) with Hello Kitty designs.

This concrete block at the train station used as a marker for halting the train to stop at the destination in Ishinomaki station has half-faded manga/anime character designs (not sure if the fading is due to the rising flood waters from the Great East Japan Earthquake of 2011).

Besides social campaigns and gentle reminders, images of popular culture characters are also found on items like stamps that are issued by the authorities to serve important administrative functions like postal needs. I visited the Japanese stamp museum at Mejiro Tokyo and conducted fieldwork there to collect stamp designs that depict anime and manga characters. I found stamps related to: Godzilla ¥80 (*Gojira* in Japanese) undated on cover; Gundam ¥50 undated on cover; spaceship Yamato ¥80; Sazaesan ¥80 undated; Captain Atom ¥50 undated on cover; Ultraman ¥80 undated on cover; Karaoke Ryuukou (popularity) ¥80 undated on cover; Doraemon stamps at ¥80 per piece; another series featuring the creator of Tetsuwan Atom and Simba the Lion valued at ¥80 per stamp. I was also able to locate special Hello Kitty stamp series with unperforated corners in sticker form

Large manga/anime figurines stand guard at street corners in the town of Ishinomaki. (Photo taken during visit in summer 2014.)

valued at ¥50 per piece. These classical works of anime and manga have been deemed important enough to be featured on commemorative stamp series found in the philatelic retail outlets in the museum.

Cosmopolitanism and Creative Production

While visiting Tokyo on a research fellowship in end-2013, I noticed the intense advertising that went on for the Broadway musical *Wicked*. It served to remind me that Tokyo was continually absorbing cosmopolitan popular cultural influence from the West just as it was producing indigenous popular culture of its own. I also visited Disneyland in my end-2013 fieldwork and the large crowds indicated American popular culture enjoys a large following in Japan. Because of the availability and presence of cutting-edge popular cultural products from the West, cross-pollination of ideas inevitably takes place. For example, I came across an *izakaya* (a Japanese pub that sells foods which complement alcohol-drinking) that displayed traditional lamps at its entrance though these lamps with

The white flying saucer-like building at the top left-hand corner of the photo is the manga museum of Ishinomaki. The town is cleared of debris and on the road to recovery from the Great East Japan Earthquake. Manga and anime cultural spaces and activities might be one option for local economy revival.

traditional shapes carried designs resembled the character Venom (from Marvel's *Spiderman* comic series and movie). Besides Japanese adaptations of American popular cultural images, unadulterated American popular culture is also featured in advertising gimmicks in hip districts like Shibuya. When I visited this district at the end of 2013, a black shiny Hummer was advertising Sean Paul's latest album. The Hummer's cool image coincided with stereotypes of American popular culture where hip hop, reggae, rap, etc. stars travel in flashy large American branded cars. American products that are familiar to Japanese consumers can also similarly be invoked through designs for marketing or retailing products in Japan. Sometimes, the context in which a foreign popular cultural icon is used may be different from the original context in which they appear. For example, a pub that I came across in Tokyo in end-2013 adapted an image

A typical public park playground featuring brightly-colored stylized manga-like character rides. This particular character is generic and not copyrighted by any anime/manga companies. Exposure to such stylized character designs gives children early exposure to stylized *kawaii*-ism (cute-ism).

that resembled Mr T from the American 1980s television series *A-team* for its aesthetic decorative needs. The commercial outlet may not be trying to relate the image to the old iconic American popular TV series, or to specifically reconnect with its cult following in Japan.

Just as nostalgia is sometimes utilized by marketers in Japan, the element of nostalgia can also be used in creative production. Japanese advertisers sometimes hire retired or former A-lister Hollywood stars to advertise Japanese products. Japanese consumers may recall or recollect these stars' previous important cinematic works nostalgically. In December 2013, I was able to find both Tommy Lee Jones and SMAP promoting the Boss line of coffee. Not all Hollywood stars appearing in Japanese commercials are former A-listers, sometimes companies like Toyota hire current A-listers like Leonardo DiCaprio to promote the Prius hybrid cars. In December 2013, the pop art world produced photos of Hollywood A-lister George Clooney posing against a white-dotted backdrop that resembled Yayoi Kusama's works. Sometimes, Tokyo icons need no promotional help from Hollywood stars because they have already been featured voluntarily in Hollywood movies, images so powerfully portrayed and widely

In more peripheral locations like the former coal mine of Ikeshima, I spotted local attempts in constructing well-known anime and manga figurines such as Doraemon and Anpanman from recycled tires and industrial equipment. The popular cultural icons made from recycled materials are then displayed in public parks. These initiatives are environmentally-friendly and also allow the residents in those areas to enjoy makeshift popular cultural art-forms.

disseminated that certain Tokyo districts became internationally well known. Some examples are discussed below.

Sometimes collaborations between American cultural icons and the Japanese popular cultural industry are accidental or coincidental. When I led a fieldtrip group to the fashionable Ura-Harajuku district, we visited the iconic Dog, a fashion studio that produced and retails some of the most cutting-edge fashion items in Japan, a brand so well-recognized that it is said that Lady Gaga was a customer of the store. Youtube videos by fans show Gaga mobbed by her own fans when she visited the store surrounded by bodyguards. In this case, the collaboration between a superstar and the

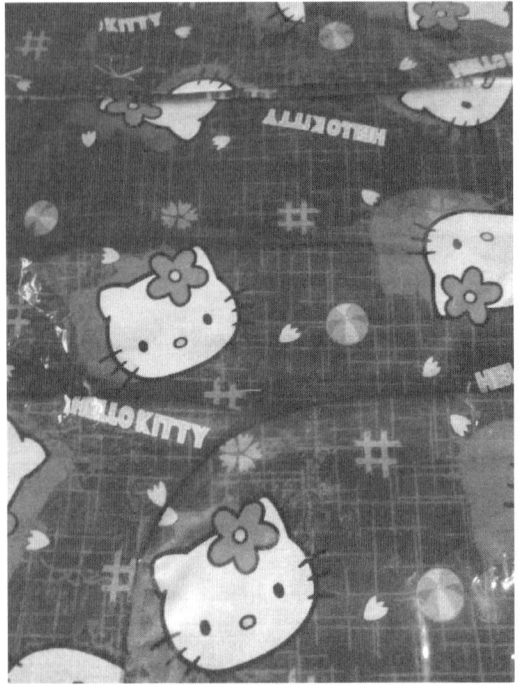

A *yukata* with Hello Kitty designs found in a recycle shop that sells secondhand goods. Recycled products like these are popular with kids during the summer *hanabi* (fireworks) season where girls like to wear summer *yukatas* to view the fireworks display.

retail outlet may be coincidental or accidental in that the American superstar happened to fancy the designs in the store which are handcrafted and unique. Dog has since become internationally known for its outlandish designs and even incorporated collaborative outreach from designers outside Japan such as Singapore.

Concluding Remarks and Limitations

It is important to note that, while this chapter has detailed to some degree, offerings in the Japanese popular cultural industry, it is by no means comprehensive. The observation studies are only a small sampling and cross-section of some products, retailing and production ecologies of a complicated creative industry. It does not pretend to be comprehensive.

The Tokyo district of Shibuya's famous crosswalk became associated with scenes from Hollywood hit movies like *Lost in Translation* and *Resident Evil*. In the former starring Scarlett Johansson and Bill Murray, camera shots gaze wondrously at a digital image of a dinosaur walking slowly across the window screen of the building on the right in the photo. In the latter, the character played by Milla Jovovich notices people on the crosswalk being attacked by zombies and eventually fights a zombie played by Japanese celebrity Mika Nakashima. (Photo taken by the author at the end of 2013 in Tokyo.)

The popular cultural industry is far more extensive with products spanning the ACG industries and beyond. This chapter can only serve as a survey of some selected facets of popular cultural consumption. In addition, while I have focused on my observations of Japanese popular culture in this chapter, it acknowledges the fact that Japan is also a major consumer of American popular cultural products; e.g. Hollywood films, Disneyland, Hard Rock Café in Yokohama and Ueno, just to name a few. Therefore, while Japanese companies produce large volumes of popular cultural materials, they also consume a lot of popular cultural products from the US (English-based products such as Thomas the Train from UK also feed

The unassuming entrance of the iconic Dog in Ura-Harajuku district.

this consumption), whose culture remains globally universalistic and extensively marketed, translated and disseminated (please refer to the chapter on universalism versus particularism for more discussion). Another limitation is that my observation studies also cover mostly traditional media and physical assets related to Japanese popular culture. As a follow-up study, it will be interesting to observe how technology will increasingly fuse with popular cultural images to form a whole new generation of products. Some examples are the cyber-idol and vocaloid Miku Hatsune who exist mostly in the digital realm but are treated like a real idol with its own existence, personality and biodata. During the summers of 2011 and 2012, I also came across Hello Kitty droids at Robosquare. The fusion of robotics with Japanese popular culture is an important trend to watch.

Section 3

Republic of Korea

Chapter 7

Hallyu Power: The Transformative Impact of the Korean Wave

Wen Xin LIM

Introduction

The Korean wave — "*Hallyu*" in Korean — refers to a surge in the international visibility of Korean culture, beginning in East Asia in the 1990s and continuing more recently in the North America, Latin America, the Middle East, and parts of Europe (Mark, 2009).[1] The term was coined by Beijing journalists in mid-1999 surprised by the burgeoning popularity of Korean popular culture in China (Kim, 2007).[2] Korean Wave has been diversifying and changing since its emergence, creating a complex range of transnational and regional connections. It can be categorized into *Hallyu* 1.0 and *Hallyu* 2.0. *Hallyu* 1.0 emphasized on the cultural export to East Asia from the late 1990s to 2007 while *Hallyu* 2.0 since the late 2007 sees the spread of Korean culture from regional to global and has been greatly influenced by the advent of social media (Dal, 2012).[3]

The Korean Wave was introduced first by Doboo Shim with the concept of "hybrid culture" (Shim, 2006).[4] After the concept was introduced,

---

[1] Mark Ravina, "Introduction: conceptualizing the Korean Wave," *Southeast Review of Asian Studies* 31 (2009): 3–9.

[2] Ju Yong Kim, "Rethinking media flow under globalization: rising Korean wave and Korean TV and film policy since 1980s" (PhD diss., Warwick Research Archive Portal, 2007).

[3] Yong Jin Dal, "Hallyu 2.0: The New Korean Wave in the Creative Industry," *International Institute Journal University of Michigan* 2 (Fall 2012): 1.

[4] Doboo Shim, "Hybridity and the rise of Korean popular culture in Asia," *Media, Culture & Society* 28, no. 1 (2006): 25–44.

some scholars regarded Korean popular culture as a fusion between East and West. Woongjae Ryoo "explores a regionally specific phenomenon and logic of transnational popular cultural flow as an example to illustrate the complexity involved in the cultural hybridization and the implications that it has on the globalization of culture" (Ryoo, 2009).[5] He also argues that the impact of the Korean wave has not only permeated popular culture but is also a measure of positive lifestyle for many Asian people (Ryoo, 2009, p. 144).[6] Ravina looks at the common features of *hallyu* across different cultures and markets and explores on the common factors that lead Korean popular culture to success in different regions (Ravina, 2009).[7] Beng Huat Chua and Koichi Iwabuchi analyze the reception of the most successful Korean dramas and provide an alternative theoretical framework to the US-centered transnational cultural studies (Chua and Iwabuchi, 2008).[8] Yoshitaka Mori highlights the historical and political effects of Korean TV consumption and points out that the Korean drama significantly changed the impression of Japanese women on Korea (Mori, 2008).[9] Jonghoe Yang compares the *Hallyu* phenomenon among the *Hallyu*-receiving countries and region including China, Taiwan and Japan (Yang, 2012).[10]

The success of the Korean Wave can be attributed to few factors including the role of government, the social-networking platform, the appealing drama plots, etc. Milim Kim studies the formation of new relationships between public and private sectors bridged by policies, the

---

[5]Woongjae Ryoo, "Globalization, or the logic of cultural hybridization: the case of the Korean Wave," *Asian Journal of Communication* 19, no. 2 (2009).

[6]Woongjae Ryoo, "Globalization, or the logic of cultural hybridization: the case of the Korean Wave," *Asian Journal of Communication* 19, no. 2 (2009).

[7]Mark Ravina, "Introduction. Conceptualizing the Korean wave," *Southeast Review of Asian Studies* 31 (2009): 3–9.

[8]Beng Huat Chua and Koichi Iwabuchi, *East Asian Pop Culture: Analysing the Korean Wave* (Hong Kong: Hong Kong University Press, 2008).

[9]Yoshitaka Mori, "*Winter Sonata* and Cultural Practices of Active Fans in Japan: Considering Middle-Aged Women as Cultural Agents," in *East Asian Pop Culture: Analysing the Korean Wave*, eds. B.H. Chua and K. Iwabuchi (Hong Kong: Hong Kong University Press, 2008).

[10]Jonghoe Yang, "The Korean Wave (*Hallyu*) in East Asia: Comparison of Chinese, Japanese, and Taiwanese who watch Korean TV Dramas," *Development and Society* 41, no. 1 (June 2012).

capital formation process, and the production and market power of visual content (Kim, 2011).[11] Sunguen Shim examines how the Korean state's policy changes have contributed to the enhancement of the competitiveness of Korean broadcasting, particularly to its overseas expansion, mainly through interviews with persons in charge of the management of terrestrial television program export (Shim, 2008).[12] Yasue Kuwahara's book *The Korean Wave: Korean Popular Culture in Global Context* has slew of essays to discuss the Korean Wave from the perspectives of production, glocalization and consumption. He argues that "it was the government industrial policies that produce Korean popular culture products and there is an effect of reception and adaptation of Korean popular culture in other countries" (Kuwahara, 2014).[13]

In other words, the *Hallyu* components — television dramas, popular music, gaming industry — through the facilitation of technological advancement, have travelled to different geographical locations, transcending national boundary and undergo adaptation, accommodation, and innovation to resonate pleasingly with audiences of different regions. This chapter critically examines the growing phenomenon of the Korean Wave and the differentiated forms of Korean Wave reception, as well as responses within and beyond East Asia region. By mapping out the growth of the Korean Wave, this chapter aims to discuss media production processes and the pivotal role of social media in transforming the conventional consumption pattern into a fan-driven trend, resulting in multiplicity of cultural trajectories in the context of creative and media industries across the world. This chapter also discusses the various implications of the Korean Wave from the economic, political, social and cultural perspectives. More importantly, it outlines how the Korean media agencies together with the platforms of social media have significantly contributed to the surge of the Korean Wave, especially in the second wave of *Hallyu*.

---

[11] Milim Kim, "The role of the government in cultural industry: Some observations from Korea's experience," *Keio Communication Review* 33 (2011).

[12] Sungeun Shim, "Behind the Korean Broadcasting Boom," *NHK Broadcasting Studies* 6 (2008).

[13] Yasue Kuwahara, *The Korean Wave: Korean Popular Culture in Global Context* (New York: Palgrave Macmillan, 2014).

Korean Wave: From a Regional to Global Phenomenon

The Korean Wave has swept across the world, elevating Korea's international image and generating positive economic implications to Korea's economy. Between 2001 and 2014, export revenue from Korean cultural industries grew by eight-fold, from US$658 million to US$5 billion,[14] and the Korean government aims to double this figure by 2017.[15] Japan is the biggest importer of Korean cultural contents with US$1.2 billion in 2011. Asian countries including Japan, China, and Southeast Asia accounted for 76.3% of Korea's total export of cultural contents in 2011 (see Table 7.1).

In the *Hallyu* 1.0 era (1990–2007), the key historical feature of the South Korea's popular cultural development was that it first boomed in its periphery, when the media conglomerates first exported their media products mainly to East Asia. Many Asian countries have embraced Korean popular culture and picked up numerous Korean cultural genres in this period, including television drama series and films. While the first phase of the Korean Wave *(Hallyu 1.0)* led to numerous ripple effects such as

TABLE 7.1. KOREA EXPORT OF CULTURAL CONTENT IN MILLION USD, 2009–2011.

	2009	2010	2011	% Share (2011)
China	581	749	1,118	27.0
Japan	664	803	1,247	30.1
Southeast Asia	458	672	796	19.2
North America	388	404	468	11.3
Europe	217	267	325	7.8
Others	126	157	189	4.6
Total	2,435	3,055	4,146	100

Source: Korea Creative Content Agency (KOCCA).

---

[14] Korea Ministry of Culture, Sports and Tourism, 2012.

[15] Katie Holliday, "Next wave of Korea craze about to start," dated 27 August 2014 in Yahoo Finance [downloaded on 29 March 2015], available at http://finance.yahoo.com/news/next-wave-korea-craze-start-222705521.html.

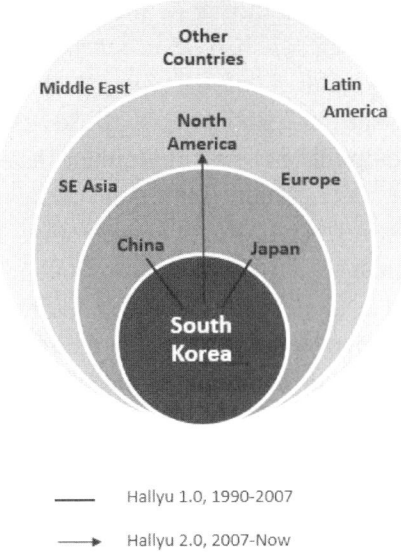

—— Hallyu 1.0, 1990-2007

——▶ Hallyu 2.0, 2007-Now

FIGURE 7.1.   THE TRANSFORMATION OF *HALLYU*.

greater awareness of South Korea in East Asia brought about by the popularity of Korean TV dramas, the sobriquet "new wave of *Hallyu*" (also known as *Hallyu* 2.0) is propelled by the worldwide success of K-pop music at a time of globalization and media liberalization. The far-reaching influence and audience-ship of *Hallyu* 2.0 stretch beyond Asia, reaching regions as far as Middle East, Latin America and Africa (see Figure 7.1).

The Korean Wave, through the facilitation of digital media and online technology, has been transforming to reach new heights of popularity.[16] Bolstered by the power of social media together with the internet presence, Korean cultural contents including the Korean movies, TV dramas and variety shows, online games, and popular music are now being spread, diffused and consumed in cyberspace even in the most remote corners of the world at an unprecedented pace. For the last few years, the dissemination of Korea's popular media contents has been facilitated by Facebook, Twitter, Youtube, Cyworld, and myriad social networking websites to

---

[16] Korea Net, "Korean Wave," in The Korea Net website [downloaded on 25 February 2015], available at http://www.korea.net/Government/Current-Affairs/Others?affairId=209.

regions where the traditional media — theatrical distributions, TV networks, and DVD/VCD sales — had never reached before.

The increasing popularity of the Korean Wave helps to improve national image, presents Korean political worldviews and more importantly serves as a cultural tool and diplomatic leverage for the South Korean government. More significantly, it creates positive spill-over effects to other industries. South Korean corporations have responded that Hallyu strengthens other commercial ventures and helps to enhance positive image and brand awareness of South Korean products in general. The South Korean government has recognized the advantage of this national phenomenon and is eager to capitalize on the success of the Korean Wave by providing public funds as well as implementing relevant policies in facilitating the development of the industry.

Increased Export of South Korean TV Programs

South Korean total export of TV programs has been increasing steadily since 2001 but remains primarily an East Asian phenomenon. With an annual growth rate of 31.5%, it amounted to US$168.9 million in 2011, 16 times more than US$10.9 million in 2001 (see Figure 7.2). Ostensibly,

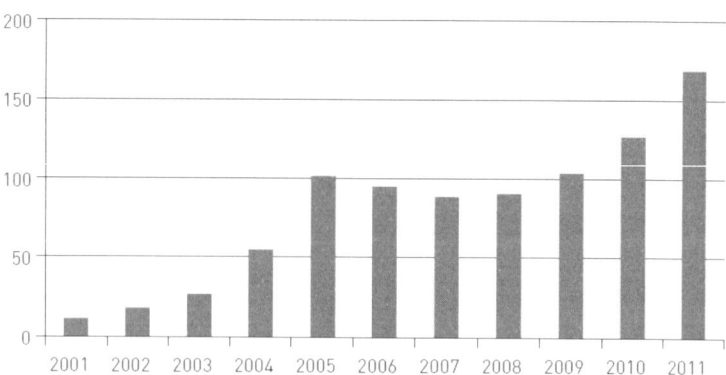

FIGURE 7.2.   KOREAN EXPORT OF TV PROGRAMS IN MILLION USD, 2001–2011.

Note: TV programs include not only dramas but also documentaries, animations, and show programs.
Source: Young Seaon Park, "Trade in Cultural Goods: A Case of the Korean Wave in Asia," *Journal of East Asian Economic Integration* 18, no. 1 (March 2014): 83–107.

TABLE 7.2. KOREAN EXPORTS SHARE OF TV PROGRAMS PER COUNTRY/REGION IN 2011.

Country/Region	Exports Share in Percentage
Japan	60.4
Taiwan	12.5
China	10.2
Hong Kong	2.4
Philippines	2.1
Singapore	1.9
Vietnam	1.7
Thailand	1.6
Myanmar	0.8
Indonesia	0.7
Others	4.6

Source: Young Seaon Park, "Trade in Cultural Goods: A Case of the Korean Wave in Asia," *Journal of East Asian Economic Integration* 18, no. 1 (2014): 83–107.

the peak year before 2007 matches with the phenomenal success of TV drama *Jewel in the Palace* (Dae Jang Geum).[17] Table 7.2 indicates the South Korean export share of TV programs for each country/region based on the US dollar amount in 2011. Japan is the biggest importer of South Korean TV programs with a 60.4% share in 2011, followed by Taiwan, China and Hong Kong.[18]

In Japan, *Hallyu* garnered explosive success around 2003 when the Japan's National Network Television (NHK) first broadcasted *Winter Sonata* on air. The impact was multiplied through the realization of the star appeal effect. For instance, the male character Bae Yong-joon became especially popular among middle-aged women, and was known as

---

[17]Young Seaon Park, "Trade in Cultural Goods: A Case of the Korean Wave in Asia," *Journal of East Asian Economic Integration* 18, no. 1 (2014): 83–107.

[18]Young Seaon Park, "Trade in Cultural Goods: A Case of the Korean Wave in Asia," *Journal of East Asian Economic Integration* 18, no. 1 (2014): 83–107.

Yon-sama to his Japanese fans.[19] The Hyundai Research Institute estimated that Bae alone had generated US$4 billion in revenue between
South Korea and Japan.[20] Tour agencies in Japan also reaped profit by
providing Korea tour packages to the drama aficionados in Japan. The
South Korean service sector (particularly tourism industry) too had a
windfall as the hotel suite where the scene of *Winter Sonata* was filmed
had at one time a waiting list for more than a month.[21]

It is reported by the *Korea Herald*[22]:

> *The number of visitors to Nami Island in Chuncheon, Gangwon
> Province, where the shooting took place shot up from about 270,000 in
> 2001 to 650,000 in 2002, right after the drama was broadcasted. The
> number is still growing, marking 2.4 million in 2011.*

The success of *Dae Jang Geum* was even more astonishing as it
went beyond East Asia, reaching out to 87 countries.[23] *Dae Jang Geum*
was first broadcasted in 2003 in Korea. It was Korea's first worldwide
television hit, which was not only popular in Asia including Japan,
China, Taiwan, India, Thailand, and Malaysia, but also in Egypt, Turkey,
Iran and Israel (see Figure 7.3). The drama is set in the 16th century
during the Joseon Dynasty, narrating the story of how a female cook
rose above social taboos and discriminations to become the first female
physician for the king.[24] It is based on a true story and portrays traditional

---

[19]The New Statesman, "How Korea got to be cool. Observations on Eastern fashions,"
dated March 2005 in The New Statesman website [downloaded on 16 July 2014], available
at http://www.newstatesman.com/node/150098.

[20]Toru Hanaki, Arvind Singhal, Min Wha Han, Do Kyun Kim and Ketan Chitnis, "Hanryu
sweeps East Asia: How Winter Sonata is gripping Japan," *International Communication
Gazette* 69, no. 3 (2007): 281–294.

[21]William Tuk, "The Korean Wave: Who are behind the success of the Korean popular
culture?" (MA diss., Leiden University, 2012).

[22]Min-young Park, "K-drama fever impacts other industries," dated 10 January 2012 in
The Korea Herald [downloaded 9 January 2015], available at http://www.koreaherald.com/
common_prog/newsprint.php?ud=20120110000723&dt=2.

[23]The Korean Culture and Information Service (KOCIS), 2015.

[24]The Korean Culture and Information Service (KOCIS), 2015.

FIGURE 7.3.   COUNTRIES/REGIONS WHERE DAE JANG GEUM WAS AIRED ON TELEVISION.

Source: Korean Culture and Information Service, 2011, Seoul, South Korea: KOCIS. Copyright 2011 by KOCIS.

Korean culture. The success of *Winter Sonata* and *Dae Jang Geum* has attracted regional recognition of the Korean Wave phenomenon, laying a good foundation for the government to introduce Korea media programming worldwide.

Korean dramas are also popular in Southeast Asia. In an article published by *Globe One*,[25] it is reported that:

> *In the Philippines, the K-drama "Boys Over Flower" was a big hit. In Vietnam, Korean dramas were also popular. Yoon Eun Hye, one of the*

---

[25] Globe One, "Power of culture — Hallyu, the Korean wave," dated 13 August 2013 in Globe One website [downloaded on 20 July 2014], available at http://globe-one.com/power-of-culture-hallyu-the-korean-wave-4636/.

members of Baby V.O.X became a superstar in Vietnam after playing a role in Korean drama "The Palace". The popularity of Korean dramas in Thailand started in 2007 when "My Girl" and "Coffee Prince" were broadcasted. In Indonesia, Hallyu began in 2002 when "Autumn in My Heart" was broadcasted on Indosiar Television and reached a viewers rating of 11%.

In addition, Korean dramas have been receiving good response in Middle East. William Tuk in his master thesis[26] stated that:

In the Middle East, Korean dramas can be found in Turkey, Jordan, Israel and Iran. "Jumong", a historical drama, was very successful in Iran in 2008 and got a rating of 85%. The actors of that show appeared in different advertisements in Iran. The dramas inspired Iranians to study and pick up the Korean language according to the Korean Culture and Information Service.

Most notably, the recent fantasy romance TV drama *My Love From the Star* (2013) has reignited the Korean Wave across East Asia. The impact of the new drama series has been greater and deeper than ever, than past generations of Korean soap operas, particularly in Mandarin-speaking regions. *My Love From the Star* set an unprecedented success in terms of viewership and streaming records, attributed to its online distribution in China. The drama went viral after its first release and received more than 600 million views on IQIYI, a Chinese video site.[27] According to the producer of the drama, HB Entertainment, the company resorted to online broadcasting due to the complicated procedure of the censorship policy adopted by the Chinese TV stations.[28] The fast-moving digital technology has transformed viewer habits in a huge dimension, allowing them to have access to nearly any program regardless of time zone and geographical location.

---

[26] William Tuk, "The Korean Wave: Who are behind the success of the Korean popular culture?" (MA diss., Leiden University, 2012).

[27] The Inside Korea, "Being Dramatic, K-Dramas continue to drive Korean Wave," dated 27 May 2014 in The Inside Korea website [downloaded on 18 November 2014], available at http://theinsidekorea.com/2014/05/dramatic-k-dramas-continue-drive-korean-wave/.

[28] Korean Culture and Information Service, "K-DRAMAS: Korean soap operas enthrall TV audiences worldwide," in *KOREA* 10, no. 5.

Advertisement by celebrity Jun Ji-hyun, the female lead of *My Love From The Star* at major tourist attraction, Oak Valley Ski Resort, Gangwon-do, Korea.

The Wall Street Journal also reported on 26 February 2014 that *My Love From the Star* is one of the most discussed and circulated topics on Sina's Weibo micro blogging platform. An article published in *The Inside Korea*, titled "K-dramas continue to drive Korean Wave",[29] corroborated the immense popularity of *My Love From the Star*:

> *"My Love From the Star" created immense interest among Chinese fans, media outlets and even in political circles was headlined in the 8 March 2014 edition of The Washington Post titled, "Could a Korean soap opera be China's guiding light?"*

Most significantly, the show successfully sparked off an idol worshipping trend, generating enormous *chimaek* (a neologism from the Korean for

---

[29]The Inside Korea, "Being Dramatic, K-Dramas continue to drive Korean Wave," dated 27 May 2014 in The Inside Korea website [downloaded on 18 November 2014], available at http://theinsidekorea.com/2014/05/dramatic-k-dramas-continue-drive-korean-wave/.

eating fried chicken and drinking beer together) craze and culture among the ardent K-drama fans in China. After the female character was depicted indulging in the delicious culinary habit, it has created a huge impact among the drama aficionados "with more than 3.7 million posts related to the Mandarin term for chimaek."[30] Riding on the bandwagon of the drama, the fried chicken restaurants in China gained a 30% increase in their sales by selling the beer and fried chicken set meal.[31] Product placement is so successful in the show that after Kim Soo-hyun's character was shown eating a bowl of noodles, the Korean instant ramen witnessed an increase in sales by 60%.[32]

Fried Chicken advertisement by celebrity Jun Ji-hyun, the female lead of *My Love From The Star* at the Gimpo Airport.

---

[30] The Inside Korea, "Being Dramatic, K-Dramas continue to drive Korean Wave," dated 27 May 2014 in The Inside Korea website [downloaded on 18 November 2014], available at http://theinsidekorea.com/2014/05/dramatic-k-dramas-continue-drive-korean-wave/.

[31] The Inside Korea, "Being Dramatic, K-Dramas continue to drive Korean Wave," dated 27 May 2014 in The Inside Korea website [downloaded on 18 November 2014], available at http://theinsidekorea.com/2014/05/dramatic-k-dramas-continue-drive-korean-wave/.

[32] The Inside Korea, "Being Dramatic, K-Dramas continue to drive Korean Wave," dated 27 May 2014 in The Inside Korea website [downloaded on 18 November 2014], available at http://theinsidekorea.com/2014/05/dramatic-k-dramas-continue-drive-korean-wave/.

There are many reasons why Korean dramas have gained such a wide following of non-Koreans. One of the very important factors is the "Beauty attracts" depicted in the drama. Korean stars, artists, singers and actors have to be good-looking to be popular. It is a common phenomenon that Korean dramas are well received among Asians, male and female, young and old, because they fall in love with the aesthetically presented celebrities in the drama. Specifically, the Korean beauty has also become the mainstream trend for girls and women in other countries.

Besides the melodramatic romance, beautiful setting, modern love affairs and historical theme which have been well portrayed in the drama, many observers also attribute the popularity of Korean dramas around the world to its emotional power. The K-dramas which have a wide-ranging genres offer interwoven themes of family, friendship, revenge, war, and business conflict which reflect the reality of life and relationships in a more tender and emotional way. The "Asian sensibilities" or the Asian qualities including traditional family values, strong sentiment of hierarchy and absence of explicit sex that demonstrated in the plot of Korean dramas resonate pleasingly in Asia and thus are warmly embraced by cross-generational viewers in Asian countries.

A report published by the Korean Culture and Information Service Ministry of Culture, Sports and Tourism[33] shows that different dramas appealed to the audiences in different countries for different reasons:

> *Americans find Korean dramas relaxing and cheerful; Europeans find the plots uncomplicated and romantic. Asians, meanwhile, discover lifestyles and trends they wish to emulate and they can also better relate the social practices. The subtle repression of emotions and intense romantic passion without overt sexuality resonates further with viewers in the Middle East. Muslim countries find the dramas "safe": they are less explicit compared to American ones, and adhere to traditions. Some say that Saudi Arabia's public broadcaster ran Dae Jang Geum and Jumong, two Korean dramas depicting life in Korea's old royal courts, with at least the partial intention of reinforcing support for and loyalty to Saudi Arabia's monarchical government.*

---

[33] Korean Culture and Information Service Ministry of Culture, Sports and Tourism, "The Korean Wave: A New Pop Culture Phenomenon," 2011.

K-Pop Sweeping Across and Beyond Asian Markets

The explosive rise of digital technologies and social media, such as YouTube, social network sites (SNSs) and smart phones, in the 21st century has become new driving engines, in fact indispensable tools in promoting *Hallyu* 2.0. Spearheaded by online gaming and K-Pop music, the Korean Wave has recently started to penetrate and make inroads into European and North American countries.[34] These two cultural genres from the Korean creative industries have brought the Korean Wave to a new milestone, encouraging and introducing cultural diversity when it comes to multimedia offerings in the global media industry.

The internet as a powerful tool to transmit and receive information, graphics and video has greatly contributed to the remarkable popularity of K-pop in the global music markets. South Korea exported US$80.9 million worth of music to the world in 2010, a 159% increase from 2009.[35] In the following year in 2011, the South Korean music industry exported US$177 million, a further 112% increase from 2010.[36] Up to 2011, K-pop videos on YouTube have been viewed 2.2 billion times in 235 countries.[37] In fact, K-pop recorded more views in the United States, Japan, Thailand, Taiwan and Vietnam than in Korea. To reiterate, K-pop is most popular in terms of viewership in Japan when considered in terms of individual states, followed by the United States and Thailand, with 240 million and 224 million views, respectively.[38] Together, East and Southeast Asia accounted for 69% of the total K-pop views on YouTube (see Table 7.3).

Most notably, data from YouTube suggest that views of Korean artists tripled in the year following the release of the runaway Korean pop hit *Gangnam Style*, which skyrocketed to 7 billion views, that is around three times the 2.2 billion views in the previous year (see Figure 7.4). Korean

---

[34] Yong Jin Dal, "Hallyu 2.0: The New Korean Wave in the Creative Industry," *International Institute Journal University of Michigan* 2 (Fall 2012): 3.

[35] Yong Jin Dal, "Hallyu 2.0: The New Korean Wave in the Creative Industry," International Institute Journal University of Michigan 2 (Fall 2012): 5.

[36] Yong Jin Dal, "Hallyu 2.0: The New Korean Wave in the Creative Industry," International Institute Journal University of Michigan 2 (Fall 2012): 5.

[37] Soo Keung Jung and Hong Mei Li, "Global Production, Circulation, and Consumption of Gangnam Style," *International Journal of Communication* 8 (2014): 2793.

[38] Soo Keung Jung and Hong Mei Li, "Global Production, Circulation, and Consumption of Gangnam Style," *International Journal of Communication* 8 (2014): 2793.

TABLE 7.3. NUMBER OF VIEWS OF K-POP VIDEOS ON YOUTUBE (2011).

Country/ Region	Number of Views of K-POP Videos on YouTube	Shares in %
Japan	423,683,759	20.3
US	240,748,112	11.5
Thailand	224,813,564	10.8
Taiwan	189,027,731	9.0
Vietnam	177,358,800	8.5
Korea	155,325,204	7.4
Malaysia	98,693,969	4.7
Indonesia	81,128,637	3.9
Hong Kong	76,937,448	3.7
Philippines	74,251,012	3.6
Singapore	68,546,360	3.3
Canada	46,477,940	2.2
Saudi Arabia	42,719,685	2.0
Mexico	34,237,580	1.6
Australia	27,132,121	1.3
France	26,591,412	1.3
Peru	25,503,082	1.2
UK	22,705,547	1.1
Brazil	21,090,241	1.0
Germany	20,114,996	0.9
Chile	13,777,557	0.7

Source: Reproduced from Soo Keung Jung and Hong Mei Li, "Global Production, Circulation, and Consumption of Gangnam Style," *International Journal of Communication* 8 (2014): 2794.

singer PSY's dancing video *Gangnam Style* created an international sensation and became the first YouTube video to exceed 2 billion views.[39] In term of viewership on K-pop videos, Asia-Pacific region dominated in

---

[39] BBC News, "Gangnam Style music video 'broke' YouTube view limit," dated 4 December 2014 in BBC News website [downloaded on 3 January 2015], available at http://www.bbc.com/news/world-asia-30288542.

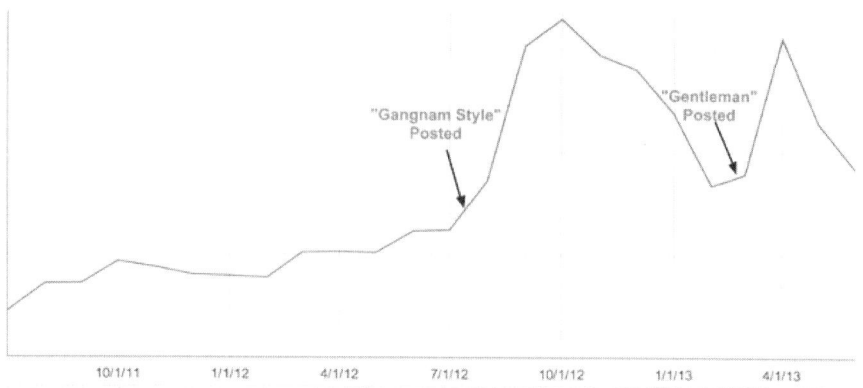

FIGURE 7.4. MONTHLY VIEWS OF TOP K-POP CHANNELS ON YOUTUBE (OCTOBER 2011–JANUARY 2013).

Source: Retrieved by the author from YouTube Trend, available at http://youtube-trends.blogspot.sg/2013/07/a-year-since-gangnam-style-k-pop-keeps.html, accessed 27 January 2015.

2012 but the market has now been replaced by countries outside of the region.[40] It was reported in the *Daily Mail*[41]:

> *The infectious video featuring PSY and a ragtag team of bizarre side-kicks galloping around Seoul spent 31 weeks on Billboard's Hot 100 list. The video earned PSY a long list of accolades, including MTV Europe, American Music and World Music video awards in 2012 and 2013. The viral hit generated countless parodies performed by people from all walks of life ranging from the Indiana Pacers fans to Philippine inmates, lifeguards, animated characters from My Little Pony and U.S. Navy midshipmen, which features members of the academy's 22nd Company busting a move in front of Bancroft Hall, on docks in Annapolis and even aboard a sailboat.* [42]

---

[40] YouTube Trend [downloaded on 27 January 2015], available at http://youtube-trends. blogspot.sg/2013/07/a-year-since-gangnam-style-k-pop-keeps.htmlm.

[41] Snejana Farberov, "Psy's *Gangnam Style* makes Internet history by galloping past 2 BILLION YouTube views," dated 31 May 2014 in Daily Mail [downloaded on 3 January 2015], available at http://www.dailymail.co.uk/news/article-2644504/Psys-Gangnam-Style-hits-2-billion-YouTube-views.html.

[42] Alex Jackson, "Midshipmen Do it Gangnam Style," dated 18 September 2012 in The Millitary News [downloaded on 28 March 2014], available at http://www.military.com/off-duty/off-beat/2012/09/18/usna-gangnam-style.html.

Exports of Korean Games

Besides Korean pop music, the online game industry has substantially gained significance as an empire in the cultural sector and is one of Korea's most significant exported cultural products. With the rapid advancement of broadband services, online gaming has become a burgeoning cultural sector with global revenues rivalling those of the film and music industries. In 2012, the export of game industry accounted for 57% of South Korea's overseas shipment of cultural goods.[43] Exports stood at US$2.6 billion in 2012, up 238% from 2007 (see Table 7.4).

By sector, South Korea's shipment of online games totalled US$2.4 billion, or 91.4% of total game export in 2012, followed by mobile game exports of US$169 million (see Table 7.5). Such exports of contents for portable devices marked a five-time growth from a year earlier, apparently from the wide distribution of smart phones and long-term evolution (LTE) network at home and abroad.[44]

Based on the 2012 figures, the size of Korean game export amounted to US$7.06 billion, accounting for 6.3% of the US$111.75 billion world game markets (see Table 7.6). Considering the huge growth potential of online games and the mobile game market, South Korea's share of the world market is expected to steadily increase.

TABLE 7.4. EXPORTS OF KOREAN GAMES IN MILLION USD, 2007–2012.

Year	2007	2008	2009	2010	2011	2012
Export	781	1,094	1,241	1,606	2,378	2,639
Growth	16.2%	40.1%	13.4%	29.4%	48.1%	11.0%

Source: White Paper on Korean Games, Ministry of Culture, Sports and Tourism (MCST) and KOCCA.

---

[43] "Games take up over half of S. Korea's cultural exports in 2012," dated 14 April 2014 in Global Post.

[44] "Games take up over half of S. Korea's cultural exports in 2012", dated 14 April 2014 in Global Post.

TABLE 7.5.   EXPORTS AND IMPORTS OF
KOREAN GAME INDUSTRY IN MILLION
USD, 2012.

	Exports	Imports
Online Games	2,410	49
Video Games	0.22	93
Mobile Games	169	83
Arcade Games	57	70
PC Games	0.052	21
Total	2,639	179

Source: White Paper on Korean Games, MCST and
KOCCA.

TABLE 7.6.   WORLD GAME MARKET SHARE OF THE 2012 KOREAN GAME
INDUSTRY IN MILLION USD (BASED ON REVENUE).

	Online Game	Video Games	Mobile Games	PC Games	Arcade Games	All
World Game Market	21,083	44,315	13,968	7,077	25,307	111,750
Korean Game Market	6,020	143	711	60	129	7,063
Market Share	28.6%	0.3%	5.1%	0.8%	0.5%	6.3%

Source: White Paper on Korean Games, MCST and KOCCA.

Korean games were exported chiefly to China, accounting for 38.6% of the total in 2012. Recording 0.4% growth from 2011, China maintained the largest market for South Korea's export, followed by Japan, accounting for 26.7% of the total; and Southeast Asia (18.8%). North America and Europe were also important, importing 7.7% and 6% of the total, respectively (see Figure 7.6).

The Korean Wave Generates Positive Spill-over Effects

Cosmetic and Skin-care Products

Wide-reaching Korean cultural popularity boosts the sales of the "Korean-made" products, presenting a huge business potential for the production companies and bringing in considerable profits for South Korea's domestic

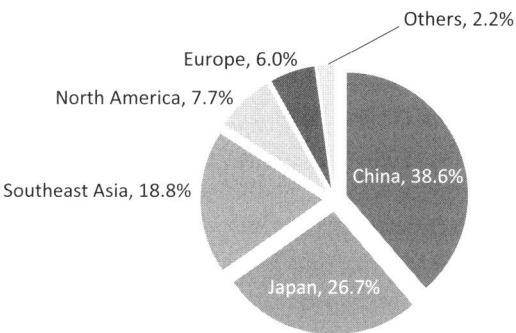

FIGURE 7.6. PROPORTIONS OF 2012 KOREAN GAME EXPORTS BY COUNTRY IN PERCENTAGE.

Source: White Paper on Korean Games, MCST and KOCCA.

entertainment enterprises. Export data from 2001 till 2011 suggest that a US$100 increase in the export of *Hallyu* cultural products resulted in a US$412 increase in sales of consumer goods, according to the Korea Export-Import Bank.[45] In a survey done by the Korean Chamber of Commerce & Industry (2012),[46] 82.2% of participating Korean corporations responded that *Hallyu* enhanced the positive image of Korea and Korean products. The industries and sectors that received the most economic impact from the phenomenon (in terms of branding for example) and sales-enhancing effects are (1) service industry, including culture (86.7%), tourism (85.7%), retail (75%) and (2) manufacturing industry, including food (45.2%), electronics (43.3%), cosmetics (35.5%), and automotive (28.1%).[47]

The Korean Wave, driven by Korean pop music and soap operas, has spilled over into its domestic beauty market including the cosmetics and skin care industries. This is achieved through celebrities' effect on

---

[45] Globe One, "Power of culture — Hallyu, the Korean wave," dated 13 August 2013 in Globe One website [downloaded on 20 July 2014], available at http://globe-one.com/power-of-culture-hallyu-the-korean-wave-4636/.

[46] Globe One, "Power of culture — Hallyu, the Korean wave," dated 13 August 2013 in Globe One website [downloaded on 20 July 2014], available at http://globe-one.com/power-of-culture-hallyu-the-korean-wave-4636/.

[47] Globe One, "Power of culture — Hallyu, the Korean wave," dated 13 August 2013 in Globe One website [downloaded on 20 July 2014], available at http://globe-one.com/power-of-culture-hallyu-the-korean-wave-4636/.

advertising campaigns, whether they feature the latest K-pop group or a veteran actor or actress, and the product placements strategy to successfully capture the heart of many K-pop fans and Korean drama fans. "Exports of related lifestyle goods amounted to US$1.067 billion in 2012, up 30.3% from a year earlier, while imports remained at US$978 million," according to the Korea Pharmaceutical Traders Association (KPTA).[48] This was the first time cosmetics exports surpassed imports.

Globe One[49] also reported that:

With active Hallyu advertising and promotion, AMOREPACIFIC, LG Household & Healthcare and MISSHA, three representative Korean

Various Korean cosmetic and skincare brands at Myeong-dong in Seoul.

[48] Korea Times, "Hallyu boosts cosmetics sales overseas market," dated 11 March 2013 in Korea Times website [downloaded on 9 January 2015], available at http://www.koreatimes.co.kr/www/news/culture/2013/03/386_131907.html.

[49] Globe One, "Power of culture — Hallyu, the Korean wave," dated 13 August 2013 in Globe One website [downloaded on 20 July 2014], available at http://globe-one.com/power-of-culture-hallyu-the-korean-wave-4636/.

cosmetics companies have increased their companies' profile in overseas market, witnessing a 30 percent increase in sales in the year of 2012.

While South Korean makeup and skincare products sell the idea of a natural, flawless, youthful, bright, fair, and dewy glowing skin after using the product, the cute packaging, natural ingredient recipe and innovative formulas adopted by the South Korean beauty brands for their marketing campaigns quickly gain brand recognition in many countries. With increasing consumer affinity in East Asia to South Korean beauty products, sales of South Korean skin care products contribute to nearly half of the overall sales of the beauty export market, followed by make-up products, with foundation and blush products contributing to one fifth of the overall market share.[50]

In term of export destinations, the number of countries that were export destinations for Korean cosmetics surged from 87 countries to 129 countries over the last decade.[51] "Japan was the largest importer of Korean-made cosmetics, purchasing US$250 million worth of products, followed by China and Hong Kong, with imports of US$209 million and US$188 million, respectively. Imports by Thailand and Taiwan stood at US$65 million and US$58 million, respectively, while Singapore and Malaysia registered US$41 million and US$33 million,"[52] according to *Korea Times*.

Korean Food

With the expanding popularity of Korean Wave, the world has shown enormous interest in the Korean culture, especially the Korean cuisine. In

---

[50] South China Morning Post, "South Korea TV dramas exploit success to push products across Asia," dated 22 June 2014 in South China Morning Post website [downloaded on 2 December 2014], available at http://www.scmp.com/business/companies/article/1538513/south-korean-tv-dramas-exploit-success-push-products-across-asia.

[51] Arirang News, "Popularity of Korean Wave leads to cosmetics export to jump six fold since 2004," dated 9 May 2014 in Arirang News website [downloaded on 25 September 2014], available at http://www.arirang.co.kr/news/News_View.asp?nseq=162119.

[52] Korea Times, "Hallyu boosts cosmetics sales overseas market," dated 11 March 2013 in Korea Times website [downloaded on 9 January 2015], available at http://www.koreatimes.co.kr/www/news/culture/2013/03/386_131907.html.

particular, the debut of the drama *Dae Jang Geum* has gained Korean cuisine a lot of attention. While Koreans take cultural pride in their food, the food recipes, methods of preparation, seasoning and pickling remain well-preserved and sophisticated. The meticulous and traditional ways of preparing Korean cuisine and also the creative food combination in the modern Korean food have interest many audiences. This has opened lucrative opportunities for South Korean food producers as well as Korean Cultural Ministry to ride on the bandwagon, and demonstrate marketing strategies, such as the stealth insertion of product placement in the Korean Drama, to promote effectively Korean traditional gastronomy and culinary creations to its overseas consumers.

The signs of Korean culinary conquest are now everywhere, with more Korean dishes such as Bulgogi, Toppoki, Bibimbap and Samgyetang entering the food-lovers' lexicon. Even Kimchi, the quintessentially Korean prickles, can now be widely accepted and consumed by foreigners. The inexpensive fermented vegetable food has gained international acclaim due to its abundance in dietary nutrition and has been listed as the top five "World's Healthiest Foods" for being rich in vitamins, fibers, and even possibly improving digestive system and reducing cancer growth.[53]

Korean cuisine has poised to become as ubiquitous around the world as Thai and Chinese cuisines. Interest in Korea and its culture has been raised in Western countries including Europe and the United States through Korean TV shows, films, and K-pop. Korean barbecues have become common in a lot of big cities, joining the ranks of hibachi grills and sushi bars.[54] It is not surprising that Korean food has started to make a landfall in many countries.

Tourism Sector

Furthermore, *Hallyu* has boosted the country's tourism sector. On the website of the Korea Tourism Organization (KTO), tourists can find the filming locations of 67 Korean dramas. Inbound arrivals jumped 9.3%

---

[53] Korea Tourism Board Organization, "Korea's Favorite Fermented Superfood: Kimchi," available at http://english.visitkorea.or.kr/enu/SH/whatToBuy/whatToBuy.jsp?action=item&cid=995700.

[54] Kim Nae-on, "Korean Pop Culture in the Eyes of the World," dated October 2015 in Korea Magazine.

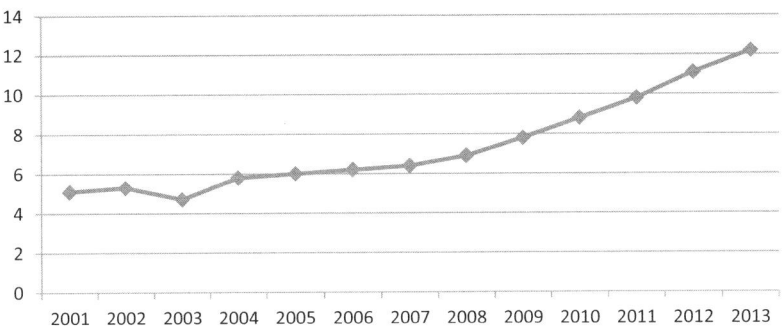

FIGURE 7.7. NUMBER OF TOURISTS ARRIVAL IN KOREA (IN MILLION) 2001–2013.

Source: Compiled by the author based on statistics from the Korea Tourism Organization, "Visitor Arrivals, Korean Departures, International Receipts and Expenditures," accessed 19 December 2014, available at http://kto.visitkorea.or.kr/eng/tourismStatics/keyFacts/visitorArrivals.kto.

to record 12.2 million visitors in 2013, statistics from the Korea Tourism Organization (KTO) show (see Figure 7.7).

Specifically, TV drama *Winter Sonata* has brought a tremendous growth in the number of foreign tourists arrival in South Korea. The number of visitors to Nami Island in Chuncheon, Gangwon province, in particular, shot up from about 270,000 in 2001 to 650,000 in 2002, right after the drama was broadcasted.[55] The island was one of the filming locations of *Winter Sonata*, especially famous for the snow-covered Metsequoia path taken by the main characters. The number of tourists registering 2.3 million in 2011 is still growing today.[56]

The KTO has noted a surge in enquiries related to the drama *My Love From The Star* from visitors since the release of the drama series in 2014. The impact of this drama series on Korean tourism appears to be resilient in Northeast Asia. The show's filming locations have become new tourist destinations for Chinese holidaymakers, according to South Korean media. One favoured destination is Petite France, a French village-themed park in Gapyeong that is not so far away from Seoul by subway. The

---

[55] "K-drama fever impacts other industries," dated 10 January 2012 in The Korea Herald.
[56] "K-drama fever impacts other industries," dated 10 January 2012 in The Korea Herald.

attraction comes not only from the setting itself, but also the mesmerising night view and landscape of Petit France, where the kiss scene of the drama was taken and subsequently created a big sensation amongst viewers.[57] *Korea Net* reported the following observation in one of its articles[58] in 2014:

> *According to the theme park staff, after the park was featured in the drama, its daily visitor numbers rose from 300 on an average weekday to 2,000 per day, and from 1,000 to 5,000 on weekends. Daily arrivals at the park have risen nearly seven-fold, with mainland tourists accounting for 60% of the rise.*

Undeniably, the Korean Wave has not only served as an entertainment industry, but also transformed and shaped the cultural practices and consumption habits of its consumers which have created a positive spill over to other industries.

The South Korean Entertainment Industry and Their Social Media Strategy

The worldwide success of Korean Wave contributes to improving and upgrading South Korea's image and its economy. The South Korean state, entertainment agencies and media companies play imperative role in promoting Korean Wave. Specifically, the advent of the information technology and the creative industry, together with the convergence of multiple factors, has contributed to the huge success of the Korean Wave. It is reported that around 1,000 entertainment agencies are active in Korea, the "big three" entertainment agencies are the most prominent, namely the SM Entertainment, the YG Entertainment, and the JYP Entertainment.[59]

---

[57] Sojung Yoon, "Tourists flock to soap opera filming locations," dated 18 March 2014 in Korea Net [downloaded on 1 April 2015], available at http://www.korea.net/NewsFocus/Travel/view?articleId=118210.

[58] Sojung Yoon, "Tourists flock to soap opera filming locations," dated 18 March 2014 in Korea Net [downloaded on 1 April 2015], available at http://www.korea.net/NewsFocus/Travel/view?articleId=118210.

[59] JoongHo Ahn, Sehwan Oh and Hyunjung Kim, "Korean Pop Takes Off! Social Media Strategy of Korean Entertainment Industry," 2014.

TABLE 7.7. THE BIG THREE KOREAN ENTERTAINMENT AGENCIES.

	K-Pop Entertainment Agencies		
	SM Entertainment	**YG Entertainment**	**JYP Entertainment**
Established Year	1995	1996	1997
Founder	Lee Soo-Man	Yang Hyun-suk	Park Jin Young
2013 Revenue	USD260 million	USD140 million	USD110 million
Current K-Pop Artists	Kangta, BoA, TVXQ, TRAX, The Grace, Girls' Generation, J-Min, SuperJunior, Shinee, f(x), EXO	Bing Bang, 2NE1, PSY, Se7en, Epik High, Gummy, Lee Hi	Wonder Girls, JOO, 2AM, 2PM, Miss A, San E, JJ Project, Baek Ah Yeon, 15&

Source: Compiled by the author based on the information from the official sites of SM Town (https://www.smtown.com/), YG Family (http://www.ygfamily.com/), and JYP Entertainment (http://english.jype.com/#/Main.aspx), accessed 29 December 2014.

These three are allegedly differentiated in their business philosophy and practices in recruiting new talents (see Table 7.7). SM Entertainment seems to place more weight on its artists' appearances, while the YG Entertainment emphasizes unique characteristics of their artists. Some liken SM Entertainment to an elite school where a thorough education is provided to its artists, ranging from acting to singing and dancing, whereas YG Entertainment tries to maximize trainee's strength instead of complementing weaknesses. JYP Entertainment has a preference for foreign language speaking abilities and puts more focus on education for its artists to communicate with international fans.[60]

It is often said that the Korean popular culture is a hybridized product of the Western hegemony and the Eastern imperialism. After the defeat of the Japanese imperialism in 1945, the southern part of the Korea Peninsula was under the military occupation and trusteeship of the United States. This caused the influx of the Western music genres such as rock, country folk, jazz and blues. Together with the Korean traditional culture which is much influenced by the Chinese culture, the Western genres and also the

---

[60] Seung-hye Yim, "In any language, JYP spells success on the global stage," dated 13 September 2013 in Korea Joongang Daily.

Japanese culture that was left behind previously, form what we call the Korean Wave today which is not cultural specific. The Korean cultural cornucopia serves as strength and advantage for the media agencies to reach out multifarious audiences from different backgrounds as the South Korean music market is too small to sustain itself. South Korean media companies were able to create hybridized forms of universalistic popular music that appeals to many different cultures. The music is co-written and co-produced by people all over the world. The choreographers are mostly foreigners while most of these K-pop songs are sung in the Korean language with some English lyrics. Nowadays songs are also recorded in the Japanese, Mandarin, or English language. By making it half-Korean in language and in style, South Korean popular cultural music aims for mass consumption by non-Korean consumers as well.

In addition, social media plays an important role in the proliferation of the Korean Wave, especially in *Hallyu* 2.0. Korean entertainment agencies developed a social media strategy with the following elements: "to align their business model with social media; to maximize various social media channels; to engage customers with on- and offline promotions; and to stimulate audience with exclusive contents."[61] With the rapid growth of social media, agencies turned their eyes to the new business model with social media. Moving beyond the conventional business model of music sales to consumers, they made use of social media like YouTube to promote artists and their music for free and sought revenues in the field of licensing, royalty, and advertisement.[62] In December 2011, to meet the growing demand of worldwide consumers, YouTube added the K-pop genre to its music page along with R&B, Rock, Pop, and Rap, the first case any specific country's music was introduced as a separate genre on YouTube.[63]

---

[61] JoongHo Ahn, Sehwan Oh and Hyunjung Kim, "Korean Pop Takes Off! Social Media Strategy of Korean Entertainment Industry," 2014.

[62] JoongHo Ahn, Sehwan Oh and Hyunjung Kim, "Korean Pop Takes Off! Social Media Strategy of Korean Entertainment Industry," 2014.

[63] JoongHo Ahn, Sehwan Oh and Hyunjung Kim, "Korean Pop Takes Off! Social Media Strategy of Korean Entertainment Industry," 2014.

TABLE 7.8. SOCIAL MEDIA PLATFORMS OF THE BIG THREE K-POP ENTERTAINMENT AGENCIES (AS OF DEC. 2014).

Social Media		SM Entertainment	YG Entertainment	JYP Entertainment
			K-Pop Entertainment Agencies	
	Joined	March 2006	January 2008	January 2008
	No. of Subscribers (mil.)	5.7	1.7	0.9
	No. of Video Views (bil.)	2.19	0.61	0.20
YouTube	Site	SMTOWN, downloaded in the *youtube.com* website on 19 December 2014, available at: www.youtube.com/SMTOWN	YG Entertainment, downloaded in the *youtube.com* website on 19 December 2014, available at: https://www.youtube.com/user/YGEntertainment	JYP Entertainment, downloaded in the *youtube.com* website on 19 December 2014, available at: https://www.youtube.com/user/jypentertainment
	Joined	March 2011	August 2010	January 2011
	Likes (mil.)	4.37	2.45	1.25
Facebook	Site	SMTOWN, downloaded in the *facebook.com* website on 19 December 2014, available at: www.facebook.com/smtown	YG Family, downloaded in the *facebook.com* website on 19 December 2014, available at: https://www.facebook.com/ygfamily/timeline	JYP Entertainment, downloaded in the *facebook.com* website on 19 December 2014, available at: https://www.facebook.com/jypnation?ref=ts&fref=ts

(Continued)

TABLE 7.8.   *(Continued)*

Social Media		SM Entertainment	YG Entertainment	JYP Entertainment
			K-Pop Entertainment Agencies	
Twitter	Joined	October 2012	November 2011	November 2010
	Followers (mil.)	2.07	1.36	0.57
	Site	SMTOWN Global, downloaded in the *twitter.com* website on 19 December 2014, available at: https://twitter.com/smtownglobal	YG Entertainment, downloaded in the *twitter.com* website on 19 December 2014, available at: https://twitter.com/ygent_official	JYP Entertainment, downloaded in the *twitter. com* website on 19 December 2014, available at: https://twitter. com/jypnation

Source: Compiled by the author based on statistics from the official social media sites of the entertainment agencies, accessed 19 December 2014.

K-Pop idols attract many fans from all around the world. While it is not always easy to connect with everyone from the diverse regions of the world, especially due to the presence of linguistic barriers, digital technology and social network sites provide convenient platforms to share pictures and status updates. Social networks give South Korean stars a chance to keep their fans updated on upcoming projects and promotions, while providing their followers with details of their daily lives. Considering the business models and current Internet environment, K-pop entertainment agencies try to diversify their social media channels such as YouTube, Facebook, and Twitter (see Table 7.8). They started official YouTube channels to promote new music videos and leveraged other social media such as Facebook and Twitter to communicate with their youth audience. At the same time, to facilitate communication with audience, major K-pop labels manage individual artistes dedicated to YouTube channel.[64] K-pop entertainment agencies also deliberately leak teasers on social media to promote new music videos or events in the hope that they go viral among K-pop fans and beyond.

Conclusion

This chapter critically analyses how the Korean entertainment and popular culture have took the world by storm with its TV dramas, pop music, online gaming etc. It discussed the transformation of the Korean Wave since the 1990s and outlined the important elements in the evolutionary process of the second wave of *Hallyu* including the role of social media platforms as well as the creative entertainment agencies in this era of digital ubiquity. It discussed the unprecedented influence of the Korean Wave from the economic, social and cultural aspects and highlighted the imperative factors contributing to the success of the Korean Wave, justifying that the Korean Wave is not simply a fortuitous phenomenon. In order to supplement the tenuous analysis for the South Korean cultural policies in promoting the Korean Wave, the next chapter will focus on the role of the South Korean government in promoting South Korean cultural products through promulgation of laws, financial supports as well as the establishment of different government bodies.

---

[64] JoongHo Ahn, Sehwan Oh and Hyunjung Kim, "Korean Pop Takes Off! Social Media Strategy of Korean Entertainment Industry," 2014.

Chapter 8

Hallyu Power: Cultural Policies of the Korean Government

Wen Xin LIM

An Overview of Korea's Cultural Policies

Korean Wave or *Hallyu* has enjoyed tremendous success in Asia since the late 1990s, and now making inroad to Europe and North America. In this chapter, I am defining K-pop comprehensively using a broad definition. In this chapter, I argue that K-pop is represented by the full spectrum of Korean cultural genres including music, dramas, lifestyle, fashion, language, and cuisine. For this chapter, I intend to analyze state policies related to the promotion of Korean Wave. Government policy is undeniably one of the most important factors to the success of the Korean Wave. The significant development of the Korean cultural commodity including movies, dramas, online gaming and popular music cannot be adequately explained without discussing the influence and the efforts of the Korean state and government. My research objective is therefore to find out, from textual analysis, the policy incentives provided for the growth of Korean popular culture.

Background

Korean cultural policy has evolved considerably over the years, from heavy state intervention underlined by protective and restrictive measures prior to the 1980s to a more market-oriented approach since the 1990s. Positive government policies are undeniably one of the most important factors for the success of the Korean Wave. In the late 1990s, after the government identified cultural industry as a strategic industry, capital and fund injected for the promotion of cultural industry has increased considerably. According to the cultural policy industries paper by Seung-ho Kwon and Joseph Kim, "the budget for cultural industry increased steeply under the Kim Dae-jung (1998–2002) government to 102.1 billion Korean Won, the first time the budget for the Ministry of Culture exceeded 1% of total government budget. The average annual budget allocation to the cultural industries almost doubled under the subsequent Roh Moo-hyun (2003–2007) and Lee Myung-bak (200–2012) governments, rising to 193.4 billion Korean Won and 321.9 billion Korean Won, respectively" (Kwon and Kim, 2013).[1]

Underlying this change was due to the transformation of the General Agreement on Tariffs and Trade (GATT) into the World Trade Organization (WTO)[2] and a fundamental shift of government's priority towards the cultural industry as a strategic sector in boosting economic development. Cultural industries were observed according to their commercial viability and economic value, and it is no longer seen as an ideological apparatus for the formation of Korea's national identity.[3] The current government policy in cultural industries can be divided into two big pillars: regulation and promotion (or development). By enacting legislation, government regulates, intervenes, and monitors the trajectory of the cultural industry. In term of promotion and development, organizations and agencies are established to support and subsidize private sector activities. Policies are also implemented with range of activities within the cultural industries, including production, distribution, marketing and consumption of cultural products. An important feature is that successive Korean governments link arts and culture with creative technology and try to promote an integrated development of the cultural industries. Instead of targeting only few selected cultural industries, the development of the cultural industry is being promoted concurrently with the expansion of mobile network, communication and multimedia industries. This forms part of the overall objective to develop

---

[1] Seung-Ho Kwon and Joseph Kim, "The cultural industry policies of the Korean government and the Korean Wave," *International Journal of Cultural Policy* 20, no. 4 (2014).

[2] This transformation indicates that all member countries of GATT, including Korea, were obliged to open their markets in media communications and culture.

[3] Nissim Otmazgin, "A tail that wags the dog? Cultural industry and cultural policy in Japan and South Korea," *Journal of Comparative Policy Analysis: Research and Practice* 13, no. 3 (2011): 307–325.

the national economy and is in line with global trends in viewing popular culture as a soft power and potential new source of exerting influence in the era of globalization.

Numerous government institutions take part in formulating and implementing policies related to the development of cultural industries. These include most importantly the Ministry of Culture, Sports and Tourism (MCST) and the Ministry of Foreign Affairs (MOFA). Institutional adjustments have also taken place from time to time as circumstances change. In particular, the structural evolution of MCST highlights the changes in Korea's government objectives and agenda in different periods of its developmental history. A more significant development in terms of the government policies towards the creative industry is the set up of the Korea Creative Content Agency (KOCCA) in 2009. KOCCA efficiently supports the growth of the cultural industry. By combining Korea Broadcasting Institute, KOCCA, Korea Game Industry Agency, Cultural Contents Center, and Digital Contents Business Group of Korea IT Industry Promotion Agency, according to Article 31 of the Framework Act on Cultural Industry Promotion,[4] the KOCCA is believed to have supported the growth of the cultural industry.

It is expected that the role of the South Korean government would remain vital in the near future. Amid the global penetration of the Korean Wave, the government is likely to bolster lawful consumption of South Korean cultural products through providing stronger institutional support and implementing legislation to prevent copyright infringement and guarantee fair trading for entertainment companies. However, the sustainability of Korean popular culture remains questionable against the backdrop of an increasingly competitive popular cultural landscape at a time of globalization. Without constant and consistent innovation, the K-pop juggernauts may face rivalry from the increasingly popular Chinese-pop and end up as a passing craze like the Japanese popular culture boom in the 1990s.

The Paradigm Shift of the Korean Government Approach

The Korean government's cultural policies have undergone a series of changes over the years. The Second World War and the Korean War have reverberated and shaped the formation of a modern cultural policy. Until the

---

[4] Korea Creative Content Agency (KOCCA), 2014.

1980s, the government was inclined to adopt protection and restriction to incoming foreign cultural products to protect and restore Korean national cultural heritage that was affected by the two wars. Restrictive measures were imposed on foreign cultures, especially the Japanese and the Western cultures, to refurbish national spirit and cultural identity. For 20 years since 1960s, the Korea government "nurtured light manufacturing industries including textile, apparel, food and beverages and later heavy and chemical industries as the key industries for economic development" (Galbraith and Kim, 1998).[5] During this period of authoritarian regime (including under the infamous Park Chung Hee regime), media policies were tailored for party's propaganda and to support government's existing economic and political agendas. The state used television broadcasting and programming to shape and change the society in accordance with its vision of rapid economic development and industrialization. Military governments suppressed creativity and stringently circumscribed cultural products that did not serve for the state's objectives.[6]

According to Marie Le Sourd, Elena Di Federico and Sung-won Yoon (2012), "the year 1994 marked the nominal beginning of democratic government that distinguished from the despotic and authoritative military government regime in the past."[7] The cultural policies of the Kim Young-sam government (1993–1997) were a "radical departure from previous governments because it recognized the potential of the cultural industries in contributing to the growth of national economic" (Kwon and Kim, 2013).[8] The government's policy focus moved from heavy regulation to independent development, from central to local, and from producer to consumer.[9] Kim

---

[5] James K. Galbraith and Junmo Kim, "The legacy of the HCI: an empirical analysis of Korean industrial policy," *Journal of Economic Development* 23, no. 1 (1998): 1–20.

[6] Nae-hui Kang, "The Vacillation of Culture in Neoliberal South Korea," School of Oriental and African Studies Working Papers in Korean Studies No. 21, 2012.

[7] Marie Le Sourd, Elena Di Federico and Sung-Won Yoon, "EU-South Korea: current trends of cultural exchange and future perspectives," European Expert Network on Culture Report, November 2012.

[8] Seung-ho Kwon and Joseph Kim, "The cultural industry policies of the Korean government and the Korean Wave," *International Journal of Cultural Policy* 20, no. 4 (2014).

[9] Marie Le Sourd, Elena Di Federico and Sung-Won Yoon, "EU-South Korea: current trends of cultural exchange and future perspectives," European Expert Network on Culture Report, November 2012.

Young-sam as a dissident politician "advocated the 'Creation of the New Korea' as a political campaign slogan and sought to improve the status of Korea in global society" through asserting cultural democracy, creativity, cultural industries and cultural tourism (Yim, 2002).[10]

There are two reasons why the government of Korea decided to fund and promote South Korean culture. First, it is recognized by the government that successful cultural products can generate considerable amount of benefit to the economy. In 1994, the Presidential Advisory Board on Science and Technology submitted a report to the president proposing that:

> *The government should promote media production as the national strategic industry by taking note of overall revenue from the Hollywood blockbuster, Jurassic Park, which was worth the foreign sales of 1.5 million Hyundai cars.*[11]

After the report was submitted, in 1994, the Korean government set up the Cultural Industry Bureau within the Ministry of Culture and Sports, and enacted the Motion Picture Promotion Law in 1995 in order to attract business fund and capital into the movie industry by providing tax incentive. In their endeavor to resuscitate and develop the cultural industry, Korea constructed the media system with the slogan "Learning from Hollywood."[12]

The moribund economy of South Korea in 1997 is the second factor that prompted the Korean government to seek for a strategic industry which aims to rejuvenate the national economy. When the Korea government first promoted cultural industry as the catalyst of the national economy, "big family-owned business groups in Korea, or *chaebol*, such as Hyundai, Samsung, and Daewoo, to name a few, expanded into the media sector to include production import, distribution and exhibition" (Shim,

---

[10] Haksoon Yim, "Cultural Identity and Cultural Policies in South Korea," *The International Journal of Cultural Policy* 8, no. 1 (2002): 37–48.

[11] Doobo Shim, "Waxing the Korean Wave," Asia Research Institute Working Paper Series No. 158, June 2011.

[12] Doobo Shim, "Waxing the Korean Wave," Asia Research Institute Working Paper Series No. 158, June 2011.

2002).[13] Yet, the brisk *chaebol* participation in the media industry was halted suddenly with the Asian financial crisis that began in late 1997.[14] The 1997 financial crisis which brought South Korea down to its rock-bottom is a turning point to veer the state-led and state-centered cultural policy and supervision towards the *laissez-faire* management style. The crisis highlighted that the country was too reliant on its *chaebols*, Korean mega-conglomerates.[15] A new industry which is independent of these conglomerates is thus needed for a stable economy in case those companies fail to meet their loan requirements or have trouble capitalizing during periods of economic doldrums. As a result, cultural industries which require only human talents and creativity quickly gained substantial attention. The Korean government then lent imperative and effortful support to the Korean popular cultural industries for the global expansion of distribution systems. Beginning of late 1990s, there was a fundamental shift which the government focused towards cultural industry as a key driver of economic development. Nissim Otmazgin noted that "cultural industries were no longer seen as an ideological tool for the preservation of Korea's national identity; rather, they were perceived in terms of their commercial viability and economic value" (Otmazgin, 2011).[16]

Kim Dae-jung (1998–2002), who called himself the "President of Culture", had implemented an increasing number of policy measures to drive the cultural industries. The government started to promote aggressively cultural products, such as television dramas, movies, animation, popular music and online games, incorporating the creativity sector into the digital economy in the late 1990s. Moreover, Kim Dae-jung government established the external infrastructure to help the growth of cultural industry by providing firms with various sources of funding. For instance, the

---

[13] Doobo Shim, "South Korea Media Industry in the 1990s and the Economic Crisis," *Prometheus* 20, no. 4 (2002): 337–350.

[14] Doobo Shim, "South Korea Media Industry in the 1990s and the Economic Crisis," *Prometheus* 20, no. 4 (2002): 337–350.

[15] Jennifer Hunter, "How Korea's government made the country cool," dated 1 August 2014 in The Star.

[16] Nissim Otmazgin, "A tail that wags the dog? Cultural industry and cultural policy in Japan and South Korea," *Journal of Comparative Policy Analysis: Research and Practice* 13, no. 3 (2011): 307–325.

"broadcast video industry promotion plan" which includes production support, human resource development, and infrastructure establishment and management was first announced by the Ministry of Culture and Tourism in 1998.[17] Under the leadership of Kim Dae-jung, the Korean Wave in popular culture started to sweep across East and Southeast Asian countries due to the exportation of television programs and films and their successful reception.

Since the early 2000s, Korea established a highly networked domestic society with the proliferation of ICT industries, and the concept of cultural industries shifted to the creative industry due to the growth of digital technologies. The Roh Moo-hyun government (2003–2007) advocated the cultural industries as the economy driving force and supported the development plan to combine the arts and strategic industries, such as electronics, mobile communication and multimedia industries.[18] Broadband and mobile connectivity began to permeate the daily life of Korean citizens and fast access to internet began to gear the Korean society towards information-intensive and knowledge-based cultures. Following the increase of competitiveness and success in the local market, export of Korean cultural products to the global markets skyrocketed and created the boom of the second wave of *Hallyu* (*Hallyu* 2.0). The potential brand values of Korean Wave have been further realized under the Lee Myung-bak government (2008–2012). By proposing "Korea, a high-class cultural nation" as its cultural policy goal,[19] Lee's government "established the Global Contents Fund in 2011 for the 'qualitative and quantitative growth of Korean cultural products in global markets'."[20]

Regulations and Supporting Policies of the Broadcasting Industry

Overall, the Korean government's policy has experienced a major shift, from protectionism before the 1980s to support and development of the

---

[17] I. Baek, "The study on the cultural policy of Korea after the democratization" (PhD diss., Dongkook University, 2009).

[18] "Cultural Industry White Paper 2004," Ministry of Culture and Tourism.

[19] Youna Kim. The Korean Wave: Korean Media Go Global (Routledge, 2013), 333.

[20] "Creative society and strong cultural nation: future contents vision and policy task," Korea Contents Agency, 2012.

cultural industry in the 1990s. Such evolution is best reflected in the changing policies regarding the broadcasting industry and the film industry. These policies have contributed significantly to the development and the rapid expansion of the South Korean audiovisual industry in overseas, including television, motion pictures and films.

As noted by Millim Kim (2011), "until the 1980s, the priority of the broadcasting regulation regime in Korea was protection and restriction."[21] The Korea government has been restricting the influx of foreign culture, especially Japanese and Western cultures, to protect the domestic broadcasting and film industries. Since the liberation of 1945, the resurgence of cultural identity by eradicating the heritage of Japanese colonialism has been a primary goal of Korea cultural policy. In 1945, a regulation was created to prohibit the import and distribution of Japanese TV programs, films, J-pop, animation and manga to remove the memory of colonization.[22] Moreover, Japanese arts, culture and creative contents were prohibited by the South Korean government before 1998. On the other hand, western popular culture was regulated based on the recognition that "western popular culture could threaten Korea's cultural traditions, which emphasized the spiritual world, morality and abstinence" (Yim, 2002).[23]

From the 1990s onwards, the Korean government's approaches changed from protectionism to support and development (see Table 8.1). According to Millim Kim:

> *This was apparent from 1988 to 1997, when the restrictive measures and supporting policies coexisted. First, the clause related to ownership for commercial broadcasting was added to the policies; second, the formation of outsourcing production programs was obliged; third, a system for human resource training for broadcasting professionals was launched. Those poli-*

---

[21] Millim Kim, "The role of the government in cultural industry: Some observations from Korea's Experience," *Keio Communication Review* 33 (2011).

[22] Haksoon Yim, "Cultural Identity and Cultural Policies in South Korea," *The International Journal of Cultural Policy* 8, no. 1 (2002): 37–48.

[23] Haksoon Yim, "Cultural Identity and Cultural Policies in South Korea," *The International Journal of Cultural Policy* 8, no. 1 (2002): 37–48.

TABLE 8.1. CHANGES IN GOVERNMENT REGULATIONS IN THE KOREAN BROADCASTING INDUSTRY.

Year	Entry Regulation	Content Regulations	Japanese Cultural Goods
1960s	Entry of foreign media company forbidden	Discussion of deliberate censorship in broadcasting	Forbidden
1970s	Entry of foreign media company forbidden	Deliberate censorship and temporary regulations	Forbidden
1980s	Entry of foreign media company forbidden	(1980–1986) Deliberation and temporary (1987) Korean Broadcasting Commission established to regulate censorship	Forbidden
1990s	Entry of foreign media company forbidden	Deliberation in the Korean Broadcasting Commission	Forbidden
2000s	Foreign media company entry permitted	(~2007) Deliberation enforced by Korean Broadcasting Commission (2008~) Changed to deliberation in the Korean Communications Standards Commission	Permitted

Source: Millim Kim, "The role of the government in cultural industry: Some observations from Korea's Experience," *Keio Communication Review* 33 (2011).

cies were practiced by the Bureau of Cultural Industry which was established under the government in 1993.[24]

Also, in order to encourage the production of television programs by domestic media companies, the South Korean government employed quota

---

[24] Millim Kim, "The role of the government in cultural industry: Some observations from Korea's Experience," *Keio Communication Review* 33 (2011).

regulation including the Broadcasting Law of 1990 and 2000 to allocate a specific number of broadcasting time to few media parties. In that way, TV schedule can be occupied by local programs produced both in-house or by autonomous producers. According to Sungeun Shim who did a vigorous research about the South Korean broadcasting industry:

> *This regulation represented one of the first measures taken to spur indus-*
> *try development as described in the Five-year Plan for Advanced*
> *Broadcasting (1995). Since the Broadcasting Law of 2000 came into*
> *effect, the domestic quota obligates cable television and satellite broad-*
> *casting, as well as terrestrial broadcasting, to air a certain quantity of*
> *domestically-produced programs. Furthermore, ceiling figures have*
> *been dictated in some cases for the volume of programs imported from*
> *one country since January 2002. Official explanation claimed that the*
> *measure would eliminate concentration on a particular country and*
> *secure diversity in the reception of international culture. In practical*
> *terms, the one-country limitation was known to be targeted at the United*
> *States for its Hollywood movies and Japan for its animation. The per-*
> *forming industry of Japan was only permitted in 1999. In 2000, anima-*
> *tion, pop music, music recordings, games and broadcasted programs*
> *from Japan were given approval (see Table 8.1)* [25]

Institutional Setting and Coordinated Efforts to Support Korean Wave

Korea's government agencies are an important force behind the Korean Wave. Various ministries, departments and agencies such as the MCST and the MOFA formulate policies and set aside money in their respective budgets to promote Korean Wave in order to boost Korea's national image in the world. In particular, MCST has played a key coordinating role in providing accurate and timely information about Korea to international audiences and assisted events that aim to bolster Korea's culture both at home and abroad. The Ministry of Culture and Communication was changed to the Ministry of Culture and established as an independent

---

[25] Sungeun Shim, "Behind the broadcasting room," *NHK Broadcasting Studies* 6 (2008).

entity from the field of public information or education in 1990.[26] Since then, in addition to its traditional responsibility of overseeing and treating the cultural industry as a propaganda machine in the name of public welfare, the Ministry of Culture has been entrusted with the role to promote and develop South Korean cultural industry through enhancing and strengthening Korea's cultural contents and innovative capacity.

Over the past 20 years, MCST has demonstrated its expanding capacity and flexibility as the key coordinator of cultural industry. MCST has undergone recurring changes of institutional structure to accommodate to the ever-changing cultural policies in different discourses and periods. The Cultural Industry Division was initiated under MCST in 1994 as the ministerial division to facilitate the development for the cultural industry. Under the Division, five departments focusing on different aspects were established, including the Cultural Industry Planning Department (see Figure 8.1). In tandem with the promotion of cultural sectors, the Ministry also spurs the robust development and expansion of Korea's technological network and services. Kwon and Kim (2013) noted that "in 2004, the Ministry formed the Game and Music Records Department, coinciding with the government's 'informatization promotion program' in the late 1990s, which influenced the rapid proliferation of personal computer ownership and broadband access."[27] Following then in 2007, the organization of the Ministry of Culture was substantially expanded and revamped. According to Kwon and Kim (2013), "the Ministry of Culture established the Game Industry Team in 2007, an independent division designed solely for the promotion of gaming industry both domestically and internationally."[28] In addition, the Copyright Industry Team was created in 2007 as the Korean government started to acknowledge and recognize the commercial importance of strong

---

[26] Kiwon Hong, "South Korea: Historical perspective: cultural policies and instruments," International Database of Cultural Policies, 29 November 2013.

[27] Seung-Ho Kwon and Joseph Kim, "The cultural industry policies of the Korean government and the Korean Wave," *International Journal of Cultural Policy* 20, no. 4 (2014). "Culture Industry White Paper 2002," Ministry of Culture and Tourism.

[28] Seung-Ho Kwon and Joseph Kim, "The cultural industry policies of the Korean government and the Korean Wave," *International Journal of Cultural Policy* 20, no. 4 (2014). "Culture Industry White Paper 2002," Ministry of Culture and Tourism.

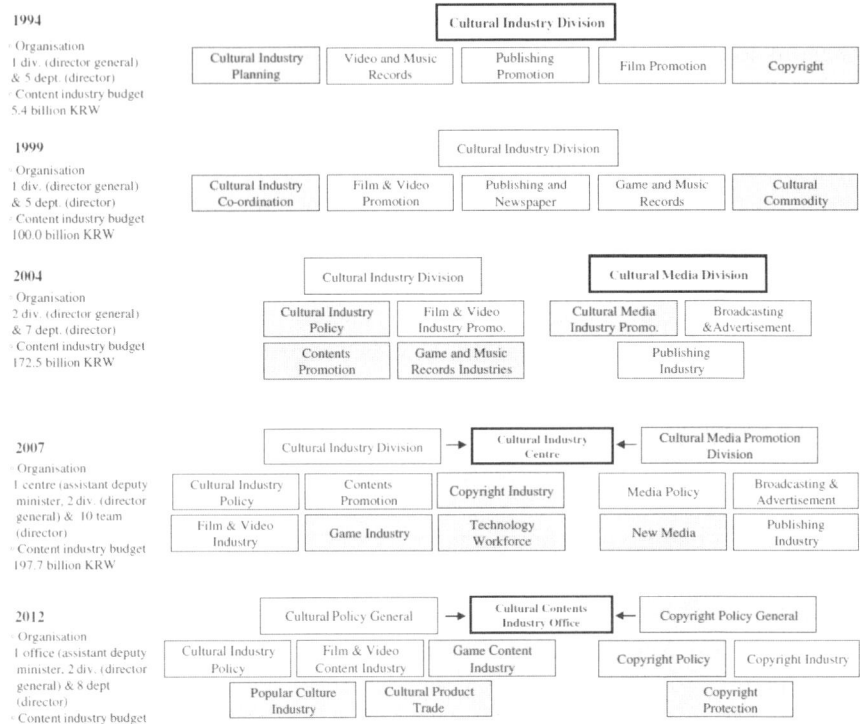

1994
- Organisation
- 1 div. (director general) & 5 dept. (director)
- Content industry budget 5.4 billion KRW

Cultural Industry Division

| Cultural Industry Planning | Video and Music Records | Publishing Promotion | Film Promotion | Copyright |

1999
- Organisation
- 1 div. (director general) & 5 dept. (director)
- Content industry budget 100.0 billion KRW

Cultural Industry Division

| Cultural Industry Co-ordination | Film & Video Promotion | Publishing and Newspaper | Game and Music Records | Cultural Commodity |

2004
- Organisation
- 2 div. (director general) & 7 dept. (director)
- Content industry budget 172.5 billion KRW

Cultural Industry Division / **Cultural Media Division**

| Cultural Industry Policy | Film & Video Industry Promo. | Cultural Media Industry Promo. | Broadcasting &Advertisement. |
| Contents Promotion | Game and Music Records Industries | Publishing Industry | |

2007
- Organisation
- 1 centre (assistant deputy minister, 2 div. (director general) & 10 team (director)
- Content industry budget 197.7 billion KRW

Cultural Industry Division → **Cultural Industry Centre** ← **Cultural Media Promotion Division**

| Cultural Industry Policy | Contents Promotion | Copyright Industry | Media Policy | Broadcasting & Advertisement |
| Film & Video Industry | Game Industry | Technology Workforce | New Media | Publishing Industry |

2012
- Organisation
- 1 office (assistant deputy minister, 2 div. (director general) & 8 dept (director)
- Content industry budget 249.1 billion KRW

Cultural Policy General → **Cultural Contents Industry Office** ← **Copyright Policy General**

| Cultural Industry Policy | Film & Video Content Industry | Game Content Industry | Copyright Policy | Copyright Industry |
| Popular Culture Industry | Cultural Product Trade | | Copyright Protection | |

FIGURE 8.1.   CHANGES IN THE ORGANIZATIONAL STRUCTURE OF MINISTRY OF CULTURE.

Sources: Derived from MCT (2007) and MCST (2012, 2013) by Seung-Ho Kwon and Joseph Kim, "The cultural industry policies of the Korean government and the Korean Wave," *International Journal of Cultural Policy* 20, no. 4 (2014).

copyright protection in terms of financial viability and in cultivation of the domestic creative firms (see Figure 8.1).[29]

In 2012, the status of MCST was further elevated under the Lee Myung-bak government. The government intended to "enhance organization and culture for the Ministry of Culture, Sports and Tourism according to the reorganization of government."[30] The Lee Myung-bak government

---

[29] Seung-Ho Kwon and Joseph Kim, "The cultural industry policies of the Korean government and the Korean Wave," *International Journal of Cultural Policy* 20, no. 4 (2014).

[30] The Korea Net, "Ministry of Culture, Sports and Tourism," in The Korea Net website [downloaded on 6 January 2016], available at http://www.korea.net/AboutUs/Ministry-of-Culture-Sports-and-Tourism.

emphasized on the idea of "cultural diplomacy" and advocated on the branding of the South Korea's national image through the establishment of Cultural Product Trade Division, which was mainly designed to invigorate and facilitate the global expansion of Korean companies and the export of Korean cultural products so as to gain international recognition.[31]

Inter-ministerial collaboration is one of the imperative factors contributing positively to promoting the development of the monolithic and overarching cultural industry. Through appropriate collaboration and tapping onto the different strengths and manpower of few ministries, it generates a virtuous and mutually beneficial cycle of growth among the selected strategic industries.[32] One typical example is the cooperation between MCST and the Ministry of Information and Communication in developing the gaming sector. One study noted that "the Ministry of Information and Communication supported research and development in advanced gaming technologies such as the development of online 3D games and the establishment of motion, sound and character databases" (Yoo, 2002).[33] Such ministerial collaboration and cooperative efforts encourage the synergistic growth of the cultural, electronics and telecommunication industries. Another division affiliated with MCST, the Korean Culture and Information Service (KOCIS), was launched in 1973 to oversee international cultural exchange and serve as a communication bridge to promote Korea cultures overseas.[34] It works on plans to provide up-to-date information and to promote positive image of Korea abroad. It also organizes and assists events such as art performances, music festivals, exhibitions and film festivals to introduce Korean culture (both traditional and contemporary) at home and abroad to offer the audiences an intensive cultural experience.

---

[31] Seung-Ho Kwon and Joseph Kim, "The cultural industry policies of the Korean government and the Korean Wave," *International Journal of Cultural Policy* 20, no. 4 (2014).

[32] "South Korea Country Report 2014," Preparatory Action Culture in EU External Relations. Seung-Ho Kwon and Joseph Kim, "The cultural industry policies of the Korean government and the Korean Wave," *International Journal of Cultural Policy* 20, no. 4 (2014).

[33] J. Y. Yoo, "Study on the promotion strategy for the online game industry," (MA diss., Ehwa Women's University, 2002). Seung-Ho Kwon and Joseph Kim, "The cultural industry policies of the Korean government and the Korean Wave," *International Journal of Cultural Policy* 20, no. 4 (2014).

[34] Korean Culture and Information Service (KOCIS), accessed 12 January 2016, available at http://www.kocis.go.kr/eng/main.do.

Furthermore, it operates the government's official multilingual website Korea.net and 28 cultural centers in 24 countries around the world.[35]

Under the MOFA, the chief agent for cultural exchange is the Korea Foundation. It aims to "promote better understanding of Korea within the international community and to increase friendship and goodwill between Korea and the rest of the world" (KOCIS, 2016) via cultural, educational and intellectual exchange.[36] According to the South Korea Country Report published in 2014:

> *The Korea Foundation has seven overseas offices, only one of which (Berlin) is in the EU; others are in China, Japan, Russia, Vietnam and the USA (Washington, DC, and Los Angeles). Established in 1991, the Foundation supports academic, cultural and intellectual cooperation exchange programmes, promotes public diplomacy initiatives and publishes journals to increase a better understanding about South Korea in the world. It also provides support to about 150 universities in 50 countries to advance Korean studies.*[37]

Together with the Korean Broadcasting Commission, MOFA officers visit faraway countries to promote Korean dramas in South America, the Middle East and Africa. The Korean government also spends tax money in translating these videos into other languages. This has resulted in the outcome that Paraguay, Peru, Iran and Swaziland are now broadcasting Korean dramas. Furthermore, the ministry is involved in promoting Korean movies in international film festivals.

In addition, a more significant development of Korea's government is the setting up of the KOCCA in 2009 to "support more effectively the growth of the creative industries sector by combining five bodies: the Korea Culture and Content Agency, the Korea Broadcasting Institute, the Korea

---

[35] Korean Culture and Information Service (KOCIS), accessed 12 January 2016, available at http://www.kocis.go.kr/eng/main.do.

[36] Korea Foundation, "Article 1, Korea Foundation Act from the Korea Foundation," in the Korea Foundation website [downloaded on 12 January 2016], available at http://en.kf.or.kr/?menuno=3774.

[37] Rod Fisher, "South Korea Country Report 2014," Preparatory Action Culture in EU External Relations, 5 March 2014.

Game Industry Agency, the Cultural Contents Centre and the Digital Contents Business Group of Korea IT Industry Promotion Agency" (KOCCA, 2016).[38] The functions of KOCCA include: "First, promote human resource development projects to acquire valuable human resources that form the basis of creativity and develop policies for the promotion of the content industry; Second, to develop the content industry into an export industry by supporting the development of specialized culture technologies from design to production, the commercialization of contents, and the promotion of various overseas expansion projects; Third, it encourages digital broadcasting projects, promotes game distribution, and carries out digitalization projects aimed at strengthening cultural content" (KOCCA, 2016).[39] The ultimate aim of KOCCA is to construct an inclusive supporting system and comprehensive structure to realize the great ambition of ranking Korea among the top five global cultural countries.

Implications and Prospects of the Korean Wave

Over the past decade, South Korea has become the "Hollywood of the East," churning out entertainment products coveted by millions of fans spanning from East Asia to Europe, and even across the Pacific to the United States. The success of the Korean Wave has been unprecedented and remarkable as it outshined its regional competitors, the Japanese and Taiwanese popular cultures, to manifest itself within and beyond the region. Based on the concept of hardware–software synergy, Korean government's support for the cultural industries has spilled over in the ICT and advanced electronics industries as the government attempted to synchronize connections between ICT sector and the entertainment and production sector through formulation and implementation of effective industrial policy at various stages of the Korean cultural industries' development.[40]

---

[38] Korea Creative Content Agency, 2014. Rod Fisher, "South Korea Country Report 2014," Preparatory Action Culture in EU External Relations, 5 March 2014.
[39] Korea Creative Content Agency, 2016.
[40] Beng Huat Chua and Koichi Iwabuchi, *East Asian Pop Culture: Analysing the Korean Wave* (Hong Kong: Hong Kong University Press, 2008), 17.

The state and the entertainment industry both share a common interest in enhancing Korea's image abroad to promote a joint national brand, brand Korea, across different sectors, spheres and products. While the Korean entertainment industry's agenda is fueled by market demand and consumers' needs, the Korean government desires to export the national cultural prowess and soft power through marketization of the Korean culture and society as a palatable lifestyle via an intricate and top–down approach.

Concluding Remarks

While the Korean Wave laps at the shores around the world, the sustainability of its cultural superiority is still questionable. In particular, the penetration of *Hallyu* into Asia's (East Asia or the whole of Asia) market sometimes leads to anti-Korean backlash in cultural powerhouses such as Japan, China and Southeast Asia, as they feel their indigenous culture is being overwhelmed and diluted by this foreign culture.[41] Against the backdrop of the increasingly competitive cultural landscape in time of globalization, there is a possibility that regional entertainment products can surpass *Hallyu* in the cultural "catch-up" process. Recent attention has been diverted to Chinese popular culture and TV reality shows. Without genuine and ongoing innovation, the Korean Wave may end up a "one-hit wonders" or a mere passing fad like the Japanese pop culture boom in the 1990s.

---

[41] Rod Fisher, "South Korea Country Report 2014," Preparatory Action Culture in EU External Relations, 5 March 2014.

Chapter 9

Korean Wave (*Hallyu*) in Singapore: Policy Implications *Hallyu* and Its Background — The Southeast Asian Context

Wen Xin LIM, Tai Wei LIM and Xiaojuan PING

The Korean wave — "*Hallyu*" in Korean — refers to a surge in the international visibility of Korean culture, beginning in East Asia in the 1990s and continuing more recently in the North America, Latin America, the Middle East, and parts of Europe.[1] Many East Asian countries have absorbed Korean popular culture and several Korean cultural genres in this period, including television programs and films. (See Annex A for table on export of Korean TV programs, for example, to other countries/regions in East Asia and Annex B on the number of viewership hits in the East Asian region and beyond for K-pop videos hosted on Youtube.) The Korean Wave has swept across the globe, elevating South Korea's international image and generating positive economic implications to South Korea's economy. The South Korean government has recognized the advantage of this national phenomenon and is eager to capitalize on the success of the Korean Wave by providing public funds as well as implementing relevant policies in facilitating the development of the industry.

Korean dramas are also popular in Southeast Asia. In the Philippines, the K-drama *Boys Over Flower* was a big hit. In Vietnam, Korean dramas were also popular. Yoon Eun Hye, one of the members of Baby V.O.X, became a superstar in Vietnam after playing a role in the Korean drama

---

[1] Mark Ravina, "Introduction: conceptualizing the Korean Wave," *Southeast Review of Asian Studies* 31 (2009): 3–9.

The Palace.[2] The popularity of Korean dramas in Thailand started in 2007 when *My Girl* and *Coffee Prince* were broadcasted. In Indonesia, *Hallyu* began in 2002 when *Autumn in My Heart* was broadcasted on Indosiar Television and reached a viewers' rating of 11%.[3] Other Southeast Asians also joined in the consumption of Korean popular cultural products through social media platforms like the Youtube viewing experience, including the Youtube hit wonder *Gangnam Style* by Psy.

This viral music video generated countless parodies performed by people from all walks of life ranging from the Indiana Pacers fans to Philippine inmates, lifeguards, animated characters from *My Little Pony* and U.S. Navy midshipmen.[4] There are spin-off benefits for firms and industries in other countries tapping into Korean star power. For example, Japan's cosmetic industry also benefits from the increased awareness of the Korean branding. The use of Korean celebrity power in this way in Japan is significant since it is one of Korea's largest export markets for lifestyle consumer products like cosmetics. In terms of consumption by individual nations, Japan was the largest importer of Korean-made cosmetics, purchasing US$250 million worth of products, followed by China and Hong Kong, with imports of US$209 million and US$188 million, respectively.[5]

Countries in Southeast Asia are also ranking consumers of Korean lifestyle products like cosmetics. Imports of such by Thailand and Taiwan stood at US$65 million and US$58 million, respectively, while Singapore and Malaysia registered US$41 million and US$33 million.[6] A Korean

---

[2]Globe One, "Power of culture — Hallyu, the Korean wave," dated 13 August 2013 in Globe One website [downloaded on 20 July 2014], available at http://globe-one.com/power-of-culture-hallyu-the-korean-wave-4636/.

[3]Globe One, "Power of culture — Hallyu, the Korean wave," dated 13 August 2013 in Globe One website [downloaded on 20 July 2014], available at http://globe-one.com/power-of-culture-hallyu-the-korean-wave-4636/.

[4]Alex Jackson, "Midshipmen Do it Gangnam Style," dated 18 September 2012 in The Millitary News [downloaded on 28 March 2014], available at http://www.military.com/off-duty/off-beat/2012/09/18/usna-gangnam-style.html.

[5]Korea Times, "Hallyu boosts cosmetics sales overseas market," dated 11 March 2013 in Korea Times website [downloaded on 9 January 2015], available at http://www.koreatimes.co.kr/www/news/culture/2013/03/386_131907.html.

[6]Korea Times, "Hallyu boosts cosmetics sales overseas market," dated 11 March 2013 in Korea Times website [downloaded on 9 January 2015], available at http://www.koreatimes.co.kr/www/news/culture/2013/03/386_131907.html.

cosmetic beauty brand Etude House for example, had expanded in Singapore from only two of its retail stores in 2009 to 18 in 2014.[7] A spokesman for Amorepacific Group, South Korea's biggest cosmetics company who owns Laneige and operates this brand, said Etude House's "turnover at its Singapore outlets has been increasing each year, and that it has the Korean wave to thank."[8]

Moreover, until as recently as 2012, Guardian, a local grocery store, did not display any Korean brands in its nationwide retail lines. However, now Singaporeans can find Korean cosmetic labels such as Yadah, Skin Watchers, Skinfactory and Dr. Jart+ (all Korean skincare brands) commonly in neighborhood pharmaceutical stores. Many of these shops are deploying K-pop and K-drama stars as ambassadors for their brands and products — for example, boy-band Shinee fronts Etude House and girl group 2NE1 member Sandara Park's images are used for promoting cosmetics brand Clio. Such star branding moves have been proven effective in encouraging fan consumption.

The Singapore Case Study

Singapore is one of the early recipient countries of K-drama (Korean TV drama) and K-pop due to its cultural, political, economic proximity with Korea as two of the four tiger economies have proactive state roles in economic development. Singapore is a nation of approximately 5.5 million (as of September 2014) of population,[9] around 11% of South Korea's population (50 million in 2014[10]), and 4.3% of Japan's (127 million in

---

[7] Samantha Boh, "Korean brands ride the wave to Singapore," dated 9 December 2013 in the mypaper.sg website [downloaded on 29 March 2015], available at http://mypaper.sg/top-stories/korean-brands-ride-wave-singapore-20131209.

[8] Samantha Boh, "Korean brands ride the wave to Singapore," dated 9 December 2013 in the mypaper.sg website [downloaded on 29 March 2015], available at http://mypaper.sg/top-stories/korean-brands-ride-wave-singapore-20131209.

[9] Department of Statistics Singapore, "Singapore Population Size and Growth by Residential Status" Population Trends 2014," September 2014, available at http://www.singstat.gov.sg/publications/publications-and-papers/population-and-population-structure/population-trends.

[10] Statista, "South Korea: Total population from 2004 to 2014 (in million inhabitants)," in the statista.com website [downloaded on 29 March 2015], available at http://www.statista.com/statistics/263747/total-population-in-south-korea/.

2014[11]). Singapore is a small consumer market in terms of population size but it represents an important aspect of K-pop cultural entry in Southeast Asia. It offers Korean companies a convenient platform to penetrate the regional Southeast Asian market. South Korean companies can invest in an important commercial, technological and trading hub in the region.

Other than being an important consumer market and a trading hub, Singapore also offers Korean and K-pop companies the opportunities to test consumer reactions to their products in a multicultural setting. The multicultural environment in Singapore complements recent Korean popular cultural trends. Korean media companies produce a hybrid form of music that appeals to many different cultures. The music is written and produced by people from around the world. The choreographers are mostly foreigners while most of the K-pop are sung in the Korean language with some English lyrics. Nowadays songs are also recorded in Japanese, Mandarin, or English. By making popular songs half-Korean linguistically, Korean music targets consumption by non-Korean consumers.

As case studies in this writing, some recent K-pop products are discussed below in the context of their resonance with local audiences and impact on local consumption of K-pop culture. The Korean TV dramas are probably one of the more recognized products with the K-pop genre. A survey conducted by the National Institute of Education (NIE) in Singapore with local female fandom has identified the elements in Korean dramas that the fans found "most attractive" include "touching storylines," "beautiful scenery" in the dramas coupled with "excellent cinematography," "good looking actors and actresses," "trendy fashion" and "nice music," and etc.[12]

The other big ticket K-pop item that reverberates with the audiences in Singapore and neighboring Malaysia are the K-pop bands. On 7 and 8 February 2015, for example, K-pop star Taeyang, member of a K-pop band Big Bang, held two concerts in Malaysia and Singapore respectively,

---

[11] Statista, "South Korea: Total population from 2004 to 2014 (in million inhabitants)," in the statista.com website [downloaded on 29 March 2015], available at http://www.statista.com/statistics/263747/total-population-in-south-korea/.

[12] Brenda Chan and Xueli Wang, "Of prince charming and male chauvinist pigs: Singaporean female viewers and the dream-world of Korean television dramas," *International Journal of Cultural Studies* 14, no. 3 (2011): 294.

receiving over 8,200 fans in total.[13] Famous K-pop star Psy, a nominated candidate for *TIME* magazine in 2012, brought *Gangnam Style* to Singapore at the Marina Bay Sands in 2013, making headlines on local newspapers with the concert hall filled to its maximum capacity.

The Online Communities

Singapore also has locally-spawned websites that cover latest K-pop trends in the city state. For example, SG K-Wave is a Korean-Wave community website, providing local Korean news and updates on events in Singapore.[14] Besides the regular entertainment inclusion, it provides coverage on "K-Fashion," "K-Travel" and "K-Food."[15] Started in 2010, the SG K-Wave's member base saw rapid growth — 6,000 members joined within a year.[16] It was chosen as the official media agency to cover the entire Alpha Entertainment / JYP Entertainment ASEAN Region Auditions in 2010, according to the website.[17] Hallyusg.net regards itself as "a versatile online media partner, providing first hand exclusives and timely updates pertaining to all aspects of Korean culture, trends, pop music and entertainment in Singapore and within the South East Asia region."[18] Its Facebook page has almost 20,000 followers at the point of this writing.[19] Other digital means for promoting K-pop stars to its Singaporean fandom can also be seen in the fact that the Embassy of South Korea in Singapore

---

[13] Koreanstardaily, "BigBang太阳马来西亚新加坡开唱引爆两国韩流热潮," dated 9 February 2015 in the koreastardaily.com website [downloaded on 29 March 2015], available at http://www.koreastardaily.com/sc/photo/56405.

[14] SG K-wave, "About SG K-wave," in the sgkwave.com website [downloaded 29 March 2015], available at http://www.sgkwave.com/about.

[15] SG K-wave, "About SG K-wave," in the sgkwave.com website [downloaded 29 March 2015], available at http://www.sgkwave.com/about.

[16] SG K-wave, "About SG K-wave," in the sgkwave.com website [downloaded 29 March 2015], available at http://www.sgkwave.com/about.

[17] SG K-wave, "About SG K-wave," in the sgkwave.com website [downloaded 29 March 2015], available at http://www.sgkwave.com/about.

[18] hallyusg, "About Hallyusg," in the hallyusg.net website [downloaded on 29 March 2015], available at http://hallyusg.net/about/.

[19] hallyusg, "About Hallyusg," in the hallyusg.net website [downloaded on 29 March 2015], available at http://hallyusg.net/about/.

Source: Screenshot of the webpage of the Embassy of South Korea in Singapore, 29 March 2015.

used an online banner featuring Korean pop stars welcoming visitors to Korea with the caption that reads "Fall in Love with Korea" (please refer to the picture above).

In Singapore, fans use social media not only to circulate and consume K-pop but also to re-create K-pop content mixing with their own creativity. In the case of K-pop, fans collaboratively re-create K-pop-related images and movies, then distribute their tailored content online or offline to other fans. A common example of such fan-driven approach is the K-pop cover song and dance products. Cover singing refers to the production of a new re-made version of an original song sung by an artiste who is not the original singer. After the K-pop hit *Gangnam Style* went viral on the Internet in 2012, a Singaporean girl earned herself instant fame by covering the song and uploading her record onto YouTube. The video clip chalked up a phenomenal hits and the singer Stepf Micayle later was invited to perform in Taiwan as well.

K-pop Influences Local Lifestyle Choices and Consumption

In terms of lifestyle choices, popular items such as food cultural choices have also emerged as options for Singaporeans to consume popular Korean culture outside the pop-songs and visual media categories (e.g. movies and TV programs). Singapore's major supermarkets, FairPrice and Giant, have increased their stock of South Korean food products, recognizing the growing popularity of South Korean cuisine and pop culture. Singapore's local major newspaper *The Straits Times* reported, from having only 200 types of made-in-Korea products in its stores in 2008, FairPrice now has doubled its stock to over 400 types.[20] Giant had expanded its range by 40% from 2011 to 2013, according to the same source.[21]

Korean cooked foodstuff restaurateurs have also leveraged on the increased supply of Korean food produce and opened up restaurants to serve Singaporeans who want more than just Korean supermarket food supply. Combining popular culture popularity and Korean cuisines, there is even a Gangnam-style Korean BBQ and Chicken opened in Singapore since 2012. Gangnam is of course a fashionable district in South Korea that was featured in Psy's Youtube global runaway hit mentioned earlier on. Meanwhile, other established American chains like Kentucky Fried Chicken (KFC) are also capitalizing on the increased recognition of Korean branding by adding Korean inspired items to its menu, such as its Spicy Korean Box and Spicy Korean Crunch Meal marketed and sold in Singapore in 2013.

There are also semi-official offices in Singapore promoting Korean culture as a whole to Singaporeans. One example is Korea Plaza. Operated by Korea Tourism Organization (KTO), Korea Plaza[22] has been running professionally in Singapore for years, providing Singaporeans information on tourism in Korea with various promotional materials and through officially organized activities. Korea Plaza activities include regular language courses, K-pop dance and Korean food making courses, including

---

[20] Gladys Chung, "The Beauty Storm," dated 24 February 2014 in the Straitstimes.com website [downloaded 29 March 2015], available at http://www.straitstimes.com/the-big-story/case-you-missed-it/story/hallyu-beauty-storm-20140224#5.

[21] Gladys Chung, "The Beauty Storm," dated 24 February 2014 in the Straitstimes.com website [downloaded 29 March 2015], available at http://www.straitstimes.com/the-big-story/case-you-missed-it/story/hallyu-beauty-storm-20140224#5.

[22] Visit Korea, "About Singapore Office," in the asiaenglish.visitkorea.or.kr website [downloaded on 28 March 2015], available at http://asiaenglish.visitkorea.or.kr/ena/OO/OO_EN_13_5_2.jsp.

courses on how to prepare the traditional Korean cuisine kimchi and classes on making *tteokbokki* (Korean spicy rice cake). To experience the Korean traditional costume, visitors are allowed to try on the *hanbok* (traditional Korean national costumes) collections and take pictures for memory. According to its website, the Plaza occasionally plays host to Korean fan club gatherings and celebrity visits, including some of the trendiest K-pop stars like Kim Jeong Hoon, Kim Gang Woo, FT Island, T-Max and Brown Eyed Girls.[23]

Tourism Benefits Both Ways

In the case of Korea Plaza, state-sanctioned agencies have helped to converge and merge Singaporean interests in Korean popular (information and promotion of K-pop stars) as well as traditional cultures (*hanbok* and traditional cuisines) into a single cohesive promotional campaign. This becomes a comprehensive one-stop promotional stop for Korean culture in general, regardless of contemporary or traditional cultures. Overall, Korean tourism benefits from this combined comprehensive approach in promoting Korean culture as a whole because the promotional message to Singaporean family units is that Korea has much to offer to both senior and junior members of the family with their varying interests in contemporary popular as well as traditional Korean cultures.

Conversely, Singapore's tourism sector also gets to benefit from increased interest in K-pop-related events as well. Singapore was picked to host the first K-pop ASEAN Festival cover dance concert on 22 November 2014. Nine troupes from ASEAN nations, including Indonesia, Malaysia, Laos, the Philippines, Thailand and Vietnam, competed at the Festival held in the Marina Bay Sands Expo. The eventual champions and winners at the Festival were Se-eon, a seven-member group from the Philippines (in first place), Defvalen from Thailand (in second place), and I-Generation from Indonesia (in third place).

---

[23] Visit Korea, "About Singapore Office," in the asiaenglish.visitkorea.or.kr website [downloaded on 28 March 2015], available at http://asiaenglish.visitkorea.or.kr/ena/OO/OO_EN_13_5_2.jsp.

Policy Implications for Singapore

To a large extent, the Korean model of promoting its popular culture has proven to be powerfully effective in many regions of the world, including in Singapore. In aspiring to be the creative hub for Asia, Singapore could draw some positive lessons from the Korean experience in cultural industrial development. For example, in the area of fan-driven approach to creative production, with institutional guidance/support, it may want to encourage talents from different disciplines into the creative industries so they can be part of this process of creating customer-tailored experiences to cater to a more demanding, "smarter" discerning consumer in the region and beyond. Major conservative Korean daily *The Korea Herald* noted that Korean soft power has demonstrated to Singapore that a country does not need to be large (be a center of the world) to exert effective soft power.[24] An ingredient for this success is attributable to the proactive role of the Korean state in promoting popular culture and this is a feature that has potential for replication in Singapore since Singapore is also an economic system where the state plays an important role.

Similarly to South Korea, Singapore being a global city-state is a melting pot and amalgamation of the East and the West, a cosmopolitan location where vibrant cultural interaction takes place. On top of that, it also exhibits great cultural diversity with distinctive Nanyang traditions and culture whereby intercultural dialogues have incorporated the different characteristics and features of various ethnicities. This serves as an excellent selling point for Singapore to leverage on its cultural and social hybridity to promote local media productions. One example is the success of the Mediacorp production *Little Nyonya* which debuted in 2008. This drama proved that the deep and compelling storyline which circles around the made-believe life-story of an extended *Peranakan* family in Malacca has successfully captured the interest of audiences. After breaking the viewership record on its own channel, the drama quickly gained attention in

---

[24] Kelly Fu and Kai Khiun Liew, "Pop culture bridges Korea and Singapore," dated 4 March 2008 in The Korea Herald Korean Wave (Korea: The Korea Herald), p. 11, hosted by National University of Singapore (NUS) website [downloaded on 26 March 2015], available at https://inetapps.nus.edu.sg/ari/docs%5Cnewspapers%5CKoreanWave-04Mar2008-newspaper.pdf.

several territories, from China, Hong Kong, the Philippines, Vietnam to the United States.[25] There is a strong revival of interest in Nyonya cuisine, Nyonya culture, Nyonya costume and also the *Peranakan* heritage in Singapore and Malaysia after the release of the drama.

As pointed out in previous sections, state presence can account for the previous and continued success of the K-pop phenomenon in Singapore. Singapore Tourism Board (STB) has tried to replicate the success of the Korean Wave in the tourism sector. It started to emulate Korean television dramas and variety shows such as *Running Man* to showcase the attractions and landmarks of Singapore to boost its tourism sector. Specifically, STB tried to map out a scenic journey in Singapore through a series of micro-movies to entice tourists from mainland China. Up to 2015, three micro-movies had been produced. The first micro-movie, *New Discoveries of Love*, features Singapore icons such as the Garden by the Bay, Marina Bay Sands, Central Business District, as well as popular food like kaya toast.[26] The story revolves around the romance story of the female character, starred by Taiwanese actress Ariel Lin Yichen, as she explores the tourist sites from Gardens by the Bay to Marina Bay Sands.[27]

The micro-movie reached out to its targeted audience through the broadcast on Youku.com and other portals like Sina.com, garnering 3.5 million views since its release.[28] In 2014, the second micro-movie starring Taiwanese actor Jimmy Lin and Chinese actress Tian Yuan was released. The film portrays Singapore as a multicultural destination for tourists to explore by showcasing the authentic local cuisine such as chilli

---

[25] Mediacorp News, "MediaCorp blockbuster drama The Little Nyonya a hit on Malaysia's cable and free-to-air channels," dated 30 November 2009 [downloaded on 7 April 2015], available at http://www4.mediacorp.sg/contentdistribution/news/index_cn.php?id=27.

[26] Grace Ng, "For Chinese tourists, it's romance of the Lion City," dated 10 May 2013 in The Straits Times [downloaded on 12 April 2015], available at http://www.straitstimes.com/the-big-story/asia-report/china/story/want-emotional-experience-come-the-lion-city-20130510">For.

[27] Grace Ng, "For Chinese tourists, it's romance of the Lion City," dated 10 May 2013 in The Straits Times [downloaded on 12 April 2015], available at http://www.straitstimes.com/the-big-story/asia-report/china/story/want-emotional-experience-come-the-lion-city-20130510">For.

[28] Yahoo News, "Royston Tan helms third micro movie," dated 23 March 2015 [downloaded on 12 April 2015], available at https://sg.news.yahoo.com/royston-tan-helms-third-micro-movie-090800876.html.

crab and also the *Peranakan* heritage. Kelly Fu and Kai Khiun Liew's *Korea Herald* article indicates that there is a formalization of exchange students between Korean and Singaporean universities, and Korean universities offer short-term scholarships to Singaporean Korean language students.[29]

Prospects for Cultural Diplomacy and Economic Exchanges

Besides serving as a model for Singapore, the success of K-pop also holds out the prospect of Track II cultural diplomacy potential for the two countries to cooperate in this field. On 25 November 2012, the Singapore embassy in Seoul hosted a reception in honor of growing exchanges between Singapore and Korea in the area of popular culture through the performance of a combined Singaporean-Korean pop group, SKarf. It was revealed by local press release in Korea and carried on the Singaporean diplomatic website that Alpha Entertainment was the production company that trained the SKarf members for two years in the genre of bubblegum pop.[30] Symbolically, "SK" stands for "Singapore" and "Korea" respectively and SKarf is a homophone that analogizes music with a scarf, implying that both can be worn comfortably by everyone.[31]

Another positive spin-off from Singaporean consumer interest in Korean popular culture is that it has provided the incentive to draw Korean companies to the island state. Because of *Hallyu*, Singaporean consumers recognizes the branding, affordability and innovativeness of Korean

---

[29] Kelly Fu and Kai Khiun Liew, "Pop culture bridges Korea and Singapore," dated 4 March 2008 in The Korea Herald Korean Wave (Korea: The Korea Herald), p. 11, hosted by National University of Singapore (NUS) website [downloaded on 26 March 2015], available at https://inetapps.nus.edu.sg/ari/docs%5Cnewspapers%5CKoreanWave-04Mar2008-newspaper.pdf.

[30] Korea Herald, "Envoy lauds K-pop's Korea-Singapore female foursome," dated 25 November 2012 in the Embassy of the Republic of Singapore Seoul Press Statements and Speeches website [downloaded on 25 March 2015], available at http://www.mfa.gov.sg/content/mfa/overseasmission/seoul/press_statements_speeches/2012/201211/20121125.html.

[31] Korea Herald, "Envoy lauds K-pop's Korea-Singapore female foursome," dated 25 November 2012 in the Embassy of the Republic of Singapore Seoul Press Statements and Speeches website [downloaded on 25 March 2015], available at http://www.mfa.gov.sg/content/mfa/overseasmission/seoul/press_statements_speeches/2012/201211/20121125.html.

popular cultural products as Asian-centric products, suitable for the skin tone, price range and lifestyle choices/tastes of Singaporeans.[32] Due to a baseline of Singaporean interest in Korean popular cultural products, Singapore's Economic Development Board (EDB) revealed that the cumulative direct investment from South Korea expanded by 12.8% from S$3.67 billion in 2010 to S$4.16 billion at the end of 2011 one year later, becoming Singapore's eighth biggest foreign investor.[33]

The spin-off benefit for Singapore does not just stop there, with more than 1,000 South Korean firms in Singapore engaging in a diverse range of commercial activities in industries as far-ranging as from F&B (food and beverages) to electronic goods. Thus, Singapore itself is becoming a platform for Korean companies to penetrate other regional markets.[34] Singapore also serves as a *de facto* laboratory for Korean popular cultural and consumer products before exporting to the Southeast Asian region due to its similarities in levels of economic development, proactive governmental role in the economy and the complementarity with South Korea. Given its multicultural makeup that reflects the racial and ethnic complexities found in East Asia, Singapore is ideal as a platform for testing out Korean popular cultural products' acceptability amongst Asian audiences before they are sent to other Asian countries. Given its highly developed legal system, efficient civil service and connectivity to the rest of the world, Singapore is also complementary to Korean penetration into new Asian markets, particularly those in Southeast Asia.

Limitations and Conclusion

There are limitations to soft power, commercial successes and reach of any popular culture. Popular culture itself inherently tends to be subjected to

---

[32] Samantha Boh, "Korean brands ride the wave to Singapore," dated 9 December 2013 in the mypaper.sg website [downloaded on 29 March 2015], available at http://mypaper.sg/top-stories/korean-brands-ride-wave-singapore-20131209.

[33] Samantha Boh, "Korean brands ride the wave to Singapore," dated 9 December 2013 in the mypaper.sg website [downloaded on 29 March 2015], available at http://mypaper.sg/top-stories/korean-brands-ride-wave-singapore-20131209.

[34] Samantha Boh, "Korean brands ride the wave to Singapore," dated 9 December 2013 in the mypaper.sg website [downloaded on 29 March 2015], available at http://mypaper.sg/top-stories/korean-brands-ride-wave-singapore-20131209.

changing trends and fashions. Therefore, to be successful and sustainably so, Korean popular culture may need to continue its spirit of innovation to come up with new products for its domestic and Asian audiences. Eventually, the uniquely Korean characteristics of K-pop may have to contend with more universally appreciated features of Korean popular culture such that audiences (particularly foreign audiences) no longer need to acquire foreign languages or acquire Korean language ability to understand, appreciate and consume those products.

In other words, what started out as particularistically Korean may eventually morph into a regional or global branding that is not idiosyncratic or uniquely constructed but one that is well-understood based on its own merits and attractive features. It is not culturally specific but universally attractive. As a multicultural entity, Singapore may be able to help in that aspect as a melting pot of different Asian cultures. Eventually the popular cultural products that succeed in Singapore in the context of multiracialism and multiculturalism may resonate with a diverse Asian audience.

ANNEX A. KOREAN EXPORTS SHARE OF TV PROGRAMS PER COUNTRY/REGION IN 2011.

Country/ Region	Exports Share in Percentage
Japan	60.4
Taiwan	12.5
China	10.2
Hong Kong	2.4
Philippines	2.1
Singapore	1.9
Vietnam	1.7
Thailand	1.6
Myanmar	0.8
Indonesia	0.7
Others	4.6

Source: Korea Communications Commission.

ANNEX B. NUMBER OF VIEWS OF K-POP VIDEOS ON YOUTUBE (2011).

Country/ Region	Number of Views of K-POP Videos on YouTube	Shares in %
Japan	423,683,759	20.3
US	240,748,112	11.5
Thailand	224,813,564	10.8
Taiwan	189,027,731	9.0
Vietnam	177,358,800	8.5
Korea	155,325,204	7.4
Malaysia	98,693,969	4.7
Indonesia	81,128,637	3.9
Hong Kong	76,937,448	3.7
Philippines	74,251,012	3.6
Singapore	68,546,360	3.3
Canada	46,477,940	2.2
Saudi Arabia	42,719,685	2.0
Mexico	34,237,580	1.6
Australia	27,132,121	1.3
France	26,591,412	1.3
Peru	25,503,082	1.2
UK	22,705,547	1.1
Brazil	21,090,241	1.0
Germany	20,114,996	0.9
Chile	13,777,557	0.7

Source: JoongAng Ilbo, "The number of views of K-POP videos on YouTube reached 2.3 billion in 235 countries" (2 January 2011).

Section 4

China

Chapter 10

Reality TV in China

Xiaojuan PING

Introduction

Reality television (TV) or reality show did not become a phenomenon in China until 2012 although it was introduced to the mainland Chinese television much earlier.[1] With accumulated experiences and acquired skills from more established foreign production teams, the Chinese reality show business has enjoyed significant increase of popularity and viewership since 2012. The *Collins English Dictionary* defines "reality show" as: a television show in which members of the public or celebrities are filmed living their everyday lives or undertaking specific challenges.[2] While in the Chinese context, reality TV or reality show (*zhen ren xiu* 真人秀) generally refers to television programs that are recorded stories or series of recorded behavior of ordinary people (rather than professional actors/actresses) within a pre-designed and constructed setting, based on a regulated format, and motivated by specific commercial goals.[3] Other more scholarly source opined that reality TV is a "specific true story about real

---

[1] China News, "Reality show alleviates Chinese anxiety (真人秀缓解国人的普遍焦虑)," dated 17 January 2014 in the Chinanews website [downloaded on 16 October 2015], available at http://www.chinanews.com/cul/2014/01-17/5749885.shtml.

[2] Collins Dictionary, "Reality show," [downloaded on 16 October 2015], available at http://www.collinsdictionary.com/dictionary/english/reality-show.

[3] CSSN, "zhen ren xiu definition," dated 30 October 2014 in the cssn.cn website [downloaded on 18 October 2015], available at http://www.cssn.cn/zt/zt_xkzt/xwcbxzt/xsyxdzrxjmfzqj/zrxjmdy/201410/t20141030_1382967.shtml translated from "由普通人(非演员)在规定的情景中,按照预定的游戏规则,为了一个明确的目的,做出自己的行动,同时被记录下来而做成电视节目".

person told in a virtue spatiotemporal setting, on a dramatized and edited/computed program with all-angle real-time filming."[4]

But there is no rigorous definition of reality show in Chinese language. It is normally defined as a concept involving — ordinary people (in contrast to professional actors/actresses), who act naturally to carry out a mission (designed by the studios or production team) with a clear goal, that is filmed and later edited as a TV show. If we deconstruct the term: "*Zhen* 真," literally means "real," indicates that these programs are non-fictional and non-fabricated; "*Ren* 人," literally means "people," requires "people" to be the core element as certain traits of the participants' personalities or behaviors should be memorable to the audiences; "*Xiu* 秀" is a transliteration of the English word "show" and it states the measures that a reality show uses to present itself, that is through virtual settings with certain designed regulations. All these elements are integrated into the programs documentarily, dramatically and entertainingly. The fact that reality show emphasizes being "live" (without scripting or role-playing), often claiming to reveal reality to its fullest, caters to certain desires of the general public, such as their curiosity into other peoples' lives, novelty-hunting when it comes to picking out the secrets of fellow human beings' lives, and our very human tendency to gossip.

This chapter thus attempts to examine the emergence and the accelerating popularity of reality TV shows (真人秀) in Chinese television as they have phenomenally generated high ratings in Chinese TV programming in recent years and have influenced Chinese people, especially the youths, in unprecedented ways. A major characteristic of reality show is the "instant sharing" of contents with television audiences/consumers in an extensively connected (by social media) society. Technological advancement, as well as prevailing popular use of smart phones, tablets, selfie-sticks and other digital-era gadgets, has largely amplified the importance of digital entertainment in the leisure activities of the young in

---

[4]CSSN, "zhen ren xiu definition," dated 30 October 2014 in the cssn.cn website [downloaded on 18 October 2015], available at http://www.cssn.cn/zt/zt_xkzt/xwcbxzt/xsyxdzrxjmfzqj/zrxjmdy/201410/t20141030_1382967.shtml translated from "特定虚拟空间中的真实故事,以全方位,真实的近距离拍摄和以人物为核心的戏剧化的后期剪辑而作成的节目".

China. Digitalization is not only a revolution in networking, education, long-distance communication and etc., but also how the young and old enjoy various digital products like reality TV shows broadcasted for smartphones and other handheld devices and readers.

Reality TV Shows in China

Reality shows were first broadcasted on Chinese television in 2000, with the Guangdong Television (GDTV) survival show *Great Survival Challenge* (生存大挑战) as arguably the trailblazing pioneer in this category of popular entertainment. The essence of these survival shows are overcoming major physical challenges imposed on the participants and the adrenaline-pumping competition between them. Excitement in overcoming challenges and financial/reward incentives in completing the mission stated in the TV show usually serve as the motivation for audiences to keep watching and even sign up to participate. The first episode of *Great Survival Challenge* filmed two male and one female participants traversing across the Chinese territorial border, marking the first-ever Chinese indigenous reality show that made headlines in several newspapers. The following episodes introduced more exciting elements such as competition mechanism, revisiting the Long March route (长征路) and cash lucky draw (RMB200,000 in episode three),[5] gaining more popularity amongst the audiences.

More recently, reality TV shows in China have diverted its focus from pure "physical" challenges to a mixture of physical, intellectual, mental and emotional elements in narrating the lives of the show participants. More specifically, dating shows (i.e. match-making that involves feeling confession and scripted flirting), competition shows (e.g. singing competition that involves story-telling about the participant's pursuit of his/her dream, usually touching and heart-rending), and family-life reality shows (e.g. celebrity's family trip to visit a museum) are among the most popular programs. These programs fall into the category of "variety show" (综艺节目).

---

[5] People.com, "Chinese Reality Show Development Report (中国真人秀节目发展报告)," dated 18 April 2006 in the people.com website [downloaded on 18 October 2015], available at http://media.people.com.cn/GB/40628/4309362.html.

The content design of Chinese variety shows is susceptible to influences from foreign variety shows, especially the ones from South Korea, Taiwan and America.

Although the Korean Wave (韩流) has seemingly dominated the Chinese reality show broadcasting, there is a variety of talent shows that use *American Idol, America's Got Talent* and *X Factor* as templates. The popular singing competition show *I Am A Singer* (我是歌手) and *China Voices* (中国好声音) are good examples of this genre. Major models of production cooperation such as franchising and joint-venture are utilized in cooperation with Korean and American production teams.

Producers Going After Viewer Interests in Reality TV Shows

There are 15 reality shows that achieved both decent economic revenue and exerted social influence on the viewers in the period leading up to January 2014 (see Table 10.1).[6] They can be divided into mainly six categories, namely talent-show/competence program, dating and social program, talk show program, scientific knowledge competition, career opportunity reality TV show, and celebrity emulation show. Four major television channels including CCTV-3, Dragon TV-2, Hunan TV-3 and Jiangsu TV-4 cover 80% of the mainstream reality shows.[7]

Stricter censorship of TV dramas and plays has contributed to the emergence of reality shows in recent years. More lucrative, attractive for sponsorships, and quicker turnover-in-filming (normally a few days, in extreme cases within one day, compared to filming for months before a single drama episode can be screened), these shows instantly gained popularity in various national television channels' programming throughout China. TV stations in more affluent coastal cities, including Shanghai (Dragon TV 东方卫视), Nanjing (Jiangsu TV 江苏卫视), Hangzhou (Zhejiang TV 浙江卫视), and Changsha (Hunan TV 湖南卫视) reaped

---

[6]China News, "Reality show alleviates Chinese anxiety (真人秀缓解国人的普遍焦虑)," dated 17 January 2014 in the Chinanews website [downloaded on 16 October 2015], available at http://www.chinanews.com/cul/2014/01-17/5749885.shtml.

[7]China News, "Reality show alleviates Chinese anxiety (真人秀缓解国人的普遍焦虑)," dated 17 January 2014 in the Chinanews website [downloaded on 16 October 2015], available at http://www.chinanews.com/cul/2014/01-17/5749885.shtml.

TABLE 10.1. POPULAR REALITY SHOWS IN CHINA (2013).

Category	English Name	Chinese Name
Talent-show/competence program	China's Got Talent	中国达人秀
	Sing My Song	中国好歌曲
	Top Million Star	星光大道
	Avenue to Spring Festival Gala	直通春晚
	I Am A Singer	我是歌手
Dating and social program	If You Are the One	非诚勿扰
	Take Me Out	我们约会吧
	Defending My Love	爱情保卫战
Talk show program	Fei De Will Watch	非常了得
	Tonight 80's Talk Show	今晚80后脱口秀
Scientific knowledge competition	Super Brain	最强大脑
	Who's Still Standing	一站到底
Career opportunity reality TV show	Opportunities of China	中国好商机
	Only You	非你莫属
Celebrity emulation show	Your Face Sounds Familiar	百变大咖秀

Source: Author based on data analyzed from baike.baidu, and China News, "Reality show alleviates Chinese anxiety (真人秀缓解国人的普遍焦虑)," dated 17 January 2014 in the Chinanews website [downloaded on 16 October 2015], available at http://www.chinanews.com/cul/2014/01-17/5749885.shtml.

the biggest benefits from this round of reality TV show boom. All four of them ranked top of the list for their ratings in reality shows in a survey in 2015 (see Table 10.2).

From these reality TV programs, several examples of the most popular reality shows are listed below:

1. *Running Man* "奔跑吧兄弟" (Zhejiang TV)[8]

Borrowed from the South Korean show *Running Man,* the storyline of the Chinese *Running Man* engages six Chinese young celebrities (aged between late 20s to early 40s) transported to a variety of locations, often

---

[8]ZJSTV, "Running Man (奔跑吧兄弟)," on the zjstv.com website [downloaded on 22 October 2015], available at http://www.zjstv.com/news/zjnews/.

TABLE 10.2. RANKING OF NATION-WIDE RATINGS FOR REALITY TV SHOWS FROM HUNAN, JIANGSU, ZHEJIANG AND DRAGON TVs AMONG URBAN HOUSEHOLDS (2013).

Rank	Program (English Name)	Program (Chinese Name)	Rating	Channel
1	Running Man	奔跑吧兄弟	7.82	Zhejiang TV
2	Here Comes Running Man	跑男来了	7.29	Zhejiang TV
3	I Am A Singer 2015 Final	我是歌手 2015 巅峰会	6.5	Hunan TV
4	Happy Camp	快乐大本营	3.72	Hunan TV
5	If You Are the One	非诚勿扰	3.69	Jiangsu TV
6	Divas Hit the Road	花儿与少年	3.57	Hunan TV
7	Day Day Up	天天向上	2.84	Hunan TV
8	It Takes A Real Man	真正男子汉	2.33	Hunan TV
9	Dad Is Back	爸爸回来了	2.32	Zhejiang TV
10	Go to Love	出发吧爱情	1.93	Zhejiang TV
11	Sisters over Flowers	花样姐姐	1.86	Dragon TV
12	Happy Comedian	欢乐喜剧人	1.73	Dragon TV
13	We Are in Love	我们相爱吧	1.7	Jiangsu TV
14	Jinxing Time	金星时间	1.52	Dragon TV
15	Hidden Energy	我看你有戏	1.45	Zhejiang TV
16	Fight for Her	为她而战	1.42	Jiangsu TV
17	We All Love to Laugh	我们都爱笑	1.41	Hunan TV
18	Start the Applauds	掌声响起来	1.32	Zhejiang TV
19	Ma'ma Mi'ya	妈妈咪呀	1.32	Dragon TV
20	Ma'ma Mi'ya (Prequel)	妈妈咪呀前传	1.31	Dragon TV

Note: Data from 1 April to 24 May 2015; based on rating reported from digital television households in 16 major cities including Beijing, Chengdu, Guangzhou, Chongqing, Hangzhou, Changsha, Nanjing, Xiamen, Xi'an, Zhengzhou, Dalian, Kunming, Wuhan, Taiyuan, Shijiazhuang, and Harbin. *Source*: Nielsen Television Audience Measurement.

a tourist site or a place with historical/cultural characteristic each week, to take on various challenges. The designated challenges include completing jigsaw puzzles after finding missing pieces hidden in corners of a building via teamwork within time limit, solving mathematical puzzles, identifying "turn coaters" in the teams, and tackling other physical challenges such as wrestling, running and charades. Each episode is designed to have a series of individual or/and team competitions.

2. *Grandpa over Flowers* "花样爷爷" (Dragon TV)[9]

The Korean backpacker travel reality show *Noona Over Flowers* is the program where the Dragon TV got inspiration for producing *Grandpa Over Flowers*. First launched in March 2015, the show was a big hit amongst Chinese audiences. It casts a group of six celebrities from different age groups going on backpack travel with a budget to Turkey. The group members, sharing an assigned budget, need to arrange their flight, accommodation, food and transportation coordinately in a foreign country. Different travel schedules and personal preferences were discernable in the interactions of the group members, some of which caused conflicts amongst the participants while other conflicts were settled more smoothly.

3. *Where Are We Going, Dad?* "爸爸去哪儿?" (Hunan TV)[10]

Another popular Korean-inspired reality TV show is *Where Are We Going, Dad?*, sharing the same title with the original show from South Korea. It is undeniably one of the best-received reality shows in China achieving No. 1 ranking for all broadcasted 16 episodes of Season 2 amongst all mainland Chinese TV channels (with the exception of CCTV)[11] in 2014. Presented by Hunan TV (sometimes nicknamed the "Mango TV" as the icon of the TV station resembles a mango), the show sends five celebrity fathers and their children on a three-day trip in each episode to various Chinese rural areas to accomplish a list of tasks including cooking without the benefits of pre-prepared materials, sleeping without proper bed,

---

[9] Dragontv, "Grandpa over Flowers (花样爷爷)," on the dragontv.cn website [downloaded on 22 October 2015], available at http://www.dragontv.cn/video/2014-06-11/fca63f39d2 f5ad3856f99cb5b177a324.html.

[10] Hunantv, "Where Are We Going, Dad? (爸爸去哪儿)," on the hunantv.com website [downloaded on 22 October 2015], available at http://www.hunantv.com/show/.

[11] Ifeng News, "*Where Are We Going, Dad?* grand finale, making rating miracle of 16 championships (《爸爸去哪儿2》大结局 十六连冠创收视奇迹)," dated 4 October 2014 on the ifeng.com website [downloaded on 18 October 2015], available at http://ent. ifeng.com/a/20141004/40323228_0.shtml.

engaging in intellectual or physical competition with other families. Chinese audiences from different generations are attracted to this show as they can relate easily their childhood or parenting stories to the celebrity parenting situations. Obviously, the seemingly candid and authentic performance of both the celebrity fathers and children, whose family lives are often kept off public scrutiny, are appealing to audiences as well.

4. *Dad Is Back* "爸爸回来了" (Zhejiang TV)[12]

Derived from the Korean reality show *Superman is Back*, Chinese reality TV *Dad Is Back* is a product of localization. As the name suggests, four celebrity families, especially fathers, are put under spotlight to take care of their children for two days without assistance from wives or other family members. It differs from the *Where Are We Going, Dad?* show as the setting is found largely at home or in familiar neighborhood locations such as parks or restaurants. The fathers' tasks are mostly daily routines, such as pacifying two-year-old, putting on clothes for the children, and multi-tasking in the kitchens for food preparation.

While none of the Chinese versions sound particularly different from their original franchises, their showcase of individualism, expressiveness and consumerism are different from the conservative official values propagated by the Chinese Communist Party (CCP). According to a report released by China's State Administration of Press, Publication, Radio, Film and Television (SAPRFT) in May 2015, it now permits the broadcast of one season of one reality show per year for every satellite broadcaster.[13] The SAPRFT also banned scripted reality shows that usually use real people as characters in staged scenes that have storylines enhanced with selective editing. Scandals about several screen celebrities involved in drug dealing, hit-and-run accidents, prostitutions and other misbehaviors have made it to the newspaper headlines from time to time. Thus, the state

---

[12] ZJSTV, "*Dad Is Back* (爸爸回来了)," on the zjstv.com website [downloaded on 22 October 2015], available at http://v.zjstv.com/zy/baba/.

[13] SAPRFT, "Socialism Core Values and Responsibilities of Broadcasting Medias (社会主义核心价值观与广播电视的责任)," dated 8 May 2015 in the sarft.gov.cn website [downloaded on 22 October 2015], available at http://www.sarft.gov.cn/art/2015/5/8/art_77_26720.html.

government attempts to ensure only positive messages are transmitted to the general public, sometimes relying on banning and limiting certain program broadcasts. It is unclear though if the government strategy would prove effective in transmitting more "positive energy" to the public, or just compels the ordinary Chinese, who constitute the largest pirate media market in the world, to migrate *en masse* to online streaming and torrent sites.[14]

Practice of Franchising and Joint-venture Models

There are two models of cooperation which Chinese television channels follow for purchasing the publishing right of introduced programs. The first model involves the actual purchase from the US and European television stations and companies while the second model is based on program offerings from South Korea after *Where Are We Going, Dad?* made its debut and became a hit in 2013. Cooperation with the US or European media companies/TV stations, which usually costs 10% of the total program funding as copyright loyalties, follows more standardized pattern. For instance, the copyright royalties of one season of *China Voices* can reach RMB20 million.[15] Accompanying the purchased copyright, a detailed "production *Bible*" will be supplied to the authorized Chinese stations as well. To ensure the Chinese version of the show keeps true to the franchise, the "*Bible*" brochure includes detailed guidelines of participant and judging panel recruitment, (indoor/outdoor) site setting-up, and filming angle and etc.

On the other hand, cooperation with Korean media companies is more flexible and, to some degree, more complex. As the success of Korean reality show is based on years of experience accumulation, original ideas, specific filming process and post-filming effects, the performance of all

---

[14]RT, "China regulator to investigate, ban 'vulgar and harmful' reality shows," dated 22 July 2015 on the rt.com website [downloaded on 22 October 2015], available at https://www.rt.com/news/310499-china-ban-reality-television/.

[15]Jiangang Liang, "Financial and economic jigsaw behind the reality show (真人秀背后的财经拼图)," dated 27 August 2015 in the JF Daily [downloaded on 22 October 2015], available at http://www.jfdaily.com/caijing/bw/201508/t20150827_1779965.html.

participants (including their make-up and costume) and advertising techniques are all important components of a show. Therefore, to be a franchisee of a Korea media company means not only purchasing the copyright but the Korean producer's (including filming and editing) all-round services; sometimes even hiring the entire production team, making the franchising fee (and therefore production fee) higher.[16]

One good example of franchising cooperation is that Zhejiang TV signed a deal with the Seoul Broadcasting System (SBS), the original producer of the *Where Are We Going, Dad?* show, to jointly produce a Chinese version of the series. Subsequently, the show became a big hit in the mainland Chinese television industry. Almost at the same time, TVB, Hong Kong's top broadcaster, had made its own version of *Where Are We Going, Dad?*, named 爸 B 也 *Upgrade* independently.[17] But the production proved to be less successful. No agreement of franchising or joint production was signed with SBS. The quality and reputation of the copycat version suffered, and some netizens even accused the Hong Kong producers of copyright infringement.

This practice of buying broadcasting rights had been widely used in Chinese variety shows until the launch of *I Am A Singer* (我是歌手), a singing competition using the reality show format. Hunan Television acquired the production rights from South Korea's Munhwa Broadcasting Corporation in 2012 and produced a localized version of the show. The Korean producers sent experts to guide their Chinese counterparts, sharing details of the creative process throughout the filming and editing, including production flow and other details that were often overlooked.

Unlike *I Am A Singer*, *Running Man* was introduced to China through another business model. Zhejiang TV jointly produced the Chinese version with its Korean partner. Instead of just sending advisers, SBS has sent its own production team including video specialists to China for the

---

[16] Jiangang Liang, "Financial and economic jigsaw behind the reality show (真人秀背后的财经拼图)," dated 27 August 2015 in the JF Daily [downloaded on 22 October 2015], available at http://www.jfdaily.com/caijing/bw/201508/t20150827_1779965.html.

[17] Ifeng News, "TVB 版《爸爸》遭吐槽: 制作小气无大牌," dated 11 December 2013 in the ifeng.com website [downloaded on 20 October 2015], available at http://ent.ifeng.com/tv/news/zongyi/detail_2013_12/11/32018102_0.shtml.

production. Because of the growing appetite of the Chinese viewers for Korean pop culture, production rights for Chinese versions of Korean shows now cost a lot more. Fees now range from US$10,000 to US$20,000 per episode, compared with US$10,000 for the whole *Running Man* program (12 episodes) about a year ago, reported by *China Daily*.[18] In the joint-venture production model, producers in Korea and China have to work together in much closer ways, thus the former is justified to ask for more than patent fees.

Almost all the endorsements and company placements in popular variety shows start with a price tag of RMB100 million in 2015.[19] *I Am A Singer* (我是歌手), *Happy Camp* (快乐大本营) and a new program *Here Comes the Idol* (偶像来了) took in a total RMB1.05 billion at the Hunan TV programs bidding auction in 2015.[20] A bid for a 15-second commercial advertisement slot came up to RMB32 million during the air-time of *I Am A Singer*.[21] According to Xinhua News, the top-ranking *If You Are the One* (非诚勿扰) sold its franchise rights to Jiangsu TV for RMB500 million in 2015. And the equally popular *Running Man* from Zhejiang TV attracted a RMB216 million price tag for its endorsement rights for its second season.[22]

---

[18] Jie Zhang, "Korean variety shows capture Chinese television, copyright fees ten-folded (韩国综艺占中国荧屏节目版权费增长10倍)," dated 20 January 2015 in the China Daily website [downloaded on 18 June 2015], available at http://www.chinadaily.com.cn/micro-reading/dzh/2015-01-20/content_13076093.html.

[19] Xinhuanet, "200 reality shows will be presented by major televisions next year (明年各大卫视推200档真人秀)," dated 20 November 2014 in the hb.xinhuanet.com website [downloaded on 22 October 2015], available at http://www.hb.xinhuanet.com/2014-11/20/c_1113326075.htm.

[20] Xinhuanet, "200 reality shows will be presented by major televisions next year (明年各大卫视推 200 档真人秀)," dated 20 November 2014 in the hb.xinhuanet.com website [downloaded on 22 October 2015], available at http://www.hb.xinhuanet.com/2014-11/20/c_1113326075.htm.

[21] Xinhuanet, "200 reality shows will be presented by major televisions next year (明年各大卫视推 200 档真人秀)," dated 20 November 2014 in the hb.xinhuanet.com website [downloaded on 22 October 2015], available at http://www.hb.xinhuanet.com/2014-11/20/c_1113326075.htm.

[22] Xinhuanet, "200 reality shows will be presented by major televisions next year (明年各大卫视推 200 档真人秀)," dated 20 November 2014 in the hb.xinhuanet.com website

Changing Taste and Mentality

Where Are We Going, Dad? has become one of China's most popular television shows, averaging more than 600 million viewers each week (and more than 640 million downloads online).[23] Sponsorship rights for the show's second season were sold for RMB312 million (about US$50 million),[24] more than 10 times higher than the sponsorship rights for the first season. Online search for *Where Are We Going, Dad?* turned up over 40 million hits on Sina Weibo.[25] Even the *People's Daily*, the official media outlet of the Chinese government, was pleased with its success. "The deep affection on display in the show is heart-warming and ignites a desire in people to return home to loved ones,"[26] the *People's Daily* reported in an op-ed. In April 2012, the Chinese Ministry of Education announced, for the first time, TV viewing guidelines to teachers and parents for healthy education development of the three- to six-year-old, indicating a growing emphasis on early childhood education.[27] The guidelines

---

[downloaded on 22 October 2015], available at http://www.hb.xinhuanet.com/2014-11/20/c_1113326075.htm.

[23] Sue-lin Wong, "Why a TV show about celebrity fathers has enraptured China," dated 20 December 2013 on theatlantic.com website [downloaded on 22 October 2015], available at http://www.theatlantic.com/china/archive/2013/12/why-a-tv-show-about-celebrity-fathers-has-enraptured-china/282562/.

[24] Sue-lin Wong, "Why a TV show about celebrity fathers has enraptured China," dated 20 December 2013 on theatlantic.com website [downloaded on 22 October 2015], available at http://www.theatlantic.com/china/archive/2013/12/why-a-tv-show-about-celebrity-fathers-has-enraptured-china/282562/.

[25] Sue-lin Wong, "Why a TV show about celebrity fathers has enraptured China," dated 20 December 2013 on theatlantic.com website [downloaded on 22 October 2015], available at http://www.theatlantic.com/china/archive/2013/12/why-a-tv-show-about-celebrity-fathers-has-enraptured-china/282562/.

[26] Sue-lin Wong, "Why a TV show about celebrity fathers has enraptured China," dated 20 December 2013 on theatlantic.com website [downloaded on 22 October 2015], available at http://www.theatlantic.com/china/archive/2013/12/why-a-tv-show-about-celebrity-fathers-has-enraptured-china/282562/.

[27] Ministry of Education, "Guidelines on Study and Development of the Three to Six Year Olds," dated October 2012 in the MOE website [downloaded on 22 December 2014], available at http://www.moe.edu.cn/publicfiles/business/htmlfiles/moe/s3327/201210/xxgk_143254.html. The original text states: "要充分发挥学前教育教科研机构和幼儿园

emphasized the important role that the mass media plays in shaping an individual's character and social development.

Thinking about what may account for the *Dad* show's unprecedented popularity, we may find several explanations. First, this show raises an important question for modern Chinese society — what is the role of father in today's Chinese family? The show features a new generation of Chinese (celebrity) fathers, who, as part of the country's burgeoning middle class, face more exposure to modern child-rearing techniques and active interactions with their children. The Confucius tradition states that filial piety is an important human trait: obeying your parents' wishes and looking after them in their old age. But Chinese parents gradually realize that listening to and respecting their children's choices may be a more appropriate way to prepare them for a modern society, considering much competition and challenges they would be facing in their adulthood. "As they raise their children, parents are growing up at the same time," said Renping Wang, a popular education expert, in an interview with the *Qianjiang Evening News*. He added, "they cannot use parenting styles from 20 years ago to guide the development of children born 20 years later."[28]

Another appealing feature of reality show is that it breaks the rules of theatrical story-telling or mechanical reciting/performing of the rehearsed lines so that they can engage in spontaneous reactions, just like every other ordinary person. In the *Dad* show, the children and their fathers show remarkable candor. "My wife is great — she's been raising our son for six years. I'm exhausted and it's only been three days. I'm buying her a bunch of flowers when we go back," confessed Guo Tao, a Chinese actor and director, who participated as a father in the show.[29] After each episode goes to air,

---

的专业优势,发挥各种大众传媒的作用,组织开展形式多样的宣传活动。要以深入浅出的语言,喜闻乐见的形式,广泛宣传《指南》的教育理念和教育方法,提高广大家长的科学育儿能力,实现家园共育".

[28] Sue-lin Wong, "Why a TV show about celebrity fathers has enraptured China," dated 20 December 2013 on theatlantic.com website [downloaded on 22 October 2015], available at http://www.theatlantic.com/china/archive/2013/12/why-a-tv-show-about-celebrity-fathers-has-enraptured-china/282562/.

[29] Translated from one celebrity father participant, Chinese actor and director Guo Tao, in *Where Are We Going, Dad?* Season 1 Episode 1, aired first on 11 October 2013 on Hunan TV. More details at http://list.hunantv.com/short/1153-109830--3-.html.

the Chinese internet and social media explode with commentaries on each celebrity's parenting style. Of course part of the appeal of the *Dad* show lies in the chance to peek into the private lives of popular Chinese celebrities and their children. Audiences revel in watching the failed attempts of celebrity fathers preparing dinner, braiding hair, and disciplining children — tasks often left to mothers in the traditional Chinese families.

Another popular reality show *If You Are the One* (非诚勿扰) on Jiangsu TV has been on many families' must-watch program list at a prime time, 21:10–22:30 every Saturday. It shows female participants bravely and explicitly expressing their motto in finding their own Mr. Right. This popular show ponders reflection and discussion about life partner selection, dating patterns, and romance/intimacy values among Chinese audiences, especially the females. Television stations across China have jumped onto the bandwagon as well, launching talk shows and reality programs about the relationship between young couples, and between parents and children.

However, another dating reality show *We Are in Love* (我们恋爱吧), broadcasted by the same Jiangsu TV, was introduced to China in January 2015 from the Korean original *We Are Married* (我们结婚了) but was taken off the air and was suspended, ostensibly for technical reasons. The official reason was that the show needed to have "more normal people falling in love on the show."[30] But there are unsubstantiated online rumors that the suspension had to do with the new rules setting stricter standards on reality show broadcasting.

Fandom Consumption

Since the movie *Far Cry*, originally a video game designed by German video game company Crytek and published by Microsoft Windows in 2004, featuring popular Chinese actress Yang Mi, made over RMB85 million of revenue from a RMB4 million investment in production,[31] the

---

[30] Beijing Daily, "We are in love suspended, "fake love" may be the cause (《我们相爱吧》突遭停播业内分析或因"假恋爱")," dated 3 June 2015 in the people.com.cn website [downloaded on 22 October 2015], available at http://media.people.com.cn/n/2015/0603/c40606-27095604.html.

[31] Ent.163, "Three reasons counting for the *Far Cry* legend, Yang Mi as a ticket box guarantee (三大原因造就孤岛》神话,杨幂成票房利器)," dated 12 March 2013 in the ent.163.

fandom economy has encouraged a new genre in the film industry — the fandom movie — to emerge in China. For the fandom movies, no specific training is required for the actors/actresses to "perform" or "act," rather what they need to do is to accompany the hardcore fans who are willing to pay for any products and services related to their idols.

Along with the winning popularity of the first two seasons of *Where Are We Going, Dad?* on TV (see Tables 10.3 and 10.4), its movie version (*Dad* movie) has collected RMB700 million ticket box revenue since its publication during the Chinese New Year season in February 2015.[32] Of the total RMB1.41 billion film revenue in this "golden holiday" season, half was attributed to movies that were adapted from reality shows.[33] The *Dad* movie demonstrated a big success of reaping revenues from consumer products associated with the movie. Movie of this kind usually requires less investment and engages in shorter production line, but brings in bigger profits. The movie version of *Running Man* released in January 2015 is another successful demonstration.

The spin-off mobile game *Where Are We Going, Dad?* (*Dad* game) was released in December 2013, and a book with the same title *Where Are We Going, Dad?* (hereafter referred as the "*Dad*" publication and other paraphernalia like game app) was published in January 2014. Players can download the *Dad* game app on their smart phone and complete tasks such as digital vegetable picking and collecting. *Dad* game has astonished the game industry with its excellent performance on the ranking of iPhone App Store Free downloads (second on the overall total download ranking and game download ranking for 24 days upon its first release[34]). The *Dad*

com website [downloaded on 12 December 2014], available at http://ent.163.com/special/gudaojinghun/.

[32] SMWEEKLY, "Spring festival movie fever dying down in 2015 (2015 年春节档已经玩不转了)," dated 3 March 2015 in the smweekly.com website [downloaded on 18 June 2015], available at http://www.smweekly.com/news/report/201503/38364.aspx.

[33] Eric, "Running Man — a freak made by fandom economy (奔跑吧!兄弟 — 粉丝经济催生的畸形儿)," dated 30 January 2015 in the movie.douban website [downloaded on 18 June 2015], available at http://movie.douban.com/review/7361602/.

[34] Hunan Daily, "*Where are we going, dad?* spin-off products got unlimited potential (《爸爸去哪儿》持续发力衍生产品潜力无限)," dated 24 January 2014 in the people.com.cn website [downloaded on 18 June 2015], available at http://culture.people.com.cn/n/2014/0124/c172318-24217549.html.

publication was well received by its fans, with its bonus features of hard-copy print-outs of the celebrity fathers and children as well as behind-the-scenes interviews with the show participants, and bloopers of film. The first two days of the book launch reached 500 copies sales alone in one Xinhua Bookstore in Beijing, and the total pre-order on Taobao hits reached over 3,000,000.[35]

TABLE 10.3. TELEVISION PREMIERE RATINGS OF *WHERE ARE WE GOING, DAD? SEASON 1.*[36]

Episode	Date	CSM46/48			CSM National Network		
		Rating	Share	Ranking	Rating	Share	Ranking
1	October 11, 2013	1.423	6.74	1	1.1	7.67	1
2	October 18, 2013	2.588	11.53	1	1.67	11.45	1
3	October 25, 2013	3.116	14.43	1	1.8	13.47	1
4	November 1, 2013	3.471	15.26	1	2.16	13.70	1
5	November 8, 2013	3.851	16.73	1	2.13	13.47	1
6	November 15, 2013	4.024	18.16	1	2.30	15.92	1
7	November 22, 2013	4.748	20.68	1	2.69	17.37	1
8	November 29, 2013	4.76	21.11	1	2.81	18.51	1
9	December 6, 2013	4.98	22.12	1	2.9	18.68	1
10	December 13, 2013	5.3	23.22	1	3.21	20.37	1
11	December 20, 2013	5.008	22.14	1	3.40	21.41	1
12	December 27, 2013	4.916	22.06	1	3.64	22.45	1

Note: CCTV channel not included.

Source: Wu Fan, "Chronology of China Television Rating in 2013, CSM Research Focus," *Rating China*, March 2014, p. 10, available at http://www.csm.com.cn/data/editor/pdf/535e081e07331.pdf.

---

[35] Hunan Daily, "*Where are we going, dad?* spin-off products got unlimited potential (《爸爸去哪儿持续发力衍生产品潜力无限》)," dated 24 January 2014 in the people.com.cn website [downloaded on 18 June 2015], available at http://culture.people.com.cn/n/2014/0124/c172318-24217549.html.

[36] Data collected from multiple sources include CSM website, Hunan TV website, 卫视小露电 blog, and 潇湘卧龙 blog, etc.

TABLE 10.4. TELEVISION PREMIERE RATINGS OF *WHERE ARE WE GOING, DAD? SEASON* 2.[37]

Episode	Date	CSM50			CSM National Network		
		Rating	Share	Ranking	Rating	Share	Ranking
1	June 20, 2014	3.927	16.82	1	2.43	14.24	1
2	June 27, 2014	3.570	15.39	1	2.06	11.59	1
3	July 4, 2014	3.605	15.81	1	2.34	14.06	1
4	July 11, 2014	3.393	15.40	1	2.12	12.67	1
5	July 18, 2014	3.08	13.73	2	1.91	11.24	2
6	July 25, 2014	3.387	14.04	2	2.62	14.27	1
7	August 1, 2014	3.485	14.78	2	2.44	13.76	1
8	August 8, 2014	3.718	16.07	2	2.79	15.59	1
9	August 15, 2014	3.640	15.45	2	2.53	14.85	1
10	August 22, 2014	3.372	14.51	2	2.27	13.27	1
11	August 29, 2014	3.296	13.45	2	2.46	13.21	1
12	September 5, 2014	2.774	11.98	2	2.18	12.53	1
13	September 12, 2014	3.067	12.96	2	1.99	11.28	1
14	September 19, 2014	2.960	13.41	2	1.90	11.68	1
15	September 26, 2014	2.844	12.47	2	1.84	10.58	1
16	October 3, 2014	2.838	14.80	1	2.09	14.34	1

Note: CCTV channel not included.

Source: Wu Fan, "Chronology of China Television Rating in 2014, CSM Research Focus," *Rating China*, March 2015, p. 8, available at http://www.csm.com.cn/data/editor/pdf/554b011b8f27d.pdf.

The popularity of the show is measured not only by advertising revenue. T-shirts, jeans, accessories, suitcases, and backpacks appeared in the show are best-sellers on Chinese e-commerce websites as fans are eager to purchase "same brand/design (同款)" items used by the celebrities; and locations featured in the shows have become travel hotspots. For example, over 100 deals were completed on Taobao featuring the same brand of a children seating equipment used by Taiwanese actor and racer Jimmy Lin

---

[37] Data collected from multiple sources include CSM website, Hunan TV website, 卫视小露电 blog, and 潇湘卧龙 blog, etc.

and his son Kimi, as well as by Taiwanese singer Cao Ge and his daughter Grace.[38] Type in keywords "Kimi's superman t-shirt/toy/mug" on Taobao website, one can see thousands of the same brand/design of Kimi's superman T-shirt or his toys available. Besides, the search for an "emergency portable toilet" for kids that was introduced in the show by celebrity father, Chinese actor Huang Lei, went viral online. Some Taobao sellers even included a snapshot of the celebrities in their online shop to attract potential fans and customers. The sunglasses that a celebrity wore on the show became another popular item for online sales. With price ranging from several dollars to hundreds, product offerings are able to satisfy demand of different customers with varying purchasing power and design preferences.

Reality TV Shows Portray Reality in China

Roughly estimated, over 200 new variety shows were screened in 2015, five times the number of the previous year,[39] among which, reality show continues to take the major share. New elements that have been introduced to reality TV shows include Chinese traditional "Peking Opera" and straight-A student experiences. However, originality and innovation are still in serious deficit in these programs. For instance, once the reality show *I Love Lyrics-memorizing* (我爱记歌词) went popular, programs featuring singing competition took over most of the channels; when *If You Are the One* (非诚勿扰) was broadcasted and went popular, all sorts of dating shows emulating this program became hits instantly; and *Keep Fighting Hubby* (老公加油), *Chinese Daddies* (中国爸爸) and *National Son-in-laws* (国民女婿) are regarded as derivations of *Where Are We Going, Dad?* (爸爸去哪儿). Some critics argue that several programs rely

---

[38]Yan Xia, "Where are we going, Dad? spin-off product gain popularity, parent-child shows stimulating consumption (《爸爸去哪儿》同款商品爆红亲自节目拉动消费市场)," dated 20 November 2013 in the media.people.com website [downloaded on 18 June 2015], available at http://media.people.com.cn/n/2013/1120/c40606-23596879.html.

[39]Xinhuanet, "200 reality shows will be presented by major televisions next year (明年各大卫视推200档真人秀)," dated 20 November 2014 in the hb.xinhuanet.com website [downloaded on 22 October 2015], available at http://www.hb.xinhuanet.com/2014-11/20/c_1113326075.htm.

on "catchy" themes such as in-law conflicts and domestic violence to attract audiences, which disrespects the families featured on the program and may have crossed the legal bottom line. As pointed out in an interview with *China Daily* by You Danni, the CEO of EE-Media, a start-up Chinese media company, "we [Chinese media] have consumed up within 10 years the results of about 40 years of research and practical experiences in reality show production from foreign countries. Now we got no more new programs to purchase from them. What will be the way ahead? We must be more creative and originative, and keep moving on."[40]

Reality TV grasps the characteristics of an era, reflecting contemporary social values in a certain society. Information and entertainment are intertwined in the Chinese reality shows and they reflect the consumerism trends in Chinese society.[41] Cultural products have been important components of consumerism in China as its mass entertainment function for satisfying and soothing inner desires is increasingly demanded by Chinese consumers. China's socio-economic transition is accompanied by environmental pollution, sky-rocketing real estate price, and other social injustices, which have left some Chinese people increasingly anxious and frustrated with life. Reality shows, to some extent, provide an imaginary solution or, at the very least, a form of escapism from these conundrums. Featuring everyday issues empathized by ordinary Chinese people at all socio-economic levels, reality shows send incessantly positive messages and energies to the Chinese society.

Reality shows assist with alleviating the anxieties that people share in contemporary Chinese society. Be it a plebian talent-show or a competition performance, these shows demonstrate a similar cultural logic: the upward mobility of an individual penetrating through social stratification by commodifying and commercializing one's talents and how one's life transformation for the better can be realized (through performing talent

---

[40] Jie Zhang, "Korean variety shows capture Chinese television, copyright fees ten-folded (韩国综艺占中国荧屏节目版权费增长10倍)," dated 20 January 2015 in the China Daily website [downloaded on 18 June 2015], available at http://www.chinadaily.com.cn/ micro-reading/dzh/2015-01-20/content_13076093.html. You's original remarks: "我们在 10 年内几乎消耗了国外40年节目的研究结果,接下来,买无所买,我们的创作之路该往 何处去?必须原创,必须往前走。"

[41] Li Li, 奇观社会的文化密码:电视真人秀的游戏规则研究, Sichuan University Press.

or art); communicational barriers between people of different social classes can be broken down (through interactions between the talents and their supervisors); and diligence/persistence with pursuing one's dream in life plus high moral behavior will eventually pay off (just like most of the talents' "experiences" revealed in the show).

Chapter 11

Yuzhaizu: A Study of Otaku Identity in Mainland China

Anying LIN

Introduction

Otaku, a word that originated in the Japanese language, is the Romanization of the Japanese word "おたく/オタク". It refers to passionate and obsessive fans of animation, manga, and other related Japanese popular culture products. Otaku culture is a subculture first developed in postwar Japan (Azuma, 2009, p. 6).[1] It has been introduced to different countries with the help of local distributors and selective appropriations of fans, and gradually becomes a huge and diverse subculture globally (Eng, 2012, p. 85).[2] Otaku culture products were first introduced into mainland China in 1980s and soon became one of the most popular culture products among children. Watching Japanese animation and reading manga are important shared childhood memories for many adolescents and young adults born after the late 1970s.

Japanese Animation

The importation of Japanese animation into mainland China is a complex story. Television sets became readily available in mainland China since

---

[1] Hiroki Azuma, *Otaku: Japan's Database Animals*, trans. J. E. Abel and S. Kono (Minneapolis, MN: University of Minnesota Press, 2009), 6.

[2] Lawrence Eng, "Strategies of Engagement: Discovering, Defining, and Describing Otaku Culture in the United States," in *Fandom Unbound: Otaku Culture in a Connected World*, eds. M. Ito, D. Okabe and I. Tsuji (New Haven, CT: Yale University Press, 2012), 85.

the 1980s (Latham, 2007, p. 43),[3] and the television stations and programs grew exponentially in the same period (Latham, 2007, pp. 46–47).[4] Amongst which, animation programs, especially those imported from Japan, was one of the most popular children's television programs (Latham, 2007, p. 70).[5] According to *Xinhua News Agency*, the national television channels of mainland China started to broadcast Japanese animations since 1981 (The Beijing News, 2006).[6] Many local television stations also imported a large number of Japanese animations based on their own programming initiatives from 1986 onwards. Until early 21st century, the cartoon and youth programs on both national and local televisions were monopolized by Japanese animation (The Beijing News, 2006).[7] Some influential works derived from the otaku list of favorites were included.[8] Such iconic works have become "classical pieces" after their airing in the main free-to-air TV channels.

However, since 2000, the State Administration of Press, Publication, Radio, Film and Television of China has issued several regulations to reduce the frequency of Japanese animation broadcasts in China. In 2000, specific censorship of animations carried out by the national government was established (The State Administration of Press, Publication, Radio, Film and Television, 2000).[9] From 2006, no foreign-produced animations are allowed during prime time children programming, which is defined as

---

[3] Kevin Latham, *Pop Culture China!: Media, Arts, and Lifestyle* (Santa Barbara, CA: ABC-CLIO, Inc., 2007), 43.

[4] *Ibid.*, 46–47.

[5] *Ibid.*, 70.

[6] The Beijing News, "Guang Dian Zong Ju Fa Bu Xin Gui: Huang Jin Shi Duan Jin Bo Jing Wai Dong Hua,"dated 13 August 2006 in Xinhua News Agency [downloaded 14 May 2014], available at http://news.xinhuanet.com/politics/2006-08/13/content_4954807.htm.

[7] *Ibid.*

[8] For example, *The Super Dimension Fortress Macross*, which is said to be the possible origin of the word "otaku;" *Neon Genesis Evangelion*, which is believed to bring the otaku culture into a new generation; and *Sailor Moon*, which is one of the most famous fighting girl animations globally, were imported and broadcasted on public TV channels during 1980s and 1990s.

[9] The State Administration of Press, Publication, Radio, Film and Television, "*Guo Jia Guang Bo Dian Ying Dian Shi Zong Ju Guan Yu Jia Qiang Dong Hua Pian Yin Jin He Bo Fang Guan Li De Tong Zhi*," dated 20 March 2000 [downloaded 14 May 2014], available

between the hours of 1700–2000 in mainland China every day (Beijing Evening News, 2006).[10] And since 2008, foreign-produced animations are completely forbidden on all national and local TV channels (The State Administration of Press, Publication, Radio, Film and Television, 2008).[11]

Despite having these regulations in place to protect and promote local animation productions, Japanese animations remain popular among children (Yang, 2006).[12] Fans could easily watch or download Japanese animations through the internet, or buy discs at a very low price legally or illegally (Yang, 2006).[13] Television has become a less important medium especially for older consumers and fans who are net-savvy (Guo and Zhang, 2003, p. 35).[14]

A survey conducted by Guo Hong and Zhang Guo Liang in 2003 interviewed 1,060 adolescents, aged mainly between 10 to 22, from primary, secondary, high schools, and universities in Beijing and Shanghai. Over 80% of responders from each age group often or at least sometimes watched animation/cartoon (Guo and Zhang, 2003, p. 31).[15] They spent over one hour on watching animation/cartoon per week on average (Guo and Zhang, 2003, p. 35),[16] and preferred watching Japanese ones amongst all cartoons/animations regardless of their age (Guo and Zhang, 2003, p. 36).[17]

---

at http://big5.mofcom.gov.cn/gate/big5/tfs.mofcom.gov.cn/article/date/i/n/cp/200212/20021200058991.shtml.

[10] Beiiing Evening News, "Jiu Xiang Xin Gui Jin Qiu 9 Yue Qi Shi Xing, Huang Jin Shi Duan Jin Bo Jing Wai Dong Hua," dated 30 August 2006 in Xinhua News Agency [downloaded 23 January 2015], available at http://news.xinhuanet.com/politics/2006-08/30/content_5026353.htm.

[11] The State Administration of Press, Publication, Radio, Film and Television, "*Guang Dian Zong Ju Guan Yu Jia Qiang Dian Shi Dong Hua Pian Bo Chu Guan Li De Tong Zhi,*" dated 9 February 2008 [downloaded 14 May 2014], available at http://www.sarft.gov.cn/articles/2008/02/19/20080221111624750711.html.

[12] Meng Yang, "Zhuang Jia Cheng Ping Bi Jin Kou Dong Hua Bu Li Yu Guo Chan Dong Hua Zhi Zuo Fa Zhan," dated 9 June 2006 in The Mirror [downloaded 14 May 2014], available at http://news.163.com/06/0812/13/2OB258OE0001124J.html.

[13] *Ibid.*

[14] Hong Guo and Guo Liang Zhang, "Zhong Guo Qing Shao Nian Yu Dong Hua Chuan Bo De Shi Zheng Yan Jiu," *Journalism Quarterly* 4 (2003): 35.

[15] *Ibid.*, 31.

[16] *Ibid.*, 35.

[17] *Ibid.*, 36.

Another survey targeting young children under 13 years old was conducted by the official state media just before new restrictions on youth programming were issued in 2006. The news report showed that, 59% of the responding children enjoyed cartoon/animation programs the most among all TV programs, and 68% of them loved Japanese animations (The Beijing News, 2006).[18] In 2010, Jian Feng Liu received 850 questionnaire responses from young people aged from 11 to 24 years old in an investigation on the animation/cartoon industry market in mainland China. 53% of the responders often watched animations and only 7% of them never did (Liu, 2010, p. 134).[19] In general, those young people had 5 to 10 years' history of watching animations (Liu, 2010, pp. 134–135).[20] 55.7% of them favored Japanese animation most, and another 10% of them preferred both Japanese and Chinese works equally (Liu, 2010, p. 135).[21]

It is worth mentioning that no significant gender differences were reported in the above surveys; that is similar number of boys and girls loved Japanese animation across age groups. To sum up, Japanese animation is believed to take up around 60% of the animation/cartoon market in mainland China, even after the restrictions on broadcasting have been in place for 10 years (Liu, 2010, p. 134[22]; Zhang, 2009, p. 94[23]).

Japanese Manga

The story of print manga is less complicated. The passion expressed by Chinese fandom towards Japanese manga broke out spontaneously since the 1990s, and the government and official channels played a minor role in generating this phenomenon. According to the printed mass media, most classical Japanese manga works had pirated versions/copies circulating in China as early as the 1990s. Furthermore, because of pirated copies, readers also have access to the latest and most "heated" (Chinese youth

---

[18] The Beijing News, "Guang Dian Zong Ju Fa Bu Xin Gui."
[19] Jian Feng Liu, "Qing Shao Nian Dong Man Pian Hao Diao Cha Ji Qi Chan Ye Mo Shi Tan Tao," *Estate Observation* 2 (2010): 134.
[20] *Ibid.*, 134–135.
[21] *Ibid.*, 135.
[22] *Ibid.*, 134.
[23] Gen Qiang Zhang, "Yu Zhai Zu De San Chong Shen Fen," *China Youth Study* 3 (2009): 94.

fans' talk for "popular") new pieces in Japan since then. Those products are mostly illegal, and are distributed by small bookstores around schools or via the internet (Ifeng Reading, 2011).[24]

Though there is a lack of official distribution channels to access Japanese manga products in China, reading them is not an experience limited only to hardcore fans. Some surveys indicated that 92.2% of the adolescents believed that Japanese manga is influential to a certain degree on their popular cultural experiences, and nine out of 10 students admitted that they had experiences of watching manga during class time for more than 10 times in their lives (Liu, 2012, p. 224).[25]

It is worth mentioning that, even under the circumstances that pirated copies are already made available in the market since the 1990s, official versions of Japanese manga have remained best-selling among imported foreign manga/comics (Ifeng Reading, 2011).[26] It is said that Japanese manga make up nearly 80% of the manga/comic market in China (Chen, 2012, p. 70).[27]

Popularity and Distribution

The introduction of animation and manga through both authorized and illegal means in the last few decades has created a dedicated sizable Japanese animation and manga fandom in mainland China, within which a hardcore otaku community emerged. However, for a long time, it is widely believed that animation and manga are only targeted at children under 12 years old. Moreover, those popular culture products are considered as negative influences on adolescences and young adults, allegedly

---

[24] Ifeng Reading, "Ri Ben Man Hua Sui Hong Yin Jin Huo Li Tai Nan," dated 21 April 2011 in ifeng.com [downloaded 14 May 2014], available at http://book.ifeng.com/yeneizixun/special/tongnianduwu/wenzhang/detail_2011_04/21/5891010_0.shtml.

[25] Han Yu Liu, "Qian Xi Ri Ben Man Hua Dui Zhong Guo Qing Shao Nian De Ying Xiang," *Blooming Season* 6 (2012): 224.

[26] Ifeng Reading, "Ri Ben Man Hua Sui Hong Yin Jin Huo Li Tai Nan."

[27] Xi Chen, "Guan Zhu Cheng Zhang Zhi Lun Ri Ben Man Hua Dui Zhong Guo Qing Shao Nian De Ying Xiang," *Science & Technology Information* 2 (2012): 70.

distracting them from their school work (Wang, 2011, p. 60).[28] Therefore, manga fans in China used to conceal their communities from the general public and escape the glare of mass media. It was until the late 2000s, that mainstream media started to pay attention to the existence of those obsessive adolescent and young adult fans, related to the import of the word "*yuzhaizu* (御宅族)," a Chinese translation of the Japanese word "otaku" imported from Taiwan. Under the label of "*yuzhaizu*" or "*zhai* (宅)" for short, the group began to acquire the status of a deviant community in mainstream society.

The size and the locations of otakus in mainland China are unclear. There are only a few existing field research studies conducted on this topic and no large-scale surveys have been carried out by scholars that the author is aware of. Fortunately, several surveys have been conducted by the private sector and the otaku communities through the internet.

The *Anonymous Social Survey of ACG Fan* conducted yearly since 2011 by *bitinn.net* is one of the most influential ones. This survey was originally a market investigation commissioned by *Animate*, one of the major animation, manga/comic, and game (ACG for short)[29] retailers based in Japan. Though the exact word "otaku" was not used in its title, "ACG fan" is also a self-defined term used by some otakus to avoid definitional confusions of "*yuzhaizu*." It is certainly questionable whether an ordinary fan of manga or anime can be equated with a hardcore fan such as the otaku. To justify my citation, the word "*zhai*" was used to refer to responders for several times in questionnaire contents in this survey as well as the result report, and the questions listed are clearly targeting at obsessive consumers. Therefore, it could be understood as analogous to a survey of otakus nation-wide.

The questionnaires were circulated through major ACG theme websites, forums, and social network. Around 3,000 people responded to its 2011 and 2012 versions (Bitinn.net, 2011; Bitinn.net, 2012),[30] and 4,856

---

[28] Wei-jia Wang, "On the Cultural Differences Between China and Japan Through the Word 'Otaku'," *Journal of Hefei University* (*Social Science*) 28, no. 6 (2011): 60.

[29] ACG is the abbreviation of Japanese animation, manga/comic and game. "ACG Fan" refers to fans of the ACG culture as its literal meaning. Some otakus prefer to use it in some occasion to avoid negative impression and definition confusions of "*Yuzhaizu*."

[30] It was 3,513 responders in 2011 and 2,929 in 2012. Bitinn.net, "Wo Men Xin Zhong De Na Duo Hua — ACG Wei Lai Diao Cha Xiao Jie Yu Hou Ji," dated 9 April 2011 in the

valid replies were received within a week in 2013's survey (Bitinn.net, 2013).[31] According to those three reports, the responders from both genders were about equal in number (Bitinn.net, 2011; Bitinn.net, 2012; Bitinn.net, 2013).[32] The age distribution of the respondents was generally in the same range across reports. Most participants' age were from 16 to 27 years old and over 50% were aged from 19 to 24. Over 60% of responders were either full-time or part-time students (Bitinn.net, 2011; Bitinn.net, 2012; Bitinn.net, 2013).[33] The reports indicated that the conceptual ideas of being an otaku or ACG fan were formed during middle school years and this identity faded gradually after graduation. The reports also found that in the identity formation stage, university students were the main force of otaku groups and the most important consumers of the industry in mainland China (Bitinn.net, 2012).[34]

The report also estimated the extent of geographical distribution of otakus based on data collected. Besides Beijing, Shanghai, Guangzhou, which are the three most-developed cities in mainland China, their surrounding cities, the mega-cluster of Chengdu-Chongqing in Southwest China, and Wuhan-Changsha in South Central China, were also hot spots of otaku activities (Bitinn.net, 2012).[35] Furthermore, according to the

---

Bitinn.net, available at http://bitinn.net/7664/; Bitinn.net, "Dong Mian Chu Xing De Lu Ya — 2012 Nian Du <ACG Ai Hao Zhe Ni Ming She Hui Diao Cha Bao Gao>," dated 5 February 2012 in the Bitinn.net, available at http://bitinn.net/9166/.

[31] Bitinn.net, "Jin Bu De Bu Fa — 2013 Nian Du <ACG Ai Hao Zhe Ni Ming She Hui Diao Cha> Fen Xi Bao Gao," dated 26 April 2013 in the Bitinn.net website, available at http://bitinn.net/10225/.

[32] In 2011, the gender ratio of male and female is 40:60. It turned to 63:37 in 2012 and became 55:45 in 2013. The report writer believed the changes were caused by questionnaire design and the route of distribution. The actual ratio based on public impression inside the community and personal experiences would be proximally 55:45 for the whole otaku population. "ACG Wei Lai Diao Cha"; "2012 Nian Du ACG Ai Hao Zhe Ni Ming She Hui Diao Cha"; "2013 Nian Du ACG Ai Hao Zhe Ni Ming She Hui Diao Cha."

[33] It is a new demographic information required for the questionnaire since 2012. Therefore, there is no data available in 2011. "ACG Wei Lai Diao Cha"; "2012 Nian Du ACG Ai Hao Zhe Ni Ming She Hui Diao Cha"; "2013 Nian Du ACG Ai Hao Zhe Ni Ming She Hui Diao Cha."

[34] "2012 Nian Du ACG Ai HaoZhe Ni Ming She Hui Diao Cha."

[35] *Ibid.*

report in 2013, over 35% of the responders to the survey lived outside the above-mentioned areas in mainland China, and over 100 responders were living abroad at the time of the survey (Bitinn.net, 2013).[36] The activities and expenditures of otakus in China were investigated as well, which showed those responders were attending activities both online and offline and spending a certain amount of money on ACG-related products (Bitinn. net, 2013).[37]

Though these surveys were not constructed and analyzed under strict academic standards, the results do provide a general picture of the population distribution of otakus in mainland China.

Generally, it is widely believed that the rise of otaku culture first appeared among Chinese youths born after the 1980s (e.g. Dong and Gao, 2012, p. 2),[38] which is the first generation of fans who grew up in an environment with easy access to Japanese animation TV programs and pirated manga. Some researchers further claimed that the majority of self-identified members of the otaku community were those born in the 1980s and aged between 20 and 36 (an example of researchers who subscribed to this view is found in the work of Zhao, 2009, p. 235).[39] However, some believed that otakuism is only a temporary identity to university students who are afraid to enter the society as a grown-up and feel detached from the reality. Such identity would fade after they get a proper full-time job and start enjoying social life outside otaku activities (e.g. Li and Gu, 2010, pp. 204–205).[40] Either way, academics agreed that the number of otakus is considerable among university students in mainland China.

According to the latest national population census in 2010, there were over 38.8 million people aged from 15 to 34 years old nation-wide, and

---

[36]"2013 Nian Du ACG Ai HaoZhe Ni Ming She Hui Diao Cha."

[37]According to 2013's report, only 12.66% of the responders spent under RMB100 in 2012 for ACG related goods. Over 43% of participants spent over RMB1,000 a year, in which around 5% of them spent over RMB10,000 in 2012. "2013 Nian Du ACG Ai Hao Zhe Ni Ming She Hui Diao Cha."

[38]Yan Dong and Qing Gao, "Gao Xiao 'Yuzhaizu' Xin Li Jian Kang Fu Dao Chu Tan," *Ji Lin Jiao Yu* 4 (2012): 2.

[39]Si Zhao, "Qian Tan 'Yuzhaizu' Xian Xiang Ji Qi Xin Li Fen Xi," *The Science Education Article Collects* 12 (2009): 235.

[40]Zhi Li and Zheng Hu Gu, "Gao Xiao 'Yuzhaizu' Xin Li Tan Xi Ji 'Chu Zhai Zhi Dao'," *Data of Culture and Education* 17 (2010): 204–205.

nearly 3.3 million of them were receiving or had received at least a university education.[41] There were also another 3.8 million young people who were high school students at the time.[42] Therefore, based on the general impression obtained from public surveys and researchers' descriptions, the otaku community is a popular and sizable one with a pool of over 3 million (university educated and above only), or even 7 million people (high school students included).

The number might be over-estimated as there are less financially endowed areas (e.g. rural villages) which have limited access to television programming and the internet. But even after eliminating the rural population, there were still over 3 million young people who were receiving or had received at least a university education, with another 2.5 million high school students in 2010.[43] That is, around 25.8% of the adolescents and young adults aged from 15 to 34 who lived in towns and cities could have come under the influence of otaku culture.[44] The percentage might be even higher if we only consider major urban cities such as Beijing, Shanghai, and Guangzhou. There are also great numbers of students overseas who are active in the mainland Chinese otaku communities.

It is also worth mentioning that, with the emergence of otakus in public sphere, related large-scale events started to make their appearance in the public as well. In the category of "youth subculture major events" occurred in 2012, Japanese animation or manga-related events, such as cosplay contest or *dojinshi* fair, took up 16 out of a total of 40 events (Zhu, Yao and Zhao, 2013, pp. 301–305).[45]

It is safe to conclude that the popularity of otaku culture among young people is a phenomenon in mainland China and has become visible in

---

[41] Population Census Office under the State Council Department of Population and Employment Statistics, National Bureau of Statistics, *Tabulation on the 2010 Population Census of People's Republic of China* (Beijing: China Statistics Press, 2012), downloaded July 20, 2015, http://www.stats.gov.cn/tjsj/pcsj/rkpc/6rp/indexch.htm.

[42] *Ibid.*

[43] *Ibid.*

[44] *Ibid.*

[45] Wen Yu Zhu, Lu Yao and Yuan Zhao, "The Youth Sub-culture Major Events (2012)," in *Annual Report of Sub-cultural Studies in China*, ed. Z. H. Ma (Beijing: Tsinghua University Press, 2013), 301–305.

recent years. The identity of those self-identified members is an intriguing topic worth further exploring.

Literature Review

Though otakus are generally described as males between the ages of 18 and 40 years old (Abel and Kono, 2009, p. xv)[46] with the core consumers in this group aged around 30 to 40 years old in Japan (Azuma, 2009, p. 3),[47] the otaku culture still projects a youthful cultural imagery through its product contents (Azuma, 2009, p. 3).[48] In mainland China, the core consumers are younger than their counterparts in Japan. As mentioned before, the first generation of otaku culture consumers have just reached their 20s to 30s by now. As a result, besides to be considered as a subculture, otaku-ology is also considered an important youth culture in the academic field in mainland China (Ma, 2013, p. 1).[49] Therefore, before going into the details of otaku identity, I will first briefly review the important theories of subculture and youth culture studies.

Subcultural and Youth Cultural Theories

According to notable scholars in the field, the term "subculture" became a key concept in analyzing young members of deviant groups with unified dressing and acting style in early 20th century, a definition that was predominantly used by scholars from the Chicago School of academics in the subject area (Bennett and Kahn-Harris, 2004, p. 7).[50] Howard S. Becker (1964, p. 9)[51] came up with the concept of "labeling" to explain the formation

---

[46] Jonathan E. Abel and Shion Kono "Translator's Introduction" in *Otaku: Japan's Database Animals*, by Hiroki Azuma, trans. J. E. Abel and S. Kono (Minneapolis, MN: University of Minnesota Press, 2009), xv.

[47] Hiroki Azuma, *Otaku*, 3.

[48] *Ibid.*, 3.

[49] Zhong Hong Ma, "The Sub-cultural Study Strategies in China in 2012," in *Annual Report of Sub-cultural Studies in China*, ed. Z. H. Ma (Beijing: Tsinghua University Press, 2013), 1.

[50] Andy Bennett and Keith Kahn-Harris, "Introduction," in *After Subculture: Critical Studies in Contemporary Youth Culture*, eds. A. Bennett and K. Kahn-Harris (New York: Palgrave Macmillan, 2004), 7.

[51] Howard S. Becker, *Outsiders: Studies in the Sociology of Deviance* (New York: Free Press 1963), 9.

of identity for those subculture members. According to him, a society constructs its own norms by making rules and labeling those who fail to obey those rules as outsiders, while the existence of the subculture community provides a way of normalization for outsiders marginalized by mainstream society (1964, pp. 1–8).[52] Those who have been stigmatized are reinforced by their subculture labels, which means they would behave according to the rules of the subculture they belong in order to fit in.

Based on this conflict model, the Birmingham Centre for Contemporary Cultural Studies (CCCS) further developed a theoretical framework using field researches of juvenile delinquency in local communities of England during 1950s and 1970s. Young people in these studies were adopting subculture as a collective reaction towards social structural changes. On one hand, the affluence of the society encouraged consumerism amongst the upper income socio-economic classes of the society and then extended it into the working class. On the other hand, the hierarchy of a society, as well as its limited career opportunities for upward mobility, remained unchanged for lower socio-economic classes. As a result, youths from the working-class were facing a consumption culture in which they did not fit in socio-economically. Subculture had been employed as a form of reactionary resistance towards the cultural changes, as well as a re-creation of their identities (Bennett and Kahn-Harris, 2004, pp. 4–6).[53]

The theoretical framework raised by CCCS, as well as the concept of "subculture," were widely influential, but have been criticized by later scholars. Several criticisms which could help in the understanding of otaku identities will be reviewed in this writing. One criticism is that the enjoyment youths gained while consuming subculture has been overlooked by CCCS. George H. Lewis (1992, p. 141) believed those musical subcultural communities formed around common interests can be better classified as a "taste cultures."[54] It is the similar tastes and mutual understanding and appreciation of the contents that created the community.

---

[52] *Ibid.*, 1–18.

[53] Bennett and Kahn-Harris, "Introduction," 4–6.

[54] George H. Lewis, "Who Do You Love? The Dimensions of Musical Taste," in *Music and Communication*, 2nd *edition*, ed. J. Lull (London: Sage, 1987), 141.

According to Simon Frith (1983, pp. 219–220),[55] those young "stylists" of subculture would switch groups and alter their identities just for fun in their leisure time. That is, instead of concerning the symbolic meaning of a particular subcultural identity, the members might just follow the "fun" they could obtain. Similar to the observation made by Frith, Andy Bennett argues that the identity of members in a subculture community is temporal and floating, in that both their boundaries and memberships have changed over time (Bennett, 1999, p. 600).[56] In fact, he preferred to avoid the term "subculture" and use the conceptual "tribes" first raised by Michel Maffesoli, which focuses on the fluid nature of the culture groups (Bennett, 1999, pp. 599–600).[57]

However, those criticisms might not be applicable to all social contexts. For example, Hilary Pilkington investigated the fandom community of rock music, which is a well-developed subculture in post-Soviet modernizing Russia (2004, pp. 119–133).[58] He found that the identities of those Russian youths were predicated upon the symbolic meaning of the behavior and performance in appreciating the music rather than enjoying the music itself (2004, pp. 121–128).[59]

Besides the criticisms mentioned above, many other scholars, including Bennett, question the presumption of the relationship between subculture and working-class identity (1999, p. 602).[60] Based on empirical observation of an urban dance-club in England, he believed that instead of re-creating tradition, consumerism provides new self-constructed identities for youths to choose from (1999, p. 602).[61]

---

[55] Simon Frith, *Sound Effects: Youth, Leisure and the Politics of Rock* (London: Constable, 1983), 219–220.

[56] Bennett, "*Subcultures or Neo-tribes,*" 600.

[57] *Ibid.*, 599–600.

[58] Hilary Pilkington, "Youth Strategies for Glocal Living: Space, Power and Communication in Everyday Cultural Practice," in *After Subculture: Critical Studies in Contemporary Youth Culture*, eds. A. Bennett and K. Kahn-Harris (New York: Palgrave Macmillan, 2004), 119–133.

[59] *Ibid.*, 121–128.

[60] Andy Bennett, "Subcultures or Neo-tribes? Rethinking the relationship between youth, style and musical taste," *Sociology* 33, no. 3 (1999): 602.

[61] *Ibid.*, 602.

Furthermore, through researches done by CCCS and the following discussions focused on young people, some scholars noticed that the members of a subculture are not restricted to young people. When these young members grow up, some of them remain ardent consumers of the subculture and the products they offer. Instead of being only a passing stage in their lives, their subcultural identities became a part of their lifelong identities. Those researchers suggest that the cultural products the interest groups consumed form their "taste of mind," and continuing this consumption behavior provides them a sense of "youthfulness" (Bennett and Kahn-Harris, 2004, pp. 10–11).[62]

In summary, the Chicago school and CCCS emphasize the symbolic value and social/class identity behind the subculture group, while later scholars pay more attention to the actual meaning of the content for the youths and also notice the fluctuation and diversity of the identities amongst fan groups and same-interest groups.

Post-subcultural Theories

There are several other theories, which could be classified as "post-subculturalism," that should be mentioned for examining otakuism. "Lifestyle" is one of the terms that has been adopted by identity theories. According to John Fiske (1989, pp. 19–55)[63] the concept of lifestyle focuses on the creativity of consumers, whereby the products they consume are cultural resources for them. Sara Thornton believed that the construction of subcultural identities needs cultural resources, including ideological ones, provided by mass media (1995, p. 177).[64] She also raised the idea of "subcultural capital," which refers to both knowledge and merchandise gained through consumption (1995, p. 121).[65] Possessing rare and hard-to-access knowledge or commodities not only draws clear boundaries between the community and ordinary consumers but also increases the status of

---

[62] Bennet and Kahn-Harris, "Introduction," 10–11.

[63] John Fiske, *Understanding Popular Culture* (London: Routledge, 1989), 19–55.

[64] Sara Thornton, *Club Cultures: Music, Media and Subcultural Capital* (Cambridge: Polity Press, 1995), 177.

[65] *Ibid.*, 121.

more dedicated fans inside the community. This theoretical framework has been effectively applied to examine how certain subcultural interest groups produce and maintain their identities through consumption and fan communication, and their relationship with the mass media (e.g. Jancovich, 2002, pp. 309–322).[66]

Post-subcultural theories highly value the active role that fans play in maintaining their communities' interest in the subcultural products. Henry Jenkins perceived members of the fandom as initiative producers rather than passive receivers (1992, pp. 24–49).[67] He described fans using all kinds of tactics to "poach" the primary text in their own way rather than applying the coding system provided by producers or writers to understand the content (1992, pp. 26–36).[68] To him, passionate fans are exploring the cultural materials and looking for new materials for appropriation in their construction of fan narratives, as well as their discussions of contents and topics. He believed the fandom could build their new cultural community with their own systems of interpretations and worldviews and even create an artistic world which is independent from mass media's control (1992, pp. 37–49).[69]

Otaku Identity

At the very beginning, the word "otaku" is only a vague self-originated identity and a descriptive term originating from the otaku community. According to Toshio Okada, the co-founder and president of the famous animation production company Gainax and later an author and a social critic who is considered to be the spokesman of the community (Saito, 2011, pp. 13–14),[70] the likely origin of the word arose from the science

---

[66] Mark Jancovich, "Cult Fictions: Cult Movies, Subcultural Capital and The Production of Cultural Distinctions," *Cultural Studies* 16, no. 2 (2002): 309–322.

[67] Henry Jenkins, Textual *Poachers: Television fans and participatory culture* (New York: Routledge, 1992), 24–49.

[68] *Ibid.*, 26–36.

[69] *Ibid.*, 37–49.

[70] Tamaki Saito, *Beautiful Fighting Girl*, trans. J. K. Vincent and D. Lawson (Minneapolis, MN: University of Minnesota Press, 2011), 13–14.

fiction fans in Japan (1996, p. 9).[71] It was first used by a small group of creative producers who later created the animation *Super Dimension Fortress Macross* and the heroine and the hero in the story used the word "otaku" to address each other. When this work became a big hit, fans started to adopt the term "otaku" as a way to address each other within the science fiction fandom community.

Nevertheless, the term was adopted by the public media with a negative connotation during the 1980s and early 1990s in Japan. In 1983, Akio Nakamori, a media columnist, used the word "otaku" in the Japanese mass media for the first time and associated it with an image of unsociable and gloomy group of animation and science fiction fans who took up a large percentage of comic or manga readership (Yi and Wang, 2012, p. 37[72]; Saito, 2011, pp. 11–12).[73] In 1988 and 1989, Tsutomu Miyazaki, an obsessive animation fan, conducted a series of child kidnappings and murders. The word "otaku" was used as a keyword in Japanese news reports covering those criminal crimes and it then became an extremely negative term associated with a "perverted" male animation/manga mania (Eng, 2012, p. 89[74]; Yi and Wang, 2012, pp. 39–40[75]; Okada, 2009, p. 41).[76]

As a member of community, Okada recalled that in early 1990s otakus tried to justify and rationalize their manga/anime interests as something acceptable and tried to present themselves positively or at least normatively to the mass majority in mainstream society in Japan (2009, pp. 53–55).[77] From his point of view, otaku was a "label" which the mainstream society used to distinguish the outliers and the otaku identity emergence during the public discourse. Moreover, Okada believed that otaku should be proud of this identity because the otaku products inherit the traditional

---

[71] Toshio Okada, *Otaku-gaku Nyumon (Introduction to Otakuology)* (Tokyo: Ohta Publishing Company, 1996), 9.

[72] Qian Liang Yi and Ling Fei Wang, *Yuzhaizu: Er Ci Yuan Shi Jie De Mi Kuang* (Suzhou: Suzhou University Press, 2012), 37.

[73] Saito, *Beautiful Fighting Girl*, trans. Vincent and Lawson, 11–12.

[74] Eng, "Strategies of Engagement," 89.

[75] Yi and Wang, *Yuzhaizu*, 39–40.

[76] Toshio Okada, *Otaku Wa Sude Ni Shideiru*, trans. T. Pu (Taipei: China Times Publishing, 2009), 41.

[77] *Ibid.*, 53–55.

Japanese aesthetic (1996, pp. 75–76),[78] and the culture is the true successor of Japan's premodern Edo-period artisan's culture (1996, pp. 224–226)[79] unlike most other modern Japanese popular culture which are under western cultural influence (1996, pp. 219–224).[80] In short, Okada believed that otakus are the "heirs of the best of Japanese culture" (Vincent, 2011, p. xiv).[81]

It is clear that based on his own experience, Okada understood the formation of an otaku identity in the context of the normalization of certain unconventional traits as a form of resistance against the social stigma and a reaction to rebuild Japanese cultural identity. When the appeal of the culture and its products was mass produced and consumed by mainstream society just like other popular cultural products, Okada declared the death of otaku there and then. This is because he believed that, though the otaku community has overcome its most difficult time, it has also lost its unconventional traits and moral codes simultaneously (Okada, 2009, pp. 100–102).[82]

This seems to echo Becker's hypothesis of how "labeling" shapes a subcultural identity (1964, pp. 1–19)[83] and CCCS's idea of re-creation of ones' identities through subculture (Bennett and Kahn-Harris, 2004, pp. 4–6)[84] reviewed earlier in this chapter. However, besides being the heirs of the true Japanese culture, Okada also believed otakus, who are "exemplary postmodern subjects" (Vincent, 2011, p. xiv),[85] could better adapt to the highly informatization world (1996, pp. 40–41).[86] In his influential book *Introduction to Otakuology*, he defined otakus as those who are highly sensitive to visual images and have the ability to process rich visual information simultaneously (1996, pp. 10–27),[87] who can read beyond texts and

---

[78] Okada, *Otaku-gaku Nyumon*, 75–76.

[79] *Ibid.*, 224–226.

[80] *Ibid.*, 219–224.

[81] Keith Vincent "Translator's Introduction — Making It Real: Fiction, Desire, and the Queerness of the Beautiful Fighting Girl" in *Beautiful Fighting Girl*, by Saito Tamaki, trans. J. K. Vincent and D. Lawson (Minneapolis, MN: University of Minnesota Press, 2011), xiv.

[82] Okada, *Otaku Wa Sude Ni Shindeiru*, 100–102.

[83] Becker, *Outsiders*, 1–19.

[84] Bennett and Kahn-Harris, "Introduction," 4–6.

[85] Vincent, "Translator's Introduction", xiv.

[86] Okada, *Otaku-gaku Nyumon*, 40–41.

[87] *Ibid.*, 10–27.

associate and take references across media platforms and genes (1996, pp. 28–32),[88] and who are extremely motivated to collect information and gain knowledge related to their favorite pieces, and are passionate to explain or share them with others (1996, pp. 33–34).[89] Furthermore, he described otakus' three distinguishable characteristics as, the ability to discover beauty of otaku products from one's unique aesthetics, to analyze the products' quality as a professional creator, and to understand the worldview/philosophy behind the products and connect them to the reality (1996, pp. 80–87).[90] Based on this definition, besides passion, it is the visual sensitivity, the information gathering, processing, and analyzing ability, as well as the extreme familiarity of otaku products that distinguish otakus from general audiences and consumers of Japanese animation/manga related culture.

Though this definition of "otaku" is not universally accepted in the same way by scholars and researchers of the popular culture field in both Japan and other English-speaking countries, most definitions generally agree that the enjoyment gained from consuming the products is important or even essential to otaku identity. Tamaki Saito, a Japanese psychologist and expert in socially withdrawal youth (*hikikomori*), further claimed that personality traits, such as "fleeing from reality," "taking refuge in fiction," and "lacking common sense," which are associated with the denial of mainstream society and against "labeling," are not the "essential aspects" of otakuism (2011, p.17).[91]

Unlike some subculture groups which could be easily distinguished by customs, styles, or rituals/behaviors, otakus are more known for their interests in "computer technology" and qualities of "encyclopedic," "fetishistic," and possessing "knowledge of particular strains of visual culture" (Vincent, 2011, p. xiii),[92] They are described as "precocious children of post-modern consumerist society" (Vincent, 2011, p. xiii).[93] After comparing otakus to more obsessed fans in a more traditional sense such as maniacs, whose passion lies in collecting goods, Saito was convinced that

---

[88] *Ibid.*, 28–32.

[89] *Ibid.*, 33–34.

[90] *Ibid.*, 80–87.

[91] Saito, *Beautiful Fighting Girl*, trans. Vincent and Lawson, 17.

[92] Vincent, "Translator's Introduction," xiii.

[93] *Ibid*, xiii.

otaku is not equal to other fans' fetishes of animation/manga and other otaku products. He believed that the spending habits of the otakus are just performance of their passion, and the thing they really consume is fictional (2011, pp. 17–19).[94] In fact, the definition of otaku in Saito's opinion is one who can understand fictional reality and be aroused by pure fictional contents (2011, pp. 24–31).[95]

The post-modern characteristics of the otaku culture and its community have been studied by many researchers. Through observing the otaku community both in Japan and in some English-speaking countries, some scholars became interested in how those fans "poached" the cultural products of animation, manga, game, and peripheral industries, in the same manner as those motivated and creative hardcore fans that Jenkins described in his post-subcultural studies (Eng, 2012, p. 85).[96] Others paid more attention to the post-modern psychological traits and identity-building exhibited through their consumption products and consuming behavior.

Japanese scholar Hiroki Azuma (2009, pp. 25–29) paid a lot of attention to the psychological needs of otakus and believed that investigating the traits and context of their consumption could provide a better understanding of otaku identity. Through observing the Japanese otaku community closely, Azuma discovered two distinct post-modern otaku features: the importance otakus placed on fictional works, and their contributions to the boom of derivative works.[97] Azuma believed that their preference of fictional world over reality among otaku community is the result of malfunctioning mainstream values and standards of Japanese society (Azuma, 2009, pp. 26–29).[98] Instead of adopting the mainstream normative values, otakus construct a community focusing on human relationships as well as alternative values and standards through animation, manga and games (2009, pp. 26–27).[99] This statement seems to echo the theory of CCCS to a certain degree like Okada but Azuma further argues that the new identity built by the otakus is neither

---

[94] Saito, *Beautiful Fighting Girl*, trans. Vincent and Lawson, 17–19.

[95] *Ibid*, 24–31.

[96] Eng, "Strategies of Engagement," 85.

[97] Azuma, *Otaku*, 25–29.

[98] *Ibid.*, 26–29.

[99] *Ibid.*, 26–27.

a denial of mainstream society values nor a re-creation of an old existing cultural tradition. Rather, it is a new set of principles and philosophies, and it is constructed through consumption and interaction with the industry. Specifically, the enthusiasm of otakus towards derivative works plays a crucial role in the new identity-building (2009, p. 27).[100]

Derivative works, which are a collection of parodies of commercially manufactured animation, manga, and game, have become a significant part of otaku culture. Those works are sold "in form of fanzines, fan games, fan figures, and the like" in fairs, exhibitions, and internet (Azuma, 2009, p. 25).[101] The derivative work market is an important and unique part of otaku culture. Although the producers are mainly amateurs, many professionals also started their careers selling their self-produced goods in this community throughout the last few decades (Azuma, 2009, pp. 25–26).[102] In some cases, even professional authors would participate in the creation of derivative products for their own established commercialized works (Azuma, 2009, p. 26).[103] Azuma claimed that, because of the nature of contents that otakus consume, commercialized products and fan-produced derivative works have similar functions and serve the needs of otakus in a complementary way (2009, p. 26).[104] Through active participation in consuming and creating derivative works, otakus are empowered to establish their own value and worldview as a community.

In fact, interactions between hardcore fans (i.e. otakus) and the animation/manga/game industry function in a similar pattern. The commercially manufactured products create the fictional universe for their customers, and otakus enjoy the worldview/settings/systems shared among series/products.

During the late 20th century, Eiji Otsuka (1989, pp. 17–19), a Japanese critic noticed that the serialized animation, manga, and other goods are usually creations based on shared settings and storylines, which he refers to as the "grand narrative".[105] Based on his observation, instead of focusing on

---

[100] *Ibid.*, 27.

[101] *Ibid.*, 25.

[102] *Ibid.*, 25–26.

[103] *Ibid.*, 26.

[104] *Ibid.*, 26.

[105] Eiji Otsuka, *Monogatari Shohiron* (*Theory of Narrative Consumption*) (Tokyo: Shi-yo-sha, 1989), 17–19.

individual short stories, otakus are more interested in the grand narrative behind the products. He took famous animation series *Mobile Suit Gundam* as an example. The individual *Gundam*-related products, such as figurines, are merely a component of the Gundam universe. While buying individual products, otakus are actually consuming the products' socio-historical background, as well as norms, beliefs, and ideologies in it (1989, pp. 17–19).[106]

This echoes to the post-subcultural idea of "subcultural capital" (Thornton, 1995, p. 121)[107] that possessing information and knowledge about a certain product is as important, or even more important than purchasing or obtaining the product itself. Interpreting messages weaved into the stories is highly valued within the otaku community; it can even be the threshold to differentiate the truly expert from the general fans.

Around the turn of the century, Azuma (2009, pp. 35–36) updated Otsuka's observation, pointing out a generational change that has taken place within the otaku community.[108] When the shift from a modern to post-modern worldview in the social and cultural contexts took place, desire for a single and complete worldview and ideology declined among the audiences in 1990s in Japan (Azuma, 2009, p. 36).[109] Inspired by the success of the animation *Neon Genesis Evangelion* and its derivative works, the otaku industry and the community altered their preferences dramatically. A set of widely applied character settings, i.e. *moe* elements, became the new shared value across products that otakus of the late 1990s sought after. That is, a database of knowledge regarding to *moe* gradually replaced the "grand narrative," and character settings alone carried symbolic meanings in the anime/manga/game works (Azuma, 2009, pp. 39–47).[110] To further elaborate this shift in fandom interactional model, Azuma used the *Neon Genesis Evangelion* as a case study. Unlike the *Gundam* series, no sequels based on the setting of the *Evangelion* world with new characters or new robots were produced. In its movie version, the production team even changed the worldview, backdrop and content of the work. Instead, amongst the large

---

[106] *Ibid.*, 17–19.
[107] Thornton, *Club Cultures,* 121.
[108] Azuma, *Otaku,* 35–36.
[109] *Ibid.*, 36.
[110] *Ibid.*, 39–47.

variety of derivative products found on the market, both commercially produced and those created by fans, are disparate stories of various characters of *Evangelion* living in completely different worlds and universes. It is the characters themselves, rather than the world they live in, that attract the otaku audiences (Azuma, 2009, pp. 36–38).[111] Azuma (2009, pp. 31–33)[112] called this element driven model of consumption a "double-layer model," and he stressed that otakus are sensitive to the double-layer structure of the products. Together with the development of a multimedia approach, which refers to creating projects across different medias, the industry even began to create stories based on elaborate character settings (Azuma, 2009, p. 48).[113] Therefore, the knowledge, the familiarity and the sensitivity to the features, concepts and elements (e.g. *moe* elements) related to all aspects of the works and their production process gradually replaced the "grand narratives" and became valuable "subcultural capital."

Several years later, Tsunehiro Uno (2008, pp. 1–20)[114] challenged Azuma's theory. Through examining influential cultural products in the 2000s, he believed that besides features like *moe*, consumers in the new century (in this case, the otakus) still dwell into the deeper implied meanings and underlying messages found in small bits of narratives embedded within the popular cultural products themselves. Although they (the consumers in the 21st century) no longer believe in the existence of a unified "grand narrative," instead, the subjective, diverse, and personal views and values of each individual character within the story (and the stories/narratives behind each of them) attract their interests.[115] In this case, again, it is the familiarity, the knowledge and the interpretations related to the products that otaku consumers valued are the most important and key to understanding the otaku identity.

Communities outside Japan were found to share some similar fan club codes and patterns of interaction as well. Lawrence Eng, for instance, studied the otaku communities in US and highlighted three ethical codes

---

[111] *Ibid.*, 36–38.

[112] *Ibid.*, 31–33.

[113] *Ibid.*, 48.

[114] Tsunehiro Uno, *Zeronendai no Sozoryoku* (Tokyo: Hayakawa Shobo, 2008), 1–20.

[115] *Ibid.*, 1–20.

amongst the otaku fandom from his own experiences as an otaku (2012, pp. 97–101).[116]

First of all, he argues that information is essential (2012, pp. 97–99).[117] Possessing content-based knowledge positively upgrades one's status within the community. That is, the more a fan knows, the more respectable he/she becomes. Information is their main source of commodity in the US otaku community.

Second, appropriation is an effective strategy for "information management, identity reconstruction, and resistance" (Eng, 2012, p. 99).[118] Eng found that the US otakus, who mostly belong to the middle class, resisted official mainstream channels and "marginalized themselves" when it came to promoting, consuming and distributing otaku products as well as their creations. Building their own community gave them power to control their own consumption when making decisions about price and value of the merchandise, and consuming products not created for US audiences, products not generally accepted in their social contexts (especially, e.g. sexual elements in the storyline), or contents on sensitive gender related issues (e.g. male otaku consuming cute and girly animations). Performing and carrying out appropriation also allowed them to construct their own characters' universes through creating and self-publishing derivative works (Eng, 2012, pp. 99–100).[119]

The third ethical feature related to otaku operating norms that Eng mentioned is about networking (2012, pp. 100–101).[120] He claimed that since the information is essential for otakus, their community could not survive without networks in either the real or virtual/online worlds, which is a feature that distinguishes it from other subculture communities in US (2012, p. 101).[121]

The similar pattern of fan-related interactions within otaku community was also observed in Australia. Craig J. Norris recalled common

---

[116] Eng, "Strategies of Engagement," 97–101.

[117] *Ibid.*, 97–99.

[118] *Ibid.*, 99.

[119] *Ibid.*, 99–100.

[120] *Ibid.*, 100–101.

[121] *Ibid.*, 101.

activities including screening, discussion, producing derivative products, and so on with other community members in Australia (2013, p. 1)[122] similar to Eng's description in US (2012, p. 87).[123]

Not surprisingly, in all these locations, the localization of otaku identities is a major topic of interest. Local impressions and images associated with the word "otaku" outside Japan can reveal a lot about otaku-ism all over the world. Generally speaking, the moral panic triggered by the Miyazaki incident did not have much impact abroad. Okada's definition and description of "otaku" in the 1990s are very influential until today in the English-speaking circles. In those countries, "otakus" usually refer to Japanese animation/manga fans without positive or negative connotations (e.g. Eng, 2012, p. 92[124]; Norris, 2003, p. 3[125]). But in negotiating complicated globalization and localization processes, various images of "otaku" and the definitions and usages of this term generate substantial debate within the anime/manga fandom communities.

According to Eng (2012, p. 92),[126] one of the most important origins of the term "otaku" within the US fandom community is the imported *Otaku no Video*, an OAV[127] produced by Gainax and written by Okada himself. Though, it is widely used within the popular cultural fandom community as a form of "self-identification," it sometimes refers to loud fans who invade others' personal space promoting otaku interests without considering others' feeling (Eng, 2012, p. 92).[128]

According to Norris, the otaku image in Australia is related to the general sci-fi (science fiction) fans who enjoy oriental spirituality and "dangerous sexuality" of animation and manga, something quite different from otaku culture he experienced in Japan (Norris, 2003, p. 3).[129] When observing that western fans are consuming "Japaneseness" found in animation and

---

[122] Craig J. Norris, "The Cross-Cultural Appropriation of *Manga* and *Anime* in Australia" (PhD Diss., University of Western Sydney, 2003), 1.

[123] Eng, "Strategies of Engagement", 87.

[124] *Ibid.*, 92.

[125] Norris, *The Cross-Cultural Appropriation*, 3.

[126] Eng, "Strategies of Engagement," 92.

[127] OAV stands for Original Animated Video.

[128] Eng, "Strategies of Engagement," 92.

[129] Norris, *The Cross-Cultural Appropriation*, 3.

manga, Norris noted that the appreciation of oriental aesthetics and a sense of the Oriental mystique (the "othering" of unfamiliar culture) is an important foundation for identity-building (2013, pp. 8–27).[130]

In summary, though the term "otaku" is used as a label to distinguish obsessive fans of a particular form of Japanese subculture from mainstream by the society, the term has been used as self-identification by fans both in Japan and in some English-speaking countries. Otaku culture is believed to be unconventional with post-modern feature/characteristics that differ from mainstream. Instead of the personality traits such as unsociable and obsessive behavior highlighted by the mass media and general public perceptions of otakus, the cultural consumption is considered as one of the essential sources of influence of the otaku identity by many researchers. The fans' emphasis on information, knowledge and familiarity with otaku materials, visual sensitivity and analytical ability related to otaku products were observed both inside and outside Japan. During the processes of globalization and localization of Japanese popular cultural products, especially for fans outside of Japan, the construction and maintenance of otaku identity is mostly an initiative shaped by unofficial networks inside the fandom community.

Reviews of Chinese-language Publicly Available Textual Documents and Literatures

Compared to the prevalence of existing literatures focusing on the subject of otaku in Japan, the US, and some other western countries, the study of this community is a rather new field in the mainland Chinese academic world. The concept of "otaku" appeared in academic journals mainly after it started to attract the attention of Chinese mass media. Therefore, I will review both academic literatures and publicly available textual documents (mainly newspapers and magazines) related to otakus in the Chinese context.

Media Perspectives of Otaku-ism

Media materials serve as important empirical data and an addition to fieldwork research by Chinese researchers. According to some scholars based

---

[130] *Ibid.*, 8–27.

in China (e.g. Li and Gu, 2010, pp. 204–205),[131] the first influential and widely cited stereotypical image of otaku portrayed by the mainstream media in mainland China is found in a news report published in the *Southern Metropolis Daily*[132] in 2008. The article described an 18-year-old boy who only enjoyed staying at home, watching animation and manga, reading books, or listening to music on his own outside of school (Wang, 2008).[133] According to the writer, the boy spoke in manga terminologies and vocabularies which are quite different from daily language used by his peers (Wang, 2008).[134] Contrary to the active consumption of animation and manga, he showed little interest in reality and routine daily activities and was poor in coping with basic living functions (like taking transportation or buying groceries). Moreover, instead of hanging out with his classmates after school, he spent considerable time chatting with fellows who led a similar lifestyle in consuming anime/manga products through internet after school. The writer of the article noted that there are more and more youths like this profiled boy in Guangzhou, and they called themselves "*yuzhaizu*," a concept borrowed from Japan. With no further details and references provided, the writer concluded subjectively that these youths are spoiled children, born after the implementation of the one child policy, who could not deal with the real life frustration and escape into a virtual life (Wang, 2008).[135]

A few days later, in response to this news story, the social investigation center of *China Youth Daily*[136] started a joint public survey with the

---

[131] Li and Gu, "Gao Xiao '*Yuzhaizu*' Xin Li Tan Xi Ji 'Chu Zhai Zhi Dao'," 204–205.

[132] *Southern Metropolis Daily* is one of the most influential Chinese newspapers based in Guangzhou province. According to *the surveillance report of newspaper competitiveness nationwide*, which was conducted by General Administration of Press and Publication of China in 2007, *Southern Metropolis Daily* ranked top 20 from 2004 to 2007 in the genre of evening paper and metro news. It was top in competitiveness nationwide in 2006 and 2007. Media Research Center of State Administration of Press, Publication, Radio, Film and Television of People's Republic of China, "Zhong Guo Bao Ye Jing Zheng Li Bao Gao (2007)," *China Newspaper Industry* 1 (2008), downloaded May 14, 2013. Available at http://paper.people.com.cn/zgby/html/2008-01/01/content_44588773.htm.

[133] Wang Ling, "Guang Zhou Chu Xian '*Yuzhaizu*' Qing Shao Nian," dated 13 March 2008 in *Southern Metropolis Daily*.

[134] *Ibid.*

[135] *Ibid.*

[136] *China Youth Daily* is an official newspaper held by the Communist Youth League of China.

news center of sina.com about "*yuzhaizu*" (2008).[137] 4,610 people participated in the survey in less than two weeks, and 56.9% of them had encountered otakus before at least at one point in their lives. Interestingly, 40.5% of the responders thought they might become an otaku before 40 years old (2008).[138] The survey also enquired its responders' opinion of otaku-ism. The result showed that though nearly half of the interviewees were worried about this "unhealthy way of life," over 30% of the responders thought its popularity was "understandable" for youths suffering from high social pressure, and nearly 40% considered otaku-ism a lifestyle choice which should not be judged by others (Wu, 2008).[139]

The discussion of "*yuzhaizu*" shortly became a hit topic in mass media. One magazine included the term "*yuzhaizu*" in its special topic *2008 Annual Fashion Dictionary* as one of the six "hot words" of the year (Ma, 2008, p. 25).[140] In the third edition of Chinese-English Dictionary edited by Wu, the terms "otaku" and "otaku girl" were included (Shanghai Translation Publishing House).[141]

The two influential news articles reviewed above triggered a wide range of discussion that can broadly represent two typical media perceptions towards otaku-ism. Otakus were either mentioned as a group of socially dysfunctional teenagers who "escaped" from the real world into the virtual world, or portrayed in a more neutral way as youths who chose to live a life heavily dependent on the internet and enjoy staying at home.

However, the obsession in consuming Japanese animation and manga, which is a fundamental feature found in the Japanese definition of otaku-ism,

---

[137] Sina.com, "Zhong Qing Bao Diao Cha: Ni You 'Yuzhai' Qing Xiang Ma," in sina.com [downloaded 14 May 2014], available at http://news.sina.com.cn/c/2008-03-18/145915173905.shtml.

[138] Sina.com, "Ni You 'Yuzhai' Qing Xiang Ma," downloaded May 14, 2014, available at http://survey.news.sina.com.cn/voteresult.php?pid=22631.

[139] Yan Wu, "Zhai Qing, Zhong Guo Shan Xian Men Ju Yi Zu," dated 31 March 2008 in China Youth Daily [downloaded 14 May 2014], available http://zqb.cyol.com/content/2008–03/31/content_2124101.htm.

[140] Ke Ma, "2008 Annual Fashion Dictionary," *Golden Age* 12 (2008): 25.

[141] "Publication: 'The Chinese-English Dictionary (Third Edition)'," Shanghai Translation Publishing House, downloaded Mar 14, 2014, available at http://www.yiwen.com.cn/news_detail.asp?cid=8&T_id=1252&Top_id=22.

has been overlooked in the narrative. Except in a few in-depth interviews (e.g. Wang, 2007, p. 22),[142] "*yuzhaizu*" tended to be roughly equated with "people who do not like going out" by mass media and general public (Wu, 2008).[143] This public understanding of otaku-ism is influenced by both media products and the direct literal interpretation of the word, for Japanese character "otaku" also means "your home" in Chinese as mentioned before.

With widespread coverage and discussions in public spaces, it is reasonable to believe that the identity of otaku will be reinforced, adopted, or resisted by the otakus in mainland China. The importance of mass media and general public has been supported by my empirical data, which I would discuss later.

Otaku Studies in Mainland China

As mentioned before, otaku studies appeared in mainland China after the term's popular use in the mass media. Some researchers claimed that the usage of the term "otaku" in the mass media of mainland China can be traced back to 2007, though no detailed evidence was provided to substantiate this claim (e.g. Li, 2012, pp. 102–108[144]; Wang, 2011, p. 32[145]; Wang, 2011, pp. 57–60[146]). Many others cited the news and/or the public survey mentioned above as the origins and evidence of the existence of an otaku community (Li and Gu, 2010, pp. 204–205[147]; Zhang, 2009, pp. 92–95[148]; Wang and Gu, 2008, pp. 41–44[149]; Zhao, 2009, pp. 235–237[150] are some of the earlier works that emerged during this period). Up till then, little

---

[142] Wei Wang, "ACG Mei You Na Me Fu Qian," *Dajiang Weekly* 12 (2007): 21.

[143] Wu, "Zhai Qing, Zhong Guo Shan Xian Men Ju Yi Zu."

[144] Yi Li, "The Development of the Word 'Otaku' in the Background of ACG Culture," *Japanese Studies and Research* 1 (2012): 102–108.

[145] Mai Qiao Wang, "Pan Dian 'Zhai' De Xin Yu Yi," *Shan Xi Jiao Yu: Gao Jiao Ban* 11 (2012): 32.

[146] Wang, "On the Cultural Differences Between China and Japan," 57–60.

[147] Li and Gu, "Gao Xiao 'Yuzhaizu'," 204–205.

[148] Zhang "'Yu Zhai Zu' De San Chong Shen Fen," 92–95.

[149] Jing Wang and Xiao Chen Gu, "'Yuzhaizu' Xian Xiang — Xin Yi Dai Mei Jie Yi Cun Zheng," *Contemporary Communications* 5 (2008): 41–44.

[150] Zhao, "Qian Tan 'Yuzhaizu'," 235–237.

covered in academic studies were found in mainland China before the mid-2000s.

Through a review of some existing literatures, I noted that, besides animation/manga industry studies and studies of specific customs and fashion trends (mostly those found in cosplay), two subject matters of interest for studies on otakus and their culture in mainland China were found, (1) the origin and semantic changes related to the word "otaku" in Chinese characters; (2) contributing social factors responsible for the rise of otaku-ism, and its impact on young generations of Chinese, especially amongst university students. Some studies go further to suggest possible solutions and countermeasures to arrest the trends.

Since the Chinese government promotes ideological campaigns and official propaganda materials which has a strong influence over intellectuals' work, many researchers, especially those from the field of education or with a membership of the *Communist Youth League*, have adopted a conflict model to understand youth cultural trends such as otaku-ism (Ma, 2013, p. 15).[151] The Birmingham school of thought (CCCS) in this area, for example, is one of the most utilized theoretical framework of analysis discernible from my Chinese-language literature review on this subject area. Under its framework, otaku culture is explained as a form of resistance to mainstream culture. A general (perhaps reductionist) understanding of those scholars is that the term "otaku" represents a certain segment of the young generation who have a poor ability to cope with reality.

Influenced by the Chinese mass media and the understanding of subculture as resistance and rebelliousness, many scholars associate otaku-ism with traits such as enjoying staying at home alone and lack of interest and ability in communication with others, in general non-sociable. Some researchers also add another criteria in defining otaku-ism which is having an obsession with a hobby related to Japanese popular culture. It is interesting that although many Chinese scholars have shown tolerance for otakus' lifestyle preferences, or even evolved a certain degree of understanding and respect for otaku-ism, being an otaku is still considered as a problematic way of life or an abnormal psychological status compared to

---

[151] Zhong Hong Ma, "The Sub-cultural Study Strategies in China in 2012," 15.

the mainstream members of society (e.g. Zhang, 2011, pp. 81–86[152]; Li and Gu, 2010, pp. 204–205[153]; Zhao, 2009, pp. 235–237[154]). Researchers, especially those in education-related fields, are concerned that such lifestyle would affect the personal development of the students as well as their performance in daily activities, especially since otaku-ism is becoming recognized as a passing phase of teenage youth. It is suggested that family, society, and school should work together which could "provide consultations" and "fix the problem" of otaku-ism (e.g. Zhang, 2011, pp. 81–86[155]; Li and Gu, 2010, pp. 204–205[156]; Zhao, 2009, pp. 235–237[157]). In short, the belief is that, with more attention, guidance and control from the responsible parties, young people will return to mainstream culture and eventually lead a conventional life.

However, in contemporary mainland China, it is somewhat challenging to identify what mainstream culture is and its relationship with other subcultures. Though official ideology and propaganda campaigns promoted by the government should be defined as "mainstream" culture, it has little real appeal for young people. The state-promoted "mainstream" culture is in danger of being marginalized and shunned by China's youths (e.g. Li, 2011, p. 297).[158] Ironically, it is the unofficial foreign cultures that are enjoying popularity amongst youths and are showing greater potential and promise of sustainability.

In fact, according to scholars who subscribe to post-modern theories, with the proliferation of internet access since 1997, youths enjoy access to a large variety of local and foreign popular culture products available on the internet freely in mainland China (Gu and Chen, 2013, pp. 279–280).[159]

---

[152] Jie Zhang, "Psychological Inquiry about 'Otaku Culture' in College Student," *She Hui Xin Li Xue* 123–124, no. 5–6 (2011): 81–86.

[153] Li and Gu, "Gao Xiao '*Yuzhaizu*'," 204–205.

[154] Zhao, "Qian Tan 'Yuzhaizu'," 235–237.

[155] Zhang, "Psychological Inquiry about 'Otaku Culture' in College Student": 81–86.

[156] Li and Gu, "Gao Xiao '*Yuzhaizu*'," 204–205.

[157] Zhao, "Qian Tan 'Yuzhaizu'," 235–237.

[158] Huan Yuan Li, "Dui Dang Dai Zhong Guo Zhu Liu Wen Hua Jian She De Li Lun Si Kao," *Charming China* 5 (2011): 297.

[159] Yi Zhou Gu and Yi Chen, "Qing Nian Ya Wen Hua Re Dian Sao Miao," in *Annual Report of Sub-cultural Studies in China*, ed. Z. H. Ma (Beijing: Tsinghua University Press, 2013), 279–280.

Foreign popular cultures, such as Japanese ACG products, drama series from US and Korea, have been consumed on a daily basis (Gu and Chen, 2013, pp. 279–280).[160] As a result, the younger generation does not struggle with values and norms of their older generations as it used to be (that is, they no longer negotiate their worldviews and beliefs with their older generation). They construct their own vocabularies, cultural practices, and philosophies. While talking about the relationship with their older generations or cultural traditions, instead of "next generation" they perceive themselves as "another kind of human being" (Gu and Chen, 2013, p. 279).[161]

This interpretation of subcultural identity resembles the identities of the third generational otaku raised by Azuma reviewed earlier. But unlike the relationship between otaku culture and Japanese youth consumers, otaku culture to the Chinese is not a local subculture. The origins of new fan-created subculture in China have its root and genesis in foreign practices that were gradually imported into China.

Concerns about foreign cultural influence through anime, manga, and games have also been raised by the nationalistic segments of the Chinese society. For example, after comparing the differences between Japanese and Chinese otaku-ism in terms of their social, cultural, and personality similarities and differences, Wei-jia Wang (2011, pp. 57–60)[162] held a rather neutral attitude towards otaku-ism. He believed that the popularity of otaku-ism in China is an inevitable outcome of social development (increasing affluence, attraction to foreign products, availability of digital technologies, etc.). He also believed that understanding otaku products provides a doorway to understanding contemporary Japan. However, he still reminded readers to be very conscious about otaku-ism's cultural implications and possible cultural invasion as a foreign-originated soft power. Xin Lan Wu is another example, as she spent a whole chapter to discuss the negative impact and possible dangers of Japanese culture popularity in her research on Japanese animations' cultural influence in

---

[160] *Ibid.*, 279–280.

[161] *Ibid.*, 279.

[162] Wang, "On the Cultural Differences Between China and Japan," 57–60.

mainland China (2012, pp. 195–223).[163] Furthermore, related to the problems and issues found in the socio-historical relationship between China and Japan, Gen Qiang Zhang (2009, pp. 92–95) directly accused otaku subculture of being a twisted worldview and distorted cultural values and influences.[164]

Based on my literature review, most observation studies were not conducted from the perspective of an otaku. The research studies also perceived otakus as a social "problem," and focused on the severity of this social "problem" and how mainstream society can fix such "problem," so as to undermine its influence and hinder its cultural proliferation.

Moreover, while discussing the content of otaku culture, most researchers mainly concentrated on visual and aesthetics features or themes found in Japanese popular cultural products. The purpose of doing so is to encourage Chinese creators to borrow positive features to improve their own products' popularity and receptivity amongst young consumers, and to serve as learning models for Chinese animation/manga companies to establish their own industry by emulating best practices.

Therefore, since the essence of otaku identity formation is believed to be based on enjoyment in consuming otaku products, it is nearly impossible to study and compare the otakus in mainland China by using existing literatures from Japan and aboard, and secondary sources such as Chinese newspapers, magazines and academic writings. Firsthand data is required.

Debating the Definition of "Otaku"

Before starting my own field research, the definition of "otaku" in Chinese context used in this chapter needs to be further clarified. As reviewed in earlier sections, the definition of "otaku" is different and controversial in Japan and English-speaking countries around the world. The use of the term "otaku" has localized in different settings (including in China) even though with the increasing popularity of Japanese popular culture

---

[163] Xin Lan Wu, *Cunzai Yu Ganzhi — Riben Dongman Zai Zhongguo De Kuawenhua Yingxiang* (Beijing: Intellectual Property Publishing House, 2012), 195–223.

[164] Zhang, "'Yu Zhai Zu' De San Chong Shen Fen," 92–95.

otakuism has been a globalized phenomenon. This is a development that resonates with the fandom situation in mainland China.

Most Chinese academic journals reviewed in this chapter debated the definitions and descriptions of the term raised by Okada in *Introduction to Otakuology* (probably the main Japanese publication referenced for the definition of otaku-ism in the context of Japan), although some other scholars have criticized his definition as being too idealistic with a tendency to glamorize the otaku community (e.g. Yi and Wang, 2012, pp. 56–60).[165] The undesirable otaku images described by Nakamori, as reviewed earlier, have also been mentioned by some journals as a counterbalancing alternative perspective to Okada's point of view. Besides, there is a very important source of a stereotypical imagery/description of otakus for general public, media, and even some academics in mainland China, as shown in the image portrayed by a Japanese TV series *Densha Otoko*.

Densha Otoko, and its associated novel and movie franchises became a big hit in 2005. It is a romance-comedy telling the story about how an otaku successfully dates a beautiful woman and becomes her boyfriend in the end with the help of the otaku societies. The hero of the story, the otaku, is portrayed as a geek who is timid and unsociable, but cute and with a kind heart (Yi and Wang, 2012, pp. 42–43).[166] According to scholars in this subject area, the popularity of *Densha Otoko* outside of Japan, especially in Taiwan, is the most important factor for popularizing the word "otaku" in the Chinese mass media. It is widely believed amongst academics in the popular culture field that the Chinese word "*yuzhaizu*" or "*zhai*" for short, as a translation of Japanese word "otaku," was utilized by the Taiwanese media in 2003 (e.g. Li, 2012, pp. 102–108[167]; Wang, 2011, p. 32[168]; Wang, 2011, pp. 57–60[169]). With *Densha Otoko*'s success, "otaku" became a hot topic in the Taiwanese mass media around 2005 and the word was subsequently adopted extensively by the mass media in mainland

---

[165] Yi and Wang, *Yuzhaizu*, 56–60.

[166] *Ibid.*, 42–43.

[167] Yi Li, "The Development of the Word 'Otaku'," 102–108.

[168] Wang, "Pan Dian 'Zhai' De Xin Yu Yi," 32.

[169] Wang, "On the Cultural Differences Between China and Japan," 57–60.

China (e.g. Wang, 2011, pp. 57-60[170]; Li, 2009, pp. 102-105[171]). It is not clear when the word was imported into mainland China's vocabulary in daily conversations, but a generally accepted fact was that it was first used by young netizens (e.g. Li, 2012, pp. 102-108[172]; Wang, 2011, p. 32[173]; Wang, 2011, pp. 57-60[174]).

It is worth noticing that though there are scenes of the otakus carrying out normal routine activities like watching and discussing animation/manga with friends or visiting a maid cafe in *Densha Otoku*'s movies and TV series, the anti-social aspects of otaku-ism like social dysfunction in interpersonal communication have been emphasized. In fact, the hero's lack of communication skills is the essential plot of the storyline. Therefore, as one of the most important references of "otaku" images for the Chinese-speaking audiences, *Densha Otoko* is one of the major sources of popular cultural products which causes the misinterpretation of "otakus" as persons who lack communication skills and are socially dysfunctional by the general public and mass media, becoming a stereotypical imagery that further influences academic thinking in China.

As mentioned in the last section, one group of scholars was interested in semantic changes of otaku in the Chinese context. Some of them believed that the word "otaku," as well as otaku culture, have been localized and developed into a very different type of culture in mainland China. Wang (2011, pp. 57-60)[175] claimed that, compared to Japanese otakus, Chinese otaku individuals do not display certain characteristics that are widely prevalent in otaku communities in other parts of the world, such as possessing proficiency in knowledge about ACG subcultural trends. Instead, two outstanding characteristics of Chinese otakus are their heavy dependence on the internet, and their desire to escape from studying and finding

---

[170] *Ibid.*, 57–60.

[171] Wei Li, "A New Interpretation of 'Zhai'," *Journal of Shanxi Normal University* 26, no. 3 (2009):112–115.

[172] Li, "The Development of the Word 'Otaku'," 102–108.

[173] Wang, "Pan Dian 'Zhai' De Xin Yu Yi," 32.

[174] Wang, "On the Cultural Differences Between China and Japan," 57–60.

[175] *Ibid.*, 57–60.

a job after graduation. Similarly, Lan Lan Gao (2010, pp. 66–71)[176] believed that, when talking about the word "*zhai*" in Chinese, it is no longer equated with the meaning of the Japanese "otaku" in the strict sense of the word, though it started as a direct translation initially. Rather, "*zhai*" refers to "homeboy" in mainland China nowadays. Yi Li (2012, pp. 102–108)[177] listed several commonly used applications and nuances of the word "otaku" in the mainland China context. One refers to people who do not like to go out in their leisure time.[178] Another characterizes people who give up finding a job and getting a career after graduation and just stay at home.[179] Other interpretations include people who have no interest in the real world and are obsessed by animation, manga, game, photography, TV drama, movie, novel, or *moe* culture; or people who are so engrossed with using and playing with technological gadgets that they ignore the human communication and daily social interactions.

However, all these discussions and debates were based on the contextual usage of the word "otaku" in conversations in the general public and the writings of the mass media. The understanding of the word "otaku" in Chinese-speaking fandom in mainland China is possibly quite different. According to members of fandom in Taiwan, the concept of "otaku" attracted the attention of Chinese-speaking otaku communities and triggered off a heated discussion in the early 1990s (Zero, 2009, pp. 20–21).[180] From these discussions, "*yuzhaizu*", as the Chinese translation of "otaku" was developed and accepted amongst fans at that time in Taiwan. Adding to this process of originating a new term, Okada's *Introduction to Otakuology* was translated by fans and disseminated extensively through the Chinese BBS in both Taiwan and mainland China since the late 1990s

---

[176] Lan Lan Gao, "'Otaku' in Japan = 'Zhainan/Zhainv' in China?," *Journal of Legends and Biographies* 1 (2010): 66–71.

[177] Li, "The Development of the Word 'Otaku'," 102–108.

[178] It is also called "*jialidun*" in Chinese, which is a term more close to Japanese word "*hikigomori*."

[179] Those young people are also called *NEET* in Japanese and other English speaking countries, which stands for "Not in Employment, Education or Training."

[180] Zero, "Tai Wan Zhai Zen Me Ren Shi 'Otaku' De?" in *Tai Wan Zhai Qi Shi Lu*, ed. A Xiu Lo Nan Jue (Taipei: Qin Lue Di Qiu Zhuan An Xiao Zu, 2009), 20–21.

(Zero, 2009, pp. 20–21).[181] Therefore, for fans in mainland China, especially those who were active in otaku community before the term of "*yuzhaizu*" or "*zhai*" was over-used by the mass media, the definition raised by Okada should be heard or even well known. It is reasonable to believe that the word "*yuzhaizu*" and Japanese word "otaku" have been both used within the fandom before the mid-2000s when the mass media and academics started to use them. Therefore, it is hard to believe that the localized definition, such as "homeboy," would be adopted by otaku community as its self-identity, especially among senior hardcore otakus.

There were scholars who held similar suspicions. They insisted that, to further discuss otaku community or otaku culture, one should distinguish the misinterpreted meanings used by the Chinese mass media from other anti-social manifestations of the term "otaku" (e.g. Li, 2012, pp. 420–421).[182] Some of them attempted to come up with definitions that could be applicable to Chinese context. Qian Liang Yi and Ling Fei Wang are two of them. After reviewing Okada's definition and other original definitions raised by Japanese researchers and also taking into account its common usage in the mainland Chinese context by both mass media and fans, they came up with a set of general criteria of otaku which they believed would be applicable to Chinese fandom and subsequently used it as a working definition for their field research (2012, pp. 61–63).[183] According to them, otaku should (1) at least be obsessed with the consuming of Japanese animation, manga/comic and game (ACG for short); (2) identify with these genres of popular culture and the activities of the fandom community and are willing to devote themselves to learning more about the culture; and (3) perform (in the case of activities like cosplay for example) the culture through interactions with fellow fans or attending activities held by the community (2012, p. 61).[184] Within these three criteria, Yi and Wang believed that the second criterion, the identity and devotion to otaku-ism, is the most important in defining an otaku. They further explained this criterion as, first, willingness to admit their identity under

---

[181] Zero, "Tai Wan Zhai Zen Me Ren Shi 'Otaku' De?", 20–21.

[182] Jie Li. "Significance of Otaku Existing in Contemporary," *Jia Mu Si Jiao Yu Xue Yuan Xue Bao* 120, no. 10 (2012): 420–421.

[183] Yi and Wang, *Yuzhaizu*, 61–63.

[184] *Ibid.*, 61.

social pressure; second, spending considerable time, energy and money to collect information and data; and third, being passionate about ACG and hoping to gain knowledge, emotional connection or a sense of belonging and identity through ACG culture (Yi and Wang, 2012, pp. 62–63).[185]

The term "*fujoshi*" often associated with otaku that needs to be clarified here before I move onto the next section. Though "*fujoshi*" is considered to be the identity of female otaku in some Japanese- and Chinese-language academic literatures (e.g. Okabe and Ishida, 2012, p. 207[186]; Ye, 2013, pp. 1–2[187]), I opined that it might not be the case in real practice. In current Chinese context, "*fujoshi*" refers to female fans who enjoy the "boys' love" (BL) element in all sorts of forms, including novel, manga, animation, game, TV series, and movie, or even fantasize about brotherly romance with historical characters and contemporary pop stars (Zhang, 2012, p. 14).[188] Therefore, in the Chinese context, a *fujoshi* does not necessarily develop a special interest in Japanese culture or animation/manga/game products. Hong Fang Zhang claimed in his report that though *fujoshi* circle shared the same cultural background with ACG fandom at the beginning, it has developed into a separate community called *tongren* community, a direct translation of the Japanese word "*dojin*," in mainland China nowadays (Zhang, 2012, p. 236).[189] My empirical experience also supports this opinion. For example, one of my potential interviewees rejected my interview invitation because she considered herself as a *fujoshi* rather than an *otaku*. In addition, she stressed that as far as she knew, the two communities had been separated completely for a long time though some ACG fans might belong to both communities.

Therefore, in this writing, I use the term "female otaku" to refer to a female who was interested in ACG culture and identify themselves with the otaku community, regardless of whether they share similar interests with the *fujoshis*.

---

[185] *Ibid.*, 62–63.

[186] Daisuke Okabe and Kimi Ishida, "Making Fujoshi Identity Visible and Invisible," in *Fandom Unbound: Otaku culture in a connected world*, eds. M. Ito, D. Okabe and I. Tsuji. (New Haven, CT: Yale University Press, 2012), 207.

[187] Kai Ye, "Lun Fu Nv De Wen Hua Ren Tong," *Modern Women* 7 (2013): 1–2.

[188] Hong Fang Zhang, *Zi Wo Yu Ta Zhe: Fu Nv Qun Ti De Hu Dong Yu Ren Tong Yan Jiu* (Master's Diss., Zhe Jiang Normal University, 2012), 14.

[189] *Ibid.*, 236.

Fieldwork Interviews and the Study of Animation and Manga Otakus

Since materials on Japanese popular culture written from the perspectives inside the otaku community are limited, and it is nearly impossible to talk about identity without hearing and processing opinions from the otaku group members themselves, I decided to collect firsthand data through fieldwork interviews to explore the issue. The definition and criteria of otakus I applied and carried out in the latter part of this writing are based mainly on Yi and Wang's definition reviewed above. The reason for utilizing their definition is because the term is comparatively clearer and has been proven to be applicable to the context of mainland China.

Participants

As discussed in the Introduction, under the section on *Popularity and Distribution*, compared to actual physical locations in specific geographical locations, cyberspace is the most important gathering place for the otaku community in China. Thus, besides my personal social network and by using snowballing technique, I have solicited informants from well-known internet-based otaku societies in mainland China including animation/manga fandom in Douban,[190] Sina Weibo,[191] and

---

[190] *Douban* is one of the most widely used Chinese Social Networking Service (SNS) websites, which allows registered users to record and provide contents about films, books, music, and events and activities. According to the reports released by Douban, it had over 75 million registered users and over 200 million unique visitors on the average from April to October 2013 (Sohu IT, 2013). The study conducted by Nielsen claimed that around 70% of internet social media users in mainland China used SNS and Douban was one of three major SNS listed (2012). *Source*: Sohu IT, "Dou Ban Xuan Bu Yue Fu Gai Yong Hu Shu Da 2 Yi Tong Bi Zeng Zhang Yi Bei," dated 13 November 2013 in *Sohu IT*, available at http://it.sohu.com/20131113/n390062939.shtml; Nielsen, "Zhong Guo She Jiao Mei Ti Shou Fang Yong Hu Diao Cha Bao Gao," dated 2012 in Nielsen [downloaded 14 May 2014], available at http://cn.nielsen.com/documents/ChinaSocialMedia.pdf.

[191] Sina Weibo, also known as Weibo or Chinese Twitter, is the most popular Chinese microblogging website with around 536 million registered users out of 564 million internet users in China. Hu Lian Wang Shi Yan Shi and Zhe Jiang Chuan Mei Xue Yuan Hu Lian Wang Yu She Hui Yan Jiu Zhong Xin, "2012–2013 Nian Weibo Fa Zhan Yan JIu Bao Gao," dated June 2013, available at http://video.zj.com/cns/20122013weibo.pdf.

Stage 1st.[192] Besides Yi and Wang's definition, the criteria set to select the informant are whether he/she consumes animation and/or manga as one of their most important activities in interest groups, with self-identification of being an "otaku."

I did not include gamers in my study because of the following reasons. Though there are also game-based fans groups within the otaku community, a large number of gamers in mainland China are addicted to non-Japanese games such as those produced by American video game company Blizzard Entertainment.[193] There is no clear-cut differentiation between gamers who play Japan-produced games and players who also play non-Japanese (mainly American)-produced games, which means most of the gamers will be interested in foreign-produced games with various cultural origins. Thus, it is a challenging task to distinguish those with a special interest in Japan-produced games, and to categorize those who fit neatly into the criteria of "otaku" defined in this chapter. Furthermore, most of the literature reviewed in the section on otaku identity, especially those using English-speaking countries as case studies, were focusing on Japanese animation and manga otakus, which might indicate the closer relationship of animation/manga fandom with otaku world in locations outside Japan.

I included informants who received tertiary education and above in this study. According to surveys reviewed earlier, university students make up the main bulk of the otaku community. By choosing university graduates, my informants would have at least four years of experience with the otaku community. Their tertiary education background helps provide more opportunities to interact with other fellow otakus in their daily lives,

---

[192] Stage 1st is a famous ACG-related theme forum, which has over 270,000 registered users and claimed to be one of the most famous otaku communities in mainland China.

[193] It is said that the players of World of Warcraft (Wow), a massively multiplayer online role-playing game (MMORPG) produced by Blizzard Entertainment, reached 3,850,000 in China by the end of 2013. Huan Qiu, "Ying Mei Te Gong Wo Di 'Wow' Zhong Guo Wan Jia Huo Da Dao 385 Wan," dated 11 December 2013 in *Huan Qiu*, available at http://tech.huanqiu.com/game/2013-12/4649899.html. Moreover, Wow is only one out of several popular games produced by Blizzard Entertainment. Qiu Gang, "You Xi Di Guo Wang Zhe Bao Xue De Cheng Gong Zhi Lu," *Reporters' Notes* 7 (2012): 52.

and in the process make observations of otakus and their communities in mainland China.

29 young adults accepted my interview requests. 22 of them, including 11 males and 11 females, met the criteria listed. There were other seven informants interviewed who did not meet the criteria defining my target group, i.e. they are either current university students (three of them), former otakus who have given up their hobbies (one of them), or fans who have the self-identity of not being an "otaku" (three of them). 22 main informants will be analyzed first while seven others will be treated separately in each section of my fieldwork analysis.

Methodology

Semi-standardized interviews[194] were conducted in this research. The informants were asked to answer a list of predetermined questions. The interviews were then carried out in an order according to the background of informants and their responses. The informants were allowed to ask questions, and follow-up questions were used by the interviewer to make clarifications. Each interview lasted 40 minutes to an hour and most interviews were either conducted through face-to-face contact, or with the assistance of a smart phone or IM software.[195] Only three informants, including one from the group of seven responders who failed to fit the criteria, were too busy to engage in a real-time interview and preferred to send their responses by emails or through the social network. All interviews were conducted in spoken Mandarin or written simplified Chinese. The demographic information collected in the interviews included age, gender, education level, occupation, place of upbringing, current residency, economic status of the family, and their subcultural identities

---

[194] Though some scholars prefer to divide interviews into two structural groups, formal and informal, or structured and unstructured interview, many scholars believe that there are continuity between the two extreme structures and at least three forms of interview should be recognized. Semi-standardized interviews allow a certain "degree of rigidity regard to presentational structure" (Berg, 2007, p. 92). Bruce L. Berg, *Qualitative Research Methods for the Social Sciences*, sixth edition (Boston, MA: Allyn and Bacon, 2007): 92.

[195] IM is short for Instant Messaging, which is a real-time communication through internet. The IM software used in this research include QQ, Skype, and MSN.

within the community of popular cultural fandom (i.e. otaku of animation or/and manga). To pinpoint their interests with precision and to categorize the different subgroups of otakus clearly, the differentiated terms of "animation otaku" and "manga otaku" were consistently and precisely mentioned by the interviewer during the interviews.

The question sets used for the interviews are divided into two parts. The first part is about their personal experiences with anime and manga culture, including when and how they came across those cultural products, subsequently became aware of their otaku identity, and continuously practiced their identities. Their surrounding environmental factors such as fellow friends, peers, social networking, and daily practices and consumption of otaku cultural products were addressed as well. The second part of the interview focused on my informants' personal observations and opinions regarding their activities both within and outside the otaku community. They were asked about their understanding of the popularity of otaku culture and how they were received or accepted by the general public and significant others; characteristics of otaku culture and the community; as well as their own definitions of the term "otaku" and their sense of belonging to this community. They were allowed to ask follow-up questions freely after the interview.

Demographic Information of My Informants

The 22 informants, half males and half females, were aged between 23 to 32 years old (Mean = 27.6, Standard Deviation = 2.5). 10 of them received undergraduate education and the rest of them either held a master's degree or were pursuing a postgraduate degree at the time of interview. In terms of occupation, besides postgraduate students, my informants came from different industries with diverse specialties (see Figure 11.1). They were all born and raised in mainland China, while five of them claimed that they had lived in more than one city during their childhood and adolescence (see Figure 11.2). Their current places of residence are shown in Figure 11.3. For those who were not physically staying in mainland China when the interview was conducted, they remained closely connected with the mainland China's otaku community, and had been communicating with other Chinese otakus on a daily basis.

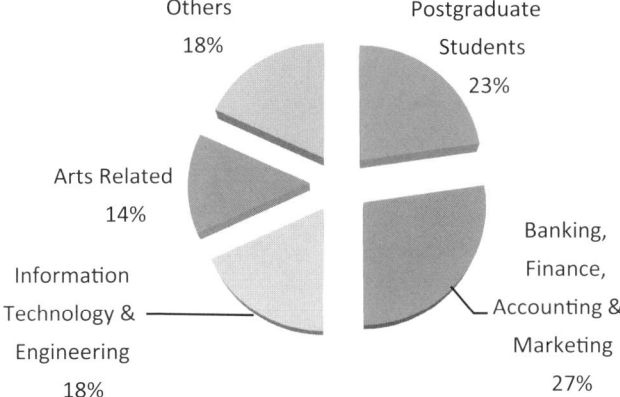

FIGURE 11.1. THE OCCUPATIONAL PROFILE AND DISTRIBUTION OF THE INFORMANTS IN MY STUDY.

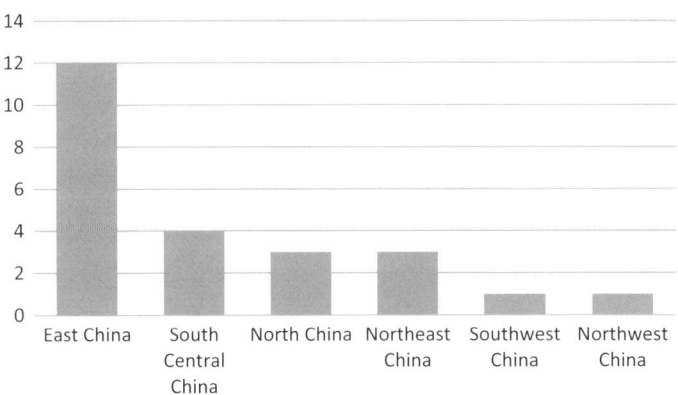

FIGURE 11.2. THE AREAS WHERE THE INFORMANTS IN MY STUDY WERE BORN AND RAISED.

It is worth mentioning that all of my informants grew up and lived in urban areas and the majority of them came from economically developed areas of mainland China (e.g. eastern China, Guangdong province in southern China and Beijing in northern China) while there were some who used to live or still lived in small towns.

Because of rapid socio-economic changes in the last half century in mainland China and the diversity of living standards across the nation, it

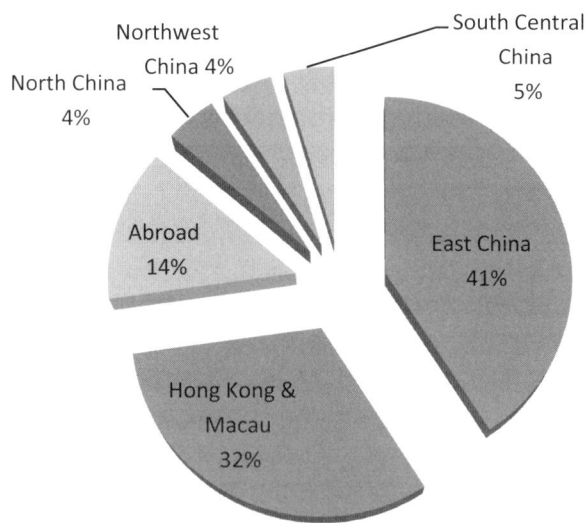

FIGURE 11.3.   CURRENT PLACE OF RESIDENCE OF THE INFORMANTS IN MY STUDY.

is very hard to define the socioeconomic status of those informants' family backgrounds. Therefore, I have consciously avoided the term "middle class" in this chapter, though all of my informants believed that they did not belong to the lower socio-economic class in China currently, and most of them, except two, believed that they were not raised in the lower income group of Chinese society.

While asked if they identified himself/herself as an animation or a manga otaku, nine of them, that is 41% of my informants, considered themselves to be an animation otaku, and three of them, that is 14%, believed that they were specifically engaged in manga otaku activities. The remaining 45% of them said they were equally familiar with both areas.

Regarding the seven other informants, they were all born and bred in eastern China and were still residing there except for one who currently lived in Hong Kong. Among three university students and one postgraduate student, one of them worked in the service industry, another served as an internet technician, and the final individual who claimed he did not qualify as an "otaku" was an animator by profession.

Turning into an Otaku

Although all my 22 informants started to consume Japanese popular culture in their early age as the Chinese researchers and mass media observed, all of them believed that they were not otakus in the first several years or first decade of their consumption habit. While being asked how they became an otaku, all except one of them provided me with details of their personal journey in their transformation from an ordinary consumer to a "true otaku."

The majority of my informants either actively explored or assumed the identity during their school years (i.e. junior and senior high school, undergraduate, and postgraduate), while 15 out of 22, that is nearly 68% of them became an otaku during senior high school years or as university undergraduates. This is consistent with the surveys reviewed in the introduction of this writing. Only one of my informants gained otaku identity after graduating from university, and another did not even aware of his/her starting point as an otaku (see Figure 11.4).

According to my informants' responses, the years of them being an otaku ranged from 2 to 16 years (Mean = 11.5; Standard Deviation = 3.9), which are much longer than some researchers' assumption of a four-year temporary identity during university years. In addition, as the demographic information shows, my informants had graduated and left their universities for five years on the average and they still held on to their otaku identity.

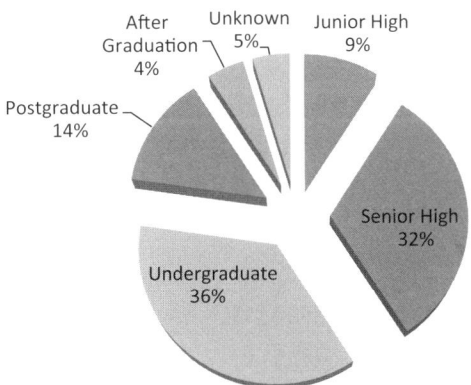

FIGURE 11.4. THE "STARTING TIME" OF TRANSFORMATION TO AN OTAKU AMONGST THE INFORMANTS IN THIS STUDY.

Therefore, to them, otaku was at least more than just a temporary identity they adopted to escape from real life difficulties such as finding jobs.

Most of my informants told me a story about how they became a conscious and serious consumer as an otaku. They related their starting point of being an otaku to a special encounter, either with otaku cultural products or with otaku communities. 16 out of 22 of my informants believed that their otaku life originated from one or several animation/manga pieces which had significant meaning to them. Half of them spent a large amount of time and energy to do their own research or create derivative works, through which they started learning the behavioral norms of otaku-ism. Another half of my informants chose to explore their horizon after exposure to inspiring works, consumed animation/manga in large volumes indiscriminately, and became knowledgeable generalists in their fields of interest. Besides consuming animation/manga, eight of them also paid their tribute to the otaku communities. According to them, it was the encounter of either magazines or online communities that not only introduced to them the knowledge of otakuology, but also inspired them to consume ACG products with critical minds, to read between the lines for textual works, and to conduct their own researches into ACG. That is, it is the communities themselves who demonstrate what it means to be an otaku in their own thinking.

All of those informants who obtained their identities through consumptions and explorations also explained the standards of "starting [out] to be an otaku" which they applied to themselves. Those criteria were related to passion, energy, and resources that they put into ACG interests in general, including starting to accumulate basic knowledge or develop aesthetic standard, developing an abstract impression towards the culture or appearance of certain behaviors (watching animation/manga under certain criteria systematically, watching animations which are recently broadcasted, or conducting serious research on anime/manga by themselves). When asked about the differences between the general ACG fans they used to be and the "true otaku" they became, the majority of them believed that starting to consuming ACG products intentionally and accumulating conceptual knowledge of the culture and its industry marked the beginning of their otaku lives.

It might be under one's expectation that the impression or understanding of Japan will be a main difference between the progressive stage of ordinary fan and otaku, due to the Japanese cultural influence embedded in otaku products and the complicated cultural-historical relationship between China and Japan. Surprisingly, only three out of my 22 informants mentioned this. Two said that they gradually developed a personal impression and understanding of Japanese culture. And only one mentioned that she used to have strong nationalistic feelings towards Japan despite her unconscious consumption of Japanese popular cultural goods. It was after getting in touch with otaku culture and becoming an otaku that made her more objective in terms of perspectives towards issues related to Japan.

Additionally, several of my informants mentioned that the availability of time and energy prior to embarking on a full-time professional career accelerated their transformation towards otaku-dom. They said that having leisure time during university years gave them an opportunity to freely explore their anime and manga interests and other features of otaku-ism. Two of them even had similar stories, that is being abroad alone as exchange or newly admitted students and having no places to go during long public holidays (i.e. Christmas) and watching some animations seemed to be a good way to kill time. After a week of extensive exposure, they were drawn to the animation world and the otaku culture.

However, not all otaku identities were obtained initiatively. Six of my informants described their otaku identity as an "accidental" discovery. They believed that they were passionate animation/manga consumers from the very beginning and no significant changes took place in their consumption habits until their exposure to the concept of "otaku" at certain points. Those exposures, mainly from the mass media or their peers, provoked their self-reflection and thereafter led to the decision of assuming the otaku identity.

For the seven other cases, as mentioned before, four of them did not consider themselves as otaku currently. One who used to be an otaku had a similar story of turning into an otaku as described above. The three who claimed they were not otaku were clearly under the influence of mass media and peers when deciding on identity adoption. Only in their cases, interactions with mass media and peers were preventing them from adopting the identity. Two of them said after communicating with their peers who belonged to the otaku communities, they did not consider themselves passionate and knowledgeable enough to be a qualified member. One of them adopted the definition of "otaku" from the Chinese mass media, and repeatedly emphasized during the interview that he was a sociable person who liked to go out and make new friends. Therefore, he claimed, despite his familiarity with otaku culture and the community, he should not be considered as an otaku.

The three current undergraduate students, two females and a male aged between 20 and 22 years old, responded quite differently to the topics regarding to the acquisition of otaku identity. In fact, none of them were sure whether he/she should be called as an otaku and had difficulties in defining otaku-ism. I will discuss this in details in latter sections of this chapter.

Based on my field data, conscious consumption was considered as a milestone which distinguishes the otaku from the general fan. Otaku communities, peers, and mass media seemed to play important roles in assisting ACG product consumers to determining their otaku identity. Besides, the environment such as the availability of time and energy (maybe also financial status, considering that most of my informants did not belong to the lower socio-economic class of society) was influential as well.

Path to Otaku-ism

Though most of my informants subjectively believed that there was a significant turning point in their otaku identity formation, all of them recalled that they were animation/manga consumers from a very young age. After comparing their entire consumption histories from childhood, there seemed to be a general path to follow towards achieving otaku identity. That is, though my informants' stories about becoming an otaku differed, they had similar experiences with animation/manga and the communities. The main differences among them are when and how they encountered their significant animation/manga experiences, and interacted with the fan community, or how they understood the concept of "otaku."

Therefore, regardless of their subjective statements in my semi-structured interviews, from my point of view, the formation of their otaku identity should be viewed as a continuous process rather than a dramatic change. I would examine their consumption histories in details and look for factors that distinguish them from their peers.

Consumption experiences in childhood and adolescence

From my informants' consumption history in animation and manga products, animation consumption usually started earlier. All my informants, except one, recalled their first encounter with Japanese animation in kindergarten or primary school. They all claimed that they watched animations/cartoons on television, mostly on local channels, regardless of their origins. According to them, all imported animations/cartoons were dubbed in Mandarin and children would watch them without being aware of the cultural origins. The only informant who failed to recall the first encounter explained that she also watched cartoons on television, but could not recall whether any of them originated from Japan. With limited supply of animation programs and products, most informants said that they just watched whatever programs that were broadcasted on television as long as they were permitted to do so by their parents. The frequency of consumption gradually decreased when they reached junior high school. Some of their cartoon viewing activities were limited by their parents since the parents regarded watching TV as having adverse effects on academic performances. At the same time, according to some of my informants, the decreasing amount of imported foreign animation caused by restrictions promulgated by the State Administration of Press, Publication, Radio, Film and Television in the first decade of the 21st century also seriously reduced their access to the anime products. Furthermore, several of my informants were even limited by their lifestyles and living conditions because they spent their weekdays in a student dormitory that was not equipped with TVs and therefore they could only access television in the weekends and holidays.

The first manga consumption experiences came later than animation for most of my informants, occurring mainly in the upper grades of primary school or junior high school. Several of them obtained their first manga series publications from their parents or relatives as gifts during this time. Some of them borrowed manga volumes from their family members (mainly older children from the extended family) or classmates. The rest used their pocket money to rent or buy manga from bookstalls or rental shops. For most of my informants, they consumed low-priced pirated copies in their initial manga consumption experiences. According to them, there used to be many manga rental shops near schools with large volume of collections, and it was about RMB0.5 to RMB5 to borrow or buy each volume, making it possible for young children to afford. Children would visit those shops during breaks or after class and return the borrowed book the next day. Some of the manga readers would read any accessible manga that they could get hold of in bookstalls and rental shops. The rest just read whatever were circulated in class or were recommended by peers. Compared to watching anime which is mainly a primary school level activity in mainland China, the habit of reading manga tends to have a longer lifespan beyond the primary school-going years. The evidence is that most of my informants could name several popular manga works circulated among classmates during their primary and high school years (mainly during the junior high school years).

When I asked whether the above animation/manga consumption experiences were shared experiences among their peers, most of them responded yes. Some of them even claimed that if one does not watch last night's animation or read recent popular manga among classmates, he/she cannot catch up with the topics with peers. One of my informants also mentioned her observation that most of her generation could understand traditional Chinese without special training because they used to watch pirated manga copies of Taiwan and Hong Kong (localities where traditional Chinese is extensively used) edition when they were young as an evidence of manga popularity. According to my informants, the differences between general consumers and serious fans or potential otaku readers only emerge later on when they grow up.

As mentioned, children were generally restricted by their parents in watching TV programs after school when they reached the age of attending junior high schools in China and there were fewer animations available at about the same period of time for my informants' generation. Most of my informants' peers gave up watching animation, found themselves a new hobby, and only consumed animation/manga occasionally during university years when online resources were available and easy to access. Instead, many of my informants changed their consumption platform to watching pirated copies of animation, mainly video CDs (VCD, an earlier format of digital video) or other computer discs (CD) formats, and later DVDs that were either borrowed or purchased before the advent of the internet era.

As for manga readers, while manga lost its popularity among peers as they grew older, most of my informants who identified themselves as manga otakus kept their reading habit. And through indiscriminate reading of manga products, those manga readers started to develop their own preferences, by following certain drawing styles, tracking their favorite authors' works, or specializing in the genres that interested them the most. My informants had colorful stories about how they discovered the "secret shop," which had the largest collections of manga in town, by word of mouth and their everlasting battle of wits with their parents who were against their animation/manga consumption but were also the informants' only source of finance to purchase animation discs and comic books. This period of time ended with the popularization of internet and free downloadable resources, which I will go into details in the next section.

Those consumption experiences in childhood and adolescence seemed to have their impact. All of my informants could clearly recall the details of popular animation/manga and some other works they had watched/read during the period. Moreover, when the free internet resources were available, some of them had purposely revisited the Japanese-language versions of the most impressionable animation TV programs that they had watched during childhood and adolescence, and some searched for animation products which had good reviews among peers but were not available for viewing during their childhoods. According to them, these practices served the purpose of re-evaluating their generation's "master pieces." Animation and manga products with worldwide popularity, such as *Dragon Balls* and *Sailor Moon*, were mentioned. Furthermore, some landmark works in otaku culture, such as *Neon Genesis Evangelion,* were brought up a number of times by different people during the interviews. These "must watch" pieces formed an important part of their childhood memory and became their initial benchmark and reference points to what constituted "good creative" works.

However, I am not saying that all my informants kept up the same level of enthusiasm towards animation/manga consistently from their very first consumption experience without any change. In fact, many of them, mainly animation otaku, had changed their main interests or targets of consumption to other products for several years or even a decade. It is usually the real life friends that tied them back to animation/manga culture. Their stories were more or less the same that they became acquainted with an ACG fan or otaku in certain point of their lives and were introduced to animation/manga pieces which evoked their childhood memory and enthusiasm. According to my informants, personal friendship connections, along with other forms of networks, served a variety of crucial function in their identity formation.

The importance of networking

Personal friendship, ACG product shops, fan magazines, and joining internet communities paved the way to otaku-ism for all my informants through providing the information, resources, and other necessary support for their activities.

As mentioned in the last section, many of my informants who once gave up ACG interests were brought back to the fandom by their networks of personal friends and fan communities. The most interesting and dramatic story was maybe the one told by a female informant who fell in love with an ACG fan during university years. In order to understand and be a part of the boy's life interests, she registered on several online otaku sites the boy used to visit and started to watch animations which had been frequently and systematically discussed on those sites (and doing detailed research on them). By now, she became a much more hardcore otaku than what the boy she fond of used to be, though she was not in any romantic relationship with another otaku for years.

Nearly all of my informants mentioned at least one real world (non-virtual) friend who shared the same interests or considered themselves as an otaku during the interview. Many of my informants were also members of ACG-related clubs during school years. After entering the era of internet, interactions with their real-life friends carrying the same interests increased. Many of my informants used the internet to keep in touch with their otaku friends whom they met at school after graduation (both high schools and universities) no matter whether they still lived in the same city or not. IM (Instant Messaging) groups, such as Tencent QQ (the most popular instant messaging software in mainland China) group consisted of class-based circles or members of a school ACG-related club, were used to share and exchange ACG-related information even after graduation.

Before the internet era, animation and manga shops, which mainly sold and rented pirated copies, were another important kind of community network which served as resources providers and information exchange platforms for my informants. Interestingly, several of them believed that many owners of anime and manga shops should be otakus or at least someone who possessed some knowledge of the field. The classical or hottest items were displayed in a conspicuous place and some of the owners would recommend masterpieces to regular customers based on client's tastes. However, this conjecture is doubtful since the Japanese animation/manga industry was quite new at that time and believed to target only at young children in mainland China. But it is highly possible that the owners and the shop assistants were the channels connecting the fans visiting the shops. That is, they were recommending or importing the hottest/most anticipated pieces based on the renting/selling records in the shops and their clients' requests, and they were passing on information and responses they heard among clients.

The appearance of ACG-related magazines in the mid/late 1990s provided a new platform for some of the informants, especially those animation viewers. As my informants recalled, before the proliferation of personal computers and internet access, print magazines were the most valuable informational channels. The editors and the authors of those magazines were mainly otakus with expertise, some of whom are still active members of online otaku communities till today. Based on the introductions, reviews and recommendations in those magazines, my informants could select specific works of interest. Those magazines were also the first platform through which my informants started to accumulate some initial knowledge about anime and manga products and the industry. Several of my informants also mentioned that those magazines usually had a column for readers to interact with editors/authors or other readers who got published in the last volume, which could be categorized as the prototype of a discussion board. It is one of the most popular column in magazines and the first place for ACG fans to create a community with people they have never met. More importantly, according to several of my informants who attributed their "turning point" to the encounters within the community, it was the critics in those magazine who first taught them to watch animation/manga from an analytical and critical perspective, or in their words it was the first time they found out that one could consume animation/manga "in this way (otaku-ism)."

Personal computers and internet accessibility, especially broadband access, had changed the lifestyles and consumption habits of my informants dramatically. Specialized anime and manga websites, BBS, discussion forums, download sites, video-viewing websites, and social networks became the main information exchange platforms and virtual gathering places. Compared to the internet, the information provided by magazines were dated and limited due to the speed of publication, and product reviews and analytical articles with equal or even better quality standards can be easily accessed through the internet. In fact, as mentioned before, some editors and authors of animation/manga magazines also wrote their own blogs, participated in online discussions, or even published their new creations online. The pirated copies of animation and manga had also been gradually replaced by free downloadable e-resources (including both legitimate and pirated contents). By vastly increasing the range and the diversity of accessible products, massive consumption and in depth research became more feasible, especially for animation lovers.

In sum, it is similar to the observation made in the US ACG fandom, that unofficial networks for information, communication, and consumption were crucial to my informants even from their early days of consumption. Besides magazines, which were also written and edited by members of the fan community, nearly all channels mentioned by my informants were unofficial ones. It was through personal connections or platforms established by otaku communities that my informants were able to keep track of the latest information or pick up their childhood passion in animation/manga and became an otaku eventually.

Seven other cases

Seven other cases in my study again revealed the similarity in their paths to otaku-ism. Animation and manga consumption were popular among peers during their childhood, including those three university students who just reached their 20s. The peak period of their otaku habits and active ACG consumption coincided with the implementation of anime restrictions and regulations as their primary school period had memories of watching Japanese animation on TV programs and sharing anime products with classmates.

Interestingly, those three young students did not show more dependence on internet-based virtual community during their identity formation than other informants. One of them only started to contact otaku communities after joining the cosplay society in her university with her friends. In addition, those three students enjoyed more financial support and tolerance of their hobby from their parents. They were allowed to buy some expensive animation/manga related goods during their high school years. However, due to the small size of the sample, these could not be inferred as generational changes.

Discussions

Most of my informants believed that their generation consumed Japanese animation and manga massively during their childhood. Only that they became conscious and serious consumers after years passed by, which distinguished them from their peers. After examining the content of all 29 interviews, it can be concluded that besides mass media influence mentioned in the last section, conscious consumption and connections with communities, including personal connections and networks built by otakus, are the most significant factors that shape the otaku identity.

Also note that, despite the fact that my informants consumed animation/manga since childhood, many of them were not aware of the cultural origin of the products at that time. It is probably the reason why only a few of my informants were sensitive to the Japanese social-cultural background of the animation/manga.

Another point worth mentioning is that, compared to animation otaku, manga otaku seems to be more independent from the communities during their identity formation process. After obtaining the resources (manga copies) from networks, manga otakus mainly consume the products and develop their consumption habits and tastes on their own. However, since 45% of my informants claimed to be both animation and manga otaku, it is hard to tell whether there is a difference between animation and manga otaku communities, or if it were only a phenomenon caused by the different nature of animation and manga consumption.

In addition, based on the stories provided by my informants, it is clear that it was the enjoyment of the content, rather than any symbolic social meaning (if any) of otaku culture that attracted my informants. The self-identified otaku informants in my study exhibited strong interest towards accumulating knowledge and information from their early stages of identity formation. It seems, though China is a country which still emphasizes ideological conflicts and class struggles in mainstream propaganda, my informants understood and enjoyed otaku identity in a more "post-modern" way that resembles both Japanese and English-speaking otaku communities. I would discuss more about this in the latter part of this writing.

Practices and Maintenance of the Otaku Identity

As the demographic profile shows, my informants believed that they had led a life as an otaku for over 10 years on average. Maintenance of their otaku identity is also an important issue worth investigating.

Since the typical otaku is believed to be an individual addicted to technology or at least a heavy internet user by some researchers (e.g. Li, 2012, pp. 102–108),[196] one might assume that people from technology-related disciplines or occupations would have better chance to gain or maintain the otaku identity. However, based on my informants' demographic information, occupation and specialization failed to demonstrate any significant correlations with the otaku identity. There were only 18% of my informants who worked in the IT industry or were engineers, and three of the post-graduate students were from arts, one was from business, and one from science. Furthermore, one of my informants was a game developer, which is a profession within the ACG industry. Based on the personal observation he shared, there were few otakus inside the industry as otakus tend to be more idealistic in game productions. Some were idealistically disappointed by the reality of the industry, e.g. profit-making motives as the top priority in any game production.

Most otakus derived their identities outside their professional lives. Investigating my informants' routine practices and consumption habits would not only reflect the fandom, but also provide the information about how their otaku identities were practiced and maintained.

---

[196] Li, "The Development of the Word 'Otaku'," 102–108.

Routine practices

Otaku interests found in the daily routines of most of my informants can be divided into four main categories: consuming animation/manga content, gathering information, participating in otaku activities and events, and contributing to otaku community through various means. There were also other lesser-known shared practices of consumption amongst otakus mentioned by several of my informants (see Figure 11.5).

Consumptions and all sorts of daily practices and activities took up a considerable portion of my informants' leisure time. Most of my informants consumed animation/manga and read otaku-related websites on a daily basis. Besides during their personal time after work, on weekends and holidays, and during lunch/dinner time, time spent on transportations and waiting for other people during appointments were also used for information gathering or even watching/reading animation/manga. The time they spent on otaku products therefore depended on their daily routines. Among my 22 informants, 16 of them had a full-time job, five were postgraduate students, and one was a freelance translator. 17 people reported that they spent more than 10 hours per week on their otaku interests. A manga otaku declared that the time she spent on discussing manga with her friends alone would exceed 10 hours per week. Several recalled that they spent more than 40 hours per week, which is equivalent to a full-time job, on ACG-related interests while they were undergraduate students. Two of my informants also admitted that they only spent around

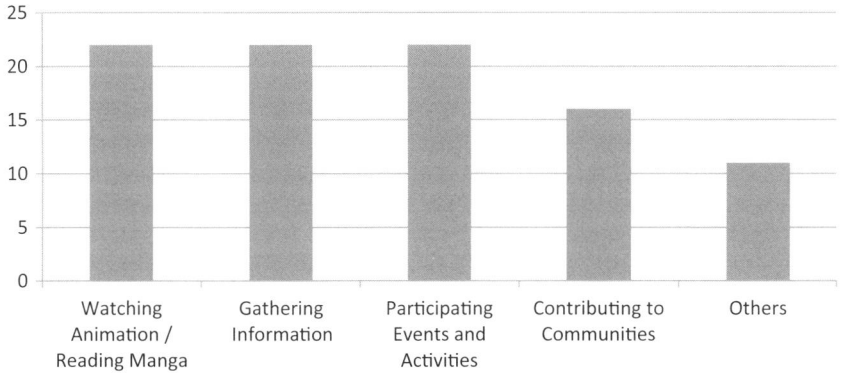

FIGURE 11.5. THE ROUTINE ACTIVITIES, LIFESTYLE HABITS AND PERFORMANCE/PRACTICE OF OTAKU AND THEIR ACTIVITIES.

one hour per week in ACG-related interests on average because the rest of their time was occupied by their professional life. One of the two further calculated that he had only one hour per day as personal time on average, and one hour per week for enjoying animation and manga was the best he could manage.

Watching animation and/or reading manga, usually on a daily or at least weekly basis, is one of the most important life routines practiced by all of my informants. Based on their responses, the pattern of consuming animation/manga content adopted by the otakus can be divided into three main categories, (1) following the newly broadcasted/published works (these fans are known as *zhuixinfan*[197]/*gen lianzai*[198]); (2) watching/reading the old pieces (they called *bujiufan/bujiuzuo*[199]); and (3) replaying/re-reading one's favorite works from time to time.

All my informants conformed to the first pattern of the consumption as they followed newly broadcasted/published animation/manga. Some of my informants were proud of the total number of years they took to follow the latest animation programs as a proof of their seniority as an otaku. Several of them believed that an otaku should show some specialized knowledge and interest in the latest animation programs or manga series, just like how a cinephilia would watch at least some new highly anticipated movies. From their tone of expressions, the knowledge accumulated and visual/audio experiences gained from watching/reading new works not only served as popular topics among otakus, but also could be regarded as a form of "subcultural capital" in the community, especially among animation fans.

---

[197]*Zhui Xin Fan* (追新番) is a word created by Chinese animation fans. *Zhui* means "follow" in Chinese and *xin fan* is an abbreviation of the Japanese word "アニメ新番組," which means new anime TV program.

[198]*Gen Lian Zai* (跟连载) means following the updates of an unfinished or newly started manga series.

[199]*Bu Jiu fan* (补旧番) is a word created by Chinese animation fans similar to the word *Zhui Xin Fan* mentioned before. It literally means the audiences have missed the opportunity of watching certain anime when it was broadcasted on TV channels and try to catch up with fellow viewers. Animation fans use the word when they are watching an old program for the first time. When it comes to manga, and not a TV program, the word *Jiu Fan* is replaced by *Jiu Zuo* (旧作), which means "old works" in Chinese.

But there seemed to be no clear benchmarks regarding how passionate an otaku should be towards newly broadcasted programs. Although most of my informants experienced a period of time in their otaku life when they were excited by new animation or manga series, they did not consume new products with the same degree of passion by the time of my interview with them. Their otaku product consumption tapered with age, time and situational contexts. Some would still spend most of their time going through new animation/manga products they could access, or even watch current anime programs based on the anime program lists from Japan. Some only selectively consumed those new pieces based on their interests. Alternatively, they would focus their consumption on certain selected genres. Some also confessed that they only watched new products recommended by friends in the fandom community or produced by their favorite animators/manga creators, or only continually updated themselves with manga contents that they had been following for years.

14 out of 22 informants conformed to the second pattern of consumption, which is watching/reading older works related to popular culture. Although two of my informants considered that the old works as something obsolete, most of my informants were aware that current animation/manga products only represented a small part of otaku culture from a longer-term historical perspective. For them, it is necessary for an otaku to gain a bigger picture of the creations, and become familiar with older sources or classical works related to their preferred genre. Moreover, some of my informants enjoyed the post-modern characteristics of otaku culture, such as parody and sarcasm. They were keen to conduct textual researches to uncover intertextual relations and to locate the "original" source of a parody or the intended target of sarcasm, as Okada's definition of "otaku" is someone who enjoyed associations and references. In addition, many of my informants were still following themes with complicated world settings and grand ideologies embedded in the content. Those informants claimed that due to the dramatic changes in the creative production process in the animation industry in Japan (e.g. characters were scripted prior to completion of storyline), most of the time, their interests could only be satisfied by older classical pieces.

The way these fans consumed older works can be further divided into three main formats. First, eight of my informants targeted the "must watch" classical/legendary pieces that were considered to be the most important or representative works by the general fandom community.[200]

Nine of them conformed to a second format, which is, when a new product attracted their attention in terms of its plot, setting, storytelling style, drawing style, music, or the voices of the characters, they would look up the bio-data of the creative production team and search for their previous works. Famous authors, directors, script writers, artists who were responsible for popular character designs or layout, music composers of well-known background music, voice actors of animated characters, or even prominent production companies were amongst some of these talented individuals and their names were frequently mentioned during my interviews. Moreover, those who mentioned these elements were excited about discussing the topic and would further comment or recommend some related words and terminologies common to the otaku community during the interview. This also resembles with Okada's criteria of otaku as someone who is able to analyze otaku products from a professional perspective of view and would like to gather information and share their opinions regarding to the works they adored. According to my informants' responses, familiarity with animation creations and unique preferences for certain artists and creators were worn as a badge of identity and fan loyalty within the otaku community.

Six of my informants consumed animation/manga content, mostly manga, in a third noticeable pattern, i.e. watch/read their favorite works repeatedly. Most of these informants in the third classified group in my study felt the quality of the newest products in anime/manga industry was not as good as it used to be, and there were not many old classic pieces left that they had not watched/read. Many of them were huge fans of old classical manga which were still serialized in a magazine. Fans of unfinished manga series recalled waiting for weeks, months, or even longer for new volumes in the series. For those manga otakus, small details that might reveal the "truth of the story" of upcoming volumes were considered as valuable insights. Re-reading older works while they waited for new issues or series helped my otaku informants to maintain their passion in their

---

[200] Some of them mentioned works such as *Mobile Suit Gundam series*, which is one of the most famous robot animation series.

favorite manga works, as well as to discover new details which might have been overlooked in the previous readings. More importantly, re-reading and discussing contents and plot developments with other fans took up a considerable percentage of their leisure time and became part of their lives, lifestyle and reading habits after years or even decades of following several manga series. An informant in her late 20s said life became so different when a manga she followed since high school ended and it felt like a closure to one stage of her life. There were also several animation fans who adopted this consumption pattern with a different motivation. For instance, one of my informants said he would go through all of his favorite directors' works once every several years and compared them to their newest productions, in terms of storytelling, visual style, and philosophy behind the storyline. For those fans, re-watching their favorite works would consistently inspire self-reflections of the worldviews and creative philosophies that their favorite creators held, as well as raise their understanding of various forms of entertainment and arts.

Besides the enjoyment of popular cultural contents, those consumption behaviors seemed to contain the prospect of accumulating specialist information and comprehensive knowledge about specific work or artist/creator, and maintaining friendship and an otaku lifestyle within the fan community, the practice of which is also associated with status in the community. Despite the existence of disparate patterns of consuming animation/manga, all these anime-watching and manga-reading routines maintained my informants' otaku identities. As some of them stated, if one were to stop watching animation or reading manga, there is nothing left in sustaining the otaku identity.

Information gathering is another aspect of the otaku consumption habits practiced by all of my informants. Moreover, most of them were not satisfied with being fed information regarding upcoming productions and anime/manga trends which were easily accessible by ordinary fans. They desired additional specialized knowledge of the products. Higher expertise and background research of the anime/manga products were required for generating the knowledge. With the help of other otaku friends and a variety of informational resources like all sorts of encyclopedia, databases, and search engines, my informants kept learning about the workings and trade secrets of the industry from their otaku friends, reading introduction articles/discussions online, or conducting their own researches to explore and uncover more knowledge about the topics in the field that they were interested in.

All of my informants were familiar with pop cultural sub-genres, commonly used terminologies and vocabularies in otaku products that they consumed, and all except one could explain in detail their own preferences with regards to these products.[201] Besides looking up on background information regarding the production crews and the creative people behind products that attracted them, they familiarized themselves with the works of famous creators, production companies, and other members of the creative teams that interested them. Some of them had special interests related to the production process and would look for articles or works that described the life and biography of the creative producers in the industry. Several of them also mentioned that they would carefully double check the facts before posting or replying posts while being engaged in discussions and debates within the otaku communities. Being considered as an unwritten manner among otakus, these habits were so basic to them that many of my informants did not practice them consciously. Several of my informants responded that they did not do anything special to gather ACG-related information. But when I asked whether they would look up on creators or companies that attracted their attention, or whether they had knowledge of certain production process/position that they mentioned earlier during the interview, their instant responses was "certainly" and added "so did everybody."

While being asked about information gathering, my informants usually emphasized that true fandom put in efforts in research. For example, several of my informants would re-organize the information that they were interested in and create their own lists of resources. Some used to spend time searching for reviews that introduced or analyzed certain animation/manga works or their creators/companies in details from a professional or academic perspective. Several of them mentioned that they used to be fans of an animation/manga piece and they would familiarize themselves with its socio-historical background and contextual settings. One manga otaku told me that she bought several books related to the period of the Renaissance because she read a romantic and fascinating manga series set in the period

---

[201] Only one informant said she still open to all genres of animation/manga.

of Renaissance. One animation otaku recalled that she once read the English version of the novel *The Catcher in the Rye*, and watched one of the representative movies of French New Wave *Breathless* because through interview articles and videos, she found out that those original texts were one of her favorite animation source of inspirations, and she wanted to understand the context of the cited words and borrowed terms in the animation. One informant shared his experiences that, when he discovered that the main characters in one of his favorite works were named after famous rock bands, he started researching all the cited characters of the story and the musical styles of the bands they were named after. Another informant also claimed that she used to spend years in her leisure time searching for websites, forums, discussions, analyze articles, behind-the-screen news, interviews, talks, event reports, etc. focusing on one of her favorite works. The practice did not end until she exhausted all available online Chinese, English, or Japanese materials related to this particular piece.

Based on my field work, there should be no doubt that Chinese otakus are also just as hardcore when reciting encyclopedic and specializing fan information ("information fetishism") as their Japanese and US counterparts. For some of my informants, enthusiasm in gathering information was one of the essential features of their identity.

Participating both online and offline activities and events was also practiced by all of my informants. The majority, that is 18 of my informants, would participate in online discussions, which mostly focused on evaluating animation/manga based on their storyline settings, aesthetic features, intertextual references, historical significance of the contents, and so on. Six of them specially mentioned that they would spend time going through fan discussions and long review articles provided by other fans. Besides discussions, they also participated or initiated other kinds of online sharing, such as sharing photos of their newly acquired figurines, voting for best animation/manga within a designated period of time, or identifying animation/manga from screenshots posted by other fans.

In addition, unlike the stereotypical image of otakus avoiding social activities and staying at home alone, my informants participated in a number of offline activities. The *dojinshi* fair is a very popular platform for otaku interactions in real world. 16 of 22 informants had participated in at least one *dojinshi* fair and some of them joined most major fairs in the city they resided in. Two of my informants, who studied abroad and never had a chance to attend a *dojinshi* fair, also expressed their strong interest towards the events and would love to attend if they could catch one. However, it is also true that not all of them were obsessive about those fairs. Four of my informants either complained that there were too many *dojinshi* fairs in mainland China then with uneven qualities, or stressed that they were not attracted to those fairs but only attended them to accompany their friends or to support their friends' products.

Besides *dojinshi* fair, six of my informants admitted they would attend offline gatherings to meet strangers acquainted through internet. Other activities mentioned by my informants include commercial exhibitions, live concerts, fan meetings of voice characters, free animation screenings, and other activities organized by private sectors or school clubs.

It is worth mentioning that, contrary to stereotypes of otaku, not all my informants enjoyed cosplay. Five of them said they had no interest in cosplay or even could not understand the psychological perspectives of cosplayers. Except for two amateur cosplayers, who used their own resources to produce professional pictures and participate in competitions, only one of my informants had experiences in cosplaying.

Making contribution to the fan community, which refers to behaviors that could provide information, resources, communication channels and platforms, creations, or unique insights to the community, is considered as an "advanced level" of otaku-ism.

Most of my participants were a contributor in the community. Similar to observations of fans in a study conducted by Mizuko Ito (2012, pp. 179–204),[202] making a contribution through participation in fan club activities would receive a mark of respect from other members in the fandom community as well as some privileges, such as attaining higher recognition, higher ranking in community forums, or greater accessibility of resources. However, my informants claimed that they participated in those activities only to repay the community, to promote their favorite works, or for their own enjoyment. Some of them even argued that "doing some-

---

[202] Mizuko Ito, "Contributors versus Leechers: Fansubbing Ethics," in *Fandom Unbound: Otaku Culture in a Connected World*, eds. M. Ito, D. Okabe and I.Tsuji (New Haven, CT: Yale University Press, 2012), 179–204.

thing" for the community or the favorite works should be one of the criteria to distinguish an otaku. According to them, one could not be regarded as an otaku, unless he/she voluntarily provides information/resources for the community, or has the impulse to promote or even produce derivative products for his/her favorite works.

There were eight informants who had experiences writing critical reviews for animation/manga pieces, while one of them was a freelance writer for animation/manga magazines and an establisher of an online animation magazine. Eight had participated in derivative works creation, including drawing and writing. Five of my informants provided resources online regularly. Four had participated in manga translation or fan-subtitling groups for animation. Other contributions mentioned by my informants include establishing websites, managing discussion boards, maintaining server for download, engaging in cosplay, and being photographer for cosplayers. The details are shown in Figure 11.6.

Judging from the details and tones of my informants' responses, these practices had certainly facilitated their belonging to otaku identity as well as to the otaku communities.

Other practices mentioned by multiple informants include regularly visiting online merchandisers or real shops which sold commercialized derivative products or books, listening to drama CD,[203] reading ACG-related

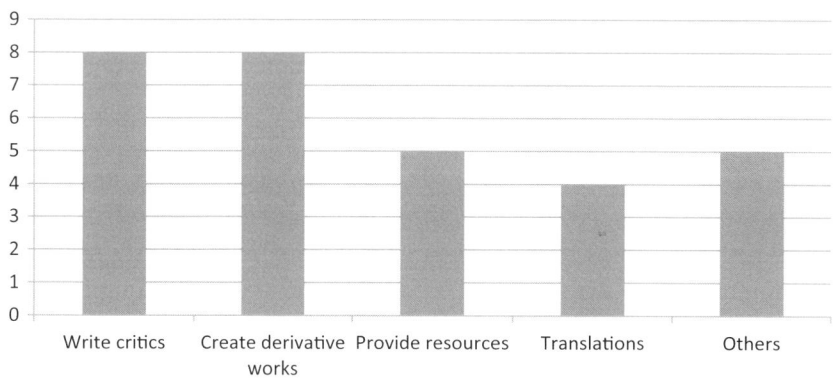

FIGURE 11.6. CONTRIBUTING TO OTAKU COMMUNITY.

---

[203] Drama CD is a Japanese word that means radio drama.

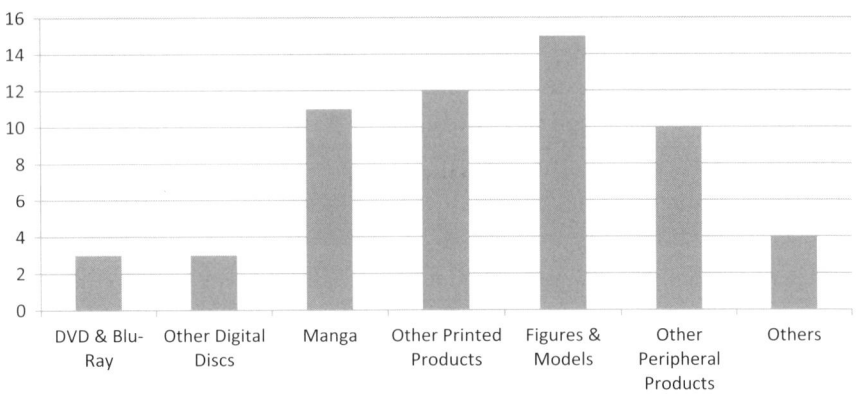

FIGURE 11.7. ITEMS OF EXPENDITURE SPENT BY MY INFORMANTS FOR PURSUING THEIR OTAKU INTEREST.

Note: Y-axis unit in the graph above represents the percentage of overall expenditures that each category of items occupies.

light novels, and consuming fan-produced derivative works (i.e. novels, drawings, videos, and games).

For **the seven other cases**, all except the one who quitted the identity, would watch animation or read manga on a daily or weekly basis, and had participated in online discussions and offline activities such as *dojinshi* fairs. However, among those three "fans," one of them did not mention information-gathering activities, and another one emphasized that she would not spend time gathering information which was one of the reasons why she believed she was not an otaku.

The informant who gave up the otaku interest used to be a passionate consumer of otaku products and an active member in both online and offline communities. According to her, the change of identity from otaku to non-otaku was due to her change in job and city of residence. After several months of busy work, late nights, and no one to talk about topics relating to otaku culture, she gradually lost the passion and gave up the interest. It is possible that without communication and emotional support from the community, it is hard to keep the passion and maintain the otaku identity.

Based on the response of three university students, it seems that with more tolerance and acceptance of the popularity of otaku culture by mainstream society, the younger generation could express and enjoy their otaku lives more freely in real lives. In addition, one of those three students that I interviewed was an amateur voice actor and singer for fan-produced products, which might indicate more well-developed derivative creation activities among younger generations.

Expenditure

As mentioned previously, after the proliferation of internet access in China, most ACG fans consume the contents of animation/manga online. Most otaku products (i.e. animation, manga, game), as well as some associated peripheral products (e.g. theme/character songs and original soundtrack, drama CD, live concert and event video, and even Japanese *dojin* productions) could be accessed or downloaded from the internet legally or illegally either free or at a very low cost, i.e. several or dozen yuan (usually less than US$10) per year through online channels or downloaded software. Fans inside the anime/manga fandom were able to access new programs or manga magazines subtitled by fan groups within several days or only hours' delay from its first broadcast or release. It is thus possible for an addicted animation/manga fan to spend a little or no finances in sustaining his/her interest but keep consuming products in a massive amount. Therefore, although otaku is described as fetishistic (Vincent, 2011, p. xiii)[204] and associated with the image of middle-aged male shopping in *dojinshi* fairs or Akihabara in Japan, buying idol-related or ACG products is not a routine practiced by otakus in mainland China.

However, it was widely agreed by my informants that expenditure on otaku interests is one of the subcultural capital valued by otaku communities. Only three of my informants, including two postgraduate students who had little disposable income, had never spent any money on products other than otaku-related Chinese-language magazines and pirated DVDs/manga. The rest listed all kinds of miscellaneous expenses, including legal copies of DVD/Blu-Ray, other digital discs,[205] manga with authorization (mainly Taiwan or Hong Kong editions), other printed

---

[204] Vincent, "Translator's Introduction," xiii.

[205] Legal copies of original sound tracks of the animation, character songs, and drama CD of animation/manga were mentioned.

products,[206] figures and models,[207] other peripheral products,[208] and other expenditures (see Figure 11.7).[209]

To most informants, those expenses were neither regular nor one-off sudden impulse. Rather, it was a consumption habit related to their economic capabilities and the individual attractiveness of available products. While being asked how much money they had spent in otaku interest, only one of them could recall numerical details of his regular monthly expenditure at around RMB240 because he would spend money on animation/manga related T-shirts on regular basis, and another who kept ledger recalled approximately RMB25,000 in the year of 2013. The rest could only provide the prices of the most expensive products/sets (i.e. manga series and DVD box) they ever bought. 77% of my informants had spent over RMB200 for a single item in their consumption history, which was much higher than the cost of magazines and pirated DVD/manga (generally between RMB5 to RMB10 per item). Over 60% of my informants had spent more than RMB500, mostly RMB700 to RMB1,000 (eight of them) on one item/set, whereas two of them spent over RMB2,000 in a single item/set (see Figure 11.8).

According to the statistics published by the National Bureau of Statistics of the People's Republic of China, the *combined* annual cash consumption expenditure for urban households in "education, culture and recreation" per capita was RMB2,033.50 in 2012, RMB2,149.69 in 2011 and RMB1,983.70 in 2010 (2013, p. 380).[210] Therefore, in the case of my informants, 77% of them had spent over 10% of one year's aver-

---

[206]Light novels, derivative drawings and books produced by fans, Japanese ACG magazines, and other products such as the artist's books were mentioned.

[207]Figures and models mentioned by my informants were (1) figures of animation/manga characters, including Garage Kit (GK), PVC Figure (PF), super deformed figurine (SD), Gashapon, and so on; and (2) scale models, mostly the model of robots.

[208]Other peripheral products mentioned include daily wearable T-shirt, stationery, accessories, dining equipment, and other goods produced by production companies or DIY by fans.

[209]Other expenditures include attending live concert, watching animated movie in cinema, and buying clothes for cosplay.

[210]National Bureau of Statistics of People's Republic of China, *2013 China Statistical Yearbook* (Beijing: China Statistics Press, 2013), 380.

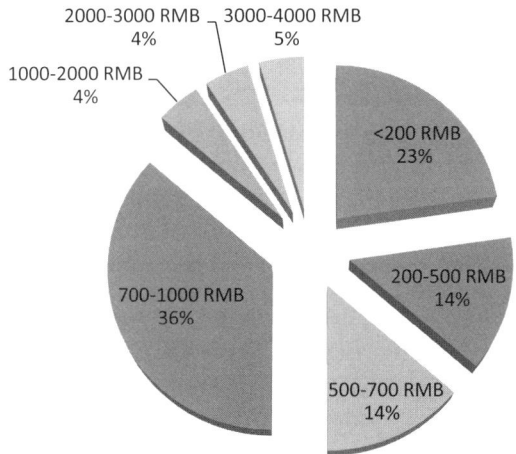

FIGURE 11.8. EXPENSES ON ANIMATION/MANJA RELATED PRODUCTS.

age individual education and leisure combined expenditure budgets on a single otaku item at least once, where around 10% of them spent urban households' average whole year's budget on one anime/manga-related item *alone*. Most of my informants believed they would spend more if they were to have better economic conditions, come across rare collectors' items, or attend live performances.

It is worth mentioning that my other seven informants consumed in a similar pattern, including those three "non-otaku" ACG fans.

The expenses my informants spent on otaku interests were considered irrational from the perspective of their family and non-otaku friends in mainland China. Some of my informants said they would not tell their parents how expensive his/her collections are. During the interview with the informant who quitted her identity, she confessed that she used to spend thousands of Chinese yuan on one plastic figure and she bought several other expensive figurines during her university years. Her husband, who was a member of musical subcultural groups, came by and overheard the conversation accidentally, and he was so surprised by the price of the products that he could not help saying "it is crazy" several times in front of the interviewers.

However, there was no general agreement among my informants about whether spending money or buying goods are important activities for otakus. Some of my informants believed an otaku should at least spend some money as a proof of their devotion to the culture. Other said they would spend money on their favorite works because it is the only way to show their support as a fan outside Japan. And the rest, especially the one who had a full-time job with stable and independent financial status and never spent any money on otaku interest related products other than private manga/DVD and magazines, disagreed the significance of expenditures to otaku identity. He explained that possession of material goods is meaningless to him. He believed some people would gain personal enjoyment from buying goods, but it is not the essence to having an otaku identity. Furthermore, my informants, who had a desire for expenditures, seemed to be spending within their means. Those who had little disposable income would spend less accordingly. This might be consistent with Saito's understandings of expenditures as a performance of their passion to otaku culture (2011, pp. 17–19).[211]

Sources and platforms

When I asked my informants about the networks through which they performed their otaku routines and purchased products, internet usage and online resources stood out again, as was the case during their identity formation periods.

Nearly all animation and manga were first consumed through the internet. The purchase of DVD/Blu-Ray and authorized manga mostly happened after my informants had watched/read the products and decided to spend money on them.

Online encyclopedias and search engines were important information gathering tools. Besides, inside the internet usage, discussion forums/BBS (electronic bulletin boards) turned out to be the most popular channels for information-sharing,[212] followed by microblogging[213] and SNS. ACG-themed

---

[211] Saito, *Beautiful Fighting Girl*, trans. Vincent and Lawson, 17–19.

[212] Besides famous forums inside otaku fandom, such as Stage1, animation/manga section of university BBS had been mentioned by several people.

[213] Surprisingly, besides Weibo, Twitter had been mentioned by three people, though it has been blocked by the Great Firewall of China and needed tools to access inside mainland China.

websites and blogs, even download websites, video websites, or online retailers (book stores such as Kadokawa Taiwan, and electronic commerce sites such as Amazon.jp) were used to access resources as well as to obtain more specialized information. According to my informants, although many of these sites were designed to provide resources and sell products rather than for information purposes, they usually provided a large array of newest updated products organized in different sections and sometimes even provided much-anticipated promotional videos, which were sufficient for some of my informants for obtaining entertainment news updates. In addition, IM had been mentioned by five of my informants,[214] and another two highlighted some software/apps that could provide additional fandom resources as well as information.[215] The details are shown in Figure 11.9. It is worth noticing that the majority of those information channels, including forums/BBS, microblogs, SNS, IM, ACG websites and blogs, download websites, and some video websites (those video websites were mainly dependent on user's uploads), were created and maintained by fellow fans.

Personal and interest group friends both online and in the real world (i.e. non-virtual) remained crucial pool of informants for them. 12 out of

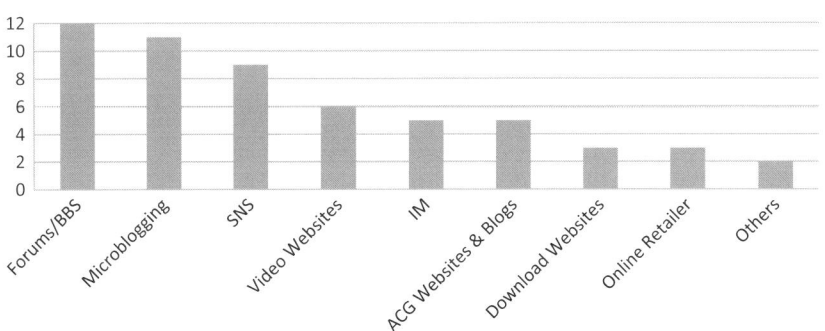

FIGURE 11.9. ONLINE INFORMATION CHANNELS.

---

[214] All five individuals were talking about using fans group in QQ, one of the most popular IM software used in China. The members of the groups they talked about were a mixture of net friends and real world friends.

[215] One of them talked about a peer-to-peer streaming video freeware. The other introduced an app on iPad to me which provided large number of newly published manga for their customers to select and watch.

22 of my informants kept gathering new program information from their peers and consumed products based on peers' recommendations. *Dojinshi* fairs, offline gatherings, and other forms of personal contact facilitated the information exchanges as well.

Finally, magazines[216] and anime/manga products stores[217] still played a role as information and consumption platform for several of my informants.

For the other seven cases, no significant differences were discovered regarding to sources and platforms they used.

To conclude, both online and real life networks were important platforms in fulfilling otaku's routine practices, consumptions, and other needs, and assisted in the maintenance of otaku identity. Compared to official channels, the communities and channels created by fans and personal connections played a more significant role.

Summary

According to my informants, watching/reading animation/manga, gathering information, attending ACG-related activities, and communicating with or contributing to otaku communities are life routines for otakus in mainland China, which not only provide the enjoyment of consumption but are also crucial to otaku's identity maintenance. On the other hand, expenditures on otaku interests are common but may not directly link to the otaku identity. Official channels again only play a little part in the life of an otaku. Both internet, mainly platforms built by otaku communities, and personal connections are the most important information and communication channels for mainland China otaku nowadays.

The Perception of Otaku Identity

After going through the process of formation, adoption, and maintenance of the otaku identity, next comes the question of how my informants

---

[216] Five of my informants still read magazines. But one of them had recently changed to subscribing to a digital magazine instead of buying printed copies, and one read the Japanese magazine *New Type*, which would provide more updated and accurate information than the news circulated in the Chinese internet.

[217] Two of them, one lived in Shanghai and one outside mainland China, would go shopping in those shops time to time.

understood their identity and situation back home regardless of the definition of "otaku" I adopted in this writing. That is, how did those young adults perceive themselves, their interest, their communities, and their relationships in the society? I will discuss their understanding of otaku first, then the perceived acceptance of their surroundings and the uniqueness of the otaku culture and the community.

Definitions of otaku

Amongst 22 of my informants, none of them entirely adopted the localized definition of otaku used by mass media such as homey boys or heavy internet users. Seven of my informants mentioned the Japanese word "otaku" and its usage in Japan, while one raised Okada's definition specifically as the source of his understanding, and another brought up the Miyazaki incident and the negative response it generated in the media response to emphasize the subcultural status of the otaku community. Therefore, as I suspected, to understand their identities, studying the mass media usage alone will not be sufficient. The definitions of otaku and self-identification with this term raised by otakus themselves would not only yield important information on how otakus draw their boundaries against general animation/manga audience, but also reveal their insights of the phenomenon of otaku-ism as members of the otaku community.

Based on their responses, one commonality stood out during the interviews. All of my informants believed that enjoyment of consuming animation/manga products is the basic requirement of being an otaku. Two of them even considered having a "love" of ACG culture alone is the only requirement for being an otaku. When they were asked for ideas about detailed qualities that can measure enjoyment or love of ACG culture, 14 of them generally described how passion should be as deep as the "true love" of life itself, and 13 informants pointed to consumption behavior of animation/manga as indicators of passion towards ACG products (see Table 11.1). There were also 10 informants who pointed out that treating animation/manga as a very important interest in life is a necessary display of enjoyment or love of popular cultural products (the main statements of how they defined "very important" have been listed in Table 11.2).

TABLE 11.1. THE STANDARD OF A "QUALIFIED" OTAKU SHOULD HAVE CONSUMED ANIMATION/MANGA.
(arranged by the number of times the statement was mentioned)

Statement 1: An otaku should have consumed a large amount of animation/manga covering various genres.

Statement 2: An otaku should either have massive consumption of animation/manga, or proficiency in several pieces that are significant to him/her.

Statement 3: An otaku should be proficient in the animation/manga or a specific genre that attract most.

Statement 4: An otaku should at least once follow the newly broadcasting animation programs in Japan (the standard for animation otaku only).

TABLE 11.2. HOW MY INFORMANTS DEFINED "VERY IMPORTANT INTEREST".
(arranged by the number of times the statement was mentioned)

Statement 1: To an otaku, animation/manga should mean something irreplaceable by any other forms of cultural products. If you only consider animation/manga as a form of dispensable expenditure, you are not qualified as an otaku.

Statement 2: Otaku is someone who has emotional attachments towards ACG culture, and the cultural products are an important source of their spiritual sustenance and comfort.

Statement 3: To an otaku, ACG interest should become a life habit, and an important part of the daily lives.

Statement 4: An otaku should be a conscious ACG products consumer.

Statement 5: As an otaku, consuming animation/manga or cultural related contents should be his/her first choice of leisure time.

Statement 6: An otaku should be someone who values ACG culture and stick to his/her opinion towards the culture. He/she will not easily give up the interest towards the culture even if it is being criticized by his/her significant others.

Statement 7: An otaku should be able to enjoy the ACG products. He/she should treat the culture as an interest rather than a career or a way of earning money and fame (in the case of derivative writers/painters and cosplayers).

Besides the love of animation/manga, other requirements cited by my informants as qualities of being passionate about ACG were quite diverse. Figure 11.10 is a summary of the criteria mentioned by them.

10 of them believed that if one did not possess enough knowledge of his/her favorite works, engaged in otaku culture, or learned more about the industry, he/she could not be called as an otaku. But two of my informants

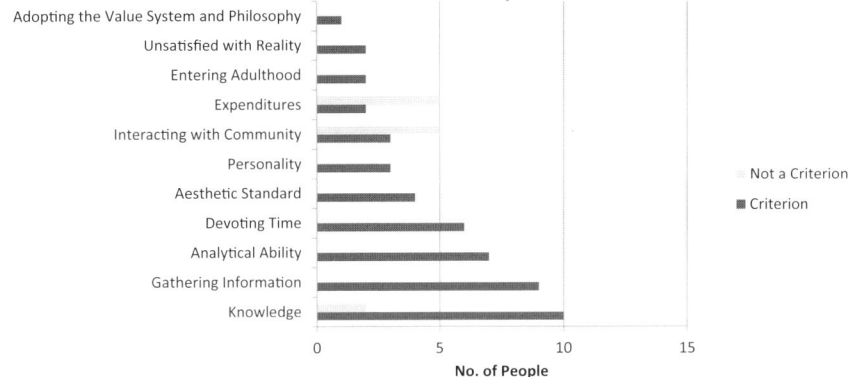

FIGURE 11.10. CRITERIA OF QUALIFYING AS AN "OTAKU" MENTIONED BY MY INFORMANTS.

said that knowledge is not essential as people would naturally gain knowledge after consuming large amount of animation/manga. Another one informant stated that knowledge should be a requirement only for advanced level of otaku-ism.

Nine of my informants insisted that an otaku by definition is someone who either is good at gathering information, or at least has curiosity and will pay effort to collect information.

Seven of them believed that an otaku should be someone who consumes the animation/products with an analytical mind. While I followed up with their responses and asked them to further explain the kind of analytical ability they were talking about in relation to otaku-level fandom, one said that an otaku should be able to form a personal opinion towards the pieces they either like or hate. Another stated that while consuming the ACG products, an otaku should be sensitive to the value system and philosophy behind the products and be capable of employing them to further reflect on the reality of life. One informant also explained that, if people were to like animation/manga only because they were attracted by the handsome looks or fascinating dresses and accessories of the characters, they are not true otakus.

Four informants listed aesthetic as a requirement, that is he/she should have his/her own taste and aesthetic standards. According to them, otaku should not only appreciate the most popular pieces, but also be adventurous enough to discover the avant-garde or experimental pieces, and be open to new styles and trends of animation/manga culture.

Behavioral habits were listed by many of them, though there seemed to be a controversy regarding the criteria. Six informants believed that otaku should be someone who spends considerable time, or the majority of their leisure time on animation/manga related consumptions, practices, and activities. Attending activities and sharing with/contribute to the fan community were only mentioned by three of my informants as criteria of being an otaku, whereas five others regarded them as unessential. Spending money on otaku interests was also mentioned by two of my informants, while another five thought it is not important at all. There was also one informant who believed that otaku should be defined as a group of people who are well-equipped with encyclopedic knowledge of otaku products and are able to relate to animation/manga contents in their daily lives.

There were also several informants who argued that the definition of "otaku" should be related to one's personality, or even philosophies and worldviews in their lives. Three of them believed an otaku should be someone who focuses more on inner thoughts and feelings than external outlook. Two of them clarified that since otaku culture is something different from the mainstream, an otaku should be someone who feels frustrated or trapped in the reality and enters the world of animation/manga with the hope of finding an alternative way of value system and life. One said that an otaku should be someone who internalizes the underlying values system and philosophy behind the popular cultural genres and products that they are into.

In addition, two of my informants believed that one could declare to be an otaku only after entering the adulthood. To those two informants, the decision of adopting the otaku identity only counts after one has explored other alternatives.

A point noteworthy to mention here is, although the priority of the interest in animation/manga was stressed, there were no requirements of loyalty towards a specific subcultural identity. Many of my informants had more than one subculture identities, and this did not pose a problem with having an otaku identity. Some of them were into other Japanese popular culture, such as Japanese TV drama, mystery novel, J-pop, or rock bands. Several of them revealed themselves as film buffs. Reading, theater performance,

American drama, online game, and so on were also mentioned during the interviews.

While being asked whether there is a universal definition of "otaku" within the otaku community itself, four of them believed yes, one claimed he was not familiar with others' opinion regarding to this subject, and the rest of the 17 informants thought that there are no general definition of "otaku" which could be accepted by the majority of the fans and otaku communities.

10 of my informants were critical that the word "otaku" had been abused not only by mass media, but also by fans. According to them, there were a lot more audiences of animation/manga compared to the past, and those new members held a variety of "misunderstanding" (by my inform-ant's standards) towards otaku-ism. Or, as some of them said, it could be interpreted as the phenomenon of a dynamically changing definition of "otaku" over the years. Some new fans may make a claim of being an otaku in order to attain a higher status inside fandom. Furthermore, it may be fashionable for some young people to do so even though they may not watch/read many animation/manga works.

Regarding the question of what causes the different understandings of the term otaku-ism, all sorts of influential factors had been listed by the 17 informants who believed that there were no general understanding of this term among fans. Nine informants proposed age/generation and years of experiences in consuming otaku culture as the main factors affecting the definition of the otaku identity. There were also eight others who suggested not having the right personality, ability, and attitudes towards otaku culture would limit one's understanding of otaku culture (e.g. a person who does not have the patience, curiosity and ability to conduct research may not understand otaku as someone with information gathering and analytical abilities). Seven of them mentioned members of different subgroups under the otaku culture might have different normative "required behavior" as a criterion for being a "qualified otaku" (an example they provided is people from cosplay circle may consider attending activities as a basic require-ment for being an otaku). Five of them believed that otaku friends and first encounters with the otaku culture would affect ones' understanding of otaku-ism. Two informants suggested that the understanding of otaku-ism could be generally divided into two categories based on the enjoyment they

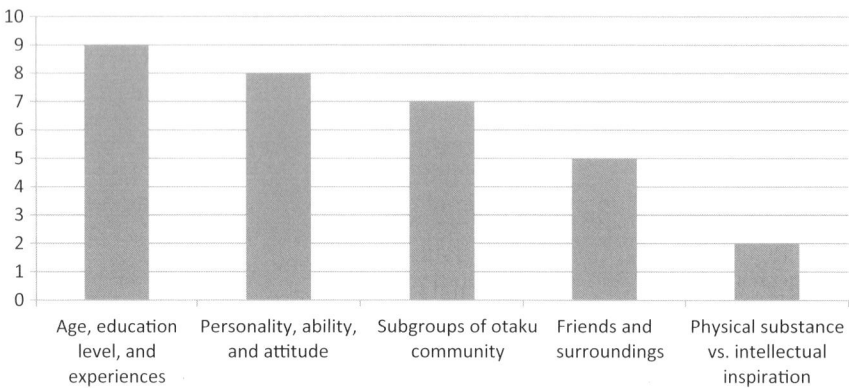

FIGURE 11.11. FACTORS BELIEVED TO HAVE AFFECTED THE UNDER-STANDING OF THE TERM "OTAKU".

pursued, the physical and materialistic appreciation, or intellectual inspiration made possible by the creative productions (see Figure 11.11).

However, amongst the 17 informants who agreed that the definition of otaku is diverse inside the community, six of them also believed that a neutral understanding of the term without attributing strict values or qualities to it is possible. They said, when one had enough exposure to the otaku community, the definition will become stricter, and will veer closer to the definition that old generations of hardcore otakus held.

Amongst the seven non-otaku cases, the informant who backtracked on the identity raised the similar criteria my informants listed above.

The three current university students in my survey, as mentioned before, seemed to have difficulties in defining or describing what they thought are the features or characteristics of an otaku. Compared to most of my 22 informants, who were interested in this topic and even asked follow-up questions several days after the interview, three student informants were uncomfortable with these questions. One of them even became upset about the discussion and said that an otaku is an otaku, and there was no need to further discuss this topic. Two of the informants adopted the stereotypical features of otakus portrayed by the public media but questioned the validity of their own definitions at the end of the interviews. One informant said that she could not provide any definition and can only describe how her friends in school animation/manga clubs behaved as possible otaku characteristics. It is also notable that while being asked whether there are any factors that might affect the definition of otaku, one of the female responders advised gender being one of the factors. She indicated that boys would consider otaku as someone who loves robot animation and plays scale models, while girls might define otaku as cosplayers. This is the only time when possible gender differences were mentioned during all interviews.

Three others who insisted that they were only fans came up with the explanations for avoiding the term "otaku." One of them associated the term "otaku" with social dysfunction and communication difficulties, which influenced him to believe that he should not consider himself as an otaku. Another mentioned that she consumed all sorts of popular cultural products indiscriminately without special emphasis on Japanese animation and manga. She also stressed that unlike a "true otaku," she had no special interests in acquiring extra specialized knowledge or biodata of the creative teams behind the products, and she had no intention of doing any additional research on her own for getting such specialized information. The third informant in this group believed he would fail to qualify as an otaku based on the time, money, and energy spent on animation/manga and otaku community compared with his otaku friends.

Perceived perceptions of otaku-ism

I asked my informants what they thought of the perceived acceptance of otaku-ism among general public. Most of my informants said that animation/manga culture had been quite popular among youths or in economically well-developed areas of China in recent years, but whether it had been widely accepted or became a mainstream in popular culture was doubtful. Some of them also stressed that, in spite of the popularity of animation/manga, the culture of otaku remained as a minority subculture.

None of my informants concealed their interests towards animation/manga, but neither would they openly declare they were otakus outside the animation/manga fandom community. Some of them even criticized the younger fans' tendencies to show off their hobbies in public and trample on others' personal social space, especially members of the public who do not appreciate their form of lifestyle.

Though none of my informants experienced any serious discrimination in real life, according to them, the stereotyped image of otaku was negative in general.

While talking about parents' attitude towards otaku-ism, all of my informants, except one, were of the opinion that their parents could not understand it.[218] Several of them said they had tried to recommend animation pieces believed to be popular among adults and general public abroad, such as those by Hayao Miyazaki, but their attempts failed. As mentioned before, many of my informants' parents were against their obsession in popular cultural products during their high school years. Their interests and related life routines had been accepted to a larger extent when they grew up. The main complaints and worries they received from their parents after entering the adulthood were that their status and habit of being an otaku were childish, and they "never grow up." Besides, a few of my informants also remarked that their family members would sometimes educate them not to "waste so much time" on an interest. One informant also mentioned that her mother was worried that she was into "Japanese things" (the informant was a fan of Japanese detective novels besides animation/manga) and told her to explore more cultural products originating from other regions of the world other than Japan.

Though the majority of my informants were not in a relationship during the interviews, several had dated otaku in the past. In fact, it seemed that they would intentionally choose those who could understand their otaku interests or, as mentioned in one case before, they adopted the interests while dating another otakus. However, not all love stories were compatible with their otaku lifestyles. One of my informants was still dealing with her emotions after her ex-boyfriend criticized her otaku interests as strange and unbearable while dating her.

According to my informants, if friends cannot at least try to understand their interests, they will not be able to continue in that friendship anymore (though the scenario never happened to any of them). As for the workplace, their colleagues either had no idea of what is otaku and did not care much, or were unaware of their otaku identities. Moreover, several of the informants told me that they had colleagues who share the ACG interests and

---

[218]The only one informant who was different said his parents had their own significant interests, and they positively encouraged him to find one and learn to enjoy life.

would sometimes ask for their recommendations for animation/manga series.

The majority of negative impressions my informants received were from their peers and general public. Watching/reading animation/manga as an adult was considered "childish" by some of their peers, along with other stereotypical image of otaku-ism. According to over half of my informants, though most of their peers enjoyed animation/manga in their childhood, many of them considered it "childish" to have otaku habits and lifestyles. Some of my informants complained that people usually mistaken otaku with persons who stay at home a lot to escape from reality, or people who are socially dysfunctional, which they believed was a misconception influenced by the mass media. There were also some informants who heard others criticizing otaku as a form of deviant and strange interest on the internet. Besides, one of my informants mentioned that people believed animation/manga were full of violence and sexual components, and therefore associated otaku with unhealthy interests/habits, which surprisingly did not come up in my survey and/or materials covered in the literature reviews. Only one informant mentioned about being criticized with a nationalistic remark. That is, in spite of the complicated historical-cultural relationship and political tensions between China and Japan, majority of my informants were never criticized because of their special interests in a Japanese culture. It is possible that people's main impression of animation/manga was based on the idea of young children's entertainment rather than a form of adult-age Japanese popular culture.

In short, all my informants' environments showed certain degree of tolerance and understanding towards otaku-ism. Some of them lived under a generally supportive atmosphere in their personal lives. The general public's perceptions of otaku that my informants mentioned were characterized as that of a group of people who are "childish" and lead an unhealthy lifestyle, but otherwise harmless as long as their academic performance are not interfered by the interests during school years, and they could manage their lives afterwards.

Most of my informants usually chose to ignore public misunderstanding and misinterpretations (in their view) unless they were in the mood for debating with non-otaku individuals, or if they were criticized by their close friends (which according to them never actually happened). Several of them considered it normal that otaku could not be understood by general public as it is a subculture after all, and it was useless to explain or defend against negative perceptions and opinions if those people just do not like otakus.

Interestingly, some of my informants agreed with some widely circulated criticisms towards otakus, such as lacking social skills, caring too little about their appearance (though none of them mentioned this point while listing the criticism they received), sometimes too loud in pursuing their interests in the general public (bad manners), and staying at home too much (too introvert). A few of them said they would reflect upon some of these criticisms as a reminder to be prudent when exercising their otaku identity.

For the other seven informants, they generally revealed similar stories as my 22 informants did, except for the three who were university students. They seemed to receive relatively more support from their family, especially financial help, compared to the others.

Their own perception of otaku-ism

Even though animation/manga products were considered childish by the general public, my informants provided a list of reasons why they found animation/manga and other otaku products so unique or attractive (see Figure 11.12).

Most of them claimed they loved watching and reading animation/manga as a form of visual arts appreciation. Some of them were fond of Japanese drawing and its minimalistic aesthetics, some believed animation/manga had more freedom in the creative phase compared to art depicting reality, some claimed it was one of the most comfortable art forms for them because they had been used to and familiar with the medium of artistic expression since childhood.

The worldview and philosophies underlined were the second most mentioned reason. Some of my informants conceptualized the otaku world as a form of altered reality, with elements that are pure, passionate, optimistic, and romantic, a constructed utopia for young people to take a rest. But in others' eyes, it is a world that is gloomy and pessimistic, with a post-apocalyptic feeling which attracted them and inspired their philosophical

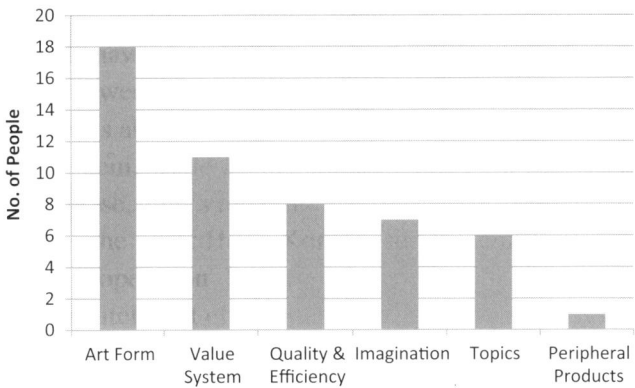

FIGURE 11.12. THE ATTRACTIVENESS OF ANIMATION/MANGA TO MY INFORMANTS.

self-reflections. Several informants mentioned that compared to American and European popular cultures, Japanese products embodied a cultural and social value based on similar cultural roots with Chinese culture, which made them easier to relate to.

Eight of my informants enjoyed animation/manga because of their higher quality production. According to them, compared to most Chinese popular TV dramas, movies, and youth literatures, ACG culture products had better qualities related to both production and contents. Moreover, the enjoyment of a 20-minute animation episode could equal a 40-minute American drama, or a movie longer than one and a half hour in terms of depth of contents and storyline covered, which is very "efficient," as they claimed. Most of my informants could also use laptops or smartphones for several minutes to read the updates of the manga series or watch a short animation episode while waiting for their instant noodles to be ready (the latter half is a popular joke among otakus).

There were also seven of them who appreciated the wild imagination in the creative process and in the storyline presented in animation/manga products which were not usually found in other forms of popular culture products.

Six of them were also attracted by the topics and current affairs discussed in animation/manga. One explained that because of the nature of the art form, it was possible to discuss sensitive and heavy topics in a casual way (e.g. depression, social withdrawal, school bullying, gender identity, sexuality, etc.). Another mentioned that the topics and themes discussed in animation/manga related to Japanese society and culture resemble the reality in China compared to American cartoons and superhero movies which are comparatively more detached from their reality.

Finally, there was one informant who provided a totally different perspective, that she loved popular culture spinning off peripheral products that are conceptually based on otaku-ism, which she thought to be unique compared to other popular culture industries.

According to the above responses, besides aesthetic satisfaction and easier acceptance, most of my informants were also after intellectual enjoyment such as appreciating the depth and variety of the topics and the values provided in the value system. As far as my informants were concerned, this aspect of otaku-ism was seldom mentioned by members outside the community and general public, but emphasized by the otaku community.

In addition to the attractiveness of otaku products, I also investigated my informants' perception towards fellow otakus and the community as a whole.

11 of them considered the otaku community as a typical subculture group and the primary similarities among otakus were the common interests or shared aesthetic standards. Several of them further claimed that there were no differences from the otaku community to other subculture groups such as film buffs.

Nine of them believed that the similarities were found in the unique behaviors and practices. That is, otakus tended to be more passionate about

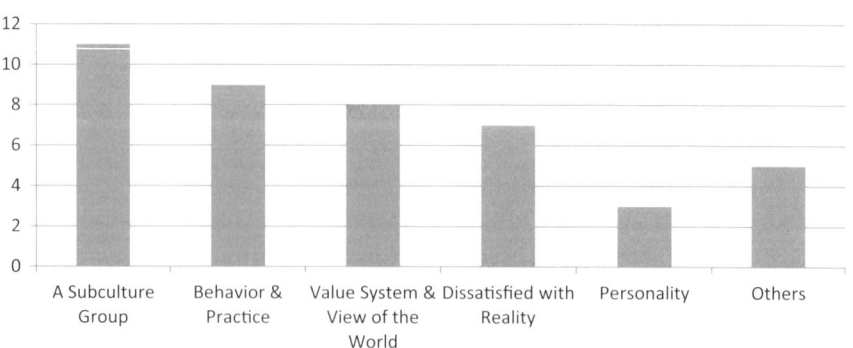

FIGURE 11.13. THE SIMILARITIES THEY BELIEVED AMONG OTAKUS.

their interests and will do research, consume peripheral products, and produce fan-based creations enthusiastically. Several also stated that otakus had a system of language and terminologies that were not shared with or well known in the general public. Therefore, it is easy for an otaku to identify another otaku in the public. They believed that these two features also distinguished otakus from other subcultural groups.

Eight of my informants, believed otakus shared similar value systems and views of the world. According to them, otakus were dreamers and persons who were idealistic with independent minds. Seven of them also pointed out that, regardless whether they believed in the same alternative system or not, members of otaku community generally questioned their reality or were dissatisfied with the mainstream/popularity in certain way. Three of them said that otakus shared similar personalities, such as introverted personalities and open to new things and ideas in general. Other shared qualities mentioned by my informants include their way of thinking, interests in Japanese culture, and attitudes towards Japan (see Figure 11.13).

In addition, though there is a popular saying in mainland China among ACG fans that it is impermeable between people living in two dimension (addicted to animation/manga) and three dimension (leading a "successful" life meeting mainstream's expectations) universe, but only one of my informants agreed with it. There were three others strongly against it and insisted it is a personal choice rather than a unique phenomenon among otakus.

When I asked whether they felt a sense of closeness or intimacy when meeting another otakus, I expected a majority answer as "no," because they had complained a lot about "pseudo-otaku" during the interview. However, 16 of 22, that is 73% of my informants said "yes." They explained that the common interests would naturally provide conversation topics, and a better chance that they could understand with each other. Some also said they will feel more relaxed if they could use the terminologies and vocabularies of the otaku community. Furthermore, some told me since it would be rare to meet another otaku, or "so-called" otaku in real life, the experiences are akin to meeting someone who shares the same secret. Three of them claimed they carefully observed the other party and might make a move after they were sure they shared similar understandings of their otaku interests and tastes.

Even the informant who turned her back on her former otaku identity said she would still feel a sense of closeness when she met another otaku, because it is like meeting someone who is doing "the same naughty thing" as she used to do.

In sum, consistent with the responses throughout the interview, most of my informants believed that otaku culture not only provided the entertainment value they enjoyed, but also satisfied deeper desires and meaning they were searching for in terms of aesthetics or worldviews. Though many of them did not believed that otakus all shared the similar goal of consumption, they still felt a sense of closeness towards other otakus or ACG fans who shared similar interests.

Discussion

According to my informants, the choice of otaku products emerged from the dissatisfaction of other popular culture products. They were either disappointed with the quality of Chinese produced popular products, or were looking for products closer to their cultural roots than western produced ones. They were attracted by the form, quality and the philosophy of animation/manga. Nevertheless, such attraction was not necessarily targeting at the Japanese culture or Japan.

Comparing my 22 informants' definitions of otaku-ism and Yi and Wang's, which I used as selection criteria while recruiting the informants in this chapter, there were some commonalities, such as the obsessiveness towards ACG and devotions to the culture. However, while Yi and Wang's operational definition relies more on practices and consumer behaviors like spending time, money, interacting with community, or attending activities, my informants' definitions tended to be more internally directed and abstract. Purchasing products, attending events, or even possessing knowledge is not essential for some of them when defining their otaku identity. They tended to see otaku-ism as a kind of talent or ability (e.g. aesthetic, information gathering and analytical abilities), or something related to life attitudes/values or philosophies. This resembles the definition raised by Okada most closely, an insider and elite of the community. It is probably the consequence of Okada's influence on Chinese otaku communities, or because most of my informants were educated members of the community regarding to their seniority in otaku community, their current jobs and living standards. It is also possible that Chinese otakus were a group of people searching for alternative life attitudes or value system in otaku-ism as Okada and Azuma described (some of them brought up this point directly).

Unlike the significant influence of mass media, the attitudes of the significant others, peers and colleagues, and general public seem to have little impact on the otaku identity. My informants were not forced to construct their community space because of being labeled and excluded by the society, and none of them adopted, maintained, or fought for asserting the otaku identity. Neither were they agitated as Japanese otakus used to do when being labeled as otaku. Many of my informants were initiatively searching for alternatives. Instead of fighting, they were merely disinterested in mainstream culture. The majority of my informants would like to keep a low profile regarding to their otaku identity and live in peace with general public. In fact, based on their perceptions, being an otaku is more like living in a parallel universe which others may not understand but will not interfere much as well. This echoes theories raised by researchers such as Azuma, except that it seems like some Chinese otakus are happy with consumption elements, and some are still looking for "grand narratives."

However, it is noteworthy that none of my informants were raised or currently lived in an environment that is strongly against ACG culture or otaku-ism. The story might be quite different for groups of otaku in mainland China facing different familial, educational or friendship networks and surroundings.

The standard my informants provided in defining otaku is generally lower than the criteria they applied to their own definitions of otaku-ism, and they believed their fellow otakus and the community might hold a lower standard towards otaku-ism. That is, although many of my informants were influenced by Okada's definition, some of them did not believe that members in the otaku community are all cultural elites or have anything special in the field of popular culture. But many of my informants were searching for high aesthetic appreciations, meanings, values, and philosophical inspiration in otaku culture, and there existed a sense of pride amongst them for being an otaku in this way. Most of my informants also expressed a sense of belonging towards the otaku community, regardless of their expectations towards other members of the community.

General Discussions and Conclusions

Based on my textual researches and fieldwork, the understanding of otaku-ism of mass media and hardcore otaku is incompatible. On the one hand, the Chinese mass media used the term "otaku" in a broader sense, which refers to socially dysfunctional youth or new lifestyle involving minimum face-to-face communication and heavy dependence on internet. Addiction to animation/manga is only one of the unimportant features shared by most members of this cultural subgroup. On the other hand, the otaku, especially senior hardcore members of otaku community, understood the term as a badge reflecting their familiarity, proficiency, and analytical capability in animation/manga culture. They not only enjoyed the entertainment value that popular culture brought about, but also enthusiastically searched for a meaning in the imaginary world that popular culture created. To them, the lack of interpersonal skills and internet addiction is a consequence of each individual's lifestyles, upbringing and living environment rather than a consequence of otaku-ism. However, both sides all agreed that the mass media is an important shaper of the otaku identity building. The debates between mass media and hardcore fans not only inspired the members of the otaku community to reflect and look at themselves but also provided them with a narrative to distinguish themselves from the general public.

My textual researches also show that the general public in China holds a tolerant attitude towards otaku-ism, which is consistent with my fieldwork results. Ultimately, Chinese culture is believed to be collective and leaves little room for personal choice compared to individualism countries. It is the belief that otaku-ism is harmless as long as the person can complete his/her tasks and manage his/her life that provides a space for otaku community to survive and develop further.

The Chinese otaku community exercised similar practices and attitude with US current otaku communities. Independent from mainstream networks, they created their own communication channels, language-use and even value systems naturally as a result of long exposure to a subculture.

In terms of consumption, though there were several important channels and networks existing in the past (such as television programs, pirated animation/manga shops and printed magazines), internet and personal relationship (including communities) are the most distinguished platforms affecting the gaining and maintaining of the otaku identity nowadays. It is the internet that provides the majority of the resources, information, and communication channels, while the personal friendship helps to introduce and keep an otaku's interests.

My fieldwork also reveals that members of the otaku community were intentionally consuming alternative value system and philosophy with different habits and styles from those that mainstream society practiced. However, most of them preferred to live in their own universe rather than fighting for being understood by the mainstream. Furthermore, they disagreed with radical behaviors (especially when exhibited in the public) and tried to accommodate themselves to mainstream social norms and standards. Although they were aware of the cultural background and origins of the otaku products, most of them were not yearning after "Japanese-ness" in contrast to the western ACG fans. They were not especially dissatisfied with Chinese culture or western culture. In fact, they were looking for similarities of Japanese and Chinese cultures in those products which aroused intimacies and will continue to consume products from other western culture as well. They seemed to be more interested in whether the products suited their taste rather than considering the origin of the culture.

It can be concluded from my field work that otaku identity is a reflection of dissatisfaction with mainstream aesthetics and consumption culture, or even the mainstream value system or reality as a whole. At the same time, it is also a taste culture and a lifestyle.

This chapter only serves as a preliminary research. Because of the small sample size, the findings require further investigation. And there are no obvious gender differences but possible variance among generations of otaku fans and otaku subgroups also need further research. Moreover, correlations between daily practice/behavior and the understanding of the otaku-ism are also worth closer examination. Last but not least, otaku community is a very special group which might provide information on Sino-Japanese relationship as well as cultural exchanges from a new perspective. The field of otaku in mainland China is a fascinating topic that requires further research in the future.

Section 5

Hong Kong

Chapter 12

Interview with a Self-identified Otaku JL, a Hong Konger Who Is a PhD Student on 30 March 2015 Monday at 9.30 pm in Singapore

Tai Wei LIM

In the previous chapter, Anna Lin's study has indicated three very important aspects of Chinese otakus. First, she considers the word "otaku" as a vague self-originated identity and a descriptive term originating from the otaku community itself. She then argues that, though the definition of "otaku" is not universally accepted in the same way by scholars and researchers of the popular culture field in both Japan and other English-speaking countries, most definitions generally agree that the enjoyment gained from consuming the products is important or even essential to otaku identity. Second, Lin and most writers agree on a common point related to hardcore fans of popular culture. Through active participation in consuming and creating derivative works, otakus are empowered to establish their own value and worldview as a community.

Third, contents knowledge is king in determining the status of otakus in the eyes of their community. It is the familiarity, the knowledge and the interpretations related to the products that otaku consumers valued that are most important and key to understanding the otaku identity, e.g. the importance of fandom information flow, familiarity with materials, shared ideas about aesthetics, and the understanding/interpretation of the popular cultural products related to the otaku identity. Lin highlights the idea that possessing content-based knowledge positively upgrades one's status within the community. That is, the more a fan knows, the more respectable he/she becomes. In fact, information is a main source of commodity in the US otaku community.

With Lin's ideas in mind, Tai Wei Lim carried out a qualitative unstructured interview where the informant was free to speak his/her mind about having an identity as an otaku. Lim had three objectives in mind for the interview. First, it functions as a useful comparative case study of a Hong Kong otaku with mainland Chinese otakus in Lin's study. The comparison may be useful given that Hong Kong (and Taiwan) is often considered to be an advanced platform for J-pop and K-pop products entering the mainland Chinese market. Second, it is a detailed in-depth look at how otakus in Hong Kong negotiate the complicated identity issues, gender differences, socio-economic strata, cultural preferences and social trends that shape their sense of aesthetics, worldviews and how they view themselves. Third, there are also some nuggets of information from the informants who compared some aspects of Cantopop with J-pop.

Interview details:

Participants: Tai Wei LIM and JL, a Hong Konger who is a PhD student
Date: 30 March 2015 (Monday)
Time: 9.30 pm
Location: Singapore

Legend for the transcript below:

Interviewer: TW: Tai Wei LIM
Interviewee: JL

TW: How do you define what you mean by otaku?

JL: My generation of otaku is by the differentiation between the normal human and us. Everybody will watch common cartoons like Hello Kitty but otaku will watch those that normal people do not watch. These animes make us think more, like psychological issues inside the anime and comic that usual people do not want to read for relaxation. I don't see otakus hiding in the room all the time like Japanese otakus. They can have social lives and meet people. The difference is what they are seeing and watching that are different from normal people. And of course even if they have their own social lives, their social lives circles are different from normal people. Normal males will have female friends. Male otakus will have friends who share similar interests and they also do chatting on otaku topics. Friends are mostly male or a high percentage of males because that is a common sense of otakus.

TW: Why do you consider yourself an otaku?

JL: Because I also watch a lot of anime that normal people do not watch. And [including anime with] some very adult issues, with a male character surrounded by a bunch of female characters centered on issues that normal people do not really care. But I watch anime [rather] than [read] comics because the latter spend more time. I consider myself an otaku because when I have free time, I prefer to watch anime [rather] than playing games or sleeping or some normal routines.

TW: What do you mean by "normal"?

JL: "Normal" is actually talking about [referring to] the average people, what they normally [do] after work, like shopping, hang out with friends and do exercise while myself and other otaku fans read the comics or visit the forum to discuss otaku news for leisure time. In this case [sense], otakus are abnormal.

TW: How did you start being an otaku?

JL: I started being an otaku in the winter of seven years ago. I was studying in Canada in a cold place, snowing all the time. At the time, I did not know skiing or skating so I stayed at home and started watching anime. I also know Japanese friends and I started watching some otaku anime and we discussed comics together, the implications of an episode.

TW: What are your spending habits as an otaku?

JL: I myself do not spend much money. I only buy some figures or buy some posters of some anime characters, or cards with logos printed on them, or go to Hong Kong animation exhibition that is an annual event in Wan Chai. I will go there. My friends go to more comic shops to rent a comic or DVD compared to me. I don't have a fixed amount of how much I spend per month. I do not yet have a chance to go to Tokyo but I plan to go. I go to Tokyo to visit Akihabara. That is one of the place I want to go.

TW: What do you know about Akihabara?

JL: I know two things. One is the collection of all the otaku shops there. It is a place for the creation of new writers or their drawings because I heard a lot of stories that a lot of people go there to get new ideas to write a new story. I want to go there because I can learn more about the anime from there, there are big collections for otaku so I can learn more from there. Other than that there are a lot of ladies and males doing cosplaying, dressed up as anime characters for fun or promoting themselves. I remember I saw from online websites that usually the fastest promotion of new things is there, like the company would usually make secret of the release date of the DVD and anime show, so they will announce it there first.

TW: Does your interest in anime culture and being an otaku motivate you to know more about Japan?

JL: Definitely so, for example, some of the otaku anime mention about the Asian god and some temple and how people worship their god and their tradition to worship the god once a year in the area (Title: "Higurashi When They Cry"). Some event to worship the god and so I want to know more about this. In the Chinese temple, there is nothing like this so I want to learn more. There's a lot of otakus talking about theme of love. They have many magical things because of love. It seems that love can change everything. When they are in trouble, some magic happens. Because of the love of friendship or couple, they can get over the trouble. Makes me want to know about Japanese culture, more focusing on the human feelings or love. That is why I am interested in Japanese culture. And some area is talking about food, that people want to try Japanese food. A lot of anime in Japan have one male character and many female characters. And the female characters always have some reason to live with the male characters, and the female will cook some delicious food and make otakus want to know about Japanese food culture.

TW: Do you consider Japanese food to be an important component of Japanese pop culture?

JL: Not really, it is not a major component but just one minor thing for the Japanese popular culture. I like it because I like cooking and trying new food.

TW: Do you face any discrimination or are people curious about your otaku habits?

JL: Usually, in Hong Kong, females would say you are so "toxic" (*dok* in Cantonese or *du* in Hanyu Pinyin, literally meaning one is poisoned deeply) because otakus watch too much anime and their lifestyles are different from other Hong Kong people, less socializing. So Hong Kong people say otakus hide themselves and do not want to face the world. But if I meet friends who also like to watch anime, they are okay with it. Even some who watch it sometime a year, they also consider them to be "toxic" because the females need to see the characteristics of the males to consider if they are "toxic" or not. If the males do not do anything and just read books, they would consider them as "toxic." If the males also go partying and also read the comics, the females would not consider them as "toxic." It depends on the percentage. How many percentage of the time is spent on the otaku "toxicity." Actually I know of female otakus, my girlfriend's female roommate. She watch anime or read comics once she has free time. "Toxic" is a word to describe male only. If we describe female, we would use "chaap" (the Japanese word in Chinese Kanji character for otaku). Actually somehow it is quite an impolite word to describe someone as "toxic," the percentage of "toxicity" is higher in someone who is "toxic" than another person who is "chaap." Let me describe it this way, if some have a good outlook on life and do some otaku stuff, we describe them as "chaap." If the guy is not looking good and people have a feeling that otakus don't like to dress themselves and look bad, then we describe them as "toxic." If someone is handsome, he is a "chaap" but otherwise "toxic."

TW: What do you think of Japanese creative industries, creativity and Cool Japan?

JL: I somehow think they are creative as I can recall, from attending a scientific seminar, they can only make some references to comics and anime, e.g. like Doraemon, in their lives. So that is creativity, from commercial things to their work and lives. There are a lot of anime that will feature some characters with magical powers and the Japanese people use some scientific explanation to make the magical powers real. For example, some random character with power may break a wall. The Japanese people [inventors] make a machine to mimic the [fictional] guy that broke the wall. The inventor or engineer, after they watch it [the manga or anime], they try to build the machine to make it come true. That is one part of creativity and the other creativity is the secondary creation ("*yeechee chongchok*" in Cantonese or "*erci chuangzuo*" in Hanyu Pinyin). An example is re-drawing some common [traditional] stories, they re-draw some very famous character to package it into another story. There are a lot of comic animators. They would make more and more production. And also the creativity is a form of business strategy, they would want the anime to be successful to make a lot of figures. Make more new episodes in order to make more money and that is the creativity for the businessman.

TW: What can Hong Kong learn from Japan's popular cultural industries?

JL: I think we should not be so narrow-minded for business or money-leading. In Hong Kong, all of the popular culture is money-leading [profit-oriented]. If they say popular culture, they would talk about how to do it for profits. In Japan, even if they know they won't make a lot of money, they will still support it. In Hong Kong, if an anime character is not so successful they will stop it. In Japan, they will go on [with a series or character that is not initially popular], they may then become successful. Many successful anime or manga artist do this for 10 years and then become successful. Hong Kong should learn from this and not be so money-leading [profit-minded]. Another thing is that in the Japanese popular culture, many of the stories is about implications or some meaning of world peace, friendship or something.

TW: Do you think that J-pop is competing with other popular cultures in Asia like K-pop?

JL: Definitely so. I can analyze two major reasons. One reason is the technological advancement because the Koreans have more technologies of making music videos or producing amazing songs or video or more technology for the singer or the stars to make them more handsome or more beautiful. When they see J-pop and K-pop, they have more appeal to the K-pop [K-pop is more appealing] because of more attractive characters. Somehow I feel that the people never care about the inner feelings. Japanese pop culture is more focused on world peace or love or friendship or something like that. K-pop and Hong Kong or Chinese pop focus more on teenage puppy love or stories about breakup or someone's engagement or something like that. So J-pop becomes less popular.

TW: What do you think of digital products in the future, digital images like Miku Hatsune?

JL: One example is Miku who will become more famous. The digital technologies will make virtual characters more realistic and make people more comfortable and more accessible to those are not otaku. It will be the trend and also the trend in Hong Kong. People who like judge a lot (criticisms), who like to judge whether a singer can sing well or outlook or style. Virtual idols can be as best as they can so people will be more satisfied because we as humans might have some imperfections. But digital idols can be perfect. For example, the voice can be like Miku that can mimic different kinds of voices and sing any songs with perfection. And their image can be rebuilt to be a perfect shape so that nobody can criticize. It can be tailored made for everyone. When it is implanted on the glass, people can see different images.

TW: What do you think are the differences between J-pop and Hong Kong popular culture?

JL: I think now the difference may be technological. For J-pop, the music videos they make are more beautiful and attractive than Hong Kong popular culture. The love or other meaning of the songs have similarities. And one more thing is that J-pop has more diversity so they can target different age groups, even the elderly can enjoy some J-pop products. But HK popular culture is more for teenagers. I remember there are more older people consuming J-pop in Japan than Hong Kong adults consuming Cantopop.

Chapter 13

A Survey of Cantopop Fandom in Hong Kong Up Till the 1980s

Elim WONG and Wilson LEE

Introduction

Fandom in Cantonese popular music (hereafter known as "Cantopop" in this chapter) in Hong Kong reflects the city's cosmopolitan culture, a place where foreign cultures can easily take root. The term "Cantopop," according to Joanna Lee's explanation, was originally coined by a correspondent of the *Billboard* magazine in 1974 as "Cantorock," and later revised as "Cantopop" to suitably indicate the turn to soft-rock music of Hong Kong music industry since the late 1970s.[1] As a result, what we now call "Cantopop" is generally equated with Hong Kong popular music, which is written in modern written Chinese but sung in Cantonese, and this chapter follows that usage of the term. Cantopop has a relatively short history in the territory compared with other popular music genres, such as western music and Shanghainese music, but Cantopop has become a mature strain of popular music in itself since the 1970s. Both fandom and musical trends have driven the development of Cantopop, which have attracted fans not only in Hong Kong, but also from other locations such as mainland China, Taiwan, Singapore and as far as North America. Given its regional and global extents, Cantopop is also an interesting topic that needs to be studied further. Through the study of Cantopop fandom in Hong Kong, one may better comprehend how Hong Kong society has undergone socio-cultural

---

[1] Joanna Ching-Yun Lee, "Cantopop Songs on Emigration from Hong Kong," *Yearbook for Traditional Music* 24 (1992): 14.

transformations in the regional and global contexts. Cantopop is usually recognized as a manifestation of local Hong Kong identity, another feature that deserves more studies.

Previous studies paid little attention to Cantopop music itself, let alone its fandom culture. At most, they described the historical development of Cantopop or some biographical accounts of particularly influential figures. Existing literatures are also mostly written in the Chinese language with a limited research scope. In discussing the general history of Cantopop, lyricists and prominent singers, Zhi-hua Huang wrote probably the first comprehensive and systematic book in 1990 to outline the historical development of Cantopop and analyzed why it became popular in the 1970s and 1980s.[2] Later in 2003, Jum Sum Wong, also known as Jim Wong 黃霑, a famous lyrics writer and music composer in Hong Kong, had periodized Hong Kong popular music history into four historical periods up till 1997 based on his rich experience in the industry.[3] Wong interpreted the musical styles in each period and gave the reasons behind the popularity of Cantopop in each historical period, but he also foresaw the decline of Cantopop and viewed it as an unavoidable trend because Cantonese, as one of the dialect of Chinese language, is difficult to market to other non-Cantonese areas, especially in mainland China, where Mandarin is the main language of communication.[4] Also, Mandarin popular music (known as Mandopop) itself, under the age of globalization, has been rising internationally exerting its strong cultural power in the past two decades for the increasing importance of Mandarin globally, because of which the influence and relevancy of Cantopop correspondingly has been diminishing.[5] More recently, Jing-zhi Liu, as a musician, studied the melody, lyrics, genre of Hong Kong Cantopop, together with

---

[2]Zhi-hua Huang, *Yueyu Liuxingqu Sishi Nian* 粵語流行曲四十年 [40 Years of Cantonese Popular Music] (Hong Kong: Joint Publishing, 1990).

[3]Jum Sum Wong, *The Rise and Decline of Cantopop: A Study of Hong Kong Popular Music (1949–1997)* (PhD diss., University of Hong Kong, 2003).

[4]*Ibid.*, 183.

[5]Yiu-Wai Chu, *Lost in Transition: Hong Kong Culture in the Age of China* (Albany, NY: State University of New York Press, 2013), 131–132.

its history.[6] Also, Liu devoted a chapter to studying 15 major composers of Hong Kong popular music. Generally, the developmental history of Cantopop and its several important leading figures are usually included into the existing literatures, but publications that study its fandom, a much larger community compared to the music producers, are relatively few.

To define whether a person is a fan, according to Henry Jenkins, is "not by being a regular viewer of a particular program but by translating that viewing into some type of cultural activity, by sharing feelings and thoughts about the program content with friends, by joining a community of other fans who share common interests."[7] An individual who commonly receives information of singers from the internet, watches TV reports of singers' interviews, reads newspaper and magazines for singers' recent activities, should not be considered as a fan since he/she does not contribute to further circulating these materials or re-creating them into other formats, such as videos or pictures, for sharing with others. Thus, the definition is related to the self-identification of fan and fan's behavior itself. This chapter tries to look at the following questions: how do external changes and transformations of a society impact on the fandom and its formation? And how do cultural capitals and resources of that particular society influence fandom? Bearing these questions in mind, this chapter, however, avoids focusing exclusively on the debates related to the definitions of fandom.

A Brief History of Cantopop Prior to the 1980s

With the economic takeoff of Hong Kong in the 1970s, the rise of Cantopop was not a coincidence. Most scholars acknowledge that Cantopop has become popular since the 1970s.[8] The popularity may be attributed to the

---

[6] Jing-zhi Liu, *Xianggang Yinyueshi Lun: Yueyu Liuxingqu, Yansu Yinyue, Yueju* 香港音樂史論：粵語流行曲, 嚴肅音樂, 粵劇 [Historical Discussion on Hong Kong Music: Cantonese Popular Music, Serious Music, Cantonese Opera] (Hong Kong: Commercial Press, 2013).

[7] Henry Jenkins, "*Star Trek* Rerun, Reread, Rewritten: Fan Writing as Textual Poaching," *Critical Studies in Mass Communication* 5, no. 2 (June 1988): 88.

[8] Huang, *Yueyu Liuxingqu Sishi Nian*, 17; Liu, *Xianggang Yinyueshi Lun: Yueyu Liuxingqu, Yansu Yinyue, Yueju*, 37.

commercialization of Cantopop in the 1970s on the one hand, and the beginning of its consumerism by the general public on the other. As a result, the emergence of Cantopop fandom is the consequence of a series of phenomena: the demand for songs sung in Cantonese, the improving quality of Cantopop, and most importantly, the increasing purchasing power, particularly among the youths. This section traces the history of Cantopop while highlighting some milestones in the emergence of Cantopop fandom in the late 1970s.

The history of Cantopop dated back as early as 1949 when a group of intellectuals came to Hong Kong from the mainland China, especially from Shanghai, due to the political instability in the mainland. Existing way before 1949 as *yuequ* (Cantonese opera songs) in Guangdong area, popular music in Hong Kong gradually transformed itself due to the influence from *shidaiqu* (generally refers to Shanghainese songs as Shanghai was once the cultural pivot in mainland) that found its way to the British colony. Many musicians in mainland China (mostly individuals formerly based in Shanghai) moved to Hong Kong since the 1950s, for example, composers Chen Ge-xin 陳歌辛 (1914–1961) and Li Hou-xiang 李厚襄 (1916–1973), and singers Bai Guang 白光 (1921–1999) and Yao Li 姚莉 (1922–); their ideas and contributions have influenced melodies of existing *yuequ* in Hong Kong. Because of the diminishing quality of *yuequ*, *shidaiqu* of the Mandarin popular music gradually became popular among audiences in Hong Kong throughout the 1950s and 1960s.[9] Conversely, though vernacular Cantonese songs gained a certain level of popularity mainly in the Southeast Asia, they were not as popular in Hong Kong's society due to its "coarse" quality.[10] In short, Hong Kong people preferred Mandarin songs and western songs at the beginning of the postwar era, with few enjoying songs in Cantonese, impeding the emergence of Cantopop songs fandom.

During the 1950s and 1960s, Hong Kong music industry was also dominated by Western popular music. In June 1960, the Radio Television Hong Kong (RTHK), an independent public broadcaster, launched a new programme, *Popular Music Night*, in which a Western DJ hosted the

---

[9] Wong, *The Rise and Decline of Cantopop*, 45–47.

[10] Wong, *The Rise and Decline of Cantopop*, 54–55.

programme in Cantonese to introduce Western popular music to its audience.[11] The Western trendsetting standard, musical style, genre and quality were then the mainstream benchmark for the Hong Kong popular music industry, and listening to popular music gradually became one of the major leisure activities in Hong Kong society. Examples that probably reflected Hong Kong society's extensive consumption of Western popular music was Pat Boone (1934–), one of the successful American singers in the 1950s to early 1960s along with another successful rock icon, Elvis Presley (1935–1977). As an international star, Boone received wide coverage from Hong Kong media when he was heading to the Philippines via Hong Kong for his concert. Before Boone's arrival at the Hong Kong Airport, four to five hundred teenagers, both male and female, waited few hours for his arrival. They asked for his autograph on commemorative albums, photos, compact discs (CDs) when they met Boone, and some of them even prepared presents for him.[12] These kinds of fan behaviors were not unique at this moment; in fact popular culture fans in Hong Kong society still exhibit such fan behavior in the 1980s and 1990s.

A monthly magazine named *gemi julebu* (literally means "fan club") in circulation since July 1967 was a popular reading among teenagers.[13] Fans purchased such publications faithfully as they were attracted by the photos of their favorite celebrities on the magazine covers and the latest celebrity news in the magazine. Jenkins categorized these fans as "Loyals" because they cherry-picked what best satisfied their interest; they intentionally purchased the publication only for the reason that they wanted more information about a specific celebrity.[14] From the regular periodicals, fans not only had a platform to seek information but also had a periodical to share photos of the same popular star with other like-minded fans, forming a community in the process. On the other hand, fan clubs in the 1960s attracted social criticisms that characterized these clubs as

---

[11] Kung Sheung Daily News 工商日報 [Commercial Daily News], dated 8 June 1960 in Kung Sheung Daily News, 7.

[12] Kung Sheung Daily News, dated 25 July 1961 in Kung Sheung Daily News, 5.

[13] Kung Sheung Daily News, dated 2 September 1967 in Kung Sheung Daily News, 10.

[14] Henry Jenkins, *Convergence Culture: Where Old and New Media Collide* (New York, NY: New York University Press, 2006), 74.

"gangster groups." Media warned parents to be careful of their children joining those "fan clubs" because they were unregistered groups of young punks (both males and females), who usually discontinued school education and gathered for rowdy overnight parties.[15] Those criticisms in the mass media claimed that the youths who were fans of particular stars and celebrities were not harmful to society initially, but became misled subsequently when they joined some "fan clubs" associated with sexual crimes during rowdy parties. These fan clubs saw several high profile police arrests of its members.

In the mid-1960s, popular songs in the Cantonese language became more visible and tended to differentiate itself from *shidaiqu* and the western popular music. Unlike the previous period, most Cantonese popular songs now became known to their audiences when they were featured in Cantonese movies. Two famous movie stars came to the front stage with several hit Cantonese songs: they are Chan Po-chu (1946–) and Siao Fong-fong (1947–). Both Chan and Siao, along with other Cantonese movie stars, received quite positive selling results of their records, yet the quality of their songs, for example the lyrics, was indeed poor.[16] These movie stars helped promote Cantonese songs to the general public through their own fan bases, and star power was independent of song quality but it helped with the songs' promotion. Moreover, local music producers and singers such as Koo Kar-Fai (1933–), Sam Hui (1948–) and Teddy Robin (1945–) who emerged in the 1960s formed a founding generation of postwar pioneers for popularizing (even regionalizing/globalizing) Cantopop later. To reflect the bigger following of local singers, the magazine of *gemi julebu* increased its contents on news about local singers and bands in its sixth issue.[17] Generally, the late 1960s, as Huang claimed, was a transition period for Cantonese popular music while Wong also considered this moment as the foundation for building the "Hong Konger" identity, resulting in the emergence of Cantopop as the outcome.[18] On the other hand, fandom culture had gradually shifted from European popular music to

---

[15] Wah Kui Yat Po 華僑日報 [Overseas Chinese Daily News], dated 16 June 1964 in Wah Kui Yat Po, 7.

[16] Huang, *Yueyu Liuxingqu Sishi Nian*, 59; Wong, *The Rise and Decline of Cantopop*, 84.

[17] Kung Sheung Daily News, dated 13 November 1967 in Kung Sheung Daily News, 6.

[18] Huang, *Yueyu Liuxingqu Sishi Nian*, 9–10; Wong, *The Rise and Decline of Cantopop*, 90.

localized Cantonese offerings, increasing in quantity, but not necessarily quality until the mid-1970s.

Between the 1960s and 1970s, Cantopop fan behaviour became group-oriented. Local singers would meet a group of fans at a particular designated place, similar to what we call "fan meetings" today. Jinfang Nightclub, located in North Point on Hong Kong Island which had been famous for the Cantonese opera became an emerging venue for such Cantopop fan activities. The Nightclub, with its "luxury decoration and equipment," was known to hold activities related to popular music every weekend with popular singers and bands making appearances to entertain customers.[19] Tsui Siu-Fung (1949–), for example, organized a fans gathering where she presented gifts to her fans and performed several keynote songs to thank them for coming.[20] Interactions between fans and singers intensified at these gatherings, both scheduled and unscheduled. To facilitate more convenient communication between fans and idols, the Cantopop band Teddy Robin and the Playboys in 1970 started writing a column, "Teddy Robin's mailbox," in a youth publication, which was published weekly every Friday at a price of 10 cents per copy.[21] With 10 cents in the late 1960s, one could afford a single journey on the Star Ferry from the Victorian Harbour in Central on Hong Kong Island to Tsim Sha Tsui on Kowloon Peninsula on the lower deck and vice versa. Through comparisons with the price of other commodities, the cost of purchasing the publication packed with information about Cantopop singers was probably affordable to most teenagers at that time, bolstering the popularity of Cantonese popular songs. Sustaining these publications and other activities could not be achieved with only a limited fan base. This implies that Cantopop singers had garnered substantial attention in Hong Kong at the beginning of 1970s, followed by the rise of Cantopop in the mid-1970s.

Several factors are responsible for the rise of Cantopop since the mid-1970s. The first is its effective coverage through the mass media. The launch of Television Broadcasts Limited (TVB) in 1967 has effectively changed the pattern of consumption of the general public within the entertainment industry.

---

[19] Wah Kui Yat Po, dated 24 April 1969 in Wah Kui Yat Po, 12.
[20] Wah Kui Yat Po, dated 14 May 1969 in Wah Kui Yat Po, 4.
[21] Wah Kui Yat Po, dated 31 March 1970 Wah Kui Yat Po, 9.

With regards to the impact on Cantopop, its full-length TV dramas usually featured Cantonese theme songs and popularized them. Most scholars acknowledge that Cantopop consolidated its position in Hong Kong entertainment industry in 1974, with releases of a renowned TV drama theme song, "*Tai Siu Yan Yun*" (A Marriage of Laughters and Tears), and a movie theme song, "*Gwai Ma Seung Sing*" (Games Gamblers Play), both of which received widespread positive responses.[22] Secondly, the emergence of many locally trained talents supported the proliferation of Cantopop. In both music composition and lyrical writing, many new faces entered the industry to enhance the diversity of Cantopop content with the introduction of multi-styles, high and low, compared with the previous period.[23] This newer generation of singers was keen to diminish the influence of Cantonese opera, and younger lyric writers composed in modern written Chinese instead of traditional literary Chinese.[24] For instance, James Wong, Lu Guo-Zhan and Cheng Kwok-Kong were three important lyrics writers in this decade who wrote numerous popular songs that helped Cantopop reach its peak during this era. Their songs focused on the themes of family and *wuxia* (martial arts heroism) which were relatively new contents for Cantopop. Apart from the reasons outlined above, Yiu-Wai Chu and Eve Leung attributed the success of Cantopop from the mid-1970s to the mid-1990s to the use of hybridization as a conceptual approach.[25] Scholars also associate the prevalence of Cantopop with the Hong Kong identity construction, and in later stages, it accounted for "the late 1980s wave of nostalgia for a disappearing Hong Kong cultural identity."[26] Conversely, Cantopop from the mid-1970s had been flourishing, creating a local brand of

---

[22] Huang, *Yueyu Liuxingqu Sishi Nian*, 10; Wong, *The Rise and Decline of Cantopop*, 92; Liu, *Xianggang Yinyueshi Lun: Yueyu Liuxingqu, Yansu Yinyue, Yueju*, 28; Wai-Chung Ho, "Between Globalisation and Localisation: A Study of Hong Kong Popular Music," *Popular Music* 22 (2003): 147; Masashi Ogawa, "Japanese Popular Music in Hong Kong: What Does TK Present?" in *Refashioning Pop Music in Asia: Cosmopolitan Flows, Political Tempos, and Aesthetic Industries*, eds. A. Chun, N. Rossifer and B. Shoesmith (London and New York, NY: Routledge, 2004), 146.

[23] Wong, *The Rise and Decline of Cantopop*, 132.

[24] Huang, *Yueyu Liuxingqu Sishi Nian*, 32.

[25] Yiu-Wai Chu and Eve Leung, "Remapping Hong Kong Popular Music: Covers, Localisation and the Waning Hybridity of Cantopop," *Popular Music* 32 (2013): 67.

[26] Gregory B. Lee, *Troubadours, Trumpeters, and Troubled Makers: Lyricism, Nationalism, and Hybridity in China and Its Others* (Durham: Duke University Press, 1996), 167.

cultural identity for this colony of Hong Kong. Since the rise of Cantopop, fandom culture of the local popular music continuously rose to a level that could compete with popular music from other countries and cultures.

In the 1970s, the fandom culture of Cantopop began to be shaped by the growing relationship between singers and fans. The role of fans then became gradually more influential than promotion through organized events held by marketing firms and production companies. In these inter-actions, fans would prepare birthday parties celebrations for their beloved singers. When Sam Hui turned 27 years old in 1975, nearly 500 fans enjoyed a birthday party with him as the guest of honour at the Hilton Hotel.[27] During the party, autograph-seeking fans had become a persistent feature of fan club activities, and, for his fans, Hui also performed three English songs and two self-composed Cantonese songs. Hui's career high-lighted the transition of the local entertainment industry from domination by the western music scene to the indigenous rise of Cantopop, and that was the reason why he sang songs in both languages during the party. Moreover, Hui is probably the most important figure in the Cantopop his-tory at that point of time, not only because his music was widespread and popular but also because of promotion by his active fan club.[28] The forma-tion of the International Sam Hui Fan Club in 1977 indicated Hui's influ-ence was not just limited to Hong Kong or Guangdong province.[29] Through the fan organizations, interactions between fans and their idols were now taking place in a vibrant manner, through face-to-face meet-ings at fan gatherings and not only by texts and words through printed publications. Their relationship became more personal than that found during the Teddy Robin era, in that singers could now understand their fans' feelings through fan club activities and mitigate their complaints or bad experiences by inviting them to concerts and performance. In one case, the Wynners, one of the most renowned bands in Hong Kong that emerged during this period, had to seek "forgiveness" from their fans by

---

[27] Kung Sheung Daily News, dated 8 September 1975 in Kung Sheung Daily News, 9.

[28] For details of Sam Hui, see Huang, *Yueyu Liuxingqu Sishi Nian*, 65–81 and Wong, *The Rise and Decline of Cantopop*, 115–123.

[29] A webpage of The Universal Sam Hui Fan Club, http://www.samhuifanclub.com/Story/menu2(1).html [downloaded 1 June 2015].

compensating them with admission to a studio programme as they needed to delay the birthday boat party for one of the members due to a schedule conflict.[30] Contrasting with the earlier promotional events in the Jinfang Nightclub, fandom activities since the mid-1970s became more large-scale and interactive, which implies that fandom was no longer an individual and personal expressions for particular singers and idols. It had become a collective group-oriented activity.

The Origin of Cantopop Fandom: Rise of Fan Clubs in the 1980s

Cantopop fandom in 1980s is incomplete without discussions on the influence of fans on the works of prominent names from that era: Alan Tam, Leslie Cheung, Anita Mui, etc. These super idols were the first batch of Cantopop singers to set up official fan clubs, and so fan club culture is regarded as a major characteristic of the 1980s Cantopop industry. The following sections survey the history of fan clubs from different perspectives to highlight the major elements, features and milestones in the history of Cantopop fandom as well as discuss the relationship between fandom and the social development of the Hong Kong society.

As early as 1981, the official fan club of Alan Tam Wing-Lun was established by his recording company PolyGram.[31] The membership quota allocated for his fan club was filled up in a short period of time.[32] The formation of Tam's club, along with Leslie Cheung and his fan club founded in 1984 and Anita Mui and hers founded in 1985, are acknowledged as the pioneering efforts in in this aspect. Fan clubs became a commonplace phenomenon in the Cantopop industry when many other idols in the 1980s followed the trend and started to communicate with fans through club activities. These include Cally Kwong Mei-Wan (1987),

---

[30] Kung Sheung Daily News, dated 7 April 1976 in Kung Sheung Daily News, 9.

[31] Alan Tam, a Hong Kong local singer who started his career as a Cantopop singer since the early 1980s, is often called by "principal" as he is experienced in the field and is willing to help the junior singers to development their singing career.

[32] Apple Dairy, "代 Cult2：八十前老歌迷專一追星追到老," in Apple Dairy [downloaded 13 May 2015], available at http://hk.apple.nextmedia.com/supplement/culture/art/20100730/14292085.

Mak Kit-Man (1988), Alex To Tak-Wai (1989) and Prudence Liew Mei-Gwan (1989). Fan clubs became a platform for developing collective identities and community as they involved interactions of more than one individual fan. However, unlike other overseas examples of popular culture fandoms, such as the recent emergence of K-pop fandom, Cantopop fandom in the 1980s to 1990s had its own unique characteristics. Before going into discussion about the characteristics of Cantopop, understanding the functions of its fan club is crucial.

Original Functions of a Cantopop Fan Club

A fan club acts as to providing an opportunity for fans to meet their idols in person. However, these organizations and the activities they organized are sometimes misused and abused. A news article reported that Cantopop fans were cheated and were forced to pay a sum of money to obtain information on the whereabouts of their idols.[33] The news was spread to the idols themselves. For example, Leon Lai, one of the "Cantopop Four Heavenly Kings" of Hong Kong, persuaded fans to join his official fan club to have the opportunity of meeting with him regularly.[34] Leon mentioned one of the most important functions for fans to enroll in a fan club is to have precious moments to meet with their idols. In 1984, Kenny Bee formed his first fan club on his birthday. At the club-launch party, the idol revealed his idea to have his own official fan club because he did not have enough time to meet with fans due to his busy schedule, and he hoped having his own fan club would facilitate his interaction with fans and getting involved in fans' activities.[35] Similar activities were visible at Roman Tam's fan club and his birthday celebration party with his fans on 2 February 1986.[36] The singer was scheduled to be away from Hong Kong

---

[33] Wah Kiu Yat Po, "歌迷戲迷為見偶像被騙，黎明呼籲保持清醒，見偶像可入歌迷會 (Fans who wanted to meet with idol were cheated, Leon Lai urged fans to stay alert, join a fan club to meet with idol)," dated 28 July 1991 in Wah Kiu Yat Po, 9.

[34] *Ibid.*

[35] Wah Kiu Yat Po, "鍾鎮濤歌迷會　二月二十三日成立　是日亞B生日雙喜臨門 (Chung Chan To fan club sets up on 23rd February, it is on Bee's birthday for double happiness)," dated 16 December 1984 in Wah Kiu Yat Po, 18.

[36] Wah Kiu Yat Po, "除夕晚廣州登台至初四　羅文年卅晚生日　歌迷會提前慶祝 (Performance at Guangzhou from New Year Eve and the Fourth of New Year, Roman

on his birthday and so the fan club organized a birthday party for him to pre-celebrate before his departure. The news also mentioned that the fan club prepared presents for Roman Tam,[37] something that has become a main activity in the fan clubs and gives the fans an opportunity to give their presents to the idol in person.

Another major function of a fan club is to foster a close relationship between idol and fans. Stars, no matter how famous, are no longer individuals who are unreachable. Take Alan Tam and Anita Mui as examples: Tam organized his fan club in 1981 and, by 1987, over 1,000 members joined the fan community and they held annual birthday parties for their idol. At 1987's birthday part of Tam, the idol teamed up with selected fans and they played games and conducted private Q&A sessions, which were activities rarely featured in a public event.[38] Such activities had become a special feature in fan clubs during this period. Enjoying a fun time with fans, Tam started an "Alan Tam Scholarship" for fans who had outstanding academic results, something meaningful given the fact that many of his fans at that time were high school students. At his birthday parties in the following years, the idol gave outstanding students a limited number of scholarships to encourage them to pursue further studies.

Mui, another idol well-known to the public, organized fan club events frequently. Not only organizing annual birthday parties as many fan clubs do, Mui's official fan club provided an extra opportunity for fans to communicate with their idol intimately. For example, in 1987, the idol went to a barbeque event held in a country park with a number of her fan club members.[39] Moreover, in every traditional festival on the Chinese calendar, Mui sent out to her fans hand-written greeting cards with her autograph.[40]

Tam's birthday on the day before New Year Eve, Fan club pre-celebrate his birthday)," dated 3 February 1986 in Wah Kiu Yat Po, 17.

[37] *Ibid.*

[38] Wah Kiu Yat Po, "阿倫及歌迷會生辰紀念 千名歌迷共慶 (Ah Lun and fan club birthday celebration), " dated 3 February 1986 in Wah Kiu Yat Po, 17.

[39] Anita Mui Archive, "歌迷會活動~1987年10月18日生日會-香格里拉 梅艷芳網上資料館," in Anita Mui Archive [downloaded 13 May 2015], available at http://www.anita-mui.com/pineapple_blog/category/anita-with/anita-fans-club/page/10/.

[40] Anita Mui Archive, "梅艷芳國際歌迷會~Menu 梅艷芳網上資料館," in Anita Mui Archive [downloaded 13 May 2015], available at http://www.anita-mui.com/pineapple_

The relationship between the idol and fans, as seen from the above example activities organized by official fan clubs, were close. Unlike nowadays, idols communicated casually with fans. In an interview with a Mui fan, she reviewed that her relationship with the idol was just like sisters. "Anita Mui was like an elder sister [to us]. She urged us not to dye our hair like she did, and not to wait outside her workplace until 2 am in weekdays. She was really considerate."[41] This fan's account demonstrated how members in her fan club valued the opportunity to get close with their idol, and without the arrangement made by the fan club, it would be harder for fans to be in touch with their busy idols.

Characteristics of Hong Kong Fandom in the 1980s

Fandom in Hong Kong displayed characteristics that can only be found in Hong Kong. One major activity of Hong Kong-based fan clubs was to participate in charity activities, and it often became news highlights in the local newspapers. Charity events like scholarship donation is a win–win approach to benefit not only fans but also the idols, who then gain popularity after the release of media coverages of these events. Most importantly, these donations and voluntary acts help people who are in need in the society. As a result, the 1980s is well known as a period of fan club-based charity events.

When Hong Kong female singer Mak Kit-man launched her official fan club in 1988, she emphasized that the aim of setting up a fan club under her name was to participate in charity events. "My fan club is not one that helps organizing gathering with my fans. Moreover, I would like my fans to work hard for the society by participating in charity activities, in order to show parents that their children are not wasting their time on the idol but showing concern on the social issues in the society,"[42] said the

---

blog/category/anita-with/anita-fans-club/page/12/.

[41] Apple Dairy, "代Cult2：八十前老歌迷專一追星追到老," in Apple Dairy [downloaded 13 May 2015], available at http://hk.apple.nextmedia.com/supplement/culture/art/20100730/14292085

[42] Wah Kiu Yat Po, "麥潔文想要歌迷會 對公益能作出貢獻 (Kit-man Mak wants her fan club to contribute to charity events)," dated 15 September 1988 in Wah Kiu Yat Po, 8.

idol. Mak liked to hold gatherings at occasions when fans can contribute to charitable events: "...for example going to barbeque with fans, and we can clean up the beach after the gathering. Isn't this meaningful to the society?"[43] In another occasion, Mak expressed her wish to participate in Walks for Millions, a fund-raising event organized by The Community Chest since 1971.[44]

Among all fan clubs in the 1980s, Alan Tam's fan club can be regarded as the most active in terms of organizing charity activities at that time. The fan club has a long history of donations made to the society in general. To name a few examples, in 1987, the fan club held an auction at Tam's birthday party and they donated over HK$10,000 to nursing homes for the elderly, along with other sundries, such as 1,000 boxes of milk, oats, face towels, sweaters and scarfs which the members collected for over three months.[45] One year later, the fan club even donated a minibus for a nursing home for the elderly. The donation was highlighted on a major local newspaper because the wife of then Hong Kong Governor David Clive Wilson, Natashi Helen Mary, was invited and was appointed as an ambassador to receive the donation on behalf of the elderly home.[46] The news article mentioned the background story behind the donation: the fan club did not have enough donations for a minibus, and although their idol offered help, the fan club rejected his offer and finally found a cheaper place to purchase the minibus for the elderly home.[47] The donation marked the very first time a local fan club organizing such large-scale donations (in terms of money collected and the scale of the ceremony). The charitable practice continued till the 1990s. On the 10th anniversary of the establishment of Tam's fan club in 1991, the singer organized a fan

---

[43] *Ibid.*

[44] Wah Kiu Yat Po, "麥潔文成立歌迷會, 要多做公益事 (Kit-man Mak sets up fan club, ask for frequent participation in charity)," dated 5 September 1988 in Wah Kiu Yat Po, 8.

[45] Wah Kiu Yat Po, "阿倫及歌迷會生辰紀念 千名歌迷共慶 (Ah Lun and fans birthday celebration with thousand fans)," 24 August 1987 in Wah Kiu Yat Po, 19.

[46] Wah Kiu Yat Po, "阿倫主持送車儀式, 港督夫人代表接受(Ah Lun hold the car donation ceremony, wife of Hong Kong Governor appointed as representative)," dated 8 May 1988 in Wah Kiu Yat Po, 3.

[47] *Ibid.*

gathering where more than 1,000 fans turned up, including both local and overseas fans, and all the entrance fees collected at the event were donated to Chi Lin Nunnery in Hong Kong for renovation works.[48]

The charitable work organized by Tam's fan club was not only beneficial to society, but some club members were also receivers of the donations. Starting from 1986, Tam set up a scholarship, The Alan Tam Scholarship, to award his fan club's members who had outstanding academic achievements. *Wah Kiu Yat Po* in 1987 recorded the winners of the award: first place went to a fan club member who obtained three As, three Bs and two Cs in the public exam Hong Kong Certificate of Education Examination (HKCEE) and she was awarded HK$15,000.[49] Another two candidates, who obtained three As, two Bs, three Ds and three As, four Cs and one D, were also awarded HK$10,000 and HK$8,000, respectively.[50] With regards to the establishment of the scholarship, the idol explained in an interview: "I am happy to see them [Alan Tam's fans] working hard [at school]. It means that they [Alan Tam's fans] are not addicted to idols and gave up study. Rather, their [academic] result is a proof of their hard work."[51] The Alan Tam fan club is the first in Hong Kong that established its own scholarship for students and this inspired other celebrities in Hong Kong, including Anita Mui. In November 1988, when the singer was invited for an interview, she expressed her desire in setting up her own scholarship for her fans too, like what Alan Tam did for his fans.[52] Furthermore, the fan club scholarship system had an impact in shaping the Cantopop fandom in the 1990s. Famous Hong Kong male singer Andy Lau Tak-wah planned to donate all income from his book project in 1991 to

---

[48]Wah Kiu Yat Po, "兩人今年同考8A, 各獲獎學金一萬元 (Two gained 8A in this year, each awarded ten thousands dollars)," dated 8 September 1991 in Wah Kiu Yat Po, 4.

[49]Wah Kiu Yat Po, "阿倫及歌迷會生辰紀念千名歌迷共慶 (Ah Lun and fans birthday celebration with thousand fans)," dated 24 August 1987 in Wah Kiu Yat Po, 19.

[50]*Ibid.*

[51]Wah Kiu Yat Po, "兩人今年同考 8A, 各獲獎學金一萬元 (Two gained 8A in this year, each awarded ten thousands dollars)," dated 8 September 1991 in Wah Kiu Yat Po, 4.

[52]Wah Kiu Yat Po, "梅艷芳想效法阿倫, 為歌迷會增設公益活動 (Mui Yim-fong wants to learn from Ah Lun, arrange charity activities for fan club)," dated 17 November 1988 in Wah Kiu Yat Po, 27.

establish his first fan club scholarship to encourage his fans to focus on academic pursuits.[53]

Hong Kong's fan clubs in the 1980s can be seen as a microcosm of a society. In a society, interactions among individuals are essential and scholars believe that cooperation between groups and individuals are essential for societal development. From their perspective, individuals are interdependent rather than independent actors, and individuals and organizational interactions, network connections and active communication are essential in building a healthy society.[54] Fan clubs in Hong Kong, as a reflection of a society, foster cooperation among organizations through the comprehensive organizational structure of fan club with their own scholarship awards and charitable donation system in the early 1980s. Being the "pioneer" in this field, Alan Tam's fan club offered voluntary help as an advisor in setting up likewise projects in Hong Kong. The best example is Kenny Bee's fan club, which was established on 23 February 1985. Members from Tam's fan club were the key players[55] in building up the foundations, from preparatory work to fan club establishment.[56] Two reasons can help explain Tam's fan club offer of help to other fan clubs: first, the two idols themselves, Tam and Bee, can forge closer friendship with each other, which allowed their fan clubs to have a friendly relationship too. Secondly, the success of Tam's fan club set a good example for the other Hong Kong idols and has become a benchmark for other clubs to follow in this area.

Since fan clubs can be seen as part of a society, naturally besides cooperation, disagreements can also occur between individuals and organizations. In 1988, Anita Mui expressed her unwillingness to continue with her fan club after disagreements and arguments broke out

---

[53] Wah Kiu Yat Po, "劉德華停拍片工作，灌錄唱片撰寫散文 (Lau Tak-wah stop acting in film, recording and writing articles)," dated 25 April 1991 in Wah Kiu Yat Po, 3.

[54] Charles Wetherell, "Historical Social Network Analysis," in *New Methods for Social History*, eds. L. J. Griffin and M. V. D. Linden *et al.* (New York, NY and Melbourne: Cambridge University Press, 1996), 126.

[55] Wah Kiu Yat Po, "鐘鎮濤歌迷會　二月二十三日成立 (Chung Chan-to fan club establish on 23rd February)," dated 16 December 1984 in Wah Kiu Yat Po, 18.

[56] *Ibid.*

amongst members of the fan club.[57] The idol was disappointed by her fans' disunited behavior and the stark contrast with Alan Tam's fan club, which always showed unity and harmony.[58] From Mui's point of view, Tam's fan club was able to set up their own elaborate scholarship awards and donation system, while her fan club failed to even agree on simple issues.[59] In this case, Tam's fan club was once again held up as an excellent example for the other Hong Kong-based fan clubs to learn from. It indicated that cooperation between individuals and organizations is essential but definitely not effortlessly achievable.

Leadership is another important societal trait. Similarly, in a fan club, members elect a chairperson for the fan club and the main duty of a chairperson is to communicate on behalf of the fan club with the recording company where the idol is affiliated. The appointment serves as a bridge to bring together the recording company and fans and to schedule fan gatherings with the idol frequently. In other words, the chairperson is the sole leader in a fan club with the responsibility to manage all affairs related to the club, including organizing fan events, communicating with fans as well as dealing with the internal disputes among members. The importance of the role has attracted media to develop interests in news and gossips about chairpersons of fan clubs, and interview them on updates and matters related to their idols.

In 1986, a news article reported Alan Tam's contract dispute with TVB in Hong Kong and the issue affected the result of the 1986's TVB award presentation.[60] The issue became the headline news of entertainment pages of major local newspapers. Hoping to get further details on the dispute, the reporter interviewed the chairperson of Tam's fan club at that time. The chairperson, Ms Angela, expressed her disappointment that her idol's songs failed to be nominated by TVB for the award. As a public figure representing the fan club of Tam, she did not comment on the

---

[57]Wah Kiu Yat Po, "覺歌迷們一盤散沙, 鼓勵向阿倫迷學習 (Fans are not united, are encouraged to learn from Ah Lun's fans)," dated 9 October 1988 in Wah Kiu Yat Po, 6.

[58]*Ibid.*

[59]*Ibid.*

[60]Alamtan.net, "1986 勁歌金曲季選 – 點解咁少入選歌? (1986 Jade Solid Gold Seasonal Nomination — Why there are so little nominated songs?)," dated 22 March 2010 in alamtam.net, available at http://www.alantam.net/?m=201003.

contract dispute or the nomination list of the 1986 Jade Solid Gold Seasonal Nomination. Having been on her position for five years, Angela instead urged fans of Tam to support their idol no matter what action he would be taking with regards to his contract dispute with the broadcasting company, even though they might not be able to see their idol's performance on TVB[61] after discontinued contract. This interview with Chairperson Angela is a good example demonstrating the important status of the fan club's chairperson to the Hong Kong music industry. Fan clubs, especially their chairpersons, have an influential role in communicating messages to the media and also commenting on news related to their idols. In the 1980s, messages from fan clubs or chairpersons were often communicated through news articles featuring media interviews before the advent of instant messaging system, Internet and mobile network.

Another important role played by the chairperson of a fan club is as an information provider for club members. A fan from Anita Mui's fan club revealed in an interview that the most exciting moment in the 1980s was to wait for the telephone call from the fan club.[62] During an era without widespread Internet access and affordable mobile devices, she spent days waiting for the latest news about the idol or fan club affairs announced by the chairperson and at one time she rushed out to see her idol's performance after receiving a phone call from the fan club at her office.[63] The above example shows that the role of chairperson is key to a fan club. Another good example is, in 1989, Alan Tam did not hold his usual birthday party with fans like he did in previous years because there was no suitable candidate to be the chairperson for his fan club then.[64]

The choice of a chairperson of a fan club can also be an interesting focus for the media in the 1980s. The Miss Hong Kong Pageant 1988

---

[61] *Ibid.*

[62] Apple Daily, "代Cult2：八十前老歌迷專一追星追到老," in Apple Dairy [downloaded 13 May 2015], available at http://hk.apple.nextmedia.com/supplement/culture/art/20100730/14292085.

[63] *Ibid.*

[64] Wah Kiu Yat Po, "與萬餘聽眾齊歡渡, 阿倫今年特別開心 (Celebrated with ten thousands of audience, Ah Lun is especially happy this year)," dated 15 August 1989 in Wah Kiu Yat Po, 12.

became a hot topic as candidate Number 9 Angela Yeung Mei-Yee was the former chairperson of Alan Tam's fan club.[65] *Wah Kiu Yat Po* reported that Yeung's participation became a major focus in the mass media because the candidate was already a public figure due to her role in Tam's fan club.[66] Yeung understood her former public role as chairperson of the fan club but asked the media to focus on her performance in the pageant rather than on her past experience as a chairperson of the fan club.[67] It is true that the fame gained as an office holder in the fan club brought Yeung public attention, but too much focus on her fandom past became an issue with her pageant career. One year after the pageant, Yeung debuted as an actress in TVB. Despite her acting career, media continued to discuss about her past experiences as the chairperson of Tam's fan club, which became an annoying issue, according to Yeung.[68] The article titled 已非歌迷會會長楊美儀懂得避忌, 不借阿倫做宣傳 (translated as "Not a chairperson of the fan club anymore, Yeung Mei-Yee knows how to avoid, not using Ah Lun to promote herself") demonstrated the eagerness for the actress to delink her name with her past in the Alan Tam fan club. To sum up, being prominent in a Cantopop fan club in the 1980s could yield substantive influence within the Hong Kong society's cultural scene. Not only were they active participants in charity and volunteers to public events, fan clubs also reflect Hong Kong society's hierarchical structure, including the role of a leader in cultural affairs.

Concluding Remarks

Before the 1980s, Shanghainese and western popular songs attracted many fans in Hong Kong society. Later, thanks to the mass media promotion and the advent of technology, Cantopop easily spread throughout Hong Kong and helped establish a Cantopop fandom culture. This transition in music

---

[65] Wah Kiu Yat Po, "楊美儀參加選美, 被視為新聞焦點 (Yeung Mei-Yee participates in pageant, seen as the news focus)," dated 14 July 1988 in Wah Kiu Yat Po, 3.

[66] *Ibid.*

[67] *Ibid.*

[68] Wah Kiu Yat Po, "已非歌迷會會長, 楊美儀懂得避忌, 不借阿倫做宣傳 (Not a chairperson of the fan club anymore, Yeung Mei-Yee knows how to avoid, not using Ah Lun to promote herself)," dated 24 August 1989 in Wah Kiu Yat Po, 34.

appreciation, as mentioned above, reflected the formation of the Hong Kong local identity as well as hybridization of external influences from mainland China, through the influx of Shanghainese talents and cultural influences. The cultural diversity of Hong Kong society did not marginalize foreign influences but hybridized and incorporated them into Cantopop music.

During its development, Cantopop fandom has not only grown on its own strength but also reflected social changes. Once Hong Kong's economic development strengthened in the 1970s, it facilitated individuals to consume more products from the entertainment industry, resulting in the formation of more organized fan clubs centered around prominent celebrities. On the other hand, as the economy took off, income inequality and other social issues emerged due to rapid social transformation, fan clubs played a role in managing those social changes by providing scholarships and charitable support for their members in need. Members of those fan clubs also became concerned with many social issues as a result. Chairpersons of fan clubs in the 1980s were public figures representing clubs, becoming unofficial spokespersons for their favorite singers or idols.

Chapter 14

K-pop Fandom in Hong Kong: A Fan's Perspective

Elim WONG

Introduction

Although Korean pop (K-pop) culture did not become widespread in Hong Kong until a decade ago with the broadcast of popular Korean dramas such as *Winter Sonata* (by Cable TV in 2001) and *Dae Janggeum* (broadcasted by TVB in 2005),[1] the origins of K-pop in Hong Kong is traceable back to 1998 when the first Korean pop music-oriented radio program *Hon Lau Zaap Gong* ("The attack of Korean wave in Hong Kong") began.[2] In the next decade, famous Korean pop singers/bands such as Rain, Park Jiyoon, Lee Hyori and Se7en gained popularity amongst Hong Kong fans. K-pop largely influenced the Hong Kong youth community through extensive promotional campaign conducted by the major entertainment companies, such as S.M. Entertainment and JYP, until the boom brought about by Korean boy bands and girl groups

---

[1] *Winter Sonata* is one of the very first Korean dramas being brought to Hong Kong market. Cable TV purchased the broadcasting right of the drama at the price of HK$1 million, which became the headline news in Hong Kong entertainment newspapers. *Dae Jangguem* was broadcasted by Television Broadcasts Limited (TVB) from 24 January to 1 May 2005. The last episode recorded over 3 million viewers and it broke the record for the most viewed TV drama series in the history of broadcasting in Hong Kong. Media Digest, "The Result of 'similar culture' — *Dae Jangguem* hits Hong Kong," in Media Digest, Radio Television Hong Kong [downloaded 30 March 2015], available at http://rthk.hk/mediadigest/ 20050614_76_120479.html.

[2] AM730, "How Korean wave was formulated?" dated 7 August 2014 in AM730 [downloaded on 30 March 2015], available at http://www.am730.com.hk/article-220541.

emerged. Idol groups and band groups are becoming major features of K-pop culture. To name a few, H.O.T, Shinhwa and G.O.D represented the first generation of K-pop group performance in South Korea. They were followed by Super Junior (since 2005), BIGBANG (since 2006), Wonder Girls and Girl's Generation (since 2007). Their mass promotion in East Asia, including the major consumers markets of Hong Kong, Taiwan, China and Japan, has attracted young people to set up fan-based communities to share information about their idols and provide a platform for fans to communicate with each other.

This chapter provides case study of a sizeable fan community dedicated to a South Korean boyband *K-group* in Hong Kong. *K-group* is a pseudonym name of the boy band which has debuted for over six years. The reason for using pseudonym names is a request from my informants to protect their privacy. Most of my informants were full-time workers who devoted their spare time to organize a voluntary fan club for *K-group*, which I fictitiously named *K-club* (a pseudonym) in this study. In protecting privacy and confidentiality, names of my informants will remain anonymous in this chapter. In order to gather first-hand materials and conduct participant observation, I joined the fan community and *K-club* in 2011 as an active member in their forum. One year later, I was nominated as one of the four administrators of the fan community *K-club* dedicated to Korean boyband *K-group* with over 5,000 members from Hong Kong, Taiwan, China and other Chinese communities and was subsequently appointed as the public relations officer and web designer.

This chapter is written based on my experience as an active member and an administrator in the *community-club*, oral interviews with the other administrators and members, as well as surveys collected in the fan club events. I aim to highlight the following characteristics of K-pop fandom in Hong Kong: (1) The coexistence of localization and globalization of fandom culture and (2) groupism as a feature to maintain fandom communities' cohesiveness in Hong Kong. Moreover, this chapter is probably one of the first English-language academic researches on K-pop fandom in Hong Kong. Its significance lies in the contents on fandom studies based on the author's personal experiences and time spent with the fan community for more than three years as an insider and participant observer to contribute to the materials in existing literatures.

It is not a comprehensive account but offers some insights into the subject matter.

Fandom — From Participants to Providers

Fandom in pop music takes on different meanings. A "fan" may be defined as one who consumes actively popular cultural products related to a particular idol or idols (i.e. their music and/or related by-products), Roy Shuker, for example, defined fans as participants who often attend concerts, collect their idol's records and goods, and discuss news related to their idols with other fans.[3] Nissim Otmazgin and Irina Lyan defined the multiple roles of fans as consumers as well as "marketers, mediators, translators, and localizers of globalized culture."[4] In this sense, fans play an important role in testing whether a particular popular cultural product is well received by local consumers and in localizing those cultural products in order to cater to the tastes of local consumers. Paul Booth further expanded the scope of fandom from individual fans of specific idols to everyone else. In his work *Digital Fandom*, he suggested that "everyone is fan of something" and we all "based part of our identity on our appreciation of that fandom."[5]

While becoming a fan is a subjective and personal choice, participation in the activities is never a solitary existence. Lisa A. Lewis pointed out that, once fans group together to share their common interests, they will soon construct their own identities, which she defined as "coherent identities for themselves" and these "individuals" share common practices as well.[6] As a result, fandom usually appears as a community. From the viewpoint of social history, every community has a close and inevitable relationship with group identity formation. For example, social historians

---

[3] Roy Shuker, "Record Collecting and Fandom," in *Popular Music Fandom: Identities, Roles and Practices*, ed. M. Duffett (New York, NY and London: Routledge, 2013), 166.

[4] Nissim Otmazgin and Irina Lyan, "Hallyu across the Desert: K-pop Fandom in Israel and Palestine," *Cross-Currents: East Asian History and Culture Review* 9 (December 2013): 70.

[5] Paul Booth, *Digital Fandom: New Media Studies* (New York, Bern, Berlin, Bruxelles, Frankfurt am Main, Oxford, Wien: Peter Lang, 2009), 20.

[6] Lisa A. Lewis, *The Adoring Audience: Fan Culture and Popular Media* (New York: Routledge, 1992).

believe that identity is "public and relational."[7] In other words, it is contextual: dependent on the external environment and specific situations; and based on interactions with others and how others perceive an individual. The construction of self-identity requires recognition by others and there is a need to distinguish an individual's unique identity from others. Characteristics of a chosen identity are shaped by the social environment which it is located in. Therefore, an identity formation process is never private and individual. Social historians view the society as a collective construct rather than the personal experiences of numerous individuals.[8] It is the sum of individuals which makes up a group. Social historians focus on the construction of social structure, which refers to the interaction among individuals and groups, and by studying social structure within a community, they are able to find out how individuals operate within a particular society.[9] In order to investigate how group identity is formed within a fan community in Hong Kong, this chapter utilizes social historical theories on identity-building in discussing the relationship between identity formation and fandom from a fan-based perspective.

The case study in this chapter is a sophisticated fan-based community *K-club* in Hong Kong. Five years old in longevity, core members of this community are longtime fans of the idol group *K-group*. The fan community is now transformed from the roles of information disseminator and forum organizer, to active organizers of local fan meetings, overseas concert trips and other fan events. The community also participates in joint fan club charitable activities with Korean, Russian, Mexican and Filipino fans. On 16 October 2015, the fan club built a forest, named The BEAST FOREST, at Kenya, together with Korean, Russian, Mexican and Filipino fans to support their idol group's debut anniversary. Although this is not the first time for the Hong Kong fan community to participate in overseas charity event for their idol group, it marks the ultimate form of fandom

---

[7]Charles Tilly, "Citizenship, Identity and Social History," in *Citizenship, Identity and Social History*, ed. C. Tilly *et al.* (New York, NY and Melbourne: Cambridge University Press, 1996), 6–7.

[8]Donald M. MacRaild and Avram Taylor, *Social Theory and Social History* (New York: Palgrave Macmillan, 2004), 83.

[9]*Ibid.*, 7.

from "participants to providers" and "observers to sponsors"[10] — members of the fan community are formally a number of "individuals" who get to know each other online. Since they share common interests, they decide to go public by becoming "providers" of the popular culture. The best example is the establishment of the fan community. They are no longer passive "observers" but "sponsors" of the culture itself by organizing activities locally and globally. I will discuss these roles in details with examples in the later sections in this chapter.

A Fan Community in Hong Kong — *K-club*

In 2009, a relatively new entertainment company from South Korea announced the debut of a male idol group *K-group*. Even before the debut of the group, members of the group were well known amongst South Korean youths as some used to be idol trainees in other top entertainment companies. *K-group* gained popularity in less than a year when one of their title songs ranked first in the South Korean popular music program M! Countdown on 25 March 2010. With the local success of *K-group*, the entertainment company decided to follow the footsteps of other media agencies to explore and expand the overseas market. *K-group* finally debuted in Japan in 2010 and released its first Japanese language album in March 2011. *K-group* came to Hong Kong for the first time in mid-2012, and followed by a joint concert in Macau two months later. The last time they visited Hong Kong was in January 2013 for another joint concert. In comparison to the Japanese market,[11] Hong Kong is a heterogeneous overseas consumer market for Korean entertainment companies to promote *K-group*.

In answering what is the reason for fans to set up non-official fan community in Hong Kong, and what is the function of non-official fan

---

[10] Sang-Yeon Sung, "K-pop Reception and Participatory Fan Culture in Austria," *Cross-Currents: East Asian History and Culture Review 9* (December 2013): 90.

[11] Since *K-group* debuted in Japan in March 2011, the boy band released six singles and two albums under the Universal Japan label. On its fourth anniversary after their debut in 2015, the company announced its newly set-up original label to release their own music from then on.

community in Hong Kong that cannot provide direct support to the group similar to those in Korea and Japan, the following sections aim to suggest the answers for the questions by studying *K-group* in details. The first group of fans in Hong Kong gathered together one year before the debut of *K-group* and they set up the first fan-site of *K-group* in Hong Kong (since 2008 but there were no updates until early 2013). This fan-site was later recognized by the entertainment company as an official fan-site of *K-group*. Unlike the official fan club of *K-group* in Hong Kong, *K-club* which was set up in 2012 does not receive any financial or logistical support from the entertainment company. From manpower recruitment to fund-raising, *K-club* relies on voluntary support from fans in Hong Kong. I chose *K-club* as an example to study fandom in Hong Kong for three reasons. First, *K-club* is the largest non-official fan-site of *K-group* in Hong Kong. By September 2015, *K-club* was welcomed by 5,487 followers on Weibo, 3,890 followers on Facebook and 3,432 followers on Instagram, which made the fan club the second largest *K-group* fan-site in Hong Kong.[12] Second, the fan community of *K-club* is the most active fan club in group purchase of *K-group*'s products (official and non-official goods). *K-club* is reputable for organizing group purchases since 2013. Besides standardized products that are usually purchasable on other fan-sites like compact discs (CDs), digital versatile discs (DVDs) and official fanlights, *K-club* is the only fan-site in Hong Kong that also helps fans to purchase non-official goods produced by Korean fan-sites, such as yearly calendars, photobooks and all kinds of accessories. Third, *K-club* owns three sub-fan-sites, each with its own accounts in Facebook, Weibo and Instagram, serving as additional information channels for members since its establishment in 2014. All these services provided for fans who are members in Hong Kong made *K-club* different from the other fanclubs of *K-group* in Hong Kong, including even *K-group*'s official fan club. The official fan club of *K-group*, although both financially and logistically supported by *K-group*'s entertainment company in South Korea, functions as a mere information hub for *K-group* and does not provide any support or services to fans. Compared with the group's official fan club,

---

[12] The official *K-group* fan club in Hong Kong had 8,763 followers on Facebook and 7,144 followers on Weibo.

K-club provides services such as organizing group-purchases of *K-group*'s official and non-official products and concert tickets. Also, *K-group* holds fan events in Hong Kong and its fan club intends to provide a platform for fans of *K-group* to communicate. These developments position *K-club* as an all-rounded and well-developed retail fan club in Hong Kong.

Assigned by the founder, I became *K-club*'s administrative staff for public relations and web design since 2013, and had spent almost two years as an active member in the fan community of *K-club*. Through my appointments, I was able to be a participant observer with access to administrative staffs and informants from the fan community. My duties include liaising with other Korean, Japanese and Chinese fan-sites of *K-group* to work out joint-promotional activities, charitable events and group purchase retailing. Also, I was responsible in dealing with enquiries from fans. Therefore, my role in *K-club* gave me opportunities to meet with fans from different backgrounds that had a wide variety of questions about the idol group.

Globalization and Localization of K-pop Fandom Culture in Hong Kong

National Chiao Tung University in Taiwan had reported on fandom culture of K-pop in Taiwan in 2012.[13] In the video clip produced by the university, it shows Taiwanese K-pop fans voluntarily organizing support events for their idols outside concert hall, for example giving out free slogan to fans or selling photo cards of the idols. The purpose of carrying out these activities for fans in Taiwan is to indicate how K-pop fan-supported events go global. For example, according to the video, giving out freebies related to the K-pop idol outside the concert hall is a culture originating from South Korea when boyband H.O.T fans started giving out photo cards to fans for free. Ever since this trend spread overseas, Taiwanese K-pop fans began to organize such free events for fans. Similar fan culture of giving out freebie gifts can be seen in Hong Kong as well. *The Wall Street Journal* noted that fans sending lunch boxes to idols is one of the many ways to

---

[13] Cast net, "應援文化, 不成文的韓流 (Support Culture, Unwritten Korean Popular Culture)," in Cast net, National Chiao Tung University [downloaded 28 April 2015], available at http://castnet.nctu.edu.tw/castnet/article/4557.

show support to K-pop idols.[14] Not that the idols cannot afford their own lunch expenses, but the care that goes into preparing the lunchbox symbolizes a deeper meaning in that fans can personally become involved in taking good care of their idol's health despite their busy schedules. Fan activities by both Korean and Hong Kong fans also focus on charitable work by providing food and beverages to needy people in South Korea, something that has become a general trend. A news report from *TIME* indicated that the donation of rice made by the fans on behalf of their idols to charities in South Korea has become an important trend in K-pop fandom culture.[15] Nowadays, K-pop fans can contribute to charitable activities on behalf of their idols by buying a rice tower product (also known as rice wreath) with the idol's name and photo displayed on it. This phenomenon is not limited to Korean fans but is also practiced by Japanese fans, which form another large K-pop consuming region.[16]

K-club, as an active fandom community in Hong Kong, rides on the globally vibrant K-pop fandom culture, including global trends related to how fans support their idol. The community purchased its first rice tower in 2013 for *K-group*'s concert in Busan, South Korea (see Picture 1). It was the first time for *K-group*'s fans in Hong Kong to donate a rice tower overseas. In the first rice tower donation, *K-club* reached the target amount within one week, which was out of the staff members' expectation.

With its first success in rice wreath donation, the fan club decided to carry on the donation activity routinely to support the idol group whenever there is a new promotional campaign organized by the idols and their management. For example, *K-club* donated three 20 kg rice bags to the

---

[14] Jaeyoon Woo, "Seoul Food: Treating Your Idol to Lunch Is the True Test of Fandom," dated 23 February 2012 in The Wall Street Journal [downloaded 28 April 2015], available at http://www.wsj.com/articles/SB10001424052970204136404577211072079207422.

[15] Krista Mahr, "South Korea's Greatest Export: How K-Pop's Rocking the World," dated 7 March 2012 in TIME [downloaded 28 April 2015], available at http://world.time.com/2012/03/07/south-koreas-greatest-export-how-k-pops-rocking-the-world/.

[16] Fans of the K-pop female group KARA formed the first community in Japan to participate in rice wreaths event in Japan, according to its agency CL Production. Source: Allkpop, "KARA's Japanese fans the first to donate rice for a concert in Japan," dated 20 April 2012 in Allkpop [downloaded 28 April 2015], available at http://www.allkpop.com/article/2012/04/karas-japanese-fans-the-first-to-donate-rice-for-a-concert-in-japan.

PICTURE 1. THE FIRST RICE TOWER DONATED BY *K-CLUB* IN 2013. PICTURE TAKEN BY THE AUTHOR WITH THE OTHER TWO ADMINISTRATORS OF *K-CLUB* OUTSIDE THE CONCERT HALL IN BUSAN.

K-group's musical performance in 2014 and 2015 and, on each occasion, the fan club arranged one administrative staff to fly over to Seoul for photo-taking opportunities with the rice tower and the idols. After a few years of rice wreath donation activities, the range of food product donations has gone beyond rice and now includes food and beverages like Korean instant noodle, milk, juice and dog food. Even natural resources like charcoal can be donated as commodities to show fans' solid support to idols. *K-club*, in responding to this new trend, had donated 90 kg of dog food to one of the idols known to be a dog lover with a pet dog at home (see Picture 2). I was appointed to visit Busan and Seoul in September 2013 and June 2014 for photo-taking with the rice tower on behalf of the fan community. Both experiences are important and remarkable in the history of Hong Kong K-pop fandom because *K-club* was the

PICTURE 2. THE FIRST DOG FOOD DONATION ORGANIZED BY *K-CLUB* IN 2014. THE DOG FOOD TOWER WAS PLACED OUTSIDE THE ENTRANCE OF THE ENTERTAINMENT MANAGEMENT COMPANY WHICH *K-GROUP* BELONGS TO.

only Hong Kong fan-site which participated in the rice donation and it showed the importance of this fan-driven club in Hong Kong fandom culture since its activity rate was higher than the official fan-site of *K-group* in Hong Kong. By the time of this article was completed, the latest rice tower donation organized by *K-club* was on 29 August 2015 when *K-group* held a concert in Seoul (see Picture 3). This recent rice tower donation event broke the record of all donations held by *K-club* in the past as 200 kg of rice was donated, instead of the usual 20 kg. Again, *K-club* was the only Hong Kong volunteer fan-site that participated in rice tower donation for *K-group*'s annual concert in Seoul in 2015.

Since the trend of supporting K-pop stars is now shifting from activities directly benefiting the idols to public donations, K-pop fandom within Korea has soon shifted their attention to a new activity — growing a future

PICTURE 3. A 200 KG RICE TOWER WAS DONATED BY *K-CLUB* ON 29 AUGUST 2015. THIS RICE TOWER WAS PLACED OUTSIDE THE CONCERT HALL IN SEOUL.

forest for their idols. A Korean company Tree Planet is a close partner working with K-pop fan clubs in this area. Although Tree Planet was not established specifically for working with fans, it aims to create "engaging means to plant the most trees in the world."[17] The company has already planted in nearly 100 forests in the name of K-pop idols funded by donations collected through the fan clubs. However, the *K-group* forest had not been planted until 2015,[18] when *K-club* saw the opportunity to build a forest in Seoul to celebrate the idol group's sixth debut anniversary in October 2015. In March 2015, administrative staff informant H contacted

---

[17] Tree Planet, "Company Info," in Tree Planet [downloaded 1 May 2015], available at http://www.treepla.net/eng/company_info.html.

[18] In 2014, fan clubs in Korea of one of the *K-group* member had built a forest in Mapo-gu, Seoul in South Korea in June 2014. It is the only forest related to *K-group* and its members.

Tree Planet for details about building a *K-group* forest in Seoul. By coincidence, a Korean fan club, Russian fan club, Mexican fan club and Philippine fan club also contacted the company on the same matter, which provided an opportunity for the five fan clubs to cooperate. This is a remarkable event since this is the first time for *K-club* to cooperate with overseas fan clubs, and *K-club* was the only party from *K-group*'s fandom community in China and Hong Kong to participate in the event. This indicates that fandom in Hong Kong is well established to keep up with the latest trends in Korea.

Because all five locations are influenced by K-pop, *K-club* has been following up closely the fan-club support trends in other parts of the world. At the same time, it developed its own unique and localized characteristics, something different from fan clubs in South Korea and Japan where fans only distribute original certified product offerings in promotional events. Two examples of localized fandom products are introduced in this section. First, the Hong Kong K-pop fandom circle tends to create products with the idols' faces or names on them and give out to fans as freebies or for sales. For *K-club*, the fan club has already produced over 50 homemade products since I joined the community in 2013 (see Picture 4). These products are mainly stationery items that are welcomed by mostly students who make up the largest group of K-pop consumers in Hong Kong, and other paraphernalia including bookmarks, notebooks, stickers and postcards/photo cards. Informants H and M were responsible for sourcing and purchasing idol-related items in *K-club*. Before joining the fan club, informant H had been working on her own online shop business to retail K-pop products. She said, "It is better to produce things that can be used everyday. In school, the students can use the [*K-group*'s] bookmark and notebook. But one thing to be taken into account is the selling price. We cannot mark it too high such that is not affordable by students."[19] Informant M, on the other hand, suggested that students love to purchase goods with their idol's face on them to support their idol.[20]

---

[19]Informant H, Interview by author. Tape recording. A cafe at Mongkok, Hong Kong, 27 April 2015, 7–9 pm.

[20]Informant M, Interview by author. Tape recording. A cafe at Mongkok, Hong Kong, 27 April 2015, 7–9 pm.

PICTURE 4. FREE IDOL PINS PRODUCED BY *K-CLUB* IN 2014.

Purchasing goods produced by *K-club* is the major source of income for the fan club. Income however is not pocketed by the fan club's administrators. Indeed, all the money collected from fans belongs to *K-club*, not the administrative staff. "All the money will be used in *K-group*'s support event, such as buying rice wreath and food support. Since we do it [organizing a fan club of idol group *K-group*] on a voluntary basis, we do not and cannot receive income from it,"[21] said Informant H, who is the designated accountant of *K-club*. In 2014, water bottles with the members' names printed on the surface were given as free gifts to fans who donated over HK$100 to *K-club* to buy rice wreath to celebrate its members' participation in a musical performance. "This [the act of giving out freebies in donation] is easier for fans to donate money, by using it [freebie gift] to attract fans,"[22] said Informant H.

   K-club, however, is a non-profit fandom community, and its main fan outreach products are based on freebies distribution to fans in Hong Kong,

---

[21] Informant H, Interview by author. Tape recording. A cafe at Mongkok, Hong Kong, 27 April 2015, 7–9 pm.
[22] *Ibid*.

PICTURE 5. AN EXAMPLE OF FREE MESSAGE CARDS PRODUCED BY *K-CLUB*. THESE CARDS WERE DISTRIBUTED FREE OF CHARGE TO FANS AT AN EVENT IN WHICH *K-GROUP* PARTICIPATED IN JANUARY 2013.

mainland China and Japan. The most common freebies among Hong Kong K-pop fandom are the photo cards and printed slogans, since they are low in production cost and easy for fans to keep and collect. *K-club* gives out photo cards and slogans whenever there are events related to *K-group*, for example concerts featuring the idol group, and fan gatherings organized by *K club* (see Picture 5). The photo cards are designed by the administrative staff members in the club and their designs follow ever-changing new concepts generated by the idol groups and their management. In other words, whenever the idol group releases a new song, there will be new photo cards designed by *K-club*. Informant P, the founder of *K-club*, who supports photo card giveaways, claimed that "I myself love to collect photo cards too! It is an interesting habit. So I think the other *K-group*'s fans will feel the same."[23]

Although the abovementioned activities are common practices in the idol fandom communities in Hong Kong, the same practices are not found in South Korea and Japan. In South Korea, fan clubs tend to produce

---

[23] Informant P, Interview by author. Tape recording. A cafe at Mongkok, Hong Kong, 27 April, 2015, 7–9 pm.

PICTURE 6. PHOTOCARDS AND POSTCARDS PRODUCED BY *K-CLUB*. THE AUTHOR AND THE OTHER ADMINISTRATORS OF *K-CLUB* DISTRIBUTED THEM OUTSIDE THE CONCERT HALL IN TOKYO IN 2014.

photo books or DVDs featuring photos and videos of their idols taken/ filmed during the club activities and events instead of relying on official photo releases. Fans in South Korea take copyright ownership of their photos and videos very seriously by restricting other fans to re-post or edit their photos and videos outside their fan-sites. The originality and creativity of the photos used in their self-made goods are highlighted in Korean fandom community and this is the major difference between fandom behavior between Hong Kong and overseas countries. In March 2014, I visited Tokyo, Japan for a concert performed by *K-group*, along with two other administrative staffs in *K-club*. We brought photo cards and postcards produced by *K-club* and had planned to distribute them outside the concert hall (see Picture 6) as well as prepared a freebie gift bags that filled with products produced by *K-club* to the members of *K-group* (see Picture 7). In the case of Hong Kong's fandom circle, fans often come over to the fan-club freebie distributors and ask for the goods, and most of the time freebie distribution tends to attract a sizeable number of fans and long queues would usually form outside the concert hall. But our experience in Japan is different. An hour before the concert, three of us went

PICTURE 7. FREEBIE GIFT BAGS PREPARED FOR THE MEMBERS OF *K-GROUP* BY *K-CLUB* IN 2014.

outside the concert hall to give out the photo cards and postcards to the fans who were waiting outside the hall, and we were rejected by some fans as they thought they had to pay us for the cards. After we explained where we were from and that our purpose for the activity was not profit-driven, they thanked us with a surprised expression, implying they had never experienced free give-outs at this kind of events. The rejection is no surprise because of the different fandom cultures between the two locations. To sum up, *K-club*, as a case study of Hong Kong fandom, explained how K-pop fandom in Hong Kong tries to keep up with global trends in fandom practices, but at the same time, produces its own localized products with unique design features. What has made Hong Kong's fandom culture so unique and different from the others? Groupism is discussed in the next section.

Groupism or Individualism?

K-pop fandom places an important premium on the identity formation amongst fans. As Lewis suggested, fandom itself is never individual and is always related to a group of "individual" fans combining their resources and efforts collectively[24]; the case study of *K-club* is an example in indicating how groupism exists in Hong Kong K-pop fandom. From my observation, however, there is a limitation to the collective behavior of K-pop fans in Hong Kong. They are not at the stage where they can actively seek mutual support from the community, and continue to emphasize individualism, or "self-identity," as suggested by Erik H. Erickson.[25] Two examples from my observation studies are utilized in this section to explain this feature.

Case Study (Event No. 1): Fan Gathering in October 2014

To best explain how fandom represents groupism, I carried out participant observation at a fans gathering in October 2014. I organized the gathering with other administrative staff members of *K-club* to celebrate the idol group's fifth debut anniversary (see Pictures 8 and 9). This is the first fan gathering organized by the fandom community. Due to seating capacity limitations, the gathering can only cater to 30 fans and registration was on a first-come-first-served basis. I was responsible for designing four games played at the gathering and all games were related to the idol group *K-group*. All 30 seats were filled within one week after the announcement on social network site (SNS) in September 2014. Over 70% of them were single participants and about 30% of them participated with one or two friends.

I distributed 30 questionnaires to all participants for research use and received 20 questionnaire responses at the end of the gathering. The information collected is kept anonymous and I have the consent from all the participants to use the data for research purpose. All these data are important to this research because it reflected the situation in Hong Kong K-pop fandom by using random and rank-and-file members from a fan

---

[24]Lisa A Lewis, *The Adoring Audience: Fan Culture and Popular Media* (New York, NY: Routledge, 1992).
[25]Erik H. Erikson, *Identity, Youth and Crisis* (New York, NY: W.W. Norton, 1968).

PICTURE 8. THE FIFTH ANNIVERSARY CELEBRATION PARTY HELD BY *K-CLUB* IN 2014.

PICTURE 9. PARTICIPANTS OF THE PARTY HELD BY *K-CLUB* IN 2014.

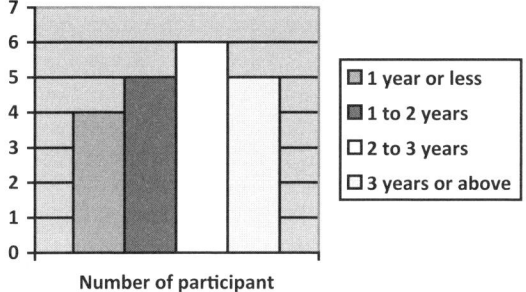

FIGURE 14.1. NUMBER OF YEARS OF PARTICIPATION IN *K-GROUP* FAN ACTIVITIES.

community instead of only surveying the administrative staffs within the community. Also, participants are from different age groups with different educational backgrounds, which provides us a cross-sectional view of K-pop fandom from diverse fandom demographics. The gathering was attended by 13 participants aged between 16 to 20 years old (65%), four aged 30 or above (20%), two aged between 21 to 25 years old (10%), and the youngest participant was aged between 10 to 15 years old (5%). Beside the diverse age group, experiences in the fandom community among participants are remarkable to note. Figure 14.1 shows the length of time of participation in *K-group* fan community. Due to the different amount of time spent in the fandom community, participants were indeed sharing different expectation to the gathering and to *K-club*.

Fans who had less than two years of experience in the fandom community tended to be more active than those who were senior members of the circle. Seven out of nine participants (77.8%) who joined fandom for less than two years had participated in rice wreath donation or other kind of donation organized by the fan-sites, both local and overseas, while only five out of 11 participants (45.5%), who had three years or above experience in fandom, did donated for *K-group* (see Figure 14.2). However, in coping with Otmazgin and Lyan's theory on fandom in encouraging fans to become providers in the community,[26] four out of 11 participants with

[26] Nissim Otmazgin and Irina Lyan, "Hallyu across the Desert: K-pop Fandom in Israel and Palestine," *Cross-Currents: East Asian History and Culture Review* 9 (December 2013): 70.

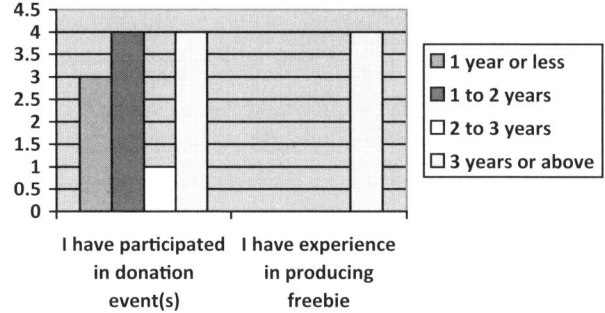

FIGURE 14.2.   NUMBER OF PARTICIPANTS WHO PARTICIPATED IN DONATION EVENT(S) AND CREATING/MAKING FREEBIES FOR THE EVENT.

three or more years of experience in joining fan clubs produced photo cards and distributed to members in the fandom circle. This behavior is usually seen amongst senior members of a fan community in Hong Kong. Since these members were individuals and not exclusive owners of any fan-sites, they made their own photo cards just for sharing with the other individuals in the circle as a way to maintain good relationship and to make new friends.

Despite the presence of different age groups and years of experience in the fandom community, 13 out of the total of 20 participants admitted that the main reason for them to join *K-club* and the fans gathering is to meet new friends. As mentioned, 70% of them came to the party alone and they aimed to make friends on that day. Informant P met new friends in the party and she kept contact with a few participants after the party. She was happy with the arrangement of the party because she can "find someone who share same interest and [they] can do things in a group, like going to concert or some events."[27] Informant H revealed she had been to a trip to Seoul with a fan she met in fans gathering in March 2015 and will be going to Taiwan for *K-group* concert with two other fans. "Now I feel even happier! I am happy to become a fan of *K-group*, and now I found friends who can talk about the boys [*K-group*'s members] with me. Isn't it amazing? I feel grateful to be a part of *K-club*," said

---

[27]Informant P, Interview by author. Tape recording. A cafe at Mongkok, Hong Kong, 27 April 2015, 7–9 pm.

Informant H.[28] Both Informant P and Informant H revealed the major significance of fandom — promoting groupism among individuals. Since identity can be formed when interaction among individuals happen, the group identity among participants is formed through interaction among members of a circle. In the case of *K-club*, the fan community provided a platform, both online (via platforms such as Facebook, Instagram, Weibo and Twitter) and offline (fans gathering and other fans-related events), for individual K-pop lovers to communicate with each other, make friends and share resources. Rather than individual interests, K-pop fandom in Hong Kong is indeed an open community and opportunity for anyone who shares the same interest to meet with each other to form group(s).

Case Study (Event No. 2): Preparation for K-group Concert 2015

Despite the fact that K-pop fandom in Hong Kong represents a collective identity since fans tend to practice the fan culture on a group basis and participate in fan community gatherings actively, the identities of the participants are not without contradictions when it comes to maximizing self-interest. The best example used to explain this contradiction is my observation on the preparation for *K-group* concert carried out by fan communities.

Ever since *K-group* announced their intention to hold the first solo concert in Hong Kong in late March, *K-club* started to prepare for the support event to the idols. Unlike donating rice wreath or other abovementioned activities, support practices for K-pop idol in Hong Kong have its unique features. *K-club* started campaigns to raise fund from fans for the idol-supporting events (e.g. preparatory activities such as providing food and beverages support). I participated in the discussions for planning these campaigns. In the discussion, some members suggested selling self-made products such as folders, stickers, postcards and the profits from such sales will all go to support the idol-related events. For example, they

---

[28] Informant H, Interview by author. Tape recording. A cafe at Mongkok, Hong Kong, 27 April, 2015, 7–9 pm.

wanted to prepare food and beverages for the idols and staffs on the concert day, and also produced props to place them outside the concert hall for fans' photo-taking. Since *K-club* was not the only fan club authorized to prepare for the support events, the fan community has to communicate with other fan-sites to prevent duplication of roles.

Internally within the fan-site community, when members of *K-club* discussed the prices, number of items and the actual uses of these items at the concert venue, some members suggested that some items might not be helpful to support idol events and the distribution of these items seemed to serve the fans' entertainment purposes rather than providing support to the idol group; but their views were rejected by other members of the fan club for the reason that "fans should get back what their money is worth for." The opposing group collected feedback from fans, which led them to believe that, since fans contributed money to the fan community, the community ought to be responsible for entertaining the fans. Therefore, providing self-made products to fans and props for photography use are essential to satisfy fans' expectations with regards to fan-club membership privileges. *K-club*'s members, in this case, valued their reputation within the fan community in terms of making fans happy and they considered this to be the most important element in the preparation process for idol-supporting activities.

Externally, *K-club* sees its preparation for supporting events as a form of rivalry with other fan-sites. Since the fan community is non-official and, in terms of membership numbers, not the largest fan-sites within the fan circle, the members care a lot about their reputation in the eyes of their rivals. As a result, the administrative staffs are ambitious in many ways: in terms of freebies, *K-club* needs to provide the largest number of gifts to fans; and in terms of food and beverages, they have to buy the largest number of items as well as the best quality items in the market. This is, however, not a phenomenon that happens only in *K-club*, as the other fan-sites that I had made contact with also intend to be the best in some ways representing *K-club*. For example, a fan community group wanted to buy the most expensive gifts for the members in the idol group, while another fan-site claimed to prepare the biggest banner in the concert hall. This kind of boasting activities intensified rivalry instincts among *K-club*'s members. At the time of this writing, the tense relationship among members of *K-group*'s fan community can be easily detected through messages posted on the social network even though the concert is yet to be held.

The point that is worth noticing for the above narrative on preparation for the concert is that, *K-group* is indeed absent from the entire discussion. A fan community, at a fundamental level, is a group of individuals gathered together to share idol's information, provide mutual help to each other and provide the best support to their idol. Nevertheless, the case study in this research shows that the original objectives of fandom are hampered by competition among fan communities, instead of fostering groupism to mobilize everyone to work on tasks that are beneficial to the idol. As long as more than one fan community are involved in a single event and rivalry emerges, self-identity will replace groupism by upholding self-interest. This applies to *K-club*, in which administrators tend to ensure that fans who have donated money to the fan club will get returns in value of some kind. Competitions between fan communities in Hong Kong are driven by self-interests, and overwhelming concerns for reputation are breaking up the cohesiveness of the community as a whole. The chat and gossip within the community with regards to "who do the best job" and "which fan community is the most supportive group" become obsessions to the participants, especially to the fan club administrations.

Conclusion

This preliminary research on K-pop fandom in Hong Kong provides an overview on fan community by looking at a particular fan club. Three major points are discernable here. First, fandom in Hong Kong transforms individual fans to idol products providers by enthusiastically making and giving out freebies and sharing idol-related information. Second, K-pop fan culture in Hong Kong selects features from other K-pop fans' cultural experiences in other parts of the world like Korea and Japan and, at the same time, creates its unique localized practices. *K-club*, for example, not only participated in the Korean-style rice wreath donation and tree-planting event but also gave out freebies to others within the fan community, which such features cannot be found outside Hong Kong (e.g. in the Japanese case). Third, fandom in Hong Kong is a creature characterized by both groupism and self-identity. This contradiction on one hand encourages group-oriented activities, and on the other hand sees individual fans emphasize on their self-identity whenever factionalism, rivalry and competition appear. This fandom world can be considered as a microcosm of Hong Kong society, as members in this society are both dependent and independent of social structures, something that the relatively new research on K-pop and its fandom and fan communities in Hong Kong will continue to examine.

Section 6

Taiwan

A Constructed "Immaginarium": Cultural Dimensions of the Taiwanese Identity Construct

Katherine TSENG

Identities: What and Why

The term "identity" may be one example that more efforts in defining a term incur more confusion in contemporary social scientific studies. In some senses, its high volatility toward contextual changes explains its much bewildering intrinsic intractableness. Serving many different purposes, the term "identity" can refer to a gamut of hard and soft issues, by which individuals converge their sense of belonging to or recognition towards certain groups. On one hand, the basis of this cognizance can be of a nostalgia characteristic, on shared memories of historical, cultural or ancestral heritages. On the other hand, it can also foster group consciousness, to fuel political activism frequently used (but not an exclusive tool) by marginalized groups to construct self-identities. An indicator to evaluate this politically-constructed consciousness is via the social interactions experienced by the individual.[1] In other words, maintaining a defined socio-political identity is an important developmental task for emerging adults.

---

[1] Jeffrey J. Arnett, "Emerging Adulthood: A Theory of Development from the Late Teens Through the Twenties," *American Psychologist* 55, no. 5 (May 2000): 469–480; Kay Deaux *et al.*, "Parameters of Social Identity," *Journal of Personality and Social Psychology* 68, no. 2 (1995): 280–291; Deborah Schildkraut, *Press One for English: Language Policy, Public Opinion, and American Identity* (Princeton, NJ: Princeton University Press, 2005).

Yet, definitions of "identity" show a lineage to inadequate-ness, elusive-ness and ubiquitous-ness.[2] Cutting the story short, the rapidly advancing integration of the globe as, commercially, a huge market, and politically, an international community that honors indiscriminately the Westphalian system of international law and order, has set a fundamental undertone for the actualization of the "nation state" and "equal and independent sovereignty" of these actors in the international system. Yet, in many parts of the world, the "nation-state" concept is a transplanted one, which conflicts with local custom and regionally developed political traditions.[3] It partially explains why this term has been ill-defined, and often applied in a non-meticulous, and contextually expedient way. In this sense, the present concept of "identity" is affiliated with a socially constructed group or community, to the extent that scholars opine that these groups, along with the attached identities, are imagined.[4]

Debates, Diversification and Development

Generally, discussions of "identity" politics and formation are informed by two major camps. Essentialists and constructivists occupy two ends

---

[2]Voluminous scholarly efforts have been dedicated to decipher the concept and development of "identity." Yet, these efforts can hardly be unified into one single formula, because this concept contains intrinsically a nature of fluidity, volatility and malleability. See Anthony D. Smith, *National Identity* (Reno, NV: University of Nevada Press, 1991); Omar Dahbour, "National Identity: An Argument for the Strict Definition," *Public Affairs Quarterly* 16, no. 1 (January 2002), 17–37; Ernest Gellner, *Nations and Nationalism* (Oxford: Blackwell, 1983); Ernest Gellner and Anthony D. Smith, "The Nation: Real or Imagined?: The Warwick Debates on Nationalism," *Nations and Nationalism* 2, no. 3 (1996): 357–370; Karl W. Deutsch, *Nationalism and Social Communication: An Inquiry into the Foundations of Nationality*, 2nd edn. (Cambridge, Mass.: MIT Press, 1966).

[3]"Nation-state" is a relatively new type of polity catalyzed by a conglomeration of factors, such as the burgeoning of enlightenment era, commercialism and industrialization, middle class and urban population, the de-secularization of politics and monarchy, prevalence of party and participatory and democratic politics, and also, the elevation of the destructiveness of war. In non-European and non-Christian areas, such as Asia and Africa, this nation-state polity is a rather abrupt formulation of political and ruling authority, where most of them are later forced to accept and adopt it via destructive wars with western imperialist intruders.

[4]Benedict Anderson, *Imagined Communities: Reflections on the Origins and Spread of Nationalism* (London: Verso, 1983).

of the spectrum. For the former, the central theme is that "nations are defined by a shared heritage, which usually includes a common language, faith and ethnic ancestry,"[5] on which an identity can be cultivated and substantiated. The constructivists, however, view identity from an introspective manner on top of the outward-looking approach. They view "identity" as a relatively stable understanding with a role-specific characteristic and self-expectation.[6] The constructivists also shed lights on the discussion, by construing identities as cognitive schemas that enable an actor to determine for itself in situations and positions where socially structured roles and understandings are required. In other words, the identity is a combination of self-expectation and projections by others perceived by an individual. In this sense, the individual is a social object.[7]

---

[5] See, Smith, *National Identity*; Gellner, *Nations and Nationalism*. Also, Rupert Emerson, *From Empire to Nation: The Rise to Self-Assertion of Asian and African Peoples* (Cambridge, MA: Harvard University Press, 1959); Liah Greenfeld and Jonathan Eastwood, "National Identity," in *The Oxford Handbook of Comparative Politics*, eds. C. Boix and S. C. Stokes (Oxford: Oxford University Press, 2009).

[6] *Ibid.*

[7] In terms of interactions between individuals and the group, scholars of political psychology have paid considerable attention to the study of national attachment as an individual group association (e.g. Richard D. Ashmore, Lee Jussim and David Wilder, *Social Identity, Intergroup Conflict, and Conflict Reduction* (Oxford: Oxford University Press, Incorporated, 2001)). Some of these studies have focused on the interrelationship between national attachment and different theoretical constructs of interests such as religious or ethnic identities (e.g. Sonia Roccas, Lilach Sagiv, Shalom H. Schwartz, Nir Halevy and Roy Eidelson, "Towards a unifying model of identification with groups: Integrating theoretical perspectives," *Personality and Social Psychology Review* 12 (2008): 280–306), authoritarianism, anomie, and general self-esteem or attitudes toward foreigners and tolerance for cultural diversity (e.g. Rebeca Raijman, Eldad Davidov, Peter Schmidt and Oshrat Hochman, "What does a Nation owe non-citizens?: National attachments, perception of threat and attitudes towards granting citizenship rights in a comparative perspective," *International Journal of Comparative Sociology* 49, no. 2–3 (2008): 195–22). Many of these studies largely differentiate between two types of national attachment: one blind, militaristic, ignorant and obedient (often called nationalism or chauvinism), and another which is genuine, constructive, critical, civic, and reasonable (often called constructive patriotism (CP); see e.g. Thomas Blank and Peter Schmidt, "National Identity in a United Germany: Nationalism or Patriotism? An Empirical Test with Representative Data," *Political Psychology* 24, no. 2 (June 2003): 289–312).

"Identity" is widely applied in a broad range of scenarios. Among these various forces, this concept lends supports to individual developments in a political and situational context in the post-colonial order. The case of Taiwan fits well into this scenario.

In the post-colonial context of "identity" formation, which the Taiwanese case intriguingly presents, a dynamic, not static, perspective should be emphasized. People living in a society which has undergone colonization and political transition are experiencing certain levels of identity crisis and interruption of identity formation. In a wide range of post-colonial literature, this identity-related protagonist is often portrayed as struggling with question of identity, national or cultural, caused by the psychological and mental conflicts triggered by the political interruption and transition, and the confrontation between the old and new order.[8] These prescriptions are reflective of a culture-oriented approach, viewing the identity as an ever-changing entity constantly being shaped and conditioned by the environment we were born into (in other words socialization). As suggested by Stuart Hall, this type of identity formation, also dubbed as a "cultural identity," searches for images which impose an imaginary coherence on the experience of dispersal and fragmentation.[9] This self-perceived identity is far from being externally fixated in some essential pasts. Rather, it is subject to the continuous interactions informed by history, culture, society and powers.[10]

This cultural perspective nourishes an advanced theory, "hybridization," by which a confluence of multiple cultures leads to the emergence of a new cultural form. Critical views related to this perspective interpret

---

[8] Alison Brysk, Craig Parsons and Wayne Sandholtz, "After Empire: National Identity and Post-Colonial Families of Nations," *European Journal of International Relations* 8, no. 2 (2002): 267-305; Matthias Koenig, Gurharpal Singh and John Rex (eds.), "Pluralism and Multiculturalism in Colonial and Post-Colonial Societies," *International Journal on Multicultural Societies* 5, no. 2 (2003).

[9] Stuart Hall, "Culture Identity and Diaspora," in *Identity: Community, Culture, Difference,* ed. J. Rutherford (London: Laurence and Wishart, 1990), 222–237; Stuart Hall, "The Global and Local: Globalization Ethnicity," in *Culture, Globalization and the World-System,* ed. A.D. King (London: Macmillan, 1991); Stuart Hall, "When was the 'Post-Colonial'? Thinking at the Limit," in *The Post-Colonial Question,* eds. R. Chamber and L. Curti (London and New York, NY, Routledge, 1996), 242–260.

[10] *Ibid.* Also, see note 11.

colonialism not as a past remembering/incident, however traumatic and perpetrating, but something that constantly intrudes and transforms our present culture and history.[11] In several occasions when a group of people/ society experienced "colonial" governance, it provides the insight that it is not only the colonization spirit that continues to shape evolving identity within the society, but also perpetuates the lingering legacy of imperialism despite the decolonization process. Furthermore, these imperialist leftover influences cast uncertain outlooks upon the political relations between these colonized societies, and their suzerain countries. In the case of Taiwan, its love–hate relationship with previous colonial master, Japan, and the intense cyclical struggles against the country with similar ancestral origins, China, provide a vivid description of the ongoing dynamic struggles within the Taiwanese cultural soul.

These rather dilemmatic perspectives that I have painted, however, cannot explain entirely the complexity and under-development of the concept "identity" in contemporary cultural studies. In this sense, several other perspectives are worth exploring before we delve into the case of Taiwan.

For one, this analysis will be conducted focusing mainly on the cultural aspects of the Taiwanese identity, and its relations with the process of identity construction and formation in Taiwan. "Political identity," for the purpose of this paper, is considered as a critical, but not a decisive factor. Yet, with its primary role in calibrating the legitimacy of the authority, the political dimension of the identity evolution in Taiwan will also be consulted. The point lies in the question: To what extent a degree of homogeneity in the political spectrum is needed as a pre-condition but, not without reservations, a convergence of the entire cultural sphere (including language, religion, morality, every-day life forms and perceptions of the world) of various groups found in the Taiwanese society. In this sense, the cultural and political dimensions of "identity" are interwoven synthetically to facilitate the workings of a modern society. On one hand, this synthesis

---

[11] Homi K. Bhabha, *Nation and Narration* (New York, NY: Routledge, 1990); also, Ien Ang, On Not Speaking Chinese: Living Between Asia and the West (London: Routledge, 2001), 24. It is argued that the emergence of a sub-national identity in Taiwan makes sense, when combining Ang's theory (Identity is ever changing) and with Bhabha's contestation ("hybridization").

constructs a normative framework (such as a Constitution) in which the preferences and identity projects of social groups are placed into a hierarchical order and reconciled with each other. On the other hand, it sets in to shape the various interpretations that the social, philosophical and national groups that make up a polity, generate in never-ending debates on how to translate those shared values, principles and goals into concrete actions and activities in everyday life and ordinary legislations.

Second, the formation of identity tends to include, although necessarily, a critical phase of "exclusion." Georg W. F. Hegel's ideas elegantly refine the conceptual pair of self-other relations, as "each is for the other the middle term through which each mediates itself; each is for himself, and for the other, an immediate being on its own accord, which at the same time is such only through this medication."[12] Samuel P. Huntington also elaborated that "we know who we are when we know whom we are against."[13] The commonality in these messages is that we first identify ourselves by relying on the existence of the differences between us and the others. By recognizing the distinction between self and others, a group/collective identity is formed.

This cognizance of a differentiated "self" versus "the others" helps accentuate the similarities between self and other in-groupers through a process of self-categorization, and to minimize the differences in self-stereotyping.[14] Furthermore, individuals gain more benefits in due course of this self-refining process, out of expectations of solidarity in behavioral

---

[12] Georg W. F. Hegel, *Phenomenology of Spirit*, trans. A. V. Miller (Oxford: Oxford University Press, 1977). For more discussions on Hegel's philosophy works, see Charles Taylor, *Hegel* (Cambridge: Cambridge University Press, 1975); Michael Baur, Georg W. F. Hegel: Key Concepts, ed. M. Baur (Abingdon: Routledge, 2014); Frederick C. Beiser, *After Hegel: German Philosophy, 1840–1900* (Princeton: Princeton University Press, 2014).

[13] Samuel P. Huntington, "The New Era in World Politics," in *The Clash of Civilizations and the Remaking of World Order* (New York, NY: Simon and Schuster, 2007), 19–39.

[14] John C. Turner stressed that social identity rests on intergroup social comparisons that seek to confirm or to establish in-group-favouring evaluative distinctiveness between in-group and out-group, motivated by an underlying need for self-esteem. See, John C. Turner, Rediscovering the Social Group: A Self-Categorization Theory (Oxford: Blackwell, 1987); John C. Turner, Michael A. Hogg, Penelope J. Oakes, Stephen D. Reicher and Margaret S. Wetherell, *Rediscovering the Social Group: A Self-Categorization Theory* (Oxford: Blackwell, 1987); John C. Turner and Penelope J. Oakes, "Self-Categorization

outcomes from the in-group members. As Socrates advised, participating in movement of collective identity is a rational deliberation outcome for the purpose of increasing personal gains.[15]

However, with everything else equal, this may be an over-simplification in some specific contexts. Special occasions do exist when multiple ethnic groups live in a polity, with a clearly outlined goal of constructing a post-modern and supra-national identity consciousness. In this sense, the European Union (EU) is an evidentiary case for identity construction in a post-modern and supra-national occasion. To a considerable extent, the European example lends referential supports to the Taiwanese identity construct. Nevertheless, dangers loom large. Over-simplification may occur when this multiplicity of identity is an outcome of deliberate political construction through policy implementation and a long-term national goal.

For the former, the European identity poses challenges to this — which is actually paradoxical to the very nature of identity formation and development — ethno-nationalist type of constitutive means. In another words, this self-others differentiation would not work in either internal or external dimensions. Internally, the "mirror" (with which the group reflects and redefines its features) and "wall" (by which the group gives itself a self-contained image which also plays a role in its external relations) functions of a group or its collective identity seem to fall out of practical use, because a visible existence of such barriers may dwindle/debilitate the internal integrity and resilience of its construction. Externally, the post-national European identity is constructed on a basis of spatio-geographical expediency, but not one with any particular polity. In other words, with the emergence of a pan-European identity consciousness, Europeans began viewing themselves as world citizens incidentally living on a single continent, and hence cannot be cosmopolitan. This self versus other distinction thus appears rather awkward and impractical for any form of application in cultural explanations.

It is in this sense that the case of Taiwan also falls into a paradigm similar to that of the European experience. The official existence of

---

Theory and Social Influence," in *Psychology of Group Influence* (2nd edn.), ed. P.B. Paulus (Hillsdale, NJ: Lawrence Erlbaum, 1989): 233–275.

[15] Francesca Polletta and James M. Jasper, "Collective Identity and Social Movements," *Annual Review of Sociology* 27 (2001): 283–305.

multiple ethnic groups in Taiwan has not only been politically imposed by politicians, but they have also received differentiated treatments from the legal authorities. This deliberate distinction in ethnicities within the Taiwanese context is designed for a long-term national goal which is preparing for the re-unification with the Chinese mainland and for removing it from the control of the communist rival regime. The identity consciousness of the Taiwanese society is thus shaped by this contextual peculiarity, in which there exists a dual normative framework, the Constitution and the National Mobilization Act (动员戡乱时期临时条款). Rights mandated in the Constitution have been partially and temporarily suspended because Taiwan was then in an emergency facing a belligerent rival communist regime in the Chinese mainland that necessitated national mobilization in the event of conflict breaking out. To fulfill this long-term national goal, certain inherent rights and interests of the people were circumscribed. Meanwhile, the government strengthened the construction of a political identity, by which people's allegiance to the government would be fortified through national campaigns and mass education. Witnessed in this purposive political identity construction, the identity formation in the Taiwanese society was thus more an outcome of a top-down rather than a *laissez-faire* bottom-up policy approach.

In this thread, a teleological perspective would better enable a good grip of the intricacy of identity construct and evolution in Taiwan.

The Identity Formation of Taiwan: Going Beyond the Political Sphere

The Cultural Dimension in Identity Construct

Before delving further to examine the relations between popular culture and identity evolution/development in Taiwan, the reception of popular culture, its cultural role and implications of cultural development, if not explicit functions of cultural promotion, deserve some preliminary discussions here.

Some scholars argue that there exist three forms of receptions of popular culture.[16] The first form is hegemonic reception, where the ideology

---

[16] Paul Graves-Brown, Siân Jones and Clive Gamble (authors & eds.), *Cultural Identity and Archaeology: The Construction of European Communities* (Psychology Press, 1996);

reflects and reinforces the domination of the ruling class. The masses are deemed to generally consent to this predisposed form of culture production. However, in an age when communication and global information dissemination are made possible because of technology advancement of the internet, this authoritarian style of culture production now has little market. In effect, there is no longer a clearly hegemonic popular culture as the regime's control over society and the social superstructure continues to erode.

The second is a negotiated form of reception, where some ground is left for expressing emotions such as anger, "without confronting the social mechanics of domination *per se*."[17] Reading the message of individuality and feelings does not directly challenge the regime's remaining political hegemony, but neither does it reflect consent. Instead, it carves out a private sphere for the individual apart from the collective one in her/his life, by institutionalizing a zone of indifference when negotiating between the two. Even if the existence of this private sphere runs short of providing a safety valve for the release of frustrations amongst the various members of society, it does offer an outlet for simply ignoring the imperatives of state authorities and opting out of the cultural world that the state tries to dominate.

The third form of reception is emancipatory, including what Miklos Haraszti called "Maverick Artists," those "willing to sacrifice the privileges of the assimilated in order to retain their independence" although "by so doing they are doomed to eek [sic] out a meager existence as fringe-dwellers

---

Michael Thompson, "The problem of the center: An autonomous cosmology," in *Essays in The Sociology of Perception*, ed. M. Douglas (London: Routledge & Kegan Paul, 1982), 302–328. For more discussion of culture and cultural rights, see Michael Thompson, Richard Ellis and Aaron Wildavsky, *Cultural Theory* (Boulder, CO: Westview, 1990); Gunnar Grendstad, Per Selle, Michael Thompson (eds.), *Cultural Theory as Political Science* (Routledge, 2003); John Storey, *Cultural Theory and Popular Culture*: *An Introduction* (Routledge, 2015); Peter Jones, "Bearing the Consequences of Belief," *Journal of Political Philosophy* 2, no. 1 (1994): 24–43; Jacob T. Levy, "Classifying Cultural Rights," in *Nomos XXXIX: Ethnicity and Group Rights*, eds. W. Kymlicka and I. Shapiro (New York, NY: New York University Press, 1997); Chandran Kukathas, "Are There Any Cultural Rights?" *Political Theory* 20 (1995): 105–139; James Johnson, "Why Respect Culture?," *American Journal of Political Science* 44, no. 3 (2000): 405–418.
[17] *Ibid.*

in a state-owned cultural desert crowded with mirages."[18] Explicit producers and consumers of this type of culture are still few, with their main forms of expression like satirical literatures or rock-and-roll music.

It is from this receptionist perspective that the role of public culture in Taiwan after 1945 could be most efficiently evaluated.

The Politics-Cum-Culture Interface

Further, the relations between a cultural and political identity merit some discussions. In the context of the Taiwanese particularity, their interactions have wielded critical influences on identity construction in Taiwan.

A cultural identity can be described as identification with and acceptance into a group that has a shared system of symbols and meanings as well as norms for conduct.[19] Generally, this shared system can be replete with a variety of recognizable elements. In Geert Hofstede's work, four categories may be attached with heavier importance: symbols, rituals, values, and heroes.[20] The former three have laid down a foundational platform, by providing epistemological instruments to reify a contextual elaboration of what the term "culture" refers to. Briefly put, symbols refer to verbal and nonverbal language. Rituals are the socially essential collective activities within this culture. Values may be the feelings not open for discussion within this culture about issues that attract judgmental evaluations. Examples are numerous, like what is good or bad, normal or abnormal, which are generally vividly present to a majority of the members of the same culture. At least, these judgements would be more than clearly discernible amongst the elite members who occupy pivotal positions in this culture.

---

[18] See, note 17.

[19] Mary J. Collier and M. Thomas, "Culture Identity: An Interpretative Perspective," in *Theories in Intercultural Communication*, eds. Y. Y. Kim and W. B. Gudykunst (Sage, 1988), 99–122.

[20] Geert Hofstede and Michael H. Bond, "Hofstede's Culture Dimensions: An Independent Validation Using Rokeach's Value Survey," *Journal of Cross-Cultural Psychology* 15, no. 4 (1984): 417–433; Geert Hofstede, "Dimensionalizing Cultures: The Hofstede Model in Context," *Online Readings in Psychology and Culture* 2, no. 1 (2011), available at http://dx.doi.org/10.9707/2307-0919.1014.

That said, it should be noted that whereas inter-cultural differences are presumed and generally detectable, intra-cultures differences are no less minor. For most of the time, these incongruences are interwoven into a plenum with tinges of characteristics so blatantly heterogeneous that purported distinctions would, without doubt, cast a laborious mission. The key lies in the perception and self-perception of every individual in this culture and the dynamism between and among these individuals and the community. Succinctly put, the identity construct of a group of people may comprise of multi-dimensional evolutions, among which their inter- and intra-dynamism constitute one major variant in due course of this identity construction.

It is under this context that the identity construct of Taiwan after 1949 could be examined in greater details, with a comprehensive inclusion of all factors that potentially influence this process of identity construction. As a result, my analytical angle shifts away from merely studying primordial feelings or political ideologies, to one stressing the ontology people have in response to this inquiry of identity construct under different contextual conditions.

Furthermore, a related issue in the Taiwanese identity construct concerns an enduring debate, albeit more in the political scenario, of "unification" and "independence."

This "unification-independence" issue has long been discussed together with the Taiwanese identity. Yet, it is important that this unification-independence dichotomy sheds critical, but not decisive, lights on the identity construction process, over-emphasis of which would not help substantiate these explicatory efforts at identity construction. Meanwhile, to assign disproportionate emphasis to this unification-independence dichotomy also runs the risks of exacerbating prevalent misunderstandings that have equalized "national identity" with the policy preferences of the Taiwanese for "unification" and "independence." But, in fact, what lies at the crux of these two political phenomena are actually two different concepts.

Preference toward unification or independence is more of a personal choice for an individual and not necessarily dependent on his/her national identity. Other pragmatic considerations generally have significant bearing to the issue. One is the factor of economics. Studies of the dissolution of the Soviet Union, which catalyzed identity changes in the societies of its republics, show that improvements in economic conditions in these locations help mitigate regional separatism and ethnic nationalism.

In the case of Taiwan, the choice of identity is often entangled with Taiwanese unification and/or independence issue. A general assessment is that in the decades when the Taiwanese community was ruled by the Kuomintang (KMT, also known as the Nationalist government) authoritarian regime, the attitudes of most people in society towards Taiwan's future political status are largely an expression of their particularistic national identity. This is less likely to change because of entrenched socio-political implications of identity-formation that have a nationalistic undertone. The only distinction lies in whether the attitude is integrated into mainland Chinese or Taiwanese nationalism.

Yet, political developments after the commencement of an era of democratization in early 1990s set off the development of the Taiwanese identity which has grown complex, requiring comprehensive intellectual explorations with multi-dimensional perspectives. Put differently, well-versed explications need to take into account political, as well as non-political factors, so as to avoid the invalidity of any single criterion for analysis or measure of validity.

Rejuvenation of a Taiwanese Identity: A Discursive Course

The KMT Authoritarian Rule: Politics as an Underlying Factor in Cultural Identity Formation

In the case of Taiwan, an issue preceding further explications of identity formation is the role of politics.

My first observation is that, before democratization starting from the 1980s, identity construction in Taiwanese society was guided by one political objective. All identity building was carried out to serve this goal, and the shaping of its policy discourses was monopolized by the ruling KMT government. This goal was underpinned by two major components. One, there was only one China in the world, which was the Republic of

China (ROC). The second component was that unification was the ultimate goal across the Taiwan Strait, which was to be conducted at the helm of the ROC.

In this context, identity construction carried out in various social aspects was conditioned upon recognition of this ultimate political goal. Furthermore, the implementation of this political goal defined parameters that distinguished the ruling class from the ruled, the elite from the commoners, the civilized and the vulgar. This distinction paradoxically matched the lines separating the late-comer mainlanders (after 1949), and migrants largely immigrating from Fujian and Guangdong provinces (from early 17th century to 1895).[21]

Succinctly put, this distinction, intentionally or not, cemented into a cultural hierarchy by rigidifying Han traditions before the onset of Communist ideology into Chinese consciousness, defined the nature of social inequality which was later solidified by rigid institutional frameworks, and justified discriminations among different generational communities of Taiwanese. In social interactions, this political goal also held great sway in moulding patterns of social behaviors, and consequently in identity construct.

This rigid political structure permeated into mob activities, or the formation of secret societies. These mobs had their political preferences, which also fell in line with their membership composition and profiles. Mob groups that draw from local Taiwanese communities tended to show predilections, if not strong identification, with the then underground anti-governmental forces. Contrarily, gangs recruiting members from the mainlander communities, such as villages for dependents of KMT troops retreating to Taiwan after 1949, became staunch supporters to the then KMT government and this pre-destined unification goal for those communities.

---

[21] The early-arriving immigrant community refers to the Holo and Hakka groups which began their migration to Taiwan from the early 17th century to 1895, before Taiwan was ceded to Japan. The indigenous community living mainly in the mountainous areas was not counted. This aboriginal minority constituted less than 3% of the population, and thus wielded a meagre influence in the evolution of the identity construct in Taiwan. The extremely minor indigenous people living in the mountainous areas, who had a different bloodline from the Austronesian race in the south and west Pacific Ocean area.

Another example is found in the sphere of religious affairs. The unification-independence dichotomy similarly served as a defining factor for the development of culture in Taiwan. Those who paid nominal homage to the KMT government's authority tended to enjoy more freedom in conducting religious affairs. The Chinese Regional Bishops' Conference in Taiwan (also known as the Catholic Church in Taiwan) was one exemplary case. On the contrary, the Presbyterian Church in Taiwan had long spearheaded the reformist position by soliciting the required dynamics by advocating freedom of thought and speech via their preaching activities. Consequently, rooms for religious activities had been significantly limited by the KMT government after it had intervened, interfered and impeded their activities via all available means.

During the KMT authoritarian era (1949 to late 1980s), entanglement between politics and almost all spheres of social life was so extensively wide that it aroused a circular question: whether the external political precondition that forced people in all walks of life to choose sides remained an open-ended question; but the contention may go another way round, which provides also contextual credits and equally powerful persuasions.

Some descriptions help to illuminate the required empirical details. Generally speaking, cultural policies after 1949 were products aimed at serving pre-destined political goals enshrining "re-unification" of the cross-strait and "extinction" of the rivalry communist regime. Popular cultural spheres were dedicated mainly to help reify the implementation of political narratives dictated by the ruling authority, leading to a large-scale re-spatialization of public and private spheres in the society. Examples are plenty, as in song and film productions that re-affirmed the orthodoxy, legitimacy and necessity of the Kuomintang (the ruling Nationalist party, KMT) ruling had mushroomed. Literary works also drew attentions to the hardship of long retreat from the Chinese mainland, and remembering of national glorious achievements.

It was thus a fair observation that popular culture is a policy product with official endorsements to boost prevailingly patriotic sentiment among the public. It represented the values for certain classes, enjoying higher political status and better-off economic conditions, and had been crafted in officially sanctioned discourses. Nevertheless, in the central and southern parts of the island of Taiwan, local communities developed their own cultural genres of various types, in vernacular dialect, the Hokkien (or in the Taiwanese variant of Minannese). These literature genres were consumed by the general public. To some extent, contemporaneous culture policies had largely internalized these preferences, due to the top-down policy implementation in a repressive manner.

This political undertone began fading into the 1980s. Momentum gathered in the international community led by the US to shift political support to the Communist government in the mainland, inflicted greater pressures on the Republican government in Taiwan. As the international reality getting harsher, credibility of the original political objective collapsed, leading to the debilitation of the ruling KMT's ability to keep internal politics and cultural development under control.

Meanwhile, burgeoning anti-authoritarian political forces mushroomed, along with various other strands of social movements. Progressing into early 1990s, this political goal, as a foundation of all social constructs of the Taiwanese identity in previous decades, had been further weakened and unable to pre-define activities in various social spheres within the Taiwanese society.

This permeating concern of politics in daily business is common. Further, its impacts can be explicated in following threads. First, how should the relations of political and non-political factors be assessed in this process? Furthermore, depending on the particularities of Taiwan's case, how has the kinetics between political and non-political factors re-configured the Taiwanese identity at present days? A related inquiry is, have these dynamisms fleshed out a "Taiwan consensus"?

After Democratization

Fading influences of politics

Entering into the 1990s, a conglomeration of economic growth, social development and democratic reform filled the vacuum left behind by this fading political goal in the course of identity construction in Taiwan. Politically, restrictions on some critical aspects in civil and political rights were lifted. Freedom was applauded in nearly all spheres. It was under this context that a political undertone for identity construction was in transition. The political undercurrent in identity construction actually continued, but had become more diversified, allowing different opinions and free choices regarding the future of Taiwan's political status to be expressed freely.

In the wake of a transformative, yet still influential, political consciousness, more room was given to cultural contents for the Taiwanese identity to thrive. In the name of democratization, restrictions on many aspects of the society were lifted, exposing society and the public to more egregious external influences. De-regulation in cultural policy-making was one welcomed incident, through which cultural vitality was boosted. This cultural vitality could be construed further from two mutually supplementary perspectives, from which a conglomeration leads to an effort in furthering the identity construct in Taiwan, something still ongoing till present day: liberalization in many aspects of social affairs entailed in the wake of democratization; and the cooperation-cum-competition relations between globalization and localization, which is also termed as the glo-calization of identity construct.

In this sense, a primary observation could be attempted. Democratization in the 1990s brought about the liberalization in various aspects in social and cultural life, which was also a welcoming development under contemporaneous international and regional context. This liberalization trend found celebrating echoes in the development at the international level. Accordingly, the force of glo-calization[22] — a conglomeration of globalization and localization — thrived and nourished this cultural vitality. The goal, while perhaps inadvertent and opaque in the beginning, nevertheless had gathered momentum in due course, to attempt to incorporate cultural contents into political parameters in the identity construct of Taiwanese. However, this process has remained inchoate, yet quickly evolving.

---

[22] Oxford Dictionaries, "Glo-calization," visited 10 September 2015, http://www.oxforddiction aries.com/definition/english/glocalization. This concept is termed as, "The practice of conducting business according to both local and global considerations." Also, see, George Ritzer, "Rethinking Globalization: Glocalization/Grobalization and Something/Nothing," *Sociological Theory* 21, no. 3 (September 2003): 193–209.

Reversing mutual-eclipsing to mutual reinforcement between cultural and political identities

Dynamism and ever-changing notions of identity at the regional and international environments laid the foundation for cultural diversity and provided expedient stimulations for cultural vitality. De-regulation of policy restrictions, in company with reforms in the political arena, had enabled an open and competitive environment for popular cultural industries. This openness and vitality were actually intertwined, lending a helping hand to each other. On one hand, society was able to hold onto the then prevailing global impulse, which in turn integrated two seemingly contradictory trends harmoniously, the "Taiwanization" (localization) and "Globalization." Described as a trend of "glo-calization," this synthesis fulfilled the vacuum left behind by fading political concerns based upon the internal societal makeup of China, and located the Taiwanese identity in the global context, which reified a sense of compensation for the Taiwanese over the Sisyphus quest for international political and legal status for its existence. Nevertheless, criticism was rife, in the sense that it was actually "Americanization" of the Taiwanese popular culture. In this aspect, social critique was not uncommon that it was the American type of consumerism that had gulped over the island, as seen in the fact that American brands had flooded in and trumped other foreign cultural ideas and commercial influences.

On the other hand, "Taiwanization" was permeating in almost all aspects of life, which actually marked the allegiance of both the producer and consumer to the local Taiwanese community. The quickly developing popularity of subcultures at the grassroot community level and elevation of cultural production in dialectic and vernacular languages provided a few demonstrating examples. An upshot was that "Taiwan," as a geographical term, had become more attractive and approachable to most Taiwanese.

In this context, the thesis advanced by Ernest Gellner in the evolution of nations and nationalism was worth remembering: that the state precedes the nation.[23] Taking into account Taiwan's particularities,

---

[23] Ernest Gellner, *Nations and Nationalism* (Ithaca, NY: Cornell University Press, 1983).

the Taiwanese identity has been featured with and nourished by this geographical insularity, and had been substantiated well before it gains momentum in historical and societal meanings. This also re-affirms the observation that the Taiwan consciousness, which is later transformed into a powerful force of civic nationalism, is mainly geographical before it gains legitimacy in the historical arena.

However, this cultural aspect of the Taiwanese identity continued to be overshadowed by the political reality which was prone to the political dynamism both across the Taiwan Strait and in the Taiwan Island. Beginning in late 1990s, a rising sentiment which was characterized by the term "de-Sinicization" set off a new era when the "Taiwanization" trend further developed, and ultimately had culminated in the eight-year reign under the Chen Shui-bian government (on behalf of the Democratic Progressive Party, DPP). Policy facilitation and mandatory instruction cultivated this trend deeply in the minds of the younger generations, exemplified by a variety of measures adopted to support it. The Name Rectification movement and a new set of curriculum guidelines in history education in secondary schools were two poignant examples. This re-affirmed a previous observation that politics, despite its fading influences, had remained a weighing factor in due course of the identity construct in Taiwan. Along this still-ongoing process, it is discernible that the relations between political and cultural identities have been subject to consistent re adjustments and re configuration in their parameters, contents and scopes.

This is what can be described as a symbiosis of politics and non-politics factors in the Taiwanese identity construct, in the context when democratic politics become robust and routine after the 1990s. Development of symbiosis between politics and non-politics factors is discernible in the Taiwanese identity construct after democratization. This politics-oriented dominance, which caused an imbalance in the relations between political and non-political issues, has been partially redressed.

This identity enhancement function of politics becomes fading. Rather than being totally obliterated, it underwent a transformation. In recent example as shown in the Sunflower movement (March 2014) and the anti-textbook guideline revision protest (January–August 2015), the younger generation has demonstrated that their opinions have been cloaked by both political beliefs and supported by palpable cultural contents. In other words, internal contradiction between politics and non-politics factors, as shown in previous generations, has been redressed. Politics and non-political factors are becoming more incorporative, which has forged a symbiosis able to accommodate all these factors.

Upon this gradually consolidated symbiosis, a Taiwanese identity which was aborted in previous occasions is reviving. For these younger generations, it is from this reviving identity construct that their behaviors and choices, political and non-political, have not demonstrated internal contradictions that may entail mutually eclipsing potentials.

In this sense, what Joseph Bosco had observed in 1992, in assessing an emerging Taiwanese popular culture,[24] still finds resounding echoes in the present day scenario. His conclusion is astonishingly resounding, that "the mainland fever" has had the ironic effect of turning all residents of Taiwan, both those arriving before and after 1949, and indigenous people, into "Taiwanese."[25] Several factors Bosco had identified remain explicatory. However, leaving aside similarity in the shifting balance of political powers, supported by local and national politicians and resurgent interests in promoting localism and an elevated sense of dignity in using dialect languages emerges in this process. Distinct from events in previous decades, the trend in identity construction upon entering the 21st century, in relation to a process of re-configuration and re-definition of popular culture in Taiwan, is not only tacitly condoned, but also voluntarily vindicated by the Taiwanese authorities. Either way, this indicates a dramatic reversal of official anti-traditionalism, anti-localism and anti-diversification in both identity construct and culture policy-making.

---

[24] Joseph Bosco, "The Emergence of a Taiwanese Popular Culture," in *The Other Taiwan*, ed. M. A. Rubistein (Armonk, NY: Sharpe, 1994), 392–403.

[25] *Ibid.* Originally, Bosco had referred to the mainland fever breaking out after 1987, at the early period of democratization, when political fetters had been lifted, and reforms being conducted in almost all aspects of social dimensions.

Conclusion

Looking back at historical developments in Taiwan, the cultural developmental landscape reveals that the identity construct is still developing, and prone to the influences from political dynamism in the Taiwanese socio-political landscape. Put differently, politics has consistently played an important role in this process. In this context, the relations between "politics" and "culture" are critical and intriguing, as they have claimed dominant positions in different stages of cultural development and led to different outcomes. Nevertheless, their interactions have provided clues to how the formation, mutation and maturization of a Taiwanese identity have been pursued, and how, in a later stage, a Taiwan consciousness is to be enlightened.

While it is difficult to summarize this ongoing process, it is discernible that a synthesis of a rapidly evolving political-cum-cultural relation and an imbalanced development of "Taiwanization" and "de-Sinicization" have set the tone for identity construction in Taiwan. Democratization justifies liberalization not only in the political, but also cultural and societal arenas, strengthening the prospects for cultural diversity and vitality. Yet, downsides remain. The dilemma faced in the political-cum-cultural dimension of accommodating "Taiwanization" and "de-Sinicization" has continued. Yet, the corresponding restraining factor of authoritarianism found in the past has withered, witnessed in the dwindling economic performance and the growing-exclusive mindset of youth reception of culture in almost all aspects, permeating among the public in these days. One consequential downside is thus, the hollowing-out of the cultural development in the Taiwan Island. In other words, when the center becomes empty, the periphery would assume the dominant position, leading and shaping future paradigms in which cultural aspects of the Taiwanese identity could thrive. As a result, the Taiwanese case of identity construction reconsiders the relationship between center and periphery of cultural formation in Taiwan and worries that the direction of cultural development in the island may be reversible and leave this newly formed culture based on freedom and autonomy with a shaky foundation for future development. In this sense, further exploration of this Taiwanese identity construct should be situated in a platform that incorporates all political, social and economic trends in Taiwan, going beyond conventional wisdom, and become more informative and sensible to all potentially influential factors.[26] Perhaps, one practical outcome of the inquiry in this writing is what cultural ideas we will leave behind for the next generations.

---

[26] In this sense, an emerging platform, dubbed as situational constructivism, provides an alternative. This is mainly developed from the study of previous Soviet republics in post-U.S.S.R. era. These post-Soviet states demonstrate similar situations as that of Taiwan. See, David D. Laitin, *Identity in Formation: The Russian-Speaking Populations in the Near Abroad* (Ithaca, NY: Cornell University Press, 1998); Igor Torbakov, "History, Memory and National Identity Understanding the Politics of History and Memory Wars in Post-Soviet Lands," in *Russian Nationalism, Foreign Policy and Identity Debates in Putin's Russia: New Ideological Patterns after the Orange Revolution*, ed. M. Laruelle (New York, NY: Columbia University Press, 2014), 41–76.

Section 7

Conclusion

Chapter 16

Conclusion: Commonalities and Convergence

Tai Wei LIM

In working on this volume, we discovered commonalities across all the country-specific case studies in the volume. It goes to show that, alongside local features, there are detectable and discernible patterns of similarities that characterize all case studies covered in this volume. Some of the major commonalities that we detected are discussed below.

Technology and Mass Media

In the course of the edited volume, we acknowledge the importance of mass media and the cultural politics it represents in shaping cultural policies. Popular culture and media have traditionally been politicized. They present a form of soft power cultural influence in shaping public perceptions and foreign policies. Dissemination of media materials is aided by the advent of technologies. Another common theme in the edited volume is that of technology. Xiaojuan Ping highlighted the point that technological advancement, prevailing popular use of smart phones, tablets, selfie-sticks and other digital-era gadgets, has largely amplified the importance of digital entertainment in the leisure activities of the young in Northeast Asia. Digitalization is not only a revolution in networking, education, long-distance communication and etc., but also how the young and old enjoy various digital products like reality TV shows broadcasted through smartphones and other handheld devices and readers.

Wen Xin Lim's South Korean case study demonstrated clearly that social media plays an important role in the proliferation of Korean Wave, especially in *Hallyu* 2.0. Korean entertainment agencies developed a social media strategy with the following elements: "to align their business model with social media; to maximize various social media channels; to engage customers with on- and offline promotions; and to stimulate audience with exclusive contents."[1] With the rapid growth of social media, agencies turned their eyes to the new business model with social media. Moving beyond the conventional business model of music sales to consumers, they made use of social media like YouTube to promote artists and their music for free and sought revenues in the field of licensing, royalty, and advertisement.[2] In December 2011, to meet the growing demand of worldwide consumers, YouTube added the K-pop genre to its music page along with R&B, Rock, Pop, and Rap, the first case any specific country's music was introduced as a separate genre on YouTube.[3]

Irrespective of handheld digital devices, social media apps or downloadable movies/songs, technological advancement led to the democratization of popular culture. Katherine Tseng argued that, in an age when communication and global information dissemination are made possible because of technology advancement of the internet, authoritarian means of culture production now has little market. In effect, there is no longer a clearly hegemonic popular culture as the regime's control over society and the social superstructure continues to erode, giving rise to a diversity of subcultural ecologies. This links us with the next common point of "identity" and cultural hybridization.

"Identity" and Cultural Hybridization

The volume also examined the common theme of "identity" through a culture-oriented approach highlighted by Tseng, Elim Wong and Wilson

[1] JoohHo Anh, Sehwan Oh, and Hyunjung Kim, "Korean Pop Takes Off! Social Media Strategy of Korean Entertainment Industry," 2013 10th International Conference on Service Systems and Service Management (ICSSSM).

[2] JoohHo Anh, Sehwan Oh, and Hyunjung Kim, "Korean Pop Takes Off! Social Media Strategy of Korean Entertainment Industry," 2013 10th International Conference on Service Systems and Service Management (ICSSSM).

[3] JoohHo Anh, Sehwan Oh, and Hyunjung Kim, "Korean Pop Takes Off! Social Media Strategy of Korean Entertainment Industry," 2013 10th International Conference on Service Systems and Service Management (ICSSSM).

Lee, viewing the identity as an ever-changing entity constantly being shaped and conditioned by the environment we were born into (in other words socialization). Almost all the writers in this volume suggest the presence of the complex process of "hybridization," by which a confluence of multiple cultures leads to the emergence of a new cultural form. Overall, popular cultural soft power is mutually reinforcing in the sense that East Asian economies work with each other and influence each other to become cool and creative but yet at the same time trend-spot global popular cultural elements for incorporation into their textual and visual imaginations and body of works.

East Asian popular cultural industry has become so sophisticated that, like industrial production systems, they have graduated and specialized production systems and testing grounds. It has the commercial and industrial potential of a creative flying geese model since Japan had in the past set the pace for the development of the creative industries. There are also differential levels of consumption, for example, Hong Kong and Taiwan are regarded as *de facto* platforms to test receptivity and reactions to popular cultural products before introduction to Chinese consumption. For the popular culture eco-system to work, besides producers, there must be consumers as well. All writings in the volume examine the important roles that consumers (specifically the fandom, including hard-core ones like otakus) play in shaping the development of popular cultural products and their creative industries.

Fandom

Tseng pointed out that rituals are the socially essential collective activities within cultures. Collective values and judgmental evaluations, like what is good or bad, normal or abnormal, are generally the outcome of negotiations by a majority of the members of the same culture. At least, these judgements would be more clearly discernible to the elite members who occupy pivotal positions in this culture and have the power to shape the outcome of its collective value system. It appears in the case of Northeast Asian fandom, popular cultural elites like otakus emphasize the ideas and concepts of groupism and collective identities when mobilizing resources for marketing campaigns, fan activities or simply exchanges of information.

In the case of Wong and Lee's Hong Kong chapter, three major points are discernible in this aspect. First, fandom in Hong Kong transforms individual fans to idol product providers by enthusiastically making and giving out freebies and sharing idol-related information.

Second, in Wong and Lee's chapter, K-pop fan culture in Hong Kong selects features from other K-pop fans' cultural experiences in other parts of the world like Korea and Japan and, at the same time, creates its unique localized practices. *K-club*, for example, not only participated in the Korean-style rice wreath donation and tree-planting event but also gave out freebies to others within the fan community, but such features cannot be found outside Hong Kong (such as in the Japanese case). Third, fandom in Hong Kong is a creature characterized by both groupism and self-identity. This contradiction encourages group-oriented activities but individual fans emphasize their own self-identity whenever factionalism, rivalry and competition appear. Wong and Lee argued that this fandom world can also be considered a miniature of Hong Kong society, while members in this society are both dependent and independent of social structures.

Politics and Socio-economic Changes

The intimate relationship between popular cultural development and environmentally induced political and social changes was also discernible in all our chapters. Social changes, societal resistance and the evolution of socio-economic values alongside economic development were intricately weaved into all the chapter contributors' narratives. In Wong and Lee's chapter, they indicated that during its development, Cantopop fandom has not only grown on its own strength but its development also reflects social changes. Once Hong Kong's economic development strengthened in the 1970s, it facilitated individuals to consume more products from the entertainment industry, resulting in the formation of more organized fan clubs centered around prominent celebrities.

On the other hand, in the Hong Kong case study covered by Wong and Lee, as the economy took off, income inequality and other social issues emerged due to rapid social transformation. Fan clubs played a role in managing these social changes by providing scholarships and charitable support to their members in need. Members of these fan clubs also became concerned with many social issues as a result. Chairpersons of fan clubs in the 1980s were public figures representing clubs, becoming unofficial spokespersons for their favorite singers or idols.

Contrasting with the high-profile public figures of Cantopop fan club leaders in Hong Kong are Anying Lin's portrayal of marginalized subcultural elites in China. She told the story that, for a long time, it is widely believed that animation and manga are only targeted at children under 12 years of age. Moreover, those popular culture products are considered as bad influences on adolescences and young adults, allegedly distracting them from their school work (Wang, 2011, p. 60).[4] Therefore, manga fans in China used to conceal their interests as well as the communities' existence from the general public and escape the glare of mass media.

It was until the late 2000s, that mainstream media started to pay attention to the existence of those obsessive adolescent and young adult fans, related to the import of the word "*yuzhaizu* (御宅族)," a Chinese translation of the Japanese word "otaku" imported from Taiwan. Under the label of "*yuzhaizu*", or "*zhai* (宅)" for short, the group began to acquire the status of a deviant community in mainstream society. The evolution of a subcultural group to mainstream acceptance was narrated in her study, alongside a growing cosmopolitan and economically prosperous China (the growth of a middle class related to increasing prosperity is discussed below). Therefore, in our chapters in the volume, we see the interesting dynamics of how the center and the periphery (and the marginalized) can alter positions in response to social dynamics. Cantopop fan club leaders who were very much cultural elites in Hong Kong society are eventually marginalized due to bad press while otakus in China (and Japan) who started off on the fringes of mainstream society eventually end up as trendsetters. The commonality amongst all our case studies demonstrates that social perceptions are often based on prevailing social conditions and fashion trends and are highly fluid and dynamic rather than remaining static in an unchanging fashion.

Perhaps, Ping's chapter about reality TV in China most dramatically demonstrated the point about the intimate nexus between socio-cultural

---

[4]Wei-jia Wang, "On the Cultural Differences Between China and Japan Through the Word 'Otaku'," *Journal of Hefei University* (*Social Science*) 28, no. 6 (2011): 60.

factors and popular cultural development in all Northeast Asian societies, certainly true in Ping's views on China. Reality show grasps the characteristics of an era, reflecting contemporary social values in a certain society. Information and entertainment are intertwined in the Chinese reality shows and they reflect the consumerism trends in Chinese society.[5] Cultural products have been important components of consumerism in China as its mass entertainment function for satisfying and soothing inner desires is increasingly demanded by Chinese consumers. China's socio-economic transition is accompanied by environmental pollution, sky-rocketing real estate price, and other social injustices, which have left some Chinese people increasingly anxious and frustrated with life. Reality shows, to some extent, provide an imaginary solution or, at the very least, a form of escapism from these conundrums. Featuring everyday issues empathized by ordinary Chinese people at all socio-economic levels, they send incessantly positive messages and energies to the Chinese society.

In her chapters, Ping pointed out that reality shows assist with alleviating the anxieties that the Chinese people share in contemporary Chinese society. Be it a plebian talent-show or a professional performance, these shows demonstrate a similar cultural logic: the upward mobility of an individual penetrating through social stratification by commodifying and commercializing one's talents and how one's life transformation for the better can be realized (through performing talent or art); communication barriers between people of different social classes can be broken down (through interactions between the talents and their supervisors); and diligence/persistence with pursuing one's dream in life plus high moral behavior will eventually pay off (just like most of the talents' "experiences" revealed in the show). The ideas of fantasy, escapism, middle-class yearnings and desires for social mobility were present in all chapters in the volume.

Middle Class as Consumers

As Cantopop, mainland Chinese reality TV shows and other strains of Northeast Asian popular cultures tried to address social inequity in the historical development in their countries of origins, externally the same

---

[5]Li Li, 奇观社会的文化密码: 电视真人秀的游戏规则研究, Sichuan University Press.

group of popular cultures are reaching out to the growing middle-class audiences of Northeast Asia. The Calvinistic ideal of attaining middle-class economic prosperity or even having access to mass consumable items when it comes to popular cultural lifestyle products resonates well with the sophisticated popular cultural marketing and distribution systems in Northeast Asia. In the tri-authored chapter by W. X. Lim, Tai Wei Lim and Ping, they studied how South Korea's media conglomerates developed many cultural products and expanded the exportation of these products to mainly East and Southeast Asia. The increasing popularity of the Korean Wave or *Hallyu* has contributed to enhancing South Korea's national image and it has been seen as a tool for public diplomacy.

Fashion trends and cultural waves are no longer driven only by the private sector and the state. Within this group of middle class consumers, a new cultural elite is emerging in the creative clusters located throughout East Asia. T. W. Lim's case study of the creative district of Akihabara is important as one of the few global nucleuses that reflects the trend physically, and universally recognized as the center of the Japanese popular cultural universe. According to Kaichiro Morikawa, a design theorist and professor at the School of Global Japanese Studies at Meiji University, Akihabara was shaped by otaku tastes in the 1990s when the retail outlets evolved from electronics retail to retailing personal computers as well as games.[6] The Comic Market also expanded in the 1990s with fanzines retailed throughout the year, along with the figurines that became popular when *Evangelion* became popular and spawned a following.[7] Messe Sanoh (games retailer), Kaiyodo (figurine manufacturer at Radio Kaikan) and Toranoana (fanzine and comic seller) were the pioneering J-pop cultural retailers that moved into Akihabara.[8] By 2009, at the peak of the *moe* (positive vibes towards made-belief cute-looking characters) movement,

---

[6]Patrick Galbraith, *The Moe Manifesto* (Tokyo, Rutland, Vermont and Singapore: Tuttle Publishing, 2014), 159.

[7]Patrick Galbraith, *The Moe Manifesto* (Tokyo, Rutland, Vermont and Singapore: Tuttle Publishing, 2014), 159.

[8]Patrick Galbraith, *The Moe Manifesto* (Tokyo, Rutland, Vermont and Singapore: Tuttle Publishing, 2014), [downloaded on 9 May 2016], available at https://archive.org/stream/TheMoeManifestoAnInsidersLookAtTheWorldsofMangaAnimeAndGaming/Moe Maifesto_djvu.txt.

Akihabara became a *bishojo* retailing area. Akihabara became the public space where private interests like *bishojo* were openly displayed, the analogy is equated with an otaku bedroom expanding into the streets of Tokyo.[9] An otaku fan naturally felt freer in this environment. Because otaku-ism has spread and proliferated globally as highlighted in T. W. Lim as well as Lin's chapters, Akihabara has become a symbolic pilgrimage destination for global middle-class and otaku consumers of Japanese popular cultural products. As a symbolic popular cultural center for J-pop, it also represents soft cultural influence for the Japanese creative industries.

Soft Power

The relationships between cultural influence, cultural diplomacy and economic benefits have led some to believe there is a connection between popular culture and "soft power." T. W. Lim's chapter noted that pink globalization has shaped the lifestyle goods consumption patterns for legions of fans. The maid cafes become constructed environments that create the fantasy of being in a comic book environment or manga world. The Japanese Ministry of Foreign Affairs (MOFA) has even appointed Lolita models as "kawaii ambassadors" due to their immense appeal.[10] In fact, Tokyo's *Diplomatic Bluebook 2006* mentioned:

> Japanese culture is currently attracting attention around the world as "Cool Japan". In order to increase interest in Japan and further heighten the image of Japan, Ministry of Foreign Affairs (MOFA) is working with the private sector through overseas diplomatic establishments and the Japan Foundation to promote cultural exchanges while taking into consideration the characteristics of each foreign country.[11]

---

[9] Patrick Galbraith, *The Moe Manifesto* (Tokyo, Rutland, Vermont and Singapore: Tuttle Publishing, 2014), 160.

[10] Manami Okazaki and Geoff Johnson, *Kawaii! Japan's culture of cute* (Munich, London and NY: Prestle, 2013), 113.

[11] Peng Er Lam, Japan Too Going After "Soft Power" in East Asian Institute National University of Singapore (EAI NUS) Background Brief No. 336 (Singapore: EAI NUS), 2007, p. 2 quoting Ministry of Foreign Affairs, Japan, Diplomatic Bluebook 2006, p. 208.

In 2009, Japan's Minister of Land, Infrastructure, Transport and Tourism Tetsuzo Fuyushiba appointed Hello Kitty as a goodwill ambassador to advocate tourism to Japan from China and Hong Kong.[12] The focus on East Asian economies is strategic, as they represent economic growth for Japan in the near future. In East Asian economies like Indonesia, economic growth is giving rise to a consuming class that is urbanized and modern, resonating with the lifestyles portrayed in Japanese manga and anime.[13]

Significantly in the economic sphere, popular cultural consumption creates positive spillover effects to other industries and therefore all Northeast Asian economies covered in this volume are capitalizing on the soft cultural power of the creative industries. W. X. Lim, T. W. Lim and Ping's co-authored chapter noted that the South Korean government recognized the advantage of this national phenomenon and is eager to capitalize on the success of the Korean Wave by providing public funds as well as implementing relevant policy in facilitating the development of the industry. In their chapter, the case study of Singapore is one of the early recipient countries of K-drama (Korean TV drama) and K-pop due to its cultural, political, economic proximity with South Korea as two of the four tiger economies with proactive state roles in economic development. Other than serving as an important consumer market, Singapore also offers Korean and K-pop companies the opportunities to test reactions to their products in a multicultural settings, springboard into the regional Southeast Asian market and invest in an important commercial, technological and trading hub in the region.

Besides serving as a model for Singapore, the success of K-pop also holds out the prospect of Track II cultural diplomacy potential for the two countries to cooperate in this field. Singapore's tourism sector also gets to benefit from increased interest in K-pop related events as well. Singapore was picked to host the first K-pop ASEAN Festival cover dance concert on 22 November 2014. Another positive spin-off from Singaporean consumer

---

[12] William Tsutsui, *Japanese Popular Culture and Globalization* (Ann Arbor, MI: Association for Asian Studies, Inc., 2010), 66.

[13] Saya S. Shiraishi, "Doraemon Goes Abroad," in *Japan Pop!* ed. T. J. Craig (Armonk, NY and London: M.E. Sharpe, 2000), 302.

interest in Korean popular culture is that it has provided the incentive to draw Korean companies to the island state.

Other than the example of K-pop, T. W. Lim's chapter noted that cross-pollination and hybridization of ideas are taking place region-wide. Popular cultural soft power is mutually-reinforcing in the sense that East Asian economies work with each other and influence each other to become cool and creative but yet at the same time trend-spot global popular cultural elements for incorporation into their textual and visual imaginations and body of works. East Asian popular cultural industries have become so sophisticated that, like industrial production systems, they have graduated and specialized production systems and testing grounds. They have the commercial and industrial potential of a creative flying geese model since Japan had in the past set the pace for the development of the creative industries. There are also differential levels of consumption, e.g. narratives noted the sequential dissemination of popular culture, for example Hong Kong and Taiwan as laboratories and platforms to test receptivity and reactions to popular cultural products before introduction to Chinese consumption.

Concluding Remarks: Important Limitations

From the chapters in the edited volume, some of the authors highlighted the limitations of popular cultural reach, even for a phenomenon like K-pop. There are limitations to soft power, commercial successes and reach of any popular culture. Popular culture itself inherently tends to be subjected to changing trends and fashions. Therefore, to be successful and sustainably so, Korean popular culture may need to continue its spirit of innovation to come up with new products for its domestic and Asian audiences. Eventually, the uniquely Korean characteristics of K-pop may have to contend with more universally appreciated features of Korean popular culture such that audiences (particularly foreign audiences) no longer need to acquire foreign languages or acquire Korean language ability to understand, appreciate and consume those products.

Governments are cognizant of these challenges. T. W Lim's chapter on J-pop highlighted this point. He noted that Japan's Ministry of Economy, Trade and Industry (METI) identified a number of challenges facing the Japanese popular cultural industry. The most well-known of all is probably the aging population which will lead to lower consumption of popular culture and creative goods overall. This will mean that Japan needs to export more popular cultural products overseas to make up for a declining domestic market. The global size of the popular cultural market is US$624 billion (2011 figure) when "trade in creative goods and services" are taken into account.[14] Japan wants to occupy more of this global market share of popular cultural products and consumption. In 2012, the METI made its ambitions public. The "creativity-based" industries make up approximately ¥2 trillion share of the global market which is expected to have a value above ¥900 trillion in 2020 and Cool Japan has set the target to increase its share in 2020 to between ¥8 trillion and ¥11 trillion.[15] Eventually, the pioneering strain of Northeast Asian popular culture that first globalized, J-pop, may hold important lessons and serve as an important reference for the other popular cultural strains in East Asia to learn from.

---

[14] Alan Wheatley, "Asian Style," dated June 2014 in Finance & Development (Washington DC: IMF, 2014), 15.

[15] Kazuaki Nagata, "Exporting culture via 'Cool Japan'," dated 15 May 2012 in Japan Times [downloaded on 23 December 2014], available at http://www.japantimes.co.jp/news/2012/05/15/reference/exporting-culture-via-cool-japan/#.VJmN10oA.

Index